PREDATORY LENDING AND THE DESTRUCTION OF THE AFRICAN-AMERICAN DREAM

Since the Great Recession of 2008, the racial wealth gap between black and white Americans has continued to widen. In *Predatory Lending and the Destruction of the African-American Dream*, Janis Sarra and Cheryl L. Wade detail salient factors that exacerbate the racial wealth gap by analyzing the economic exploitation of African Americans, with a focus on predatory practices in the home mortgage context. They also examine the failure of reform and litigation efforts ostensibly aimed at addressing this form of racial discrimination. This research, augmented by first-hand narratives, provides invaluable insight into the racial wealth gap by vividly illustrating the predation that targets African-American consumers and examining the intentionally obfuscating settlement terms of cases brought by the U.S. Department of Justice, States Attorneys, and municipalities. The authors conclude by offering structural, systemic changes to address predatory practices. This important work should be read by anyone seeking to understand racial inequality in the United States.

Dr Janis Sarra is Professor of Law at the University of British Columbia, Peter A. Allard School of Law, and was the founding Director of the National Centre for Business Law. Over 100 superior and appellate court judgments have cited her books and publications in corporate, finance, securities, and insolvency law. Dr Sarra is a member of the Canadian delegation to United Nations Commission on International Trade Law WG V.

Cheryl L. Wade is the Dean Harold F. McNiece Professor of Law at St John's University School of Law, New York. A member of the American Law Institute, Professor Wade has written over thirty-five book chapters, essays, and law review articles exploring the intersection of race, law, and business.

Predatory Lending and the Destruction of the African-American Dream

JANIS SARRA
Professor of Law
The University of British Columbia
Peter A. Allard School of Law

CHERYL L. WADE
Harold F. McNiece Professor of Law
St John's University School of Law

CAMBRIDGE
UNIVERSITY PRESS

University Printing House, Cambridge CB2 8BS, United Kingdom

One Liberty Plaza, 20th Floor, New York, NY 10006, USA

477 Williamstown Road, Port Melbourne, VIC 3207, Australia

314–321, 3rd Floor, Plot 3, Splendor Forum, Jasola District Centre, New Delhi – 110025, India

79 Anson Road, #06-04/06, Singapore 079906

Cambridge University Press is part of the University of Cambridge.

It furthers the University's mission by disseminating knowledge in the pursuit of education, learning, and research at the highest international levels of excellence.

www.cambridge.org
Information on this title: www.cambridge.org/9781108496063
DOI: 10.1017/9781108865715

First published 2020

A catalogue record for this publication is available from the British Library.

Library of Congress Cataloging-in-Publication Data
Names: Sarra, Janis Pearl, 1954- author. | Wade, Cheryl L. (Cheryl Lyn), 1956- author.
Title: Predatory lending and the destruction of the African-American dream / Janis Sarra, University of British Columbia, Vancouver, Peter A. Allard School of Law, Cheryl Wade, St. John's University School of Law.
Description: Cambridge, United Kingdom ; New York, NY : Cambridge University Press, 2020. | Includes bibliographical references and index.
Identifiers: LCCN 2020000446 | ISBN 9781108496063 (hardback) | ISBN 9781108811583 (ebook)
Subjects: LCSH: Discrimination in mortgage loans--United States. | Predatory lending--United States. | African Americans--Economic conditions.
Classification: LCC HG2040.2 .S27 2020 | DDC 332.7/208996073--dc23
LC record available at https://lccn.loc.gov/2020000446

ISBN 978-1-108-49606-3 Hardback
ISBN 978-1-108-81158-3 Paperback

Co-author Cheryl L. Wade dedicates this book to her mother, Evelyn Wade Hickson, her late father, Benjamin F. Wade, and her maternal grandparents, John W. Ford and Pattie F. Ford. Due to their brilliance, strength and endurance in pursuing their own African-American dreams, Cheryl and her brother, Vernon F. Wade, had countless joyful moments in a home purchased as a result of her parents' vision and labour. It was a purchase that was co-signed, literally and figuratively, by her grandparents.

Co-author Janis Sarra dedicates this book to her family for their continuing support, including her life partner, Dr Ronald Book Davis, her children Samantha, Danielle, and Alexander, her wonderful granddaughters Amadea, Jolie, Carmen, and Magdalena, and her mother, Lucy. She is deeply privileged to have a home for her family.

Contents

Figures

Tables

Foreword

For most Americans, homeownership is a major source of wealth-building. Thus, the housing foreclosure crisis, an aspect of the 2008 global financial crisis, and the concomitant loss of real and potential wealth financially devastated many Americans. This book focuses on an important but often underreported story about why African Americans, who only recently gained wider access to homeownership, were especially hard hit. More than a decade later, the plight of African Americans continues to receive little attention in discussions about the housing crisis. This book exposes how opaque financial transactions undercut black homeownership and why all Americans need to be mindful of what happened to African Americans.

The authors, who are legal experts in banking, finance, corporate governance and accountability, use financial market theory, corporate theory, bankruptcy principles, and critical race theory to document how large financial institutions *intentionally* targeted black homeowners and mortgage applicants using predatory lending schemes. They acknowledge that other racial and socio-economic groups were similarly victimized by these sub-prime lending schemes, but argue persuasively that anti-black biases, including racialized stereotypes of African Americans, contributed to the targeted predatory lending schemes applied to black homeowners and mortgage applicants. The authors link the success of these lending practices to African Americans' long-standing lack of access to housing and mortgages due to racial discriminatory practices by lending institutions and realtors. Given this history of discrimination, and the resulting pent-up demand for housing, African Americans were especially appealing targets.

The consequences of the 2008 housing crisis continue to reverberate through the African-American community. The generational progress of blacks into the middle class that started in the mid twentieth century not only stopped after 2008, but also declined significantly as a result of mortgage foreclosures triggered by sub-prime lending schemes. This book contains hard evidence supporting the authors' arguments, as well as moving personal narratives of many African Americans victimized by the predatory lending practices.

Parts of this book will appeal to a wide range of readers. You do not need to be a lawyer or financial expert to understand their arguments. The authors' explanation of the mechanics of the financial markets is accessible to all readers. Yet those readers interested in financial details will appreciate the authors' in-depth examination of the various legal settlements with financial institutions presented in Chapter 8. The examination documents how most relief efforts focused on investors, not homeowners. This story is a gripping account of the failure of governments, large and small, to protect consumer borrowers from misleading and often intentionally deceptive lending practices. Even if readers decide to forego the details in Chapter 8, the other chapters explain why the problems leading to the 2008 housing crisis are structural. These structural impediments explain why post-crisis reforms have not eliminated the problems that triggered the crisis. As proof, the authors, in Chapter 9, describe how a decade after the crisis, new forms of predatory lending schemes continue to target the same vulnerable population.

The authors conclude by asking whether, given the motivations for predatory lending schemes targeting African Americans, the law can provide adequate remedies. In Chapter 10, they offer a variety of suggested remedies. Because African Americans occupy a distinct historical, social and economic position, any effective reform must acknowledge the long and continuing anti-black bias that affects all aspects of American life. The authors caution that reforms alone will not eradicate the racism that caused so many African Americans to suffer during the 2008 housing crisis.

Taunya Lovell Banks
Jacob A. France Professor of Equality Jurisprudence
University of Maryland
Francis King Carey School of Law

Acknowledgements

Our sincere thanks to the courageous individuals who shared their stories with us.

Thanks to Alice Nicholson, New York, for sharing her extensive experience and sage advice. Thanks also to Victoria L. Brown-Douglas, New York; Professor Taunya L. Banks, University of Maryland; and Charles Ferrell and the Charles H. Wright Museum of African-American History, Detroit. Thanks to Dr Rizwaan Mokal for his cogent advice on Chapter 10 and to Professor Bruce Markell for clarifying some aspects of U.S. bankruptcy law. We are profoundly grateful to multimedia artist Tomashi Jackson for permission to use her painting, "Ms. Marlene on Dean Street (History Upside Down)" on the cover of this book. Many thanks also to Ms Marlene Saunders who is depicted in the painting after having won her battle to keep her home. We also thank Constance Tilton of the Tilton Gallery for connecting us to Tomashi Jackson and her beautiful work.

On the related song project, we sincerely thank Bethany Baptist Church, Jamaica, New York, Carolyn Bowie, Jane Brewton, Pastor Craig Scott Brown, Sr, Victoria L. Brown-Douglas, Moretta Butler, Ena D. Davis, Helen Eastman, Shirley Erves, Marie Francois, Penny Gardner, Michael Garrett, L. Priscilla Hall, Jac-Lyn Hayward, Bruce D. Lennon, Lewis McCain, Karen Montgomery, Alice Nicholson, Dexter Romain, Nancy Scott, Alex Silverman, Sophia Thomas, Crystal Thompson, Jenisha Thompson and Vernon R. Williams.

Thanks also to MaryGrace Johnstone, Law III, the Peter A. Allard School of Law, the University of British Columbia, for her research and administrative support in checking references, and in particular for her excellent research for the appendix on the settlement of sub-prime litigation. Thanks to Priyaa H. Menon, Becky Jackaman, Cameron Daddis and Matt Gallaway of Cambridge University Press for their production assistance and to Gregory Ronczewski of Bowen Island, Canada for his cover design.

Cheryl L. Wade thanks her Mom for giving her all that she needed to pursue her own dreams. Thanks also to Arthur Lee Kindred and Patricia S. Brim for pointing us in the right direction for invaluable information and sources.

1

Introduction

More than a decade after the 2008 financial crisis, African Americans and other individuals are still struggling to hold on to their homes. In this book, we examine specifically the inequitable treatment of African Americans under the United States' current financial system. From 2008 to the third quarter of 2018, the ten-year anniversary of the commencement of the global financial crisis, there were more than 17 million home foreclosures in the United States. Millions of Americans lost their homes and life savings as a result of the sub-prime mortgage debacle. A disproportionate number of these individuals are African American. This important untold story is not just about the working poor. Millions of middle-class and high-income African Americans who qualified for regular fixed-rate, long-term mortgages were steered to sub-prime mortgages because lenders were capitalizing on years of structural racism, shattering the dreams of home ownership for African Americans. For the most part, white American borrowers who had credit histories identical to the credit histories of African-American borrowers were not targeted for sub-prime mortgages.

Since the global financial meltdown, there has been substantial reform to the banking sector in terms of new capitalization requirements and mechanisms to resolve bank financial distress.[1] However, while there has been some regulatory reform in respect of the financial products and services that precipitated the financial crisis – such as securitization, collateralization, and sub-prime mortgage and other asset-backed securities – these reforms have been pathetically weak. Moreover, the actual relief given to families suffering the devastating effects of the meltdown was

1 Resolving bank insolvency means using a series of mechanisms to restructure banks in financial distress. See the discussion in Janis Sarra, "A Bridge Over Troubled Waters – Resolving Bank Financial Distress in Canada" in Janis P. Sarra and Justice Barbara Romaine, eds, *Annual Review of Insolvency Law 2017* (Toronto: Carswell, 2018), 255–341.

woefully inadequate, and, as this book reveals, tracking it has been like watching a "shell game" that masks actual relief.[2] The lack of attention to reform of the structural features of financial markets has resulted in a failure to address much of the harm, and safeguards have not been put in place against future predatory lending.

In 2019, hundreds of thousands of African Americans and others continue to fight foreclosure. Many financial professionals have taken credit for having averted a complete global meltdown of the financial system at the time the crisis commenced. Although that view has some merit, it ignores the critical issues of at what cost and to whom? For millions, the crisis continues today.

It is now well documented that lenders, brokers, and mortgage servicers engaged in conduct that was fraudulent and misleading.[3] The mortgage market charged excessively high rates and fees, engaged in high-pressure sales tactics, imposed unnecessarily harsh prepayment penalties, and distorted loan structures to avoid the application of consumer protection statutes. A number of factors contributed to the sub-prime mortgage collapse. One significant cause was securitization, which created rapidly accelerating market pressure to sell highly risky mortgages. In the sub-prime context, securitization created incentives for misconduct and fraudulent lending, rather than serving as a risk management tool. This book analyses how these developments were possible due to deeply embedded racism in the United States. African Americans were four times as likely as similarly situated white Americans to pay sub-prime rates on their mortgages, even when controlling for factors such as borrower income and property location.[4] Potently durable stereotypes about African Americans are at the heart of the sub-prime mortgage debacle. Black Americans were targeted for predatory lending more than any other group because of the intractability of the myth of black intellectual inferiority and enduring anti-black bias that foments their economic exploitation, thus leaving a legacy of intergenerational harm that impedes wealth accumulation by black Americans.

By telling the stories of Americans of African descent who were victimized by predatory lending in this book, we provide the narratives that counter one predominant account of predatory lending that blames the individuals harmed.

[2] A shell game is a game involving sleight of hand in which three inverted cups or nutshells are moved about and contestants must spot which is the one with an object underneath; "a swindle involving the substitution of something of little or no value for a valuable item," Merriam-Webster Dictionary, "shell game."

[3] See, for example, the Financial Crisis Inquiry Commission, *Final Report of the National Commission on the Causes of the Financial and Economic Crisis in the United States, Submitted Pursuant to Public Law 111–21* (Washington, DC: FCIC, January 2011), xv, https://fcic-static.law.stanford.edu/cdn_media/fcic-reports/fcic_final_report_full.pdf (hereafter FCIC Report). The FCIC was established as part of the Fraud Enforcement and Recovery Act.

[4] FCIC Report, 110.

For decades, African Americans have been compared to other groups that emigrated to the United States – groups that have amassed wealth and financial security after generations of pursuing the American Dream. Why are disproportionately higher numbers of black Americans living in poverty? Why is there a significant gap between the wealth of African-American households and white American households, and why has the gap widened so dramatically in recent years? This book provides one overlooked but dramatically salient explanation for the racial wealth gap.

The approach by lenders and their agents in the United States to the targeting of African Americans for predatory loans is best explained by the theory that U.S. racial categories are social constructs that justify the exploitation of disadvantaged groups. U.S. racial categories have no basis in biological reality. The constructs and the attributes that attach to the socially constructed racial groups validate the exploitation of people of colour. We suggest that the harm that results from systemic and structural racism cannot be mitigated without understanding how white Americans benefit. This understanding is just as important as acknowledging the ways that African-American borrowers were disadvantaged.

Predatory Lending and the Destruction of the African-American Dream offers a comprehensive account of the harms to African Americans victimized by predatory mortgage lending. The discussion in this book is uniquely informed by a combination of critical race theory, financial market theory, post-racialism critique, corporate law theory, and bankruptcy law, drawing on the strengths of the authors to conceptualize a new paradigm for addressing the losses associated with predatory mortgage practices and their continuing harms.

The structural nature of racism undergirds the predatory lending scams in the 2000s, along with the inertia over a decade later that precludes help for black Americans victimized by these practices. Institutional policies in private organizations such as banks and other financial institutions, and the institutional policies of public bodies such as housing agencies and the court system, provide little or no redress for black Americans who were victimized by predatory lending and for individuals who continue to be scammed. These policies entrench and exacerbate the racial wealth gap that has existed since the first enslaved Africans were brought to the shores of what is now the United States. We posit that post-racial ideology eclipsed understanding of the impact of predatory lending on African Americans, their families, and communities. A burgeoning new U.S. market, non-prime mortgages, has in the past two years moved into the sub-prime market space. It is another form of predatory lending that many pundits and policymakers had concluded could never happen again.

Although coalitions among people of colour and marginalized white Americans are desirable, it is also important to understand the ways that racism in general, and economic discrimination in particular, impact different groups differently. This book devotes time and attention to black Americans.

We chart a way forward that requires a normative shift in lending practices in which lenders can be held more accountable for their behaviour. We consider the parameters of what is possible under the current U.S. federal administration cloaked under the guise of populism. We examine the continuing disconnection between ostensibly well-meaning bureaucracies in the managing of loss mitigation and the experience of individuals in their homes and communities. We examine, specifically, the plight of mortgagors in three of the cities hardest hit by the sub-prime crisis and recount stories of their loss and of the frustration of their legal advocates. We examine the strategic lobbying efforts of the mortgage industry at various key decision junctures regarding ameliorative legislation and reflect on the role and limits of regulatory oversight.

We tackle several critically important questions. What are the intergenerational harms caused by the continuing crisis and what mechanisms might be available to change that trajectory? What can be accomplished structurally in an era of deregulatory priority? What are the current implications for middle-class and working-class Americans of all races with respect to the most recent developments?

The book is structured as follows. Chapter 2 introduces the topic of foreclosure and outlines the theoretical contributions and principles drawn upon throughout the book. It traces the specificity of the discriminatory targeting of African Americans for predatory schemes. Chapter 3 examines the predatory and sub-prime lending that occurred in the years leading up to the collapse of the sub-prime mortgage market during which mortgage lenders developed numerous new products with opaque and predatory terms. At the time of the sub-prime market collapse, 20 per cent of homes in the U.S. mortgage market were being purchased with sub-prime loans. A "dual mortgage market" emerged, in which borrowers of colour were served primarily by sub-prime lenders, while white American borrowers were served primarily by conventional lending institutions.

Chapter 4 examines state, federal, and other studies that have documented how African Americans specifically were targeted for predatory and sub-prime lending even when they qualified for traditional mortgages. We grapple in this chapter with the crucial but still unanswered question of why African Americans were targeted by situating the discussion in the context of centuries-old anti-black bias in the United States. In Chapter 5, we examine the sub-prime market collapse and the impact it had on consumer borrowers who had these predatory sub-prime mortgages. The chapter juxtaposes the series of measures by the U.S. Department of the Treasury to slow the run on capital through temporary guarantees and direct bailouts with the government's failure to be responsive to the plight of millions of mortgage borrowers.

Chapter 6 discusses how lenders lobbied the U.S. Senate not to enact meaningful reform, which resulted in a vitally important missed opportunity to give a lifeline to millions facing foreclosure through bankruptcy reform. Bankruptcy forgiveness could have been an immediate and highly effective strategy to deal with the millions of home foreclosures at the height of the crisis. Chapter 7 explores other reforms implemented, ostensibly in response to the crisis, suggesting that the federal government's efforts to protect homeowners were well intentioned but ineffective for millions of borrowers. Regulators allowed the very same predatory lenders who had created the problems to administer the programs.

Chapter 8 examines legal actions brought against predatory sub-prime lenders and servicers. It briefly summarizes the results of allegations of fraud and violation of various federal and state securities and financial services law by looking at the lawsuits against firms that issued predatory residential mortgage-backed securities. The chapter also provides contextual analysis relating to claims brought against lenders under anti-discrimination law. Chapter 9 reveals that there are now new iterations of predatory lending in the form of non-prime loans, as well as continued abusive practices in mortgage modifications. The U.S. government ended its modification programs in 2016 and handed authority for modification back to the private sector.

Chapter 10 turns to a normative discussion on how we should approach default for home mortgage borrowers. It explores whether there is a possibility for a paradigm shift, such as a complete reconceptualization of mortgage lending, terms, and conditions, responses leading up to and upon default, and prevention of foreclosures. We also consider, in the face of a regulatory lacuna, whether an investment community that is concerned with environmental, social, and governance factors could be enlisted to pressure mortgage originators and servicers to remedy their conduct. By exercising their investment power, socially responsible investors could meaningfully shift the trajectory of financial markets with respect to mortgage lending.

I RESEARCH METHODOLOGY FOR THIS BOOK

Our research methodology was multifaceted. We reviewed the extant literature on the financial crisis and sub-prime meltdown. We examined many state and federal government reports on the causes. We also examined the congressional transcripts of testimony by numerous market players, regulators, and consumer groups.

We travelled to Detroit, New York, and Baltimore in September 2018, three of the cities hit the hardest by foreclosures. We interviewed individuals and their lawyers for first-hand accounts of what has been occurring in the decade since the financial crisis began and how the harm is still being perpetrated more than ten years later. Several of these stories are recounted in their entirety in this book. These first-hand accounts debunk the victim blaming myth that many undeserving people were given mortgages that they should not have received.

Our methodology for Chapter 8, which examines settlements of lawsuits brought by state and federal authorities, was to read many public documents, including the court-approved settlement orders, the reports of the monitors appointed under the settlements, and as much other information as we could cull from other sources. Although there are more than 5,000 pages detailing the settlements, the actual relief given to the millions victimized by foreclosure is cloaked in non-transparent reporting. We supplemented examination of the public documents with interviews of the monitors by which we sought clarification of the reported amounts.

In this book, we have consciously avoided using the phrase “post-crisis” because for millions of African Americans in the United States, the financial crisis continues.

2

Foreclosure: At What Cost and to Whom?

Home is where the heart is
So the saying goes
You chase your dreams in poetry
and pay for them in prose
Then comes the dreadful day you find
that you've been sold a lie:
It was just a little loan, now they've taken every-thing you own
and you're standing on your own
Wondering why?

Homes and Hearts, 2018[1]

This chapter introduces the topic of foreclosure and includes discussion of the theoretical frameworks and principles that can inform deeper consideration of the foreclosure issues of the past decade and going forward. It examines how lender predation differs among U.S. consumer borrowers according to the consumers' race and provides interviews with African Americans who are currently fighting foreclosure and interviews with these individuals' lawyers. Our investigation traces the specificity of the discriminatory targeting of black Americans for predatory schemes. We also include a framing discussion with respect to the mortgage-backed securities market, market practice, and regulatory oversight at the commencement of the global financial crisis. We examine the huge gap between what regulators believed was occurring and what was really happening in the practice of mortgage lending on the ground. We explore the deeper connection between market design and its consequent incentives for self-dealing as primary drivers in continuing harmful

1 Excerpt from gospel song composed by Alex Silverman, "Homes and Hearts" (October 2018), Live Canon, www.livecanon.co.uk/foreclosurefollies, with research input from and collaboration with Cheryl Wade and Janis Sarra.

conduct in financial markets. Our objective in this chapter is to give readers who may have only passing familiarity with critical race theory and financial market theory a solid context in which to read the rest of this book.

I FORECLOSURE

Much has been written about the sub-prime mortgage market meltdown in the United States and the millions of foreclosures on homes that occurred in the past decade. The term house "foreclosure" means a legal process in which the lender that has advanced capital to a consumer borrower by way of a mortgage loan and lien on the real property takes possession of the house when a borrower has stopped making payments. The lender, or whoever holds the mortgage when in default, then attempts to recover the outstanding amount of the loan by forcing the sale of the house that was used as the collateral for the loan. Foreclosure is a common method in the United States to address default in loan payments, as it is in some other regions of the world. Of note, however, is that foreclosure is less common in countries such as the United Kingdom, which has a mortgage possession process that has a series of steps in which consumers are protected and can negotiate accommodations before a house is repossessed for failure to make payment.[2]

It is now well established that during the U.S. sub-prime mortgage debacle, there was particularly egregious conduct by lenders and their agents that ultimately led to millions of foreclosures. Mortgage brokers gave fraudulent information to borrowers. Exorbitant fees were paid to lenders and their brokers based on volumes of loans sold. Credit rating agencies failed to appropriately rate and value mortgage-backed securities.[3] Complex derivatives hedging transactions eventually precipitated the meltdown.[4] Sub-prime lending in the United States surged to $1.2 trillion in 2005[5] and, by 2006, sub-prime lending accounted for 23.5 per cent of all mortgage originations. Of the $600 billion of sub-prime loans originated in 2006, most were securitized.[6] Prior to 2007, the foreclosure rate was historically less

[2] UK Government, "Repossession" (2019), www.gov.uk/repossession.

[3] William K. Black, "The Two Documents Everyone Should Read to Better Understand the Crisis" *Huffington Post* (28 March 2009), www.huffingtonpost.com/william-k-black/the-two-documents-everyon_b_169813.html (hereafter Black, "Two Documents"); Fitch Ratings, "The Impact of Poor Underwriting Practices and Fraud in Subprime RMBS Performance" *Huffington Post* (28 November 2007), http://big.assets.huffingtonpost.com/FraudReport8Nov07Fitch.pdf (hereafter Fitch Ratings).

[4] Janis Sarra, "Embedding Fairness as a Fundamental Norm in Financial Markets" in Janis P. Sarra, ed, *An Exploration of Fairness, Interdisciplinary Inquiries in Law, Science and the Humanities* (Toronto: Carswell, 2012) (hereafter Sarra, "Embedding Fairness").

[5] Financial Crisis Inquiry Commission, *Final Report of the National Commission on the Causes of the Financial and Economic Crisis in the United States, Submitted Pursuant to Public Law 111–21* (Washington, DC: FCIC, January 2011), xv, https://fcic-static.law.stanford.edu/cdn_media/fcic-reports/fcic_final_report_full.pdf (hereafter FCIC Report), 13. All references to dollars in this book are references to U.S. dollars, unless otherwise noted.

[6] FCIC Report, 70.

than 1 per cent.[7] By 2010, 1 in every 11 outstanding residential mortgage loans in the United States was at least one payment past due, portending massive numbers of impending foreclosures.[8]

The U.S. National Commission on the Causes of the Financial and Economic Crisis in the United States (called the U.S. Financial Crisis Inquiry Commission (FCIC)) concluded that there was a systemic breakdown in accountability and ethics in the mortgage lending market.[9] The commission observed that the soundness and the sustained prosperity of the financial system and the economy rely on notions of fair dealing, responsibility, and transparency, but that a serious erosion of standards of responsibility and ethics created, and then exacerbated, the financial crisis.[10] The commission found greed, hubris, and misdeeds that resulted in systemic failures, concluding that corrosion of mortgage-lending standards and the mortgage securitization pipeline lit and spread the flame of contagion and crisis.[11]

As noted in the introduction, from 2008 to the third quarter of 2018, there were more than 17 million home foreclosures in the United States,[12] causing Americans to lose their homes and life savings. For example, foreclosure cases comprised almost one-third of all court cases state-wide of the New York Supreme Court civil caseload, which at the end of 2015 had almost 90,000 foreclosure cases pending.[13] The docket of weekly numerous foreclosure auctions in Kings County, New York reflected that the zip codes of the properties involved neighbourhoods comprised almost entirely of black Americans.[14] The impact of discriminatory lending practices is devastating. According to the Federal Reserve Bank, black Americans held 8.7 per cent of U.S. home loans in 2006. In 2014, black Americans held only 5.2 per cent of the nation's home loans;[15] their losses from sub-prime loans diminished their ability to re-enter the housing market.

7 FCIC Report, 402.

8 FCIC Report, 402.

9 FCIC Report, xxii.

10 FCIC Report, xxi.

11 FCIC Report, xxiii.

12 FCIC Report; the precise figure is 17,463,253: ATTOM Data Solutions, "US Foreclosure Activity Drops to 12-Year Low in 2017" (18 January 2018) at Graph – U.S. Historical Foreclosure Activity and Rates, www.attomdata.com/news/foreclosure-trends/2017-year-end-u-s-foreclosure-market-report/. Fifty per cent of all loans actively in foreclosure as of the end of 2017 were originated between 2004 and 2008.

13 State of New York, Unified Court System, *2015 Report of the Chief Administrator of the Courts* (New York: Unified Court System, 2015), 4, New York Courts, http://ww2.nycourts.gov/sites/default/files/document/files/2018-06/2015ForeclosureReport.pdf.

14 State of New York, Unified Court System, "Kings County Supreme Court Foreclosure Sales: September to November 2018" (2019), New York Courts, www.nycourts.gov/courts/2jd/kings/civil/foreclosuresales.shtml.

15 United States, Board of Governors of the Federal Reserve System, *Residential Mortgage Lending in 2016: Evidence from the Home Mortgage Disclosure Act Data* (Washington, DC: Federal Reserve Bulletin, November 2017), 9, Federal Reserve, www.federalreserve.gov/publications/files/2016_hmda.pdf.

Hundreds of civil enforcement lawsuits rose out of sub-prime mortgages involving borrowers and the investors who invested in mortgage-backed securities. For example, Ocwen Mortgage Financial Corporation[16] settled civil law enforcement lawsuits for $2.1 billion for its misconduct that resulted in premature and unauthorized foreclosures, violations of homeowners' rights and protections, and the use of false and deceptive documents and affidavits.[17] We discuss these settlements in Chapter 8.

Hundreds of thousands of people who qualified for regular mortgages were steered to sub-prime mortgages because of the huge fees and interest amounts being extracted by lenders and mortgage brokers. African Americans were particularly targeted for sub-prime mortgages and predatory loans, often when they could afford traditional fixed-rate long-term mortgages.[18] Predatory loans have exorbitantly high fees at the point they are originated and usually include complex interest resetting terms that are frequently not understood by borrowers.[19] That black consumers were particularly targeted is emblematic of continuing racism that exists in the United States today.

While it is evident that some mortgages were given inappropriately to consumers who would never have been able to continue to make payments, the blame for these practices falls squarely on the lenders and their agents. Several studies have documented a widespread lack of financial literacy among consumers, who stood to lose their life savings if a mortgage transaction went badly,[20] but even financially literate consumers in many cases were unable to protect themselves from the architecture of complex predation designed by sophisticated lenders. One study found that "banks knowingly preyed on black mortgage-seekers when it came to issuing

[16] Ocwen Financial Corporation of Atlanta, Georgia, and its subsidiary, Ocwen Loan Servicing, and two companies later acquired by Ocwen: Homeward Residential Inc and Litton Home Servicing LP. Ocwen specializes in servicing high-risk mortgage loans.

[17] Montana Department of Justice, "Attorney General Fox Announces $2.1 Billion Joint State-Federal Settlement with Ocwen Mortgage" (20 December 2013), https://dojmt.gov/attorney-general-fox-announces-2-1-billion-joint-state-federal-settlement-with-ocwen-mortgage/#more-30699. See the discussion in Part VII of this paper.

[18] American Civil Liberties Union, "Justice Foreclosed: How Wall Street's Appetite for Subprime Mortgages Ended Up Hurting Black and Latino Communities" (October 2012), www.aclu.org/sites/default/files/field_document/justiceforclosed-singlepage-rel4.pdf (hereafter American Civil Liberties Union, "Justice Foreclosed"); Cheryl L. Wade, "Fairness, Narrative, Empathy, and the US Racial Wealth Gap" in Janis P. Sarra, ed, *An Exploration of Fairness, Interdisciplinary Inquiries in Law, Science and the Humanities* (Toronto: Carswell, 2012) (hereafter Wade, *Fairness*). Sam Thielman, "Black Americans Unfairly Targeted by Banks before Housing Crisis, Says ACLU" *The Guardian* (23 June 2015), www.theguardian.com/business/2015/jun/23/black-americans-housing-crisis-sub-prime-loan.

[19] American Civil Liberties Union, "Justice Foreclosed," 6.

[20] Manisha Padi, "Consumer Protection Laws and the Mortgage Market: Evidence from Ohio" (2018) (Working Paper), 6, Manisha Padi, https://manishapadi.com/workingpapers/, referencing the National Low Income Housing Coalition, "Findings from the HB 4050 Predatory Lending Database Pilot Program" (1 April 2007), https://nlihc.org/resource/findings-hb-4050-predatory-lending-database-pilot-program (hereafter Padi, "Consumer Protection Ohio").

sub-prime mortgages" and racial discrimination was key to predatory lending that accelerated the financial collapse.[21] In some cases, the mortgages were designed to fail, with the lender anticipating default of the loan and realization of the property in foreclosure.[22]

Legislative reforms to bank regulation since 2008 have focused on bank resolution and "bail-in," and almost no attention has been paid to the massive losses financially and emotionally experienced by the borrowers from foreclosure. Other statutory reforms aimed at addressing the most egregious conduct of lenders and servicers has proven inadequate as discussed in Chapter 9. In focusing a spotlight on these issues, it is important to set a public policy context for the harms that continue to occur and the failure of legislators to adequately address the structural failures underpinning the sub-prime mortgage crisis.

II THEORETICAL FRAMEWORK AND PRINCIPLES THAT INFORM DEEPER CONSIDERATION OF THE FORECLOSURE ISSUES

This book draws on several theoretical frameworks that inform both our insights and our recommendations going forward, including Rawlsian notions of justice,[23] theories of fairness in financial markets,[24] and critical race theory. To assess the sub-prime mortgage meltdown and the massive number of foreclosures in the past decade, it is important to consider principles against which to measure what occurred in the years leading up to, during, and after the meltdown.

A starting place for assessing mortgage and other financial markets is a notion of fairness as an overarching, fundamental principle. "Fairness" as a concept can be viewed as the capacity to take the perspective of another and to adjust conduct and decisions to take account of others' perspectives to achieve more equitable outcomes.[25] Perspective-taking can deepen the understanding of financial markets and encourage a substantive aspirational goal of more equitable treatment of individuals who are differently situated.[26] Currently, the notion of fairness in financial markets is limited primarily to creating "equal opportunity to participate in the market."[27] Yet the rules

21 Sarah Burd-Sharps and Rebecca Rasch, "Impact of the US Housing Crisis on the Racial Wealth Gap Across Generations: An Independent Report Commissioned by the American Civil Liberties Union," Social Science Research Council (June 2015), www.aclu.org/files/field_document/discrimlend_final.pdf (hereafter Burd-Sharps and Rasch, "Impact").

22 American Civil Liberties Union, "Justice Foreclosed," 6.

23 John Rawls, *A Theory of Justice* (Cambridge, MA: Harvard University Press, 1971) (hereafter Rawls, *Theory*); John Rawls, *Political Liberalism* (New York: Columbia University Press, 1996) (hereafter Rawls, *Political*).

24 Sarra, "Embedding Fairness," 193–240.

25 Sarra, "Embedding Fairness," 193.

26 Sarra, "Embedding Fairness."

27 Janis Sarra, "Modernizing Disclosure in Canadian Securities Law: An Assessment of Recent Developments in Canadian and Selective Jurisdictions" (Paper prepared for the Task Force to Modernize Securities Law in Canada, 2006).

and practices that have arisen have had direct and indirect distributive consequences that widen wealth disparities.[28] Of course, financial markets are not entirely responsible for the unfairness in wealth distributions; rather, such markets are part of a complex system of social, political, and economic influences and historical inequitable endowments of wealth.[29]

Aristotle observed that fairness is a key human trait that humans need to flourish and perform fundamental social practices well.[30] Immanuel Kant advanced the idea that each individual's actions should be guided by the notion that such actions would become a universal law or norm; that what can be determined as fair is the result of that universal perspective-taking.[31] Yet as this book reveals, perspective-taking alone will not allow a retooling of the system of mortgage lending to embed a fairness norm because the decision-makers continue to be the most economically privileged in our society.[32] Even if they try to be other-regarding, decision-makers may not have the insight or capacity to fully understand the fair or unfair outcomes of particular policy choices or to shift fundamental norms. Or the decision-makers may lack empathy altogether and ignore the possibility or desirability of other-regarding considerations.

Co-author Sarra has written:

> Just as markets are dynamic, our conception of how fairness values should be inculcated into the regulatory structure of oversight of markets needs to be dynamic and responsive to problems identified. Markets are socially constructed, but their norms and standards are the result of a complex interplay between the most powerful market actors, supervisory authorities, elected representatives, and the judiciary and other adjudicators. The issue is whether the rules advance our collective notions of what is fair or just ...[33]

John Rawls observed that one way of testing for fairness of the law is to regard it as fair insofar as it treats the interests of all those individuals subject to it with equal concern.[34] The law should not countenance favourable treatment simply on the basis of wealth, gender, race, ethnicity, tribe, family, sexual orientation, social status, or political affiliation.[35] Thus, the legal regime for mortgage origination, servicing, and realization should aspire in good faith to treat borrowers

[28] Sarra, "Embedding Fairness," 194.

[29] Sarra, "Embedding Fairness," 195.

[30] Aristotle, *Nicomachean Ethics*, trans. W. D. Ross (Kitchener: Batoche Books, 350 BCE/1999).

[31] Immanuel Kant, *Kant: Political Writings*, ed. Hans Reiss, trans. H. B. Nisbet (Cambridge: Cambridge University Press, 1991).

[32] Sarra, "Embedding Fairness," 200.

[33] Sarra, "Embedding Fairness," 203.

[34] Sarra, "Embedding Fairness"; and Rawls, *Theory*.

[35] Ronald Davis, Stephan Madaus, Alberto Mazzoni, Irit Mevorach, Rizwaan J. Mokal, Barbara Romaine, Janis Sarra, and Ignacio Tirado, *Micro, Small, and Medium Enterprise Insolvency* (Oxford: Oxford University Press, 2018), 29 (hereafter Davis et al, *Insolvency*).

with concern equal to how it treats wealthier or more powerful market actors, and to treat them with equal concern regardless of their race or ethnic origin. The requirements of good faith and equal concern are two of law's primary substantive goals,[36] and with respect to financial markets, they should apply to both substantive and procedural law.

Mortgage debt was historically aimed at encouraging home ownership, a concept that is deeply embedded in legal systems globally and has become an indispensable component of the U.S. economy. The availability of mortgages to enable purchase of homes can have a broad social and economic role in financial security and economic development.[37] However, as discussed throughout this book, U.S. policies encouraging home ownership through mortgage availability were racially skewed and worked to disenfranchise African Americans.

Mortgage debt and lending law principles should instead accord equal concern to the interests of all stakeholders affected and must guide the creation of tools and processes that reflect society's policy choices within the complex combination of financial, corporate, property, tax, and welfare laws. It must create ascertainable and transparent rules that parties understand before they enter into the credit arrangement.[38]

In thinking about a framework going forward as discussed in Chapter 10, we can draw on Rawlsian notions of hypothetical choice position in which all those individuals affected by peculiar circumstances and thus subjected to processes shaped by mortgage law principles are regarded as possessing identical information about the range of options available. Critically, however, the individuals would have no information about their own identity, attributes, interests, or stake.[39] In this state of ignorance as to whether they would be among the privileged few or the millions of disadvantaged, they would be required to agree on the design of a mortgage regime.[40] In this hypothetical choice, each person's concerns are given equal weight by every participant in the bargain, since each has an equal chance of discovering that a particular set of interests is in fact their own.[41] Rizwaan Mokal observes that if parties do not know who they will turn out to be once a state of ignorance is removed, commercial market rules must equally take into account the interests of all the people they might find themselves to be.[42]

[36] Davis et al, *Insolvency*, 30.

[37] Janis Sarra, *Creditor Rights and the Public Interest, Restructuring Insolvent Corporations* (Toronto: University of Toronto Press, 2003).

[38] Davis et al, *Insolvency*, 36.

[39] Rawls, *Theory*.

[40] Rizwaan J. Mokal, "On Fairness and Efficiency" (2003) 66 *Modern Law Review* 452, 452–9 (hereafter Mokal, "Fairness and Efficiency").

[41] Rizwaan J. Mokal, *Corporate Insolvency Law – Theory and Application* (London: Oxford University Press, 2005) (hereafter Mokal, *Theory*), 80–1.

[42] Mokal, *Theory*, 81.

Importantly, having one's interests accorded equal concern in the choice of mortgage law principles does not equate to being given identical treatment.[43] To show equal concern towards each of the law's subjects may require differential legal treatment responding to relevant differences among them, in terms of wealth disparities, information asymmetries, and vulnerability to harm.[44] Currently, the mortgage debt regime in the United States favours sophisticated and well-resourced repeat players, such as banks, financial firms, mortgage originators, and mortgage servicers, as well as their principals, directors, and investors. The effects of a system that allows rapid foreclosure and realization of assets disproportionately and inequitably affects weaker, less sophisticated parties – the borrowers.

Underpinning fairness is also the need for timely and effective processes for the resolution of any disputes, including legal processes for individuals seeking to remain in their homes when creditors are trying to foreclose on them. It requires effective processes for individuals to seek remedies for any wrongdoing connected with origination or administration of the mortgage debt.

Timely and effective resolution processes should be underpinned by accessibility, transparency, certainty, and accountability.[45] Yet as this book reveals, none of these important procedural protections were present in the system of mortgage modifications and foreclosures. By accessibility, we mean having in place mechanisms that reduce barriers to individuals seeking relief from oppressive loan terms or seeking remedies for misconduct by mortgage lenders and servicers. By transparency, we mean transparency in processes to resolve loan default, meaningful rights to receive notice of pending foreclosure or other actions, the opportunity to be heard before a court renders a decision on foreclosure, and transparency of outcomes. As Chapter 8 will illustrate, there has been a lack of transparency in the actual outcomes of the many lawsuits arising out of abusive conduct in the mortgage market.

Certainty refers to both legal certainty regarding the actual content of the rules and practical certainty in respect of the ability of the process to ensure timely and adequate enforcement of the law. Individuals are entitled to know their respective rights and remedies.[46] Accountability is required because consumer borrowers' interests have been harmed. Yet no one has been held accountable such that the abusive practices that occurred have stopped, creating incentives for further misconduct in respect to mortgage lending and servicing in the future.

As co-author Sarra observed elsewhere, markets are socially constructed. Race, like markets, is a social construct and, like markets, involves a "complex interplay" among many individuals, organizations, and systems. The work of critical

[43] Mokal, *Theory*, 10–11, citing Ronald Dworkin, *Sovereign Virtue: The Theory and Practice of Equality* (Cambridge, MA: Harvard University Press, 2000).

[44] Davis et al, *Insolvency*.

[45] Davis et al, *Insolvency*, 42.

[46] Davis et al, *Insolvency*, 44.

race theorists is essential to understanding the economic exploitation of African-American mortgagors. Critical race theory helpfully informs consideration of the historical and economic contexts in which the law and financial markets operate. It provides a methodology for "studying and transforming the relationship among race, racism, and power" and places into perspective the relevance of "group- and self-interest."[47] Richard Delgado and Jean Stefancic observed:

> Unlike some academic disciplines, critical race theory contains an activist dimension. It not only tries to understand our social situation, but to change it; it sets out not only to ascertain how society organizes itself along racial lines and hierarchies, but to transform it for the better.[48]

Our goals, embodied in this book, align with the activist dimension of critical race theory and the attempt to not only understand the complex issue of racially discriminatory mortgage markets, but also to offer recommendations for reshaping such markets for the better.

Several fundamental observations of critical race theorists provide important insights that may mitigate the wealth-destructive impact of racial discrimination in the home mortgage context. Most critical race theorists conclude that "racism is ordinary, not aberrational ... the usual way society does business."[49] This observation is realistic, rather than merely bleak and pessimistic. Without understanding racism's ordinariness, it will flourish and thrive because it will be overlooked. The realization that racism is ordinary requires a heightened vigilance of all those individuals who claim to abhor it to mitigate the harm it causes. Understanding the ordinariness of racism reduces the likelihood that racism's casualties will be blamed for racism's consequences. This understanding will help to avoid the kind of victim blaming that we describe in Chapter 4, where some placed much of the condemnation for the foreclosure crisis on the individuals who were targeted for predatory loans.

Derrick Bell, the critical race movement's "intellectual father figure,"[50] articulated a fundamental critical race theory called "interest convergence," which we discuss in Chapter 10. Bell explained that *Brown* v *Board of Education* reversed state-sanctioned segregation only because the interests of white and black Americans converged.[51] Obviously, black Americans' interests revolved around the dismantling of segregation. White Americans' interests in reversing state-sanctioned segregation focused on rehabilitating the global reputation and standing of the United States

47 Richard Delgado and Jean Stefancic, *Critical Race Theory: An Introduction*, 3rd ed. (New York: New York University Press, 2001), 2–3 (hereafter Delgado and Stefancic, *Critical Race Theory*).

48 Delgado and Stefancic, *Critical Race Theory*.

49 Delgado and Stefancic, *Critical Race Theory*, 7.

50 Delgado and Stefancic, *Critical Race Theory*, 5.

51 See Derrick A. Bell, Jr, "*Brown v Board of Education* and the Interest Convergence Dilemma" (1980) 93 Harvard L Rev 518 (hereafter Bell, "*Brown v Board of Education*").

after the shame of centuries of slavery, degradation, torture, and exploitation of African Americans.[52] Bell concluded most Americans have little incentive to address racism because it benefits affluent white Americans financially.[53] Poor and working-class white Americans are similarly uninterested in eliminating racism because of the psychic benefits they enjoy as a result of embracing the privilege that whiteness affords in a racist U.S. social system.[54] In Chapter 10, we explain that the interests of white and black Americans converged only briefly in the immediate aftermath of the economic crisis that was precipitated by predatory lending and subsequently disappeared as a result of the racially skewed remedies that we describe in Chapters 6–8.

Another foundational tenet of critical race theory, the value of narrative, is central to the crux of this book. We describe the stories of the African Americans we interviewed and the ordeal they continue to endure more than a decade after having been targeted for predatory loans. Race theory's legal storytelling principle encourages people of colour to "recount their experiences with racism and the legal system and to apply their own unique perspectives to assess law's master narratives."[55] We provide narratives that enable assessment of the legal system and the financial markets.

Also invaluable to the discussion in this book is the work of race theorists about white privilege. Acknowledging white privilege is an important step towards revealing the systemic nature of racism. Stephanie Wildman and Adrienne Davis explain this idea:

> calling someone racist individualizes the behavior, ignoring the larger system within which the person is situated. To label an individual a racist conceals that racism can only occur where it is culturally, socially and legally supported. It lays the blame on the individual rather than the forces that have shaped that individual and the society that the individual inhabits. For white people this means that they know they do not want to be labeled racist. They become concerned with how to avoid that label, rather than worrying about systemic racism and how to change it.[56]

As we note in Chapter 3, it is imperative that analysis of predatory mortgage lending includes consideration of the systemic privileges and benefits that lenders, investors, and other market participants reaped in addition to examination of the ways that borrowers were disadvantaged.

[52] See Bell, "*Brown v Board of Education.*"
[53] See Bell, "*Brown v Board of Education.*"
[54] See Bell, "*Brown v Board of Education.*"
[55] Delgado and Stefancic, *Critical Race Theory*, 9. See also Richard Delgado, "Legal Storytelling: Storytelling for Oppositionists and Others: A Plea for Narrative" (1989) 87 Michigan L Rev, 2411.
[56] Stephanie Wildman and Adrienne Davis, "Language and Silence: Making Systems of Privilege Visible" in Richard Delgado, ed, *Critical Race Theory: The Cutting Edge* (Philadelphia: Temple University Press, 1995), 573 (hereafter Wildman and Davis, "Language").

When co-author Sarra wrote about fairness and financial markets elsewhere, she framed the issue by asking whether market regulation advances "collective notions of what is fair or just." Critical race theory provides a lens through which we examine the possibility of achieving fairness or justice for African Americans. The narratives of the African Americans we provide in this book reveal that they are not part of the collective that shapes notions of fairness and justice, which becomes even clearer upon consideration of the historical context that we provide in Chapter 4.

The failure of black homeownership as a pathway to economic parity parallels the failure of black entrepreneurship as a similar mechanism for African American upward mobility. In other words, black homeownership is a failed experiment in the same way that black entrepreneurship is. Both were supposed to serve as a road map for African Americans to achieve economic stability and financial equality with white Americans. The failure of both is attributable not to imagined or real deficiencies of the homeowners and entrepreneurs, but to systemic and structural racism. We describe the systemic racism inherent in the structure of racially discriminatory mortgage practices in this book. Systemic racism similarly erodes the possibility of wealth accumulation and economic fairness for black Americans through black entrepreneurship. Black entrepreneurs typically pay higher insurance rates than their white counterparts, face discrimination from suppliers of goods and services, have trouble finding investors, grapple with regulations that are applied in ways that discriminate, and are impeded by the intergenerational wealth gap that is exacerbated by predatory mortgage lending.[57] The question we face in this book is whether capitalism can work for African Americans. Perhaps another version of capitalism that includes anti-racism efforts, reparations, and redress when discrimination occurs will move U.S. society and financial markets closer to achieving economic justice for African Americans.

The difficulty of attaining economic justice for African Americans can be illustrated by the inapplicability of Rawlsian notions of the hypothetical choice position. It may be possible for individuals to have identical information about options for mortgage law principles, but the premise that individuals will have no information about their own identity may be unworkable in the United States. Even if it were hypothetically possible that a person would not know, or could set aside, information about his or her racial identity, the invisibility of white privilege would skew most white Americans' ability to give equal weight to the interests of African-American mortgage market participants. Rawls' theory may not work in a highly racialized society because it requires white Americans to consider the possibility that being black will erase the privileges their whiteness provides because that privilege is invisible to them. Many, if not most, white Americans embrace U.S. notions of meritocracy, and in more recent years, post-racialism. According equal concern to

57 See Aaron Ross Coleman, "Black Capitalism Won't Save Us" *The Nation* (22 May 2019), www.thenation.com/article/nipsey-killer-mike-race-economics/. See also Robert Suggs, "Rethinking Minority Business Development Strategies" (1990) 25 Harvard Civil Rights-Civil Liberties L Rev 101.

the interests of black Americans would require full acknowledgement of the role of racism in twenty-first century America, along with acceptance and understanding of the vulnerability of all black Americans – poor, working class, middle class, and even affluent. The invisibility of white privilege,[58] coupled with a nationwide failure to acknowledge the depth of black exploitation, make equal concern for black borrowers practically impossible for almost all white Americans.[59]

The intentionality of predatory and racially discriminatory mortgage practices explains the nation's failure to acknowledge the depth of black exploitation, and the impossibility of the goal that white Americans would have equal concern for black borrowers. Our discussion in this book is not shaped by recent critical race scholarship about implicit bias. The term implicit bias suggests that the bias "is generally outside the awareness and control of a person."[60] We are clear that the targeting of African Americans by predatory lenders and other actors related to such lending was, and continues to be, intentional.[61] The anti-black bias we describe in this book is not accidental or coincidental, and even though the bias may not be overtly or explicitly expressed, it is not implicit bias as that term is used in recent scholarship. It is clearly within the "awareness and control of a person." Nor is the discrimination we describe unconscious racism as that term was used in Charles Lawrence's foundational 1987 article on the topic.[62]

In the context of gender diversity in corporate boardrooms, Aaron Dhir persuasively argues that implicit cognitive biases likely explain boardroom homogeneity. "The presence of unconscious bias in the board appointment process ... generates a complex set of barriers for" women directors.[63] Dhir explains that when it comes to implicit biases, "judgments are instinctively and unintentionally generated, and may even contradict the individual's explicit philosophies and beliefs."[64] In Chapter 4,

58 Wildman and Davis, "Language."

59 Most black Americans, and very few white Americans, would agree with Derrick Bell about the reality and extent of black economic exploitation. "[B]lack people have been used to enrich this society and to serve as its proverbial scapegoat." Derrick Bell, "White Superiority in America: Its Legal Legacy, Its Economic Costs" (1988) 33 Villanova L Rev, 767 (hereafter Bell, "White Superiority"). The article continues, "A major function of racial discrimination is to facilitate the exploitation of black labor, to deny [African Americans] access to benefits and opportunities that would otherwise be available, and to blame all the manifestations of exclusion-bred despair on the asserted inferiority of the victims." Bell, "White Superiority," 767.

60 Justin D. Levinson and Robert J. Smith, eds, *Implicit Racial Bias Across the Law* (Cambridge: Cambridge University Press, 2012), 3.

61 See, generally, Carol Necole Brown, "Intent and Empirics: Race to the Subprime" (2010) 93 *Marquette Law Review* 907, showing "that the disparities in subprime lending experienced by black borrowers result from intentional reverse redlining and steering by lenders."

62 Charles R. Lawrence III, "The Id, the Ego, and Equal Protection: Reckoning with Unconscious Racism" (1987) 39 *Stanford Law Review*, 317.

63 See Aaron A. Dhir, *Challenging Boardroom Homogeneity: Corporate Law, Governance, and Diversity* (Cambridge: Cambridge University Press, 2015), 47 (hereafter Dhir, *Challenging Boardroom Homogeneity*).

64 Dhir, *Challenging Boardroom Homogeneity*, 49.

we describe how predatory lenders intentionally targeted African-American homebuyers, and in Chapter 9, we chronicle the continuing predation against African-American consumers. The intentionality of the predation is unmistakable. It is not instinctive, nor does it contradict lenders' explicit beliefs about black Americans and the ease with which they can be targeted. In Chapter 4, we provide historical context that explains the derivation of consciously held beliefs about African Americans from centuries-old stereotypes.

III A FOCUS ON AFRICAN AMERICANS AS SPECIFIC TARGETS OF PREDATORY LENDING

When discussing race and racism in the context of predatory lending, most authors focus on practices that targeted African-American and Latino-American (Latinx) borrowers. The narratives we gathered for this book, however, describe the ordeals suffered by black or African-American families, rather than those endured by members of the Latinx community. This focus is not because the interests of African Americans in this context are more salient or complex than those of Latinx and other Americans. In the twenty-first century, the American dream of homeownership appears to be close to unattainable for many people of colour and even for some white Americans.[65] But here, we set aside the pertinent economic interests of other Americans to focus on the particular concerns of African Americans.

While coalitions among people of colour and marginalized white Americans are desirable, it is also important to understand the ways that racism, in general, and economic discrimination, specifically, impact different groups differently. A close look at the economic issues that plague Latinx, Asian Americans, Native Americans, and some white Americans is imperative. However, we agree with Stephanie Wildman and Trina Grillo who advocate for the devotion of scholarly time and attention to one issue at a time – race or gender, for example – without the reflexive and mindlessly automatic drawing of analogies among disparate issues.[66] Similarly, we think it is important to spend some time discussing race in a way that examines the concerns of one racial group at a time – without lumping together the economic interests of all people of colour. Of course, discussions about race and economics should include the concerns of white Americans who live at the margins of our economy, but these Americans also deserve an exploration of their issues that is separate from discussions about other groups.

65 See e.g. Nancy Isenberg, *White Trash: The 400-Year Untold History of Class in America* (UK: Penguin Publishing, 2016) (hereafter Isenberg, *White Trash*). "First known as 'waste people,' and later 'white trash,' marginalized Americans were stigmatized for their inability to be productive, to own property, or to produce healthy and upwardly mobile children – the sense of uplift on which the American dream is predicated." Isenberg, *White Trash*, xiv.

66 Trina Grillo and Stephanie Wildman, "Obscuring the Importance of Race: The Implication of Making Comparisons between Racism and Sexism (or Other-Isms)" (1991) 40:2 Duke L J 397.

Unfortunately, the already complex discussion we undertake in this book is further complicated by semantics. Throughout this book, we use the terms "African American" and "black American" interchangeably. We acknowledge that many understand the group that is denominated African American to include only the descendants of Africans who were enslaved in the United States. Those individuals with this view would argue that the term black American is more inclusive and appropriately reflects the intra-racial diversity of individuals victimized by predatory lending who we interviewed. Some of our interviewees had emigrated to the United States from the Caribbean, and at least one individual is a first-generation immigrant from Africa. The families of some of our other interviewees have been in the United States for decades, or perhaps generations. The most accurate term for the individuals we interviewed, specifically, and those targeted by predatory lending, in general, may be "people of African descent who live in the United States." The clumsiness of this term, and the general controversy about the language used to discuss black people living in America reveal the complex nature of racial reality in the United States. These complexities make extremely difficult any discourse about race and racism in the United States. The difficulties that are inherent in the U.S. discourse about race make opaque the context or factual background that precipitated the drain of wealth from black families and black communities as a result of predatory lending practices. In this book, we sort through some of the racial complexity by revealing previously unheard narratives and providing context not considered until now.

We want to be clear that in using the term African American, we do not intend to exclude individuals of Caribbean descent and recent African immigrants. We simply conclude that, contrary to the beliefs of some, the term African American is appropriate because it encompasses what the subjects of this book have in common – African ancestry (for some much more recent than for others) and individuals who have chosen to make a home in the United States, also known as America. Identifying this controversy about semantics is important at the outset because it demonstrates that black Americans are not monolithic, which is essential to understand when grappling with the issues that we discuss in this book. Critical race and feminist legal theorists have long advocated against taking an essentialist approach when discussing race, gender, and other aspects of individual identity that ignore important differences among members of a particular group.[67]

[67] Gender essentialism is "the notion that a unitary, 'essential' women's experience can be isolated and described independently of race, class, sexual orientation, and other realities of experience." Angela P. Harris, "Race and Essentialism in Feminist Legal Theory" (1989–1990) 42 Stan L Rev, 581, 585. Extrapolating from this definition of gender essentialism is the idea that something similar happens in racial discourse when there is an attempt to define an essential black experience, or Latinx experience, that is independent of gender, class, sexual orientation, national origin, and other aspects of an individual's background.

It is important to take an anti-essentialist approach that acknowledges the differences in class, gender, sexual orientation, ancestry, and background among black people living in the United States.[68]

But, while it may be useful to acknowledge how national origin, class, gender, and other factors intersect with race, it is equally helpful to understand that in most contexts, discriminators rarely see these distinctions, especially when it comes to the discriminatory targeting of black Americans for predatory schemes. Lenders target black Americans for predatory loans without regard to whether they are African immigrants, of Caribbean descent, or African Americans whose families have been in the United States for many generations. In other words, the anti-essentialist intra-racial distinctions among black people that can be made are irrelevant and most likely invisible to predatory lenders.

The theory that U.S. racial categories have no basis in biological reality, but are social constructs that justify the exploitation of disadvantaged groups provides important context for understanding why lenders targeted black Americans for predatory loans.[69] Centuries ago, a racial category in the United States was created

[68] Inextricably linked to essentialism is intersection theory. The ground-breaking article on intersectionality explores the marginalization of black women in both "feminist legal theory and antiracist policy discourse because both are predicated on a discrete set of experiences that often does not accurately reflect the interaction of race and gender." Kimberle Crenshaw, "Demarginalizing the Intersection of Race and Sex: A Black Feminist Critique of Antidiscrimination Doctrine, Feminist Theory and Antiracist Politics" (1989) 1 *University of Chicago Legal Forum*, 140. Similarly, and most relevant to the discussion in this article, is the importance of acknowledging other intersections such as race and national origin. This distinction becomes troublesome, however, when some who are of Caribbean descent, or who are only the first, second, or third generation to emigrate from Africa believe that negative stereotypes about the descendants of Africans enslaved in the United States (i.e. African Americans) are true. One of the stereotypes that is most relevant to our discussion in this article is the notion that African Americans who have been in the United States for many generations are lazy and lack the requisite ambition to pursue homeownership.

[69] Ian F. Haney-López, "The Social Construction of Race: Some Observations on Illusion, Fabrication, and Choice" (1994) 29 Harv Cr-CL L Rev 1, 27 (hereafter Haney-López, "Social Construction of Race"): "[H]uman interaction rather than natural differentiation must be seen as the source and continued basis for racial categorization." But even though race is a social construction (i.e. a societal creation), it is "materially relevant" because, for example, the creation of a racial category denominated as "black" comes with stereotypes and prejudgments that affect individuals, institutions, and society in general; see Ann McGinley, "Policing and the Clash of Masculinities" (2015) 59 How LJ, 221– 241. "Race essentializes and stereotypes people, their social statuses, their social behaviors and their social ranking. In the United States and South Africa, one cannot escape the process of racialization; it is a basic element of the social system and customs of the United States and is deeply embedded in the consciousness of its people." Audrey Smedley and Brian Smedley, "Race as Biology Is Fiction, Racism as a Social Problem Is Real: Anthropological and Historical Perspectives on the Social Construction of Race" (2005) 60 *Am Psychologist* 16: 22 (hereafter Smedley and Smedley, "Race as Biology Is Fiction"). "Skin color, hair texture, nose width, and lip thickness have remained major markers of racial identity in the United States.… However, physical features and differences connoted by them are not the effective or direct causes of racism and discrimination. It is the culturally invented ideas and beliefs about these differences that constitute the meaning of race." Smedley and Smedley, "Race as Biology Is Fiction," 20.

and its members were called Negro, and eventually Afro American, then black, and then African American. Differences in culture, class, ethnicity, and national origin were unseen and irrelevant in the creation of this racial category, but its creation was essential to the justification of the enslavement of the members of this racial group. Not only was the racial group a creation of society, but the characteristics attributed to the group were also a social construction. Members of the group were constructed as lazy, ignorant, and subhuman. These stereotypes justified their enslavement and exploitation. In this book, we consider the durability of these centuries-old stereotypes along with twenty-first century racial animus as the factors that explain, at least in part, why lenders targeted black Americans for predatory sub-prime mortgages.

3

Predatory Lending Practices Prior to the Global Financial Crisis

The 2008 financial crisis resulted in an exponential increase in foreclosures of residential homes in the United States, but there were serious issues regarding mortgage lending practices and foreclosures prior to the financial crisis. This chapter examines the predatory and sub-prime lending that occurred in the years leading up to the collapse of the sub-prime mortgage market, during which time mortgage lenders developed numerous new products with opaque and predatory terms. As noted in the introduction, a dual mortgage market emerged in which sub-prime lenders primarily served African Americans, while conventional lending institutions primarily served white borrowers.[1] Even after controlling for differences in borrower and neighbourhood risk characteristics, African-American and Latinx borrowers were more likely to receive sub-prime loans and/or loans with other risky product features than similarly situated white borrowers.[2]

This chapter examines the various mechanisms used in predatory mortgages, including inappropriate and sometimes fraudulent conduct such as misleading terms, false estimates, and inadequate disclosure. It examines the racism underpinning high-pressure sales tactics and punitive prepayment penalties. Brokers were compensated in up-front fees from the borrower, from the lender, or both, so performance of the loan did not matter to them. Fees were often paid without the borrower's knowledge.[3] Many borrowers mistakenly believed mortgage brokers acted

1 Debbie Gruenstein Bocian, Wei Li, and Carolina Reid, "Lost Ground, 2011: Disparities in Mortgage Lending and Foreclosures" (2011) Center for Responsible Lending, 8, University of North Carolina, www.responsiblelending.org/mortgage-lending/research-analysis/Lost-Ground-2011.pdf (hereafter Bocian et al, "Lost Ground").

2 Bocian et al, "Lost Ground," 8.

3 Financial Crisis Inquiry Commission, *Final Report of the National Commission on the Causes of the Financial and Economic Crisis in the United States, Submitted Pursuant to Public Law 111–21* (Washington, DC: FCIC, January 2011), 90, https://fcic-static.law.stanford.edu/cdn_media/fcic-reports/fcic_final_report_full.pdf (hereafter FCIC Report).

in borrowers' best interests.[4] One common fee the lender paid to the broker was the "yield spread premium," which meant that on higher-interest loans the lending bank would pay the broker a higher premium, giving the incentive to sign the borrower to the highest possible rate.[5]

These practices and many others created a pernicious downward cycle for African Americans in terms of loss of wealth and of homes. Housing is particularly important to the economic security of African Americans. Home equity constitutes 60 per cent of black household wealth, compared with 45 per cent for whites,[6] meaning that foreclosure is even more devastating on personal wealth.[7] Loss of equity investment in the home thus has a disproportionately harmful effect on African Americans' financial security. A study by the Pew Research Center in 2009 found that there is a growing racial wealth gap between white and black households. While 15 per cent of white households had no or negative wealth, 35 per cent of black households had no or negative economic wealth.[8]

Only three years into the crisis, the Financial Crisis Inquiry Commission (FCIC) found that four million families had already lost their homes to foreclosure with another four and a half million pending foreclosures or mortgagors seriously behind on their mortgage payments.[9] By 2011, $11 trillion in household wealth had vanished, including retirement accounts and life savings completely lost.[10]

I COLLUSION BY MARKET PLAYERS

The FCIC documented many unethical and illegal practices in the period leading up to 2008.[11] There was collusion among financial institutions, brokers, and disreputable home improvement contractors or other vendors targeting vulnerable groups, including racial minorities, immigrants, and the elderly.[12] Many mortgage products

4 FCIC Report, 90.
5 FCIC Report, 90.
6 Mechele Dickerson, *Homeownership and America's Financial Underclass: Flawed Premises, Broken Promises, New Prescriptions* (Cambridge: Cambridge University Press, 2014), 193 (hereafter Dickerson, *Homeownership*).
7 American Civil Liberties Union, "Justice Foreclosed: How Wall Street's Appetite for Subprime Mortgages Ended Up Hurting Black and Latino Communities" (October 2012), www.aclu.org/sites/default/files/field_document/justiceforclosed-singlepage-rel4.pdf (hereafter American Civil Liberties Union, "Justice Foreclosed"), 12.
8 Rakesh Kochhar et al, "Twenty to One: Wealth Gaps Rise to Record Highs between Whites, Blacks and Hispanics" (2011), Pew Research Center, www.pewresearch.org/wp-content/uploads/sites/3/2011/07/SDT-Wealth-Report_7-26-11_FINAL.pdf (hereafter Kochhar et al, "Twenty to One").
9 FCIC Report.
10 FCIC Report, xv.
11 FCIC Report.
12 Christopher Peterson, "Predatory Structured Finance" (2007) 28:5 *Cardozo Law Review* 2185–2189, 2215–2216, https://ssrn.com/abstract=929118 (hereafter Peterson, "Predatory Structured"); Celeste M. Hammond, "Predatory Lending: A Legal Definition and Update" (2005) 34 Real Est L J 176 (hereafter Hammond, "Predatory Lending").

had no caps on the amount of interest that could be charged over time. Often variable rates were not disclosed in the loan documents.

Regulatory capture was a huge issue, allowing the collusion to thrive. There was a global wave of deregulation across all aspects of financial markets. International banking standards under Basel II effectively allowed banks and other financial institutions to regulate their own governance and capital adequacy. Financial institutions were viewed as too-big-to-fail. In the United States, there was rapid rise in what is referred to as the "shadow banking sector," non-deposit taking banks and lenders that did not come under the regulatory oversight of banking, weak as it was becoming. Deregulation meant that mortgage lending was not subject to effective oversight either by firm principals or by regulators. The structure of credit rating also contributed to the market meltdown because the companies selling the financial products compensated the credit rating agencies for ratings, creating incentives for favourable ratings.

II "REDLINING" AND DISCRIMINATORY ZONING SET THE STAGE FOR PREDATORY LENDING

The Federal Home Loan Bank System was created in 1932 to "promote home ownership in the United States," but, as Meshra Baradaran points out, it also "initiated a century of devastating race inequality" as the agencies created to facilitate mortgage lending practiced racially discriminating "redlining."[13] The Federal Home Loan Bank Board commissioned the creation of "residential security maps" for over 200 cities, creating a red line around almost all the minority neighbourhoods and deeming them ineligible for mortgage financing.[14] It prevented access for people in these communities to this cheaper source of mortgage credit. Coupled with the fact that racial covenants in many neighbourhoods prevented the sale of homes to non-white Americans, it effectively prohibited access to the most cost-effective mortgages.[15]

In addition, the Federal Housing Administration (FHA) refused to provide insurance for loans to African Americans or anyone who wanted to buy a home in redlined neighbourhoods.[16] Given that lenders would not approve low-cost loans unless they were federally insured, and because the FHA would not insure loans to

13 Mehrsa Baradaran, *How the Other Half Banks: Exclusion, Exploitation, and the Threat to Democracy* (Cambridge, MA: Harvard University Press, 2015), 46–47 (hereafter Baradaran, *How the Other Half Banks*).

14 Baradaran, *How the Other Half Banks*, 47.

15 Baradaran, *How the Other Half Banks*, 47.

16 Douglas Massey, "Origins of Economic Disparities: The Historical Role of Housing Segregation" in James Carr and Nandinee Kutty, eds, *Segregation: The Rising Costs for America* (New York: Routledge, 2008).

purchase homes in racially mixed neighbourhoods,[17] redlining increased the cost of mortgages for African Americans. This lack of access to mortgage loans and insurance also exacerbated white flight from redlined neighbourhoods and resulted in serious deterioration of many inner-city neighbourhoods.[18] Even white borrowers who were interested in living in racially mixed neighbourhoods faced barriers to doing so because they could not get a low-cost FHA-insured mortgage in such neighbourhoods.[19]

Moreover, many cities in the United States enacted and enforced racial discrimination in zoning laws, prohibiting African Americans and Latinx would-be homeowners from purchasing homes in white neighbourhoods.[20] Racial segregation persisted even after the U.S. Supreme Court found these laws to be unconstitutional because state and federal courts enforced real property covenants that prevented white homeowners from selling their homes to non-white Americans.[21] Combined with real estate brokers and federal agencies steering African Americans away from white neighbourhoods, *de facto* racial segregation continued even after racially restrictive covenants were struck down.[22] Mechele Dickerson notes that although the 1968 Fair Housing Act and the 1974 Equal Opportunity Credit Act made it illegal to engage in discriminatory lending practices, African Americans and Latinx consumers faced discrimination in access to mortgages, being unable to buy low-cost, low-risk government-insured mortgage loans.[23]

Even after race-restrictive covenants were found illegal, cities enacted racist ordinances. When the ordinances were struck down, private deeds contained restrictive covenants.[24] Moreover, even where they were legally allowed to move into white neighbourhoods, African-American families were subjected to harassment, destruction of their homes, and violence. In some instances, police authorities told them they would no longer respond to calls regarding property destruction or harassment if they continued to live in the neighbourhood.[25] Dickerson notes that in addition to the risk of being physically injured or killed, African Americans who bought homes in white communities often were unable to obtain insurance because insurers had concluded that the risks of vandalism or having the home torched were high.[26]

17 Dickerson, *Homeownership*, 149.
18 Baradaran, *How the Other Half Banks*, 47.
19 James Carr and Nandinee Kutty, "The New Imperative for Equality" in James Carr and Nandiness Kutty, eds, *Segregation: The Rising Costs for America* (New York: Routledge, 2008), 1.
20 Dickerson, *Homeownership*, 13.
21 Dickerson, *Homeownership*.
22 Dickerson, *Homeownership*.
23 Dickerson, *Homeownership*, 13.
24 Dickerson, *Homeownership*, 155.
25 Dickerson, *Homeownership*, 156.
26 Dickerson, *Homeownership*.

III CARELESS AND PREDATORY LENDING COMMENCED PRIOR TO THE GLOBAL FINANCIAL CRISIS

In the period leading up to the collapse of the sub-prime mortgage market, there was ample evidence of careless and predatory lending practices. Christopher Peterson lists numerous ways in which sub-prime mortgage lending involved inappropriate and sometimes fraudulent conduct.[27] He notes that it involved one or more of fraud, misleading terms, false estimates, broker commissions for loans that exceeded a risk-adjusted price, inclusion of overpriced or unnecessary insurance, unnecessarily harsh prepayment penalties, inflated appraisals, forgery, and distorted loan structure to avoid the application of consumer protection statutes.[28] Sales people allocated insufficient time to review documents at closing, engaged in mark-ups on third-party services, repeated refinancing of loans over a short period of time to capture closing costs, and incorrectly calculated interest and other charges.[29]

1 *Predatory Products*

There was acute unfairness in the mortgage market in terms of the products sold to African Americans and the processes for dealing with issues or concerns as they arose. Not only did the market exhibit a careless disregard for consumer borrowers in the types of products offered, thus the antithesis of being "other-regarding," it met not a single one of the criteria for substantive and procedural fairness, including accessibility, transparency, certainty, and accountability.

Various mortgage products offered teaser interest rates in the first few months or first year, with rapidly accelerating percentage interest rates in the three months to a year following origination, many with no caps on how high interest rates could increase over time.[30] Often variable rates were not disclosed in the loan documents. Mortgage brokers sold mortgages with low down payments, and credit was granted with little or no inquiry into the credit worthiness of individuals.[31] Mortgage lenders aggressively promoted these products, the terms of which

27 Peterson, "Predatory Structured," 2215.

28 Peterson, "Predatory Structured."

29 Peterson, "Predatory Structured."

30 Jennifer S. Taub, *Other People's Houses* (New Haven, CT: Yale University Press, 2014) (hereafter Taub, *Other People's Houses*).

31 Taub, *Other People's Houses*, 4–5, 47–49. Taub traces the origins of the 2008 foreclosure crisis to the 1980s when industry successfully lobbied federal and state regulators to liberalize lending laws, and savings and loan companies and associations (S&L) to attract billions in wholesale funding and enable them to make high yielding, risky real estate development loans and to invest in assets that were junk bond status. She also observes that in the late 1980s private investors received billions in tax breaks and government guarantees to purchase the good assets of failed S&L, leaving behind the bad assets, the cost of which was paid by taxpayers.

were poorly explained or not disclosed.[32] The breadth of these loans contributed to what was already a housing bubble in terms of soaring property values and mortgage sales.

Payments were initially lower for interest-only mortgages because none of the principal was being paid off even when the borrower was diligently making all payments. In many cases, the full amount of the interest was not being paid monthly. Then, when the teaser rate period ended, the interest-only mortgages became fully amortized with the unpaid interest added to the principal to form a higher principal balance than the initial loan.[33] In the three years prior to 2005, interest-only loans went from 1 per cent of mortgages to 37 per cent of mortgages.[34]

The development of adjustable-rate mortgages (ARM) had pre-crisis origins, but these mortgages soared in numbers and market share in the several years leading up to the 2008 financial crisis. The Center for Responsible Lending defines ARM as loans with any one of the following characteristics: ARM with interest rate resets of less than five years, negative amortization, or interest-only payment schedules.[35] The Consumer Financial Protection Bureau notes the difference between a traditional mortgage and an ARM:

> The difference between a fixed rate and an adjustable rate mortgage is that, for fixed rates the interest rate is set when you take out the loan and will not change. With an adjustable rate mortgage, the interest rate may go up or down. Many ARMs will start at a lower interest rate than fixed rate mortgages. This initial rate may stay the same for months, one year, or a few years. When this introductory period is over, your interest rate will change, and the amount of your payment is likely to go up.[36]

By 2004, "option-ARM" became popular because monthly payments were lower than more traditional mortgages, with many borrowers making only the minimum payments required.[37] By 2005 and 2006, 10 per cent of all mortgage borrowers in the United States took out option-ARM loans, which meant the amount owing on their mortgage rose every month despite diligence in making payments.[38]

[32] Janis Sarra, "Embedding Fairness as a Fundamental Norm in Financial Markets" in Janis P. Sarra, ed, *An Exploration of Fairness, Interdisciplinary Inquiries in Law, Science and the Humanities* (Toronto: Carswell, 2012) (hereafter Sarra, "Embedding Fairness").

[33] Dickerson, *Homeownership*, 79.

[34] Dickerson, *Homeownership*, 80.

[35] "Higher rate is defined as first-lien loans for which the annual percentage rate (APR) was 300 basis points or more above Treasury rates of comparable maturity" (Bocian et al, "Lost Ground," 4).

[36] Consumer Financial Protection Bureau, *What is the difference between a fixed-rate and adjustable-rate mortgage (ARM) loan?* (25 September 2017), www.consumerfinance.gov/ask-cfpb/what-is-the-difference-between-a-fixed-rate-and-adjustable-rate-mortgage-arm-loan-en-100/.

[37] FCIC Report, 106.

[38] FCIC Report, xx.

For example, Countrywide began issuing "pay-option ARM" in 2000, and by 2004 they were a large part of Countrywide's loan originations.[39] In some instances, pay-option ARM borrowers were able to make payments that were less than the interest that accrued on the principal balance each month. The difference between the amount of interest that accrued on the loan and that lower payment is called negative amortization and was added to the principal balance of the loan. If the loan's principal balance reached a certain amount, frequently 110 per cent or 115 per cent of the original loan amount, the loan payment reset to the amount necessary to amortize the principal balance. This reset could result in substantially higher payments for borrowers, resulting in a form of what became known in the industry as "payment shock."[40] By 2005, 68 per cent of pay-option ARM loans originated by Countrywide and Washington Mutual (WaMu) had low- or no-documentation requirements.[41] The FCIC found that many mortgage lenders wilfully disregarded a borrower's inability to pay.[42]

Jennifer Taub observes that ARM low teaser interest rates were often 1 per cent, which was then reset upwards after one to three months and then adjusted each month afterwards.[43] Despite the interest reset rate, the consumer often was not immediately aware of the changes in interest rate because the monthly payments did not change in the first year, but rather, the accumulating interest was added to the loan principal.[44] Brokers received commissions and higher fees for steering consumers into sub-prime predatory mortgages with higher interest rates. Lenders at all levels of the mortgage food chain were rewarded for volume of sales of these deceptive mortgages. During this period, earnings in the financial sector for mortgage executives averaged $3.4 million annually, the highest of any industry.[45]

A second feature of ARM involved payment options, which were inaccurately explained or not explained at all. Borrowers were encouraged to make monthly interest-only payments, which were marketed as an option that kept payments to a reasonable level; the borrowers did not understand that the principal amount was never being paid down. Minimum payment options, which involved paying only a fraction of the interest accruing, added the deferred interest to the amount of the loan so that the borrower was going even further into debt although making all the mortgage monthly payments. Both options resulted in the borrower never paying down the loan and the amount of debt accumulating rapidly. Borrowers would be

39 Bank of America Settlement Agreement Annex 1 Statement of Facts (21 August 2014), Department of Justice, www.justice.gov/iso/opa/resources/4312014829141220799708.pdf (hereafter Bank of America DOJ Settlement, Annex 1).

40 Bank of America DOJ Settlement, Annex 1.

41 FCIC Report, xxiii.

42 FCIC Report, xxiii.

43 Taub, *Other People's Houses*, 126.

44 Taub, *Other People's Houses*.

45 FCIC Report, 63.

almost immediately underwater in terms of their capacity to pay. Lenders received the value of all the payments until the borrower defaulted and then were able to foreclose and repossess, thus realizing the full value of the property.[46]

Lenders marketed ARM to borrowers with limited income who were drawn in by the low interest rates and not informed about the short, medium, and long term consequences.[47] If they were told about the re-amortization, they were told not to worry about it as they would likely be earning more in the future and would be able to make payments by the time of the re-amortization, or they could always sell their home or refinance.[48] By 2006, between 70 per cent and 80 per cent of mortgage borrowers were only paying the monthly minimum.[49] For companies such as WaMu, 95 per cent of borrowers were paying only the monthly minimum.[50]

A study by two Federal Reserve economists estimated at least 38 per cent of borrowers with ARM did not understand how much their interest rates could reset at one time, and more than half underestimated how high their rates could reach over several years.[51] The same lack of awareness extended to other terms of the loan, for example, the level of documentation provided to the lender. Another way lenders sold mortgages quickly was to require less information about the borrower.[52] Stated income, low-documentation, or sometimes no-documentation (no-doc) loans had emerged for people with fluctuating or hard-to-verify incomes, such as the self-employed.[53] In return, lenders charged a higher interest rate. By 2007, no-doc loans were 9 per cent of all outstanding loans.[54] "Most borrowers didn't even realize that they were getting a no-doc loan," observed Michael Calhoun, president of the Center for Responsible Lending. "They'd come in with their W-2 and end up with a no-doc loan simply because the broker was getting paid more and the lender was getting paid more and there was extra yield left over for Wall Street because the loan carried a higher interest rate."[55]

[46] Taub, *Other People's Houses*, 126.
[47] Taub, *Other People's Houses*, 129.
[48] Taub, *Other People's Houses*, 127.
[49] Taub, *Other People's Houses*.
[50] Taub, *Other People's Houses*.
[51] United States, Board of Governors of the Federal Reserve System and Department of Housing and Urban Development, *Joint Report to the Congress Concerning Reform to the Truth and Lending Act and the Real Estate Settlement Procedures Act* (Washington, DC: HUD, July 1998), 56, HUD, www.huduser.gov/portal//Publications/pdf/HUD-11647.pdf.
[52] FCIC Report, 110.
[53] FCIC Report, 110.
[54] FCIC Report, 110.
[55] FCIC Report, 90, citing Griffith Garwood, Director, Division of Consumer and Community Affairs, Board of Governors of the Federal Reserve System, Consumer Affairs Letter CA 98-1 "To the Officers and Managers in Charge of Consumer Affairs Examination and Consumer Complaint Programs" (20 January 1998), FCIC, https://fcic-static.law.stanford.edu/cdn_media/fcic-docs/1998-01-20%20Federal%20Reserve%20Consumer%20Affairs%20Letter%20CA%2098-1%20(To%20the%20Officers%20and%20Managers%20in%20Charge%20o.pdf.

The "2/28" or "3/27" mortgages, also known as hybrid-ARM, were ostensibly created to allow credit-impaired borrowers the opportunity to repair their credit.[56] During the first two to three years, a lower interest rate meant a manageable payment schedule and enabled borrowers to demonstrate they could make timely payments. Eventually, the interest rates would rise sharply, and payments would double or even triple, leaving borrowers with few alternatives. If the borrowers were deemed creditworthy, then they could refinance into a similar mortgage or one with a better interest rate, often with the same lender. If the borrowers were unable to refinance, then they were unlikely to be able to afford the new higher payments and would have to sell the home and repay the mortgage. If the borrowers could not sell or make the higher payments, then they would have to default.[57] These complex subprime mortgages overwhelmed borrowers when interest rates shot up after an introductory time period.[58] If the borrower could not pay or refinance, then the lender would foreclose and benefit from sale of the home in a rising real estate market.[59]

The market was flooded with exotically named mortgages: Alt-A, low-doc, or ninja (no income, no job, no assets) loans, "piggyback mortgages," or "pick-a-pay ARM."[60] New variants on ARM, called "exploding ARM," featured low monthly costs at first, but payments could suddenly triple if borrowers were unable to refinance.[61] Loans with negative amortization would eat away the borrower's equity.[62] Some borrowers naively trusted mortgage brokers who earned more money placing them in risky loans than in safe ones.[63]

A piggyback mortgage was a predatory mortgage arrangement in which a lender offered a first mortgage for perhaps 80 per cent of the home's value and a second mortgage for another 10 per cent or even 20 per cent.[64] Borrowers liked these arrangements because their monthly payments were initially cheaper than a traditional mortgage plus the required mortgage insurance, and the interest payments were tax deductible.[65] Lenders liked them because the smaller second mortgage, even without mortgage insurance, could potentially be sold to the government-sponsored entities.[66] At the same time, the piggyback mortgages added risks. These mortgages placed the pressure of paying two mortgages on the borrower, considerably

56 FCIC Report, 105.
57 FCIC Report, 105.
58 FCIC Report, 105.
59 FCIC Report, 105.
60 FCIC Report, 6.
61 FCIC Report, 7.
62 FCIC Report, 7.
63 FCIC Report, 7, citing Julia Gordon and Michael Calhoun (Center for Responsible Lending), interview by FCIC (16 September 2010), http://fcic.law.stanford.edu/interviews/view/60 (hereafter Gordon and Calhoun, Interview).
64 FCIC Report, 110.
65 FCIC Report.
66 Government-sponsored entities are discussed in Chapter 4.

increasing the risk of inability to pay and eventual default and foreclosure. A borrower with a higher combined loan-to-value (LTV) had less equity in the home.

In a rising market, should payments become unmanageable, the borrower could always sell the home and come out ahead. However, should the payments become unmanageable in a falling market, the borrower would owe more than the home is worth.[67] Piggyback loans, which often did not require down payments, guaranteed that many borrowers would end up with negative equity if housing prices fell, especially if the appraisal had overstated the initial value.[68] By September 2005, those borrowers with piggyback mortgages were four times as likely as other mortgage holders to be 60 or more days delinquent.[69]

The Center for Responsible Lending found a pervasive practice of yield-spread premiums, which are monetary incentives for mortgage brokers to inflate rates on sub-prime loans. Black Americans were particularly targeted for mortgages in which yield-spread premiums accrued to brokers.[70] As a former loan officer for Wells Fargo testified in *Baltimore* v *Wells Fargo*, "Since loan officers made more money when they charged higher interest rates and fees to borrowers, there was a great financial incentive to put as many minority borrowers as possible into sub-prime loans and to charge these borrowers higher rates and fees."[71] For example, on an interest-only mortgage of about $600,000, Wells Fargo charged $20,000 just for its fee to originate the loan.[72] Lenders had direct incentives to lend irresponsibly. Often the loans were sold by the mortgage originator immediately, and the mortgagor did not know that the company she or he had borrowed from no longer held the debt, unless the mortgagor had occasion to make an inquiry about their mortgage. In some cases, the loan originator just continued to transfer the payments to the loan purchaser, without the consumer borrower even being aware of the sale of the mortgage.[73] Many African-American mortgage payors had trouble finding out who to contact if they had queries about payments or even how to ascertain who actually held the mortgage that had been sold several times.[74]

These predatory practices inflicted on the borrower side of the market were accompanied by equally inappropriate behaviour on the lending side, which really

67 FCIC Report, 110.
68 FCIC Report.
69 FCIC Report, 110.
70 Gordon and Calhoun, Interview, 4.
71 Declaration of Tony Paschal in *City of Baltimore* v *Wells Fargo Bank*, No 8-062 (JFM), Document 133 Plaintiff Memorandum (D Md filed 16 October 2009), 9, Civil Rights Litigation Clearinghouse, www.clearinghouse.net/chDocs/public/FH-MD-0001-0009.pdf (hereafter *Baltimore* v *Wells Fargo*, Plaintiff Memorandum), cited in American Civil Liberties Union, "Justice Foreclosed," 8, 24.
72 American Civil Liberties Union, "Justice Foreclosed," 13.
73 Taub, *Other People's Houses*, 14.
74 Alice Nicholson, lawyer specializing in foreclosures, interview, New York, September 2018 (on file with authors) (hereafter Nicholson, Interview).

accelerated the conditions for market failure. Sub-prime and Alt-A mortgage–backed securities depended on a complex supply chain, largely funded through short-term lending in the market, which would become critical as the financial crisis began to unfold.[75] These loans were increasingly collateralized by highly rated mortgage securities backed by increasingly risky loans. Independent mortgage originators such as Ameriquest and New Century, without access to deposits, typically relied on financing to originate mortgages from warehouse lines of credit extended by banks, from their own commercial paper products, or from money borrowed in the repo market (repurchase agreements market), essentially collateralized short-term loans. For commercial banks such as Citigroup, warehouse lending was a multibillion-dollar business.[76]

Institutions relied for their operating cash on short-term funding through the commercial paper and the repo markets.[77] But just prior to the financial meltdown, commercial paper buyers and banks became unwilling to continue funding them, and repo lenders became less and less willing to accept sub-prime and Alt-A mortgages or mortgage-backed securities as collateral.[78] They also insisted on ever-shorter maturities, eventually of just one day, inherently destabilizing demand, because it gave them the option of withholding funding on short notice if they lost confidence in the borrower.[79] Another sign of problems in the market became apparent when financial companies began to report more detail about their assets under the new mark-to-market accounting rules, particularly about mortgage-related securities that were becoming illiquid and hard to value.[80]

Taub points out that accounting rules exacerbated the incentives for misconduct because they allowed the deferred unpaid interest to be booked as income since it was eroding the borrowers' equity in the home.[81] Then, at five years, the ARM mortgage would "recast," meaning that the terms allowed the lender to establish a new monthly payment that was based on a new larger principal amount that included the original principal plus all the accumulated interest.[82]

Also, African Americans were more likely to be offered sub-prime loans that carried prepayment penalties, so that it was impossible to refinance the high-interest mortgage.[83] Although 2 per cent of traditional mortgages contained prepayment penalties, the Home Mortgage Disclosure Act data revealed that 70 per cent of sub-prime mortgages in the period leading up to the financial crisis contained

[75] FCIC Report, 113.
[76] FCIC Report, 113.
[77] FCIC Report, 234.
[78] FCIC Report, 234.
[79] FCIC Report, 234.
[80] FCIC Report, 234.
[81] Taub, *Other People's Houses*, 127.
[82] Taub, *Other People's Houses*.
[83] Dickerson, *Homeownership*, 167.

prepayment penalties; and the likelihood that the sub-prime mortgage contained a prepayment penalty was 30 per cent higher if the borrower lived in a postal code area that had a high percentage of African Americans and other minority Americans.[84] By 2010, 25 per cent of African Americans who received a mortgage from 2004 to 2008 had lost their homes to foreclosure or were seriously delinquent in payments, compared with 12 per cent of white borrowers.[85]

2 *One First-hand Account*

Before turning to the reasons for collapse of the sub-prime mortgage market, here is one account among the millions of how individuals were affected by predatory lending. The following narrative of a couple in Queens, New York illustrates how people who qualified for traditional mortgages were steered into inappropriate products and the continuing painful legacy of these sub-prime mortgages. The husband was a litigation administrative manager for a large New York law firm. These words are his in September 2018, exactly ten years after the sub-prime market meltdown:

> My wife was pregnant, and we lived in an apartment. In 2007, we bought a home. We got a loan even though no one checked my income. I didn't have a lawyer but the loan didn't look right to me, so I said, "I can't sign this", and two days later, Wells Fargo came back to me with another loan, which we thought looked better and must be alright. I made my payments regularly, but when the financial crisis hit, hundreds of lawyers and staff were laid off from my firm. I was forced to take a buyout and lost my job. I notified Wells Fargo right away about the loss of income. My wife stayed home with our child, but after her leave, they laid her off too. I worked for a major law firm; my wife was a bookkeeper/manager in the accounting department of a hotel. So many people were laid off then—because of the downturn. Wells Fargo worked out a deal for me where I made trial payments, but the idea was really to drain our savings and then push us out. I had trouble making the payments, so I asked the bank about the formula they used to come up with the amount I was supposed to pay. I appealed the bank's decision, but I never got an explanation for the Wells Fargo formula.
>
> I went to all ends to get help. One time when I went on vacation, I took all my mortgage documents with me to the Florida Wells Fargo office. On another occasion, I drove from New York City to Philadelphia with all my documents. I slept in the car, got in line and tried to get advice from the Philadelphia office. That office was decorated with balloons, they were giving out Wells Fargo t-shirts, they took all the documents, but I got no help. Wells Fargo then sent letters to come to hotels

[84] Debbie Gruenstein Bocian, Keith S. Ernst, and Wei Li, "Race, Ethnicity and Subprime Home Loan Pricing" (2008) 60 *J Econ & Bus*, 110–111.

[85] Debbie Gruenstein Bocian, Wei Li and Keith S. Ernst, "Foreclosures by Race and Ethnicity" (18 June 2010) Center for Responsible Lending, www.responsiblelending.org/mortgage-lending/research-analysis/foreclosures-by-race-and-ethnicity.pdf; and Bocian et al, "Lost Ground."

for "education." But the purpose of the centres was to offer us $5,000 or $10,000 to move and then take our house.

My wife and children—we're still in our home. We are fighting the bank. I know several friends who were able to get large loans with no documents—then the property was gone. I know people who have committed suicide. When I went to my doctor, I found out that I have high blood pressure. I can't sleep at night. I'm impatient and I find myself yelling at my wife and my children. My wife has shut down. [The couple starts to cry.] I have to get up in the middle of the night to pray. It's hard to explain all of this to my children. I don't know whether my marriage will survive this stress. I thought I was intelligent. I work hard. I don't use drugs. What did I do wrong? This takes so much out of me. I want to give up. I've spent over $50,000 on lawyers. I'm trying to hold family together. What do I have to do?

His lawyer observes that the Obama administration–initiated mortgage modification program[86] was ineffective. The banks claim that they will help, but they don't. Based on thousands of foreclosures she has been involved in, she observes that there are huge issues with appropriate serving of notice and with short sales.[87] The practice of "nail and mail," nailing to the door (the notice may or may not still be there when the borrower comes home) and then putting a foreclosure notice in the regular surface mail, means that individuals are frequently not given notice of the foreclosure proceeding and it is over before they receive notice, if they ever receive it. She also reports that the courts have become impatient with foreclosures and want to clear the files from their dockets, so they are allowing this short-circuiting of proper notice. Yet failing to appear leaves the borrower without recourse: if you did not answer the notice, you have no claim.[88] As discussed in Chapter 2, meaningful notice and the opportunity to be heard are fundamental to the underlying principle of fairness. That the courts would be complicit in denying individuals these rights so they can clear their dockets is highly inappropriate. Yet those individuals and families victimized by foreclosure do not have access to the information or resources to appeal these decisions.

Lawyer Alice Nicholson also notes that lenders have agreed in many cases to take a reduced amount for six months when clients are unemployed, essentially taking the unemployment benefit cheque amount. Then the lender comes back after six months with a bill for the deficiencies, asking for a lump sum to catch up on the payments, knowing that the homeowner cannot pay.[89] Thus, the whole plan is to foreclose on the borrower.[90] The other very common practice is to offer a trial modification for homeowners who are employed, and at the end of the three-month trial modification, say they are still reviewing and not making a decision on permanent modification as they are supposed to.

[86] The modification program is discussed in Chapter 7.
[87] Short sales are discussed in Chapter 7.
[88] Nicholson, Interview.
[89] Nicholson, Interview.
[90] Nicholson, Interview.

Like many others, this couple had to file for bankruptcy to effect a stay of the foreclosure, but this measure is temporary, at best, as discussed in Chapter 6.

3 *Predatory Refinancing and Loss of Equity*

It is important to understand that predatory mortgage financing was not just targeted at individuals entering the housing market for the first time. Predatory lenders also targeted individuals who had owned homes for some time and had built up a great deal of equity, many even having fully paid for their homes. ARM were aggressively sold as re-financing mortgages. Lenders told borrowers that they could free up some money by taking a mortgage on their equity or cut their interest rates in half, but did not tell them about the accumulating interest.[91] They were not informed that refinancing would cost thousands of dollars in application fees and penalties.[92]

The amount of mortgage debt per household in the United States rose from $91,500 in 2001 to $149,500 in 2007. The FCIC found that millions of Americans traded away decades of equity built up in their homes.[93] Even where consumers had accumulated equity savings, predatory lenders took advantage of them. The FCIC found that there was an advertising barrage that bombarded potential borrowers, urging them to refinance their homes: "Direct-mail solicitations flooded people's mailboxes, loan officers offering the latest loan products: 1 percent loans! (But only for the first year.)"[94]

These practices reveal how unfairness was embedded in the market. Mortgage originators and brokers masked the actual costs of the loans in their sales pitches. They knew that they would not be held accountable for misrepresentations because the mortgages would be sold on in the market before the ink was dry on the loan documents, which leads to the next discussion: the role that securitization played in precipitating and then exacerbating the meltdown of the sub-prime mortgage market.

4 *Securitization as a Significant Cause of the Sub-prime Meltdown*

There were a number of contributing factors to the sub-prime mortgage collapse; however, there is no doubt that a significant cause was securitization, which created a rapidly expanding market for highly risky mortgages.[95] Securitization, if used

[91] Nicholson, Interview, 129, observing that the federal Truth in Lending Act did not mandate clear disclosure of the risk of these loans.

[92] Nicholson, Interview.

[93] FCIC Report, 7.

[94] FCIC Report, 9.

[95] American Civil Liberties Union, "Justice Foreclosed," 22. A. Mian and A. Sufi, "The Consequences of Mortgage Credit Expansion: Evidence from the U.S. Mortgage Default Crisis" (2009) 124:4 *The Quarterly Journal of Economics* 1449–1496 (hereafter Mian and Sufi, "Consequences").

appropriately, can help a lender spread risk of defaults on mortgages and other loans. However, in the period leading up to the financial crisis, securitization grew exponentially, without appropriate regulatory oversight. Securitization has many forms. Common is where a lender (originator) packages a pool of residential mortgages and sells them to a separate entity, which may be in the form of a trust or special purpose entity (SPE), the entity paying for the bundle of mortgages by issuing debt securities to capital markets participants. These securities are referred to as residential mortgage-backed securities (RMBS) in the United States. Payment obligations under the securities are met from collecting payments from the pool of mortgages held by the trust or SPE. Since payments were coming from a number of mortgages, investors believed these debt securities were less risky than debt securities on a single operating company.

In the sub-prime context, responsible securitization never occurred. Securitization allowed lenders to bundle mortgages into packages of securities and sell them on in the market, shedding the risk in exchange for significant upfront fees and commissions.[96] Securitization lowered incentives to monitor the granting of credit at the outset, which also led to misconduct by originating mortgage lenders.[97] The poor credit assessment at the front end of the mortgage lending decision meant that some people who did not qualify for traditional mortgages were led to believe that they could have the American dream of home ownership. Others did qualify but were nonetheless steered into sub-prime mortgages. School boards, municipalities, and other public institutions were among the many investors that believed the mortgage-backed securities were low risk and invested tax dollars in these financial products.

The sub-prime mortgage securitization process created a channel through which risky mortgages were conveyed and sold throughout the financial system. This channel was essential to the origination of the burgeoning numbers of high-risk mortgages.[98] The originate-to-distribute model undermined responsibility and accountability for the long-term viability of mortgages and mortgage-related securities and contributed to the poor quality of mortgage loans.[99]

Mian and Sufi, as well as others, have documented how the rise of securitization, coupled with deregulation of the financial sector in the United States, allowed lenders to spread loan risk across multiple parties, creating incentives for more risky lending.[100] High-risk loans were bundled into tranches and resold in the market as securities investments, resulting in much higher returns to the originating lenders than more traditional 25-year fixed-rate mortgages.[101] The tranches

96 Sarra, "Embedding Fairness."
97 Sarra, "Embedding Fairness."
98 FCIC Report, xix.
99 FCIC Report, 125.
100 Mian and Sufi, "Consequences," 1449–96.
101 Sarra, "Embedding Fairness."

were ostensibly arranged by categories of risk, but in reality many were rated A regardless of their credit-worthiness. Securitizing originators quickly sold their loans and shed their own risk; their own capital only invested in any given loan for a short period of time.[102] This lack of capital at risk increased the incentives for misconduct.

The FCIC described a typical securitization deal that is helpful to repeat here to understand the complexity of the transactions. The deal, named CMLTI 2006-NC2, involved $947 million in mortgage-backed bonds. In 2006, New Century Financial originated and sold 4,499 sub-prime mortgages to Citigroup. Citigroup then sold them to a legal entity that Citigroup sponsored, which was created as a separate legal entity so that the assets would not be on Citigroup's balance sheet.[103] The separate entity would own the mortgages and issue the tranches. The entity purchased the loans with cash that it had raised by selling the securities these loans would back. The 4,499 mortgages carried the rights to the borrowers' monthly payments, which the Citigroup's separate entity divided into 19 tranches of mortgage-backed securities. Each tranche gave investors a different priority claim on the flow of payments from the borrowers, and a different interest rate and repayment schedule.[104] The credit rating agencies assigned ratings to most of these tranches and investors relied heavily on these ratings. Tranches were assigned ratings by the rating agencies based on their riskiness: from AAA, the highest rating for the safest investments, to AA, A, BBB, and BB; and these ratings were further distinguished with '+' and '–'.[105] Below the senior tranches and next in line for payments were eleven mezzanine tranches, so named because they sat between the riskiest and the safest tranches. The mezzanine tranches were riskier than the senior tranches and were paid a correspondingly higher interest rate.[106] The last to be paid was the most junior tranche, called the "residual" or "first-loss" tranche, which was set up to receive whatever cash flow was left over after all the other investors had been paid. This tranche would suffer the first losses from any defaults of the mortgages in the pool and commensurate with this high risk it provided the highest yields.[107] In the Citigroup deal, as was common, this tranche was not rated at all. While investors in the lower-rated tranches received higher interest rates because they knew there was a risk of loss, investors in the AAA tranches did not expect payments from the mortgages to stop.[108] For each mortgage, the brokers received an average fee from the borrowers of $3,756 or 1.81 per cent of

[102] Peterson, "Predatory Structured," 2221.
[103] FCIC Report, 71.
[104] FCIC Report, 71.
[105] FCIC Report, 71.
[106] Three of these tranches in the Citigroup deal were rated AA, three were A, three were BBB (the lowest investment-grade rating), and two were BB, or junk, FCIC Report.
[107] FCIC Report, 71.
[108] FCIC Report, 72.

the loan amount.[109] On top of that, the brokers also received yield spread premiums from New Century for 1,744 of these loans that averaged $2,585 each.

Consider what this deal meant for the consumer borrowers measured against the principle of fairness. First, the party with whom they negotiated the mortgage was long gone and they could not trace who actually held the mortgage if they experienced any problems with respect to payments or had queries about shifting interest rates. In some cases, multiple parties held actual interest in the property. Second, the brokers received many thousands of dollars in fees and yield spread premiums that the consumer borrower paid for without being informed about them. Third, the shedding of risk through the selling of tranches of bundled mortgages meant that no one on the lender side cared about the risk profile of an individual mortgage, which in turn created incentives to sell masses of mortgages without assessing credit worthiness or capacity to pay.

Moreover, by moving loans off their books, commercial banks reduced the amount of capital they were required to hold as protection against losses, thereby improving their earnings, but meaning that there was little capital serving as a safety net within the commercial bank. Securitization also let banks rely less on deposits for funding, because selling securities generated cash that could be used to make loans. Banks could also keep parts of the securities on their books as collateral for borrowing, and fees from securitization became an important source of revenues.[110] If many loans were pooled into one security, investors believed that a few defaults would have minimal impact. The idea was that risk-averse investors would buy tranches that paid off first in the event of default but had lower yields. Return-oriented investors would buy riskier tranches with higher yields.[111] Borrowers under these mortgages continued to make their monthly payments, unaware that the mortgage had been distributed to investors holding mortgage-backed securities, and that they would be dealing with entirely different and largely uninterested counterparties should they encounter any difficulties.

Adam Levitin and Susan Wachter have observed that fee-based mortgage securitization encouraged a greater supply of mortgage credit, but equally, put pressure on brokers as intermediaries to issue greater numbers of mortgages to generate fee income for the lending institutions.[112] There was such demand for RMBS that there was increasing pressure to sell mortgages that would be available to be bundled and sold to investors. The incentives were wrong at every level of the decision chain, the broker selling the mortgage, the intermediaries taking the fees and the profits from

[109] FCIC Report, 91.
[110] FCIC Report, 43.
[111] FCIC Report, 43.
[112] Adam Levitan and Susan Wachter, "Explaining the Housing Bubble" (2012) 100:4 *Georgetown Law Journal* 1177–1183.

securitizing the loans, and the pressure by mortgaged-back investors to have increasing short-term returns on their investment.

There is also a great deal of evidence that the securitization industry encouraged predatory lending in communities of colour, which caused much of the bubble that eventually led to the crash, an issue discussed at length in the next chapter.[113] On the credit decision side, lenders were drawing consumers' attention to current payment rates as good deals without drawing their attention to the costs of future payments or to the fact that their loans would be securitized.[114]

On Wall Street, where many of these loans were packaged into securities and sold to investors around the globe, the expression "IBGYBG" (I'll be gone, you'll be gone) became common for referring to deals that brought in big fees up front while risking much larger losses in the future.[115] Soon after borrowers signed the mortgage documents, the loans were put into the packages described above and sold in bulk to securitization firms, including investment banks such as Merrill Lynch, Bear Stearns, and Lehman Brothers, and commercial banks and savings and loan associations (often referred to as 'thrifts' in the United States) such as Citigroup, Wells Fargo, and WaMu.[116] From there, the firms would repackage the loans into residential mortgage–backed securities that would mostly be stamped with A, AA, or AAA ratings by the credit rating agencies and sold to investors. Investors purchased these mortgage-backed securities because they believed them to be safe investments and because they yielded higher returns than other equally rated investments.[117]

Securitization also destroyed an important element of traditional lending: the relationship of the local bank and the borrowers in the community in which they are located. Such relationships in the past meant that banks were part of local communities and were more likely to forebear on enforcement of in-default mortgages or to negotiate new more affordable terms when borrowers encountered temporary financial setbacks due to job loss or medical expenses.[118] With securitization, the relationship between sub-prime borrowers and lenders is non-existent and often in flux as mortgages are sold on to other investors or entities several times. The crucial

[113] American Civil Liberties Union, "Justice Foreclosed," 5.

[114] O. Bar-Gill and E. Warren, "Making Credit Safer" (2008) 157:1 *University of Pennsylvania Law Review* 1–101. O. Bar-Gill, *Seduction by Contract: Law, Economics, and Psychology in Consumer Markets* (Oxford: Oxford University Press, 2012).

[115] FCIC Report, 8, citing Robert Kuttner, interview by FCIC, 5 August 2010.

[116] FCIC Report.

[117] FCIC Report. See also the United States Senate Permanent Subcommittee on Investigations, Staff Report, *Wall Street and the Financial Crisis: Anatomy of a Financial Collapse* (Washington, DC: U.S. Senate, 2011), www.hsgac.senate.gov/imo/media/doc/PSI%20REPORT%20-%20Wall%20Street%20&%20the%20Financial%20Crisis-Anatomy%20of%20a%20Financial%20Collapse%20(FINAL%205-10-11).pdf.

[118] Sarra, "Embedding Fairness."

decision to pursue a foreclosure or renegotiate a delinquent mortgage is made, in the case of a securitized loan, by an agent who acts on behalf of investors,[119] a party uninterested in preservation of the community.

One study observed that in the first year of the financial crisis, securitized mortgages issued without a guarantee from government-sponsored entities accounted for more than half of the foreclosure starts, despite their relatively small market share.[120] Another empirical study by the National Bureau of Economic Research revealed that by 2012 the foreclosure crisis was not only a sub-prime sector event, but also had expanded, causing many prime borrowers to lose their homes. That negative equity, in which the amount of the mortgage is greater than the value of the home, was a significant cause of foreclosure rather than irresponsible borrower behaviour.[121]

5 *Collateralization Offloaded Risk*

In many cases, the securities sold in securitization processes were repackaged again (resecuritized) into collateralized debt obligations (CDO), often composed of the riskier portions of these securities. The effect of resecuritizing was that the senior tranches of the securities artificially pulled up the credit rating of the riskier tranches of debt even though the lower tranches had significant credit risk. These CDO were then sold to ordinary people, often as low- or medium-risk investments when, in fact, they were high risk.[122]

Most of these CDO received AAA ratings, creating the illusion of a safe and secure investment.[123] It was not clear anymore who the owner or owners of the mortgages were because they had been bundled, sliced, repackaged, insured, and sold as incomprehensively complicated debt securities to an assortment of investors.[124]

Collateralization meant that the originating lender had immediately shed its risk and then proceeded to lend again in the market because others had acquired the risks of bad loans, which rapidly increased the amount of debt outstanding.[125] This practice resulted in a situation whereby once the bank extracted the fees on the originating loan, the bank passed the risk along to various tranches of debt that in turn resulted in less front-end assessment of credit worthiness. When credit was

119 Sarra, "Embedding Fairness." 5.

120 S. Agarwal et al, "Policy Intervention in Debt Renegotiation: Evidence from the Home Affordable Modification Program" (2017) 125:3 *J Polit Econ* 654–658 (hereafter Agarwal et al, "Policy Intervention").

121 Fernando Ferreira and Joseph Gyourko, "A New Look at the US Foreclosure Crisis: Panel Data Evidence of Prime and Subprime Borrowers from 1997 to 2012" (2015) National Bureau of Economic Research (Working Paper 21261), 27, NBER, www.nber.org/papers/w21261 (hereafter Ferreira and Gyourko, "A New Look"). Negative equity was defined in the study as "when the current loan-to-value (LTV) ratio is greater than one."

122 Sarra, "Embedding Fairness," 208.

123 Sarra, "Embedding Fairness," 8.

124 FCIC Report, 7.

125 FCIC Report.

granted, it was "covenant light," without the traditional terms and conditions that ensured monitoring and early intervention.[126]

Even during the levelling off and subsequent decline of the housing market beginning in 2006, issuance of CDO and "synthetic CDO" continued unchecked, which greatly expanded the exposure to losses when the housing market collapsed and intensified the impact of the collapse on the financial system and the economy.[127] During this period, speculators fuelled the market for synthetic CDO, essentially 'betting' on the future of the housing market. Managers of these synthetic CDO products had potential conflicts of interest in trying to serve the interests of customers who were betting mortgage borrowers would continue to make their payments and of customers who were betting the housing market would collapse.[128] There were also potential conflicts for underwriters of mortgage-related securities to the extent they shorted the products for their own accounts outside of their roles as market makers.[129]

By 2004, creators of CDO backed by mortgage-backed securities were the dominant buyers of the BBB-rated tranches of mortgage-backed securities, and their bids significantly influenced prices in the market for these securities. By then, mortgage-backed securities accounted for more than half of the collateral in CDO.[130] By 2005, the creators of CDO were buying virtually all the BBB tranches. Just as mortgage-backed securities provided the cash to originate mortgages, now CDO were providing the capital to fund mortgage-backed securities.

The relational aspects of financial markets were severely impaired through securitization and collateralization, which set the stage for failure.[131] In previous years, a bank would be a company's primary senior lender with an ongoing interest in business relationships as well as an interest in the local community in terms of deposit accounts and spin-off business relationships.[132] The same was true for small businesses, including sole proprietorships. On the residential side, debt transactions carried covenants which mortgage borrowers undertook to meet specific expectations, and the lender monitored compliance, often intervening informally in governance when it detected early stage problems. In turn, investors and other borrowers benefited from the positive externalities associated with this oversight and early intervention.[133] However, the nature of debt shifted, and the objective of preserving long-term relationships was no longer a priority for senior lenders because the risk had been, in their view, offloaded to investors. Of course, what was not transparent was the seriously interconnected nature of these transactions.

[126] FCIC Report.
[127] FCIC Report, 212.
[128] FCIC Report, 212.
[129] FCIC Report, 212.
[130] FCIC Report, 130.
[131] Sarra, "Embedding Fairness," 207.
[132] Sarra, "Embedding Fairness."
[133] Sarra, "Embedding Fairness."

The FCIC concluded that declining demand for riskier tranches of mortgage-related securities led to the creation of an enormous volume of CDO composed of the riskiest tranches, which fuelled further demand for sub-prime and non-prime mortgage securitization, contributing to the housing bubble.[134] Many risky CDO-squared, credit default swaps, synthetic CDO, and asset-backed commercial paper programs that invested in mortgage-backed securities ended up on the balance sheets of systemically important institutions and contributed to their failure or near failure during the financial crisis.[135]

Key over-the-counter (OTC) derivatives implicated in the financial crisis were credit default swaps (CDS). CDS are a type of financial product developed originally to protect lenders from the risk of default and help them leverage more capital.[136] They were sold to investors to protect against decline in the value of mortgage-related securities backed by risky loans.[137] In the period leading up to the financial crisis, CDS were sold to provide protection against default to purchasers of the top-rated tranches of CDO, which facilitated the sale of those tranches by convincing investors they had hedged their risk. However, they also greatly increased the exposure of the sellers of the CDS protection to the housing bubble's collapse. Synthetic CDO, which consisted in whole or in part of CDS products, enabled securitization to expand even as the mortgage market dried up and provided another means of speculating on the housing market.[138] Issuance of synthetic CDO jumped from $15 billion in 2005 to $62 billion in 2006.[139] Synthetic CDO enabled sophisticated investors to place bets against the housing market or pursue more complex trading strategies. Investors, usually hedge funds, often used CDS to take offsetting positions in different tranches of the same CDO security. That way, the investors could make some money as long as the CDO performed, but they stood to make more money if the entire market crashed.[140] By layering on correlated risk, they spread and amplified exposure to losses when the housing market did collapse. A total of $225 billion in CDO were issued in 2006 alone, the FCIC estimating that 27 per cent of collateral was derivatives, compared with only nine per cent the year prior.

Given that the CDS purchaser did not have to have any "skin in the game" in terms of mortgage value at risk, it fostered a massive speculative market of CDS purchasers who did not own any value in the underlying securities.[141] This speculation resulted in excessive leveraging along every segment of the "toxic mortgage supply chain."[142]

134 FCIC Report, 155.
135 FCIC Report, 155.
136 Sarra, "Embedding Fairness."
137 FCIC Report, xxiv.
138 FCIC Report, 155.
139 FCIC Report, 191.
140 FCIC Report, 191.
141 Sarra, "Embedding Fairness."
142 Taub, *Other People's Houses*, 224–46.

CDS offered the seller a potential upside for what they believed was a relatively small risk of a potentially large downside. The purchaser of a CDS product transferred to the seller the default risk of an underlying debt. The debt security could be any bond or loan obligation. The CDS buyer made periodic payments to the seller during the life of the swap. In return, the seller offered protection against default or specified credit events such as a partial default.[143] If a credit event such as a default occurred, the CDS seller would typically pay the buyer the face value of the debt.[144]

But a CDS purchaser can use the swap to speculate on the default of a loan the purchaser does not own. These CDS products are often referred to as "naked CDS" and can inflate potential losses and corresponding gains on the default of a loan.[145] In the housing boom, CDS were sold by firms that failed to put up any reserves or initial collateral or to hedge their exposure. In the run-up to the crisis, American International Group (AIG), the largest U.S. insurance company, would accumulate a one-half trillion dollar position in credit risk through the OTC market without being required to post one dollar's worth of initial collateral or make any other provision for loss.[146] The value of the underlying assets for CDS products outstanding worldwide grew to $58.2 trillion at the end of 2007.[147] The amounts are almost unfathomable.

In June 2005, derivatives dealers introduced the "pay-as-you-go" CDS, a complex instrument that mimicked the timing of the cash flows of real mortgage-backed securities.[148] Because of this feature, the synthetic CDO into which these new swaps were bundled were much easier to issue and sell.[149] CDS products allowed CDO managers to create synthetic and hybrid CDO more quickly than they could create cash CDO.[150] Second, they enabled investors in the CDO, including the originating banks, such as Citigroup and Merrill, to transfer the risk of default to the issuer of the CDS, such as AIG and other insurance companies.[151]

Derivatives are financial contracts whose prices are determined by, or derived from, the value of some underlying asset, rate, index, or event. They are not used for capital formation or investment; rather, they are instruments for hedging business risk or for speculating on changes in prices, interest rates, etc. Derivatives come in many forms. The most common are OTC swaps and exchange-traded futures and options. They may be based on commodities, interest rates, currency rates, stock indexes, and credit risk.[152] The derivatives

143 Sarra, "Embedding Fairness."
144 FCIC Report, 50.
145 FCIC Report, 50.
146 FCIC Report, 50, citing data provided by AIG to the FCIC, CDS notional balances at year-end.
147 FCIC Report, citing Bank for International Settlements, semi-annual OTC derivatives statistics.
148 FCIC Report, 190.
149 FCIC Report.
150 FCIC Report, 195.
151 FCIC Report.
152 FCIC Report, 45–6.

markets are organized as exchanges or as OTC markets, although some recent electronic trading facilities blur the distinctions.[153]

In September 1998, the Federal Reserve Bank of New York orchestrated a $3.6. billion recapitalization of Long-Term Capital Management (LTCM) by 14 major OTC derivatives dealers.[154] Federal Reserve Chair Greenspan championed derivatives and advocated deregulation of the OTC market and the exchange-traded market.[155] In December 2000, Congress passed the Commodity Futures Modernization Act of 2000 (CFMA), which in essence deregulated the OTC derivatives market and eliminated oversight by the U.S. Commodity Futures Trading Commission (CFTC) and the U.S Securities and Exchange Commission (SEC).[156] The SEC did retain anti-fraud authority over securities-based OTC derivatives such as stock options, and the regulatory powers of the CFTC relating to exchange-traded derivatives were weakened but not eliminated; however, the CFMA effectively shielded OTC derivatives from virtually all regulation or oversight.[157] This deregulation set the stage for even riskier market practices.

Among U.S. bank holding companies, 97 per cent of the notional amount of OTC derivatives, which were millions of contracts, were traded by just five large institutions in 2008: JP Morgan Chase, Citigroup, Bank of America, Wachovia, and HSBC, many of the same firms that would find themselves in trouble during the financial crisis.[158]

The instruments grew more and more complex. CDO were constructed out of CDO, creating CDO-squared, and when firms ran out of real product, they started generating cheaper-to-produce synthetic CDO, which were composed not of real mortgage securities but of bets on other mortgage products.[159] None of the principal actors – the mortgage brokers who scouted the loans, the lenders that issued the mortgages, or the financial firms that created these financial products – had "enough skin in the game," referring to their own capital at risk.[160] They all believed they could off-load their risks relating to these toxic mortgages and other structured financial products at a moment's notice to the next person in line.[161] Yet, when borrowers stopped making mortgage payments, the losses were huge, amplified by derivatives, and when the "music stopped," the losses were concentrated in a group of systemically important financial institutions.[162]

153 FCIC Report, 46.
154 FCIC Report, 47–8.
155 FCIC Report, 48.
156 FCIC Report.
157 FCIC Report.
158 FCIC Report, 50.
159 FCIC Report, 8.
160 FCIC Report, xxiv.
161 FCIC Report.
162 FCIC Report.

Thus, the 2000 legislation to ban the regulation of OTC derivatives by the federal and state governments contributed significantly to the crisis.[163] Without any oversight, OTC derivatives rapidly spiralled out of control and grew to many millions of derivatives contracts worth $673 trillion in notional amount. These products lacked transparency, capital, and collateral requirements. Speculation was wildly out of control and interconnections among firms were not appropriately understood, which concentrated the risk in this market.[164]

Highly speculative markets for CDS products emerged. For example, AIG sold $79 billion in CDS protection, which helped to launch and expand the sub-prime market and, in turn, to further fuel the housing bubble.[165] AIG, which was not required to put aside capital reserves as a cushion for the protection it was selling, was bailed out when it could not meet its obligations.[166] The government ultimately committed more than $180 billion because of its concern that AIG's collapse would trigger cascading losses throughout the global financial system.[167]

CDS products enabled creation of synthetic CDO, essentially bets on the performance of real mortgage-related securities, which in turn amplified the losses from the collapse of the housing bubble by allowing multiple bets on the same securities and spreading them throughout the financial system.[168] Goldman Sachs packaged and sold $73 billion in synthetic CDO from July 2004 to May 2007.[169] Synthetic CDO created by Goldman Sachs referenced more than 3,400 mortgage securities, and 610 of them were referenced at least twice.[170]

Peterson observes that securitization facilitated capitalizing "fly-by-night companies that specialized in fraud, deceptive practices, abusive collections, and other predatory behaviour."[171] He argues that the notion of predatory lending has been cast too narrowly and that predatory-structured finance recognizes that businesses that sponsor securitization of residential mortgage loans are aware of and capable of preventing mortgage predation; and that liability rules alone are inadequate because they excuse many of the most culpable parties from accountability.[172] He suggests that financial technology has outpaced consumer protection law, which has effectively deregulated much of the consumer mortgage market because the terminology of those statutes frequently leaves predatory home-mortgage loans beyond their scope.[173]

163 FCIC Report.
164 FCIC Report.
165 FCIC Report, xxiv.
166 FCIC Report, xxv.
167 FCIC Report.
168 FCIC Report, xxiv.
169 FCIC Report.
170 FCIC Report, xxv.
171 Peterson, "Predatory Structured," 2189. See also Stephen Lubben, "Beyond True Sales: Securitization and Chapter 11" (2004) 1 NYU J L & Bus, 89.
172 Peterson, "Predatory Structured."
173 Peterson, "Predatory Structured," 2190, 2276.

Peterson cogently documents Lehman Brothers' lending practices prior to its collapse, in which it knowingly profited from predatory loans.[174] Lehman Brothers' collapse resulted in huge losses to investors. It also was implicated directly in predatory lending. "Lehman assisted Household Finance in securitizing sub-prime mortgage loans during a period when Household Finance was indisputably engaging in predatory lending."[175] Although Lehman Brothers escaped liability for its role in predatory lending, a coalition of State Attorneys General sued Household Finance for deceptive, fraudulent, unconscionable, and statutorily prohibited lending practices. Household Finance eventually agreed to what was, at the time, the largest predatory lending settlement in U.S. history, almost half a billion dollars.[176] Lehman Brothers was also a major underwriter of Delta Funding Corporation, a firm specializing in sub-prime mortgage lending. During this business relationship, Delta Funding Corporation settled a predatory lending lawsuit with the New York Attorney General for targeting low income minorities in Brooklyn and Queens and giving loans with monthly payments larger than customers' monthly income, thus "virtually guaranteeing default on the loan."[177]

Lehman Brothers also was involved closely with First Government Mortgage, another company accused of predatory lending, which signed an enforcement agreement with the Department of Housing and Urban Development.[178] Peterson observes that "Instead of shunning First Government, Lehman bought one of its subsidiaries after convincing the Office of Thrift Supervision to allow Lehman to keep the subsidiary's savings and loan charter, despite protests by consumer organizations over predatory lending."[179] Lehman Brothers was also the primary underwriter for Conseco Finance Company, a subsidiary of the large insurance company. Conseco Finance Company, once the nation's largest originator of mobile home loans, was the subject of dozens of lawsuits for predatory lending, including chronically using inflated appraisals of mobile homes to justify loans padded with unnecessary fees and vulture-like insurance policies.[180] Lehman Brothers was the primary financier for First Alliance, a notorious predatory lender. It gave First Alliance a warehouse line of credit from which to originate loans and then purchased those loans immediately after First Alliance made them, in turn packaging and collateralizing the loans to offload them in sales to investors.[181]

The FCIC concluded the financial crisis reached cataclysmic proportions with the collapse of Lehman Brothers.[182] Lehman Brothers, like other large

[174] Peterson, "Predatory Structured," 2222–5.
[175] Peterson, "Predatory Structured."
[176] Peterson, "Predatory Structured."
[177] Peterson, "Predatory Structured."
[178] Peterson, "Predatory Structured."
[179] Peterson, "Predatory Structured."
[180] Peterson, "Predatory Structured."
[181] Peterson, "Predatory Structured."
[182] FCIC Report, 343.

derivatives dealers, experienced serious runs on its derivatives operations that played a role in its failure.[183] Its massive derivatives positions greatly complicated its bankruptcy, and the impact of AIG's and Lehman Brothers' failure through interconnections with derivatives counterparties and other financial institutions contributed significantly to the severity and depth of the financial crisis.[184] Lehman Brothers' bankruptcy resulted, in part, from significant problems in its corporate governance, including poor risk management, exacerbated by compensation to its executives and traders based predominantly on short-term profits.[185] The Lehman Brothers' bankruptcy affected approximately 6,000 subsidiaries and affiliates with $600 billion in assets and liabilities, more than 100,000 creditors, and 26,000 employees.[186] Its failure triggered default clauses in derivatives contracts that allowed its counterparties the option of seizing its collateral and terminating the contracts.[187] After the parent company filed for bankruptcy, about 80 insolvency proceedings of its subsidiaries in 18 foreign countries followed. In the main bankruptcy proceeding, claims exceeding $873 billion were filed against Lehman Brothers.[188]

6 *Third-party Mortgage Servicers Engaged in Egregious Conduct*

Securitization of mortgage-backed securities resulted in expansion of third-party mortgage servicing to collect and distribute payments.[189] Servicers collected and processed mortgage payments from borrowers, took out any escrow payments for real estate taxes and insurance, paid themselves servicing fees, and then forwarded the remaining funds for disbursement to investors. Sometimes payments were forwarded to a trust on behalf of investors. Fees were based on the interest, and servicers received much higher fees when borrowers had ARM

183 FCIC Report.
184 FCIC Report.
185 FCIC Report.
186 FCIC Report, 339.
187 FCIC Report.
188 FCIC Report, 340.
189 Patricia McCoy et al, "Systemic Risk Through Securitization: The Result of Deregulation and Regulatory Failure" (2009) 41 Conn L Rev, 1327, 1329–33, 1336–38, 1343, 1369–72 (2009); Peterson, "Predatory Structured," 2213–21 discussing how securitization enabled predatory lending; Anna Gelpern and Adam Levitin, "Rewriting Frankenstein Contracts: The Workout Prohibition in Residential Mortgage-Backed Securities" (2009) 82 S Cal L Rev 1075, 1080–1112. Trusts holding securitized mortgages had to be passively managed to get preferential tax treatment; Jean Braucher, "Humpty Dumpty and the Foreclosure Crisis: Lessons from the Lackluster First Year of the Home Affordable Modification Program (HAMP)" (2010) 52 Ariz L Rev, 727, 745–746 (hereafter Braucher, "Humpty Dumpty"), noting that "not only were servicers' interests not necessarily aligned with those of investors, but there were many potential conflicts among investors because of their different interests in securitized mortgage pools."

because the loans required more processing to adjust interest rates and had higher levels of default to process.[190] Servicers received additional fees if they met performance targets for loss mitigation, which created incentives for them to be aggressive in pursuing payments from mortgage borrowers. They also were allowed to retain late fees, which encouraged a practice of delaying posting of payments so that they were considered late even where the borrower paid on time.[191]

Many of the investment banks that were securitizing mortgages had vertical operations so that entities that were servicing the sub-prime mortgages were related; however, Levine notes that they often avoided the retail origination of loans to avoid being subject to fair lending and consumer protection claims.[192] For example, Bear Stearns launched EMC Mortgage Corporation. Bear Stearns approved mortgage loans, securitized them, and passed them to EMC Mortgage Corporation to collect borrowers' monthly payments.[193] Morgan Stanley purchased mortgage servicer Saxon Capital for essentially the same purposes.[194] This practice resulted in a situation in which the investment banks and their subsidiaries were taking a cut of fees at each stage of the lending, securitization, and servicing process.[195] Instead of third-party mortgage servicers, they were related-party mortgage servicers with all the potential for conflicts of interest entailed in such arrangements.

Servicers engaged in a range of misconduct. They inflated amounts owing, claiming outrageous fees for small administrative tasks, lost borrowers' cheques, thus making them late when they had to resubmit – all done with impunity because mortgagors did not have the information or resources to detect or complain about false charges.[196] As noted earlier, borrowers who encountered problems had no one to negotiate with because servicers were just the conduit for processing payments, not the party with the residual interest in the mortgage. Servicers often lost or claimed that they had lost loan files and required borrowers to submit documentation several times. Since their task was to collect money and

190 F. Raiter, "Credit Rating Agencies and the Financial Crisis" (testimony before the U.S. House of Representatives, Committee on Oversight Governance and Reform, 22 October 2008) (hereafter Raiter, "Credit Rating").

191 Raiter, "Credit Rating," 24.

192 Jeffrey Levine, "The Vertical Integration Strategy" (2007) 67:5 *Mortgage Banking* 58, 60–61 (hereafter Levin, "Vertical Integration").

193 Levin, "Vertical Integration," 60–4.

194 Levin, "Vertical Integration."

195 G. Morgenson and G. Fabricant, "Countrywide's Chief Salesman and Defender" *New York Times* (11 November 2007), www.nytimes.com/2007/11/11/business/11angelo.html.

196 Gretchen Morgenson, "Borrowers Face Dubious Charges in Foreclosures" *New York Times* (5 November 2007), www.nytimes.com/2007/11/06/business/worldbusiness/06iht-06mortgage.8207232.html.

they were compensated for the recovery of late fees and fees to foreclose, there was no incentive to negotiate any modifications.[197]

After the sub-prime market began to collapse, most servicers resisted or outright fought against modifications, particularly any reduction in payments. One Federal Reserve Bank of Boston study found that of 600,000 modifications only 3 per cent had any reduction in payments.[198] Some servicers forced borrowers to sign waivers of their right to any remedies for fraud and other misconduct if they wanted to get a modification.[199]

Where servicers negotiated modifications, the monthly payments were often higher. Moreover, servicers of securitized mortgages usually operated subject to pooling and servicing agreements with explicit and implicit restrictions on loan modification.[200] One example would be limits on the percentage or dollar number of modifications without permission from investors, which, of course, could never be obtained.[201] The principals of the servicers, the investment banks, often delayed making decisions on permanent modifications because they had to write down their capital.[202]

In some instances, people presenting themselves as servicers commenced scams called some variation of "foreclosure rescue companies." They would locate borrowers through public foreclosure notices, offer to help negotiate modification, charge thousands of dollars in fees, and then do nothing.[203] Some of them even faked documents telling borrowers that they got a modification agreement.[204] When the California government shutdown 200 so-called foreclosure rescue businesses

197 *Montgomery County, Maryland et al* v *Bank of America Corporation et al*, No 18-03575 (ADC), Document 1 Complaint and Demand for Jury Trial (D Md So Div filed 20 November 2018), para 365, citing P. Goodman and J. Flores, "Lucrative Fees May Deter Efforts to Alter Troubled Loans" *New York Times* (29 July 2009).

198 M. Adelino, K. Gerardi, and P. Willen, "Why Don't Lenders Renegotiate More Home Mortgages? Redefaults, Self-Cures and Securitization" (2009) Federal Reserve Bank of Boston (Public Policy Discussion Paper No 2009-4), 3.

199 Mary Kane, "Loan Servicers Work the Fine Print in Obama Foreclosure Plan" *Washington Independent* (30 July 2009).

200 United States, Internal Revenue Service, *Revenue Procedure* 2007–72 (Washington, DC: IRS, 6 December 2007). Diane Thompson, "Why Servicers Foreclose When They Should Modify and Other Puzzles of Servicer Behavior: Servicer Compensation and Its Consequences" (October 2009) National Consumer Law Center (Working Paper), 12–13 (hereafter Thompson, "Why Servicers Foreclose").

201 Thompson, "Why Servicers Foreclose," 38–9; A. Pinedo and A. Baumgardner, "Federal Mortgage Modification and Foreclosure Prevention Efforts" (2009) 41:4 Unif Comm Code LJ 319–45.

202 J. Nocera, "From Treasury to Banks, an Ultimatum on Mortgage Relief" *New York Times* (11 July 2009).

203 John Leland, "Swindlers Find Growing Market in Foreclosures" *New York Times* (15 January 2009) (hereafter Leland, "Swindlers").

204 Leland, "Swindlers."

operating without a licence, over half the people in these companies had been previously involved in the mortgage industry.[205]

The *New York Times* quoted one partner at the Federal Loan Modification Law Center ('FedMod') as saying: "We just changed the script and changed the product we were selling."[206] FedMod charged $3,495 fees upfront to borrowers, who in some cases, gave the last of their resources or opened up lines of credit to pay the fees. FedMod gave its salespeople a 30 per cent commission on each sale and one FedMod employee testified to never having seen an actual modification.[207] The article notes that while FedMod was sued in 2009 for deceptive and unfair practices, no sooner are some businesses shut down as others open up, always staying ahead of authorities.[208]

IV THE SUB-PRIME MORTGAGE MARKET COLLAPSE

The U.S. housing market began to collapse almost two years prior to the commencement of the 2008 global financial crisis. The value of homes plummeted and defaults on mortgage payments rose significantly.

Financial institutions had created, bought, and sold mortgage securities they never examined or knew to be defective. These institutions were depending on billions of dollars of borrowing that had to be renewed each and every night, secured by sub-prime mortgage securities.[209] The FCIC found that trillions of dollars in risky mortgages had become embedded throughout the financial system because mortgage-related securities were packaged, repackaged, and sold to investors around the world. Lenders made loans that they knew borrowers could not meet payments on and that could cause massive losses to investors in mortgage securities.[210] Major financial institutions knew a significant percentage of loans did not meet their own underwriting standards or those of the originators, but they still sold those securities to investors.[211]

As financial markets began to collapse, stagnant income and rising unemployment, particularly in the African-American and Latinx communities, combined with rising interest rates and depressed housing values, resulted in massive numbers of defaults and foreclosures.[212] Of 45 million outstanding

[205] P. Goodman, "Subprime Brokers Resurfaces as Dubious Loan Fixers" *New York Times* (20 July 2009) (hereafter Goodman, "Subprime"); D. Lawder, "US Agencies Pledge Crackdown on Mortgage Fraud" *Reuters* (17 September 2009).

[206] Goodman, "Subprime."

[207] Goodman, "Subprime."

[208] Goodman, "Subprime."

[209] FCIC Report, xvii.

[210] FCIC Report, xxii.

[211] FCIC Report, xxii.

[212] Dickerson, *Homeownership*, 11.

mortgages by 2011, more than 12 million were underwater and one in seven families with a mortgage had outstanding mortgage debt that was greater than the value of the house.[213]

The housing bubble in the United States had been fuelled by low interest rates, easy and available credit, scant regulation, and toxic mortgages.[214] When the bubble burst, hundreds of billions of dollars in losses in mortgages and mortgage-related securities precipitated a market crash. Financial institutions had significant exposures to those mortgages and had borrowed heavily against them; and these losses were magnified by derivatives such as synthetic securities.[215] Banks that had borrowed heavily to purchase mortgage-backed securities began to experience financial distress as they were excessively leveraged and did not have the liquidity to turn over the mortgage-backed paper in the market.

High leverage, inadequate capital, and short-term funding made many financial institutions extraordinarily vulnerable to the downturn in the market in 2007. The investment banks had leverage ratios, by one measure, of up to 40 to 1.[216] This ratio means that they had $40 of debt to $1 of assets. Leverage at many institutions was even greater than reported when considering off balance-sheet exposures such as those of Citigroup, and derivatives positions such as those of AIG.[217] Merrill Lynch held $55 billion in "'super-senior" and supposedly "super-safe" mortgage-related securities that resulted in billions of dollars in losses.[218]

This combination of excessive borrowing and risky investments was related to failures of corporate governance and regulation. Too many financial institutions had borrowed to excess, leaving them vulnerable to financial distress or ruin if the value of their investments declined even modestly.[219] For example, as of 2005, the five major investment banks – Bear Stearns, Goldman Sachs, Lehman Brothers, Merrill Lynch, and Morgan Stanley – were operating with extraordinarily thin capital.[220] For the firms with a leverage ratio of 40 to 1, a less than 3 per cent drop in asset values could wipe out a firm's capital.[221] Much of their borrowing was short-term, in the overnight market – meaning the borrowing had to be renewed daily.[222] At the end of 2007, Bear Stearns had $11.8 billion in equity and $383.6 billion in liabilities and was borrowing as much as $70 billion daily in the overnight market.[223]

[213] Dickerson, *Homeownership*, 11–12.
[214] FCIC Report, xxii.
[215] FCIC Report, xvi.
[216] FCIC Report, 230.
[217] FCIC Report, 230
[218] FCIC Report, xix.
[219] FCIC Report.
[220] FCIC Report.
[221] FCIC Report.
[222] FCIC Report.
[223] FCIC Report, xx.

Leverage often was hidden in derivatives positions, in off balance-sheet entities, and through "window dressing" of financial reports available to the investing public.[224] The heavy debt was exacerbated by the risky assets financial institutions were acquiring with that debt.[225] By the end of 2007, Lehman Brothers had amassed $111 billion in risky commercial and residential real estate holdings and securities, twice what it had held just two years prior and more than four times its total equity holdings.[226] As massive losses spread throughout the financial system in the fall of 2008, many institutions failed or would have failed without the government bailouts.[227] Credit markets seized up, trading ground to a halt, and the stock market plunged.

Lack of transparency contributed greatly to the crisis: the exposure of financial institutions to risky mortgage assets and other potential losses were unknown to market participants, and many firms did not know their own exposures.[228] The opaque, deregulated OTC derivatives market created a web of millions of interconnected counterparty credit risks, exposing the system to a contagion of spreading losses and defaults.[229] Enormous positions concentrated in the hands of systemically significant institutions that were major OTC derivatives dealers added to uncertainty in the market and systemic risk. The bank runs on these institutions included runs on their derivatives operations through novations, collateral demands, and refusals to act as counterparties.[230]

A series of actions, inactions, and misjudgments left the country with stark and painful alternatives – either risk the total collapse of the U.S. financial system or spend trillions of taxpayer dollars to stabilize the system and prevent catastrophic damage to the economy.[231] The government chose to rescue a number of financial institutions deemed too big to fail because they were so large and interconnected with other financial institutions or so important in one or more financial markets that their failure would have caused a previously unheard of volume of losses and failures to spread to other institutions.[232]

At the time of the sub-prime market collapse, sub-prime lending was worth $600 billion, and one in five home loans in the U.S. mortgage market were sub-prime loans.[233] Ferreira and Gyourko observed that even for loans that had slightly less risk,

[224] FCIC Report.
[225] FCIC Report.
[226] FCIC Report, xx.
[227] FCIC Report, 386.
[228] FCIC Report.
[229] FCIC Report.
[230] FCIC Report
[231] FCIC Report.
[232] FCIC Report, 386.
[233] Katalina Bianco, "The Subprime Lending Crisis: Causes and Effects of the Mortgage Meltdown" (May 2008) *CCH Federal Banking Law Reporter*, 6.

consumers were exposed to the risks of financial contagion and market contraction, thus unable to sell their homes.[234] Selling a home at a much lower value than originally purchased meant that millions lost any savings they had invested in the home and any equity value that they had built up in payments. It also meant that they had greater debts than when they purchased the home. The firms that had aggressively marketed and given sub-prime mortgages when housing pricings were buoyant, or had let people borrow against their home equity, now refused to let them refinance their high-cost mortgages; yet the depressed housing market meant that it was impossible to sell their homes for a sum that would allow them to pay off their mortgage debt.[235] For many, negative equity meant still having to make mortgage loan payments after losing their homes.

1 *The Shadow Banking Sector Seriously Exacerbated the Misconduct*

In the United States, there had been a rapid rise in what is referred to as the "shadow banking sector," non-deposit taking banks and lenders that did not come under the regulatory oversight of banking authorities, as weak as it was.[236] Many of these firms already have been referred to in this chapter. A brief description of this system is important because it sets the stage for lack of accountability in the types of mortgages and other financial products sold to African Americans and others. It is also important for understanding how regulatory oversight must be improved in the future.

U.S. regulators had permitted the growth of the shadow banking system, laden with short-term debt and non-transparency of the multitrillion-dollar repo lending market, off balance-sheet entities, and the use of OTC derivatives, without adequate capital and liquidity protections.[237] Deregulation meant that mortgage lending was not subject to effective oversight either by firm principals or by regulators.[238]

At the commencement of the financial crisis, the six largest financial institutions held 67 per cent of all assets in the financial system.[239] The phenomenal growth of investment banks and other entities in the shadow banking system was the result of the ability of these financial institutions to freely operate in capital markets beyond

234 Ferreira and Gyourko, "A New Look." C. Mayer, E. Morrison, and T. Piskorski, "A New Proposal for Loan Modifications" (2009), 26 A Yale J on Reg 417; C. J. Mayer, K. M. Pence, and S. M. Sherlund, "The Rise in Mortgage Defaults" (2008) 23:1 *J Econ Perspect*. 27–50.

235 Dickerson, *Homeownership*, 11.

236 FCIC Report, xx.

237 FCIC Report.

238 FCIC Report, 55. In November 1999, Congress passed and President Clinton signed the Gramm-Leach-Bliley Act, Pub L 106–102 (GLBA), which lifted most of the remaining Glass-Steagall-era restrictions.

239 Baradaran, *How the Other Half Banks*, 58.

the reach of the regulatory oversight to which deposit-taking banks were subject.[240] Their activities were very profitable and very risky.[241] Yet regulators looked to financial institutions to police themselves – "deregulation" was the buzzword.[242] In stark contrast to historical practice when local mortgage lenders took full responsibility for making and servicing 25-year loans, the firms used structured financial products to turn sub-prime and other mortgages into complex investments.[243]

For a sizeable fee, many of these Wall Street investment banks brokered or provided short-term financing to large corporations through commercial paper. Commercial paper is unsecured corporate debt that is not backed by any pledge of collateral. These loans were cheaper because they were short-term – often for less than nine months, sometimes as short as two weeks, and eventually, as short as one day. The borrowers usually "rolled over" the loans when they came due, and then rolled them over again and again. Because only financially stable corporations were able to issue commercial paper, investors considered it a very safe investment.[244] By 2000, commercial paper issued in the market had risen to $1.6 trillion.[245]

The second major shadow banking market that grew significantly was the market for repurchase agreements – "repos." Wall Street securities dealers often sold Treasury bonds with their relatively low returns to banks and other conservative investors, then invested the cash proceeds of these sales in securities that paid higher interest rates. The dealers agreed to repurchase the Treasury bonds – often within a day – at a slightly higher price than that for which they sold them. This repo transaction, which was in essence a loan, made it inexpensive and convenient for shadow banking firms to borrow. Because these deals were essentially collateralized loans, the securities dealers borrowed nearly the full value of the collateral, and repos were rolled over frequently.[246]

Investment banks could employ far greater leverage, unhindered by oversight of their safety and soundness or by capital requirements outside of their broker-dealer subsidiaries, which were subject to a net capital rule. The money market funds and the investment banks that sponsored many of them were not subject to the same supervision as banks.[247]

Ultimately, it became clear that the shadow banking system was very fragile due to high leverage, short-term funding, risky assets, and inadequate liquidity.[248] When the mortgage market collapsed and financial firms began to abandon the

[240] FCIC Report, 27.
[241] FCIC Report, 27.
[242] FCIC Report, 27.
[243] FCIC Report, 27.
[244] FCIC Report, 30.
[245] FCIC Report, 31.
[246] FCIC Report.
[247] FCIC Report, 33.
[248] FCIC Report, 255.

commercial paper and repo lending markets, some institutions depending on them for funding their operations failed or, later in the crisis, had to be rescued.[249] Interconnections created contagion as the crisis spread even to markets and firms that had little or no direct exposure to the mortgage market.[250] The financial sector, which grew enormously in the years leading up to the financial crisis, had wielded great political power to weaken institutional supervision and market regulation of the shadow banking system and the traditional banking system.[251] This deregulation made the financial system especially vulnerable to the financial crisis and exacerbated its effects.[252]

2 *The Complicity of Credit Rating Agencies*

The structure of credit rating also contributed to the market meltdown.[253] The "hard-wiring" of credit ratings into certification of products in the United States amplified these problems, as did conflicts of interest in the compensation of credit rating agencies.[254] The companies selling the financial products paid the credit rating agencies for rating their products.[255] The function of credit rating agencies was to rate the quality of mortgage-backed securities; however, they used outdated tools that failed to consider liquidity risk, thus rating various investment products as safe investments when they were not.[256] Credit rating agencies embraced mathematical models as reliable predictors of risks, which replaced judgment in many instances.[257] Black reports that the rating agencies never reviewed loan files before giving AAA ratings and that had they reviewed even small samples of sub-prime loans, they would have rated them as toxic waste.[258] Rating agency Fitch reviewed a small sample of sub-prime loan files after the market collapse and found "the appearance of fraud or misrepresentation in almost every file," which could have been identified with adequate assessment and underwriting.[259]

[249] FCIC Report, 255.

[250] FCIC Report.

[251] FCIC Report.

[252] FCIC Report.

[253] Sarra, "Embedding Fairness," 208.

[254] Sarra, "Embedding Fairness."

[255] Sarra, "Embedding Fairness," 208–9.

[256] Sarra, "Embedding Fairness."

[257] FCIC Report, xix.

[258] William Black, "The Two Documents Everyone Should Read to Better Understand the Crisis" *Huffington Post* (28 March 2009), www.huffingtonpost.com/william-k-black/the-two-documents-everyon_b_169813.html (hereafter Black, "Two Documents").

[259] Fitch Ratings, "The Impact of Poor Underwriting Practices and Fraud in Subprime RMBS Performance" *Huffington Post* (28 November 2007), 4, http://big.assets.huffingtonpost.com/FraudReport8Nov07Fitch.pdf (hereafter Fitch Ratings).

Investment banks paid handsome fees to the credit rating agencies to obtain the desired ratings on structured financial products.[260] Wall Street firms such as Salomon Brothers and Morgan Stanley became major players in these complex markets and relied increasingly on quantitative analysts ("quants").[261] The increasing dependence on mathematics let the quants create more complex products and let their managers say that they could better manage those products' risks.[262] The high ratings erroneously given to CDO by credit rating agencies encouraged investors and financial institutions to purchase them and enabled the continuing securitization of non-prime mortgages.

Thus, the credit rating agencies were highly complicit in the financial meltdown because the mortgage-related securities at the heart of the crisis could not have been marketed and sold without their ratings approval.[263] From 2000 to 2007, Moody's rated nearly 45,000 mortgage-related securities as AAA.[264] In 2006, 83 per cent of the mortgage securities rated AAA were ultimately downgraded.[265] Flawed computer models, the pressure from financial firms that paid for the ratings, competition for market share, and the absence of meaningful public oversight exacerbated the role of credit-rating agencies in the collapse of the market.[266]

The FCIC concluded that the credit rating agencies abysmally failed in their central mission to provide quality ratings on securities for the benefit of investors.[267] They did not heed the many warning signs indicating significant problems in the mortgage market. The FCIC found that Moody's continued issuing ratings on mortgage-related securities using its outdated analytical models rather than making the necessary adjustments.[268] The clear failure of corporate governance at Moody's failed to ensure the quality of its ratings on tens of thousands of mortgage-backed securities and CDO. The business model under which firms issuing securities paid for their ratings seriously undermined the quality and integrity of those ratings. Thus the FCIC concluded that the rating agencies placed market share and profit considerations above the quality and integrity of their ratings.[269]

Why is it important to understand this complicity in a book on consumer mortgage foreclosure? Investors and major firms relied unquestioningly on credit rating agencies as their arbiters of risk,[270] which fuelled investor demand for high

260 FCIC Report, 44.
261 FCIC Report.
262 FCIC Report.
263 FCIC Report, xxv.
264 FCIC Report.
265 FCIC Report.
266 FCIC Report.
267 FCIC Report, 212.
268 FCIC Report.
269 FCIC Report.
270 FCIC Report, xvii.

short-term returns, thus creating market pressure to amplify sales to unwitting consumers, including many African Americans. The person purchasing a home simply wanted mortgage financing at a reasonable price and on reasonable terms, but did not realize that there were these complex structures creating market pressures to make quick returns on what, for the individual, was supposed to be a safe and secure life investment in a home.

3 *The Role of the Government-sponsored Entities in the Sub-prime Meltdown*

U.S. government-sponsored entities (GSE) have historically provided liquidity in the U.S. mortgage market by buying private mortgage loans using funds generated from bonds they issue in the capital markets.[271] During the Great Depression, the Reconstruction Finance Corporation chartered the Federal National Mortgage Association, referred to as "Fannie Mae." Fannie Mae was to buy mortgages that the Federal Housing Administration (FHA) insured and that adhered to the FHA's underwriting standards, thereby virtually guaranteeing the supply of mortgage credit that banks and thrifts could extend to homebuyers.[272] In 1968, the government split Fannie Mae into two entities, the second being the Government National Mortgage Association, referred to as "Ginnie Mae," and assigned many of Fannie Mae's loan guarantee operations to Ginnie Mae. Ginnie Mae is a wholly owned government corporation that is part of the Department of Housing and Urban Development (HUD).[273] Two years later, the thrifts persuaded Congress to charter another GSE, the Federal Home Loan Mortgage Corporation, referred to as "Freddie Mac," to help the thrifts sell their mortgages. The legislation also authorized Fannie Mae and Freddie Mac to buy conventional, fixed-rate mortgages that the FHA or the Department of Veterans Affairs did not back.[274] The U.S. federal administration and Congress subsequently reorganized Fannie Mae and Freddie Mac as publicly traded corporations.

Fannie Mae and Freddie Mac had dual public and private missions: to support the mortgage market and to maximize returns for shareholders. They did not originate mortgages; they purchased them from banks, thrifts, and mortgage companies, and either held them in their portfolios or securitized and guaranteed them. The Federal Reserve provided services such as electronically clearing payments for GSE debt and securities as if they were Treasury bonds, so Fannie Mae and Freddie Mac could borrow at rates almost as low as the Treasury paid.[275]

[271] Dickerson, *Homeownership*, 43.
[272] FCIC Report, 38.
[273] Dickerson, *Homeownership*, 43.
[274] Dickerson, *Homeownership*, 38.
[275] Dickerson, *Homeownership*, 39.

Banks had been unsuccessful in attempts in the early 1980s to securitize mortgages, in part due to previous state prohibitions on the sale of securities.[276] Fannie Mae and Freddie Mac were deployed to buy up old low-interest loans and securitize them.[277] Prior to then, Freddie Mac and Fannie Mae only financed new home loans that the savings and loan companies and associations (S&L or 'thrifts') originated, thus fulfilling their mandate to support new homeowners.[278] This deregulation allowed S&L to avoid state prohibitions on selling securities widely. They were selling these pass-through mortgage-backed securities across the United States, and the S&L off-loaded much of their risk on to Freddie Mac and Fannie Mae because these GSE were providing guarantees and legal exemptions.[279]

Very important to understand is that from their inception until about a decade before the financial crisis, the GSE could not purchase nor securitize sub-prime loans within their permitted loan limits.[280] However, in the 1990s, the federal government allowed the GSE to purchase riskier, high LTV loans made to borrowers with lower credit ratings. Once the GSE could purchase these higher risk loans, the private sub-prime market grew exponentially as private mortgage originators could off-load their risk on to the GSE. Within ten years, sub-prime mortgage lending went from 9 per cent of all mortgage originations to 20 per cent.[281] Sub-prime mortgage originations skyrocketed from $160 billion in 2001 to $600 billion in 2005.[282]

From 2005 to 2006, the GSE ramped up their purchase and guarantee of risky mortgages, but they suffered from many of the same failures of corporate governance and risk management as in other financial firms.[283] Fannie Mae's quest for bigger market share, profits, and bonuses led it to ramp up its exposure to risky loans and securities as the housing market was peaking.[284] In 2007,

[276] Taub, *Other People's Houses*, 68.

[277] Dickerson, *Homeownership*, 43.

[278] Dickerson, *Homeownership*.

[279] Taub, *Other People's Houses*, 178–180. Taub observes that without the Alternative Mortgage Transaction Parity Act of 1982 and the Depository Institutions Deregulation and Monetary Control Act of 1980, "neither sup-prime loams nor high risk Option ARM and other negative-amortizing lending could have flourished"; Taub, *Other People's Houses*, 224–5. Moreover, the Secondary Mortgage Market Enhancement Act of 1984 removed legal barriers that had previously blocked development of a private mortgage securities market, leading to a proliferation of these products; Taub, *Other People's Houses*, 228–9. See also the Federal Deposit Insurance Corporation, *History of the Eighties: Lessons for the Future Vol 1, An Examination of the Banking Crises of the 1980s and Early 1990s* (Washington, DC: FDIC, 1997), www.fdic.gov/bank/historical/history/vol1.html, especially at Chapter 4, The Savings and Loan Crisis and Its Relationship to Banking, www.fdic.gov/bank/historical/history/167_188.pdf (hereafter FDIC Report).

[280] FDIC Report, 78.

[281] Dickerson, *Homeownership*, 78.

[282] Dickerson, *Homeownership*, 78.

[283] FCIC Report, xxvi.

[284] FCIC Report, xix.

Freddie Mac also was increasing its purchases of riskier loans, expanding into Alt-A and other interest-only loans.[285] Fannie Mae and Freddie Mac had a combined leverage ratio of 75 to 1, which was shockingly high.[286] Their $5 trillion mortgage exposure and market position were significant, thus resulting in their dramatic failure. The GSE had participated in the expansion of risky mortgage lending and declining mortgage standards, thus adding significant demand for less-than-prime loans.[287]

The FCIC examined the role of the GSE in the financial crisis and found they had a highly problematic business model as publicly traded corporations with the implicit backing of, and subsidies from, the federal government. The public mission was blurred by private pressure for returns to shareholders.[288] The FCIC concluded that the business model of Fannie Mae and Freddie Mac was fundamentally flawed.[289] Risky lending and securitization resulted in significant losses at Fannie Mae, which, combined with its excessive leverage permitted by law, led to the company's failure.[290]

Corporate governance, including risk management, also failed at the GSE in part because of skewed compensation methodologies.[291] The Office of Federal Housing Enterprise Oversight (OFHEO) lacked the authority and capacity to adequately regulate GSE.[292] The GSE exercised considerable political power and were able successfully to resist legislation and regulatory actions that would have strengthened oversight of them and restricted their risk-taking activities.[293] In early 2008, the federal government and the GSE decided to increase the mortgage activities and risk of GSE to support the collapsing mortgage market, despite the unsound financial condition of the institutions.[294] Although these actions provided support to the mortgage market, they led to increased losses at GSE, which were ultimately borne by taxpayers. They reflected the conflicted nature of the dual mandate of GSE.[295]

The FCIC found that Fannie Mae and Freddie Mac contributed to the crisis, but were not a primary cause, and GSE mortgage securities did not contribute to the significant financial firm losses that were central to the financial crisis.[296] "They relaxed their underwriting standards to purchase or guarantee riskier

[285] FCIC Report, 183.
[286] FCIC Report, 230.
[287] FCIC Report, 230.
[288] FCIC Report, xxvi.
[289] FCIC Report, 323.
[290] FCIC Report.
[291] FCIC Report.
[292] FCIC Report.
[293] FCIC Report.
[294] FCIC Report.
[295] FCIC Report.
[296] FCIC Report, xxvi.

loans and related securities in order to meet stock market analysts' and investors' expectations for growth, to regain market share, and to ensure generous compensation for their executives and employees – justifying their activities on the broad and sustained public policy support for homeownership."[297] The delinquency rates on the loans they purchased or guaranteed were significantly lower than those purchased and securitized by other financial institutions.

Because lenders could originate loans that the FHA would then insure and sell as government-backed mortgages to the GSE in the secondary market, there were huge incentives for mortgage originators to sell many more mortgages and then use the sale proceeds to originate more loans.[298] When Congress set goals that required GSE to increase the number of loans they bought, the GSE expanded into sub-prime mortgages, which they previously had not purchased; these loans lacked most of the financial safeguards the GSE benefited from previously, such as low LTV, down payment requirements, and fixed-interest rates.[299] Fannie Mae and Freddie Mac were placed into conservatorship in 2008.

4 *Failure of Regulatory Oversight*

Reference has been made throughout this book to the many types of deregulation that occurred in the years leading up to the financial collapse. Regulators lacked the independence and strength of oversight necessary to safeguard financial stability in the United States. The financial sector had become a much more dominant force in the U.S. economy. From 1978 to 2007, the amount of debt held by the financial sector in the United States soared from $3 trillion to $36 trillion.[300] On the eve of the crisis, financial sector profits constituted 27 per cent of all corporate profits in the United States.[301] The FCIC concluded that the financial crisis was the result of human action and inaction, in which financial market participants and the federal government ignored or discounted warning signs and failed to manage evolving risks within a system essential to the well-being of the American public.[302] The FCIC found that the crisis could have been entirely avoided.

The warning signs were everywhere, yet regulators ignored them: an explosion in risky sub-prime lending and securitization, an unsustainable rise in housing prices, widespread reports of egregious and predatory lending practices, dramatic increases in household mortgage debt, exponential growth in financial firms' trading activities, and largely unregulated derivatives and short-term repo lending markets.[303]

[297] FCIC Report, xxvi.
[298] Dickerson, *Homeownership*, 46.
[299] Dickerson, *Homeownership*, 47.
[300] FCIC Report, xvii.
[301] FCIC Report.
[302] FCIC Report.
[303] FCIC Report.

A month before Lehman Brothers' collapse, the Federal Reserve Bank of New York was still seeking information on the exposures created by the Lehman Brothers' more than 900,000 derivatives contracts.[304]

The FCIC concluded that regulators failed to adequately supervise the safety and soundness of financial firms, thus allowing them to hold inadequate capital and take inordinate risk in activities such as non-prime mortgage securitization.[305] The FCIC found that the Federal Reserve failed to set prudent mortgage-lending standards that could have stopped the flow of toxic mortgages.[306] Ignoring all the warning indicators, days before the collapse of Bear Stearns in March 2008, the SEC Chair Christopher Cox expressed "comfort about the capital cushions" at big investment banks.[307]

The FCIC also concluded that widespread failures in financial regulation and supervision resulted in the devastating instability of the nation's financial markets.[308] Years of deregulation and reliance on self-regulation by financial institutions that was actively pushed by the powerful financial sector, championed by former Federal Reserve Chair Greenspan, and supported by successive administrations and Congresses, stripped away key safeguards.[309] The FCIC identified gaps in the oversight of critical areas with trillions of dollars at risk, such as the shadow banking system and the OTC derivatives markets.[310] The FCIC also found that the federal government permitted financial firms to pick their preferred regulators in a race to the weakest supervisor.[311] In some instances, regulators had ample power but neglected to use it, such as the power to end runaway mortgage securitization.[312]

The SEC failed to enforce adequately its disclosure requirements governing mortgage securities, exempted some sales of such securities from its review, and pre-empted states from applying state law to them, thereby failing in its core mission to protect investors.[313] The Federal Reserve failed to recognize the cataclysmic danger the housing bubble posed to the financial system and refused to take timely action to constrain its growth. It believed that it could contain the damage from the housing bubble's collapse.[314] Collapsing mortgage-lending standards and practices created conditions that were ripe for mortgage fraud.[315]

[304] FCIC Report, xxi.
[305] FCIC Report, 279.
[306] FCIC Report, xvii.
[307] FCIC Report, xxi.
[308] FCIC Report, xviii.
[309] FCIC Report.
[310] FCIC Report, xviii.
[311] FCIC Report.
[312] FCIC Report.
[313] FCIC Report, 187.
[314] FCIC Report.
[315] FCIC Report.

Regulators failed to identify poor governance practices in the financial institutions and continued to rate the firms they oversaw as safe and sound even in the face of mounting troubles, often downgrading them just as they collapsed financially.[316] This failure was caused by many factors, including beliefs that regulation was unduly burdensome, financial institutions were capable of self-regulation, and regulators should not interfere with activities reported as profitable.[317] Large commercial banks and thrifts, such as Wachovia and IndyMac, which had significant exposure to risky mortgage assets, were subject to runs by creditors and depositors.[318]

The Federal Reserve realized far too late the systemic danger inherent in the interconnections of the unregulated OTC derivatives market. Its failure to require disclosure meant that it lacked the information needed to act in a timely and effective way.[319]

The FCIC also concluded that the Federal Reserve did not employ the authority the Home Ownership and Equity Protection Act (HOEPA) granted to it.[320] In 2000, the Federal Reserve revisited the rules protecting borrowers from predatory conduct, and after hearings, the staff offered two reform proposals, neither of which were adopted.[321] The first would have effectively barred lenders from granting any mortgage, not just the limited set of high-cost loans defined by HOEPA, solely on the value of the collateral and without regard to the borrower's ability to repay. For high-cost loans, the lender would have to verify and document the borrower's income and debt; for other loans, the documentation standard was weaker because the lender could rely on the borrower's payment history. The staff memo explained such a rule would mainly "affect lenders who make no-documentation loans." The second proposal addressed practices such as deceptive advertisements, misrepresenting loan terms, and having consumers sign blank documents – acts that involve fraud, deception, or misrepresentations.[322] Federal Reserve officials rejected both staff proposals, and while the Federal Reserve did make very minor modifications to HOEPA in 2001, it stated that it did not want to interfere with the flow of credit or create unnecessary creditor burden.[323] The FCIC found that nothing improved with this minor rule change.

The Federal Reserve's failure to stop predatory practices frustrated and infuriated consumer advocates and some members of Congress. Yet their accounts of abuses were brushed off as anecdotal.[324] In particular, the Federal Reserve failed to meet its

[316] FCIC Report.
[317] FCIC Report.
[318] FCIC Report.
[319] FCIC Report.
[320] FCIC Report, 84.
[321] FCIC Report, 93.
[322] FCIC Report, 93, citing an internal staff document of the Federal Reserve Board, *The Problem of Predatory Lending* (Washington, DC: Federal Reserve Board, 5 December 2000), 10–13.
[323] FCIC Report, 94.
[324] FCIC Report, 95.

statutory obligation to establish and maintain prudent mortgage lending standards and to protect against predatory lending.[325]

This failure to engage in regulatory oversight did not arise in a vacuum. The financial industry exerted pressure on policy makers and regulators. In the decade leading up to 2008, the financial sector expended $2.7 billion in reported federal lobbying expenses and paid another $1 billion in campaign contributions.[326] In the period leading up to the financial crisis, there was a lack of political will to fundamentally protect society and to temper the conduct of financial institutions.[327] That lack of political will continues to exist today in new forms of predatory lending.

Without effective regulatory oversight, financial institutions acted recklessly by taking on too much risk with too little capital.[328] The large investment banks and bank holding companies focused their activities increasingly on risky trading activities that produced phenomenal profits, but also enormous exposures to financial risk.[329]

The Federal Reserve's policies and pronouncements encouraged rather than inhibited the growth of mortgage debt and the housing bubble.[330] Lack of regulatory oversight resulted in a significant failure of accountability and responsibility throughout each level of the lending system, from corporate boardrooms to individuals interacting with consumers.

Earlier in this chapter, we discussed the complicity of credit rating agencies. Neither the SEC nor any other regulator regulated the credit rating agencies adequately to ensure the quality and accuracy of their ratings. Not only did federal banking supervisors fail to rein in risky mortgage lending practices, but the Office of the Comptroller of the Currency and the Office of Thrift Supervision pre-empted the applicability of state laws and regulatory efforts to national banks and thrifts, thus preventing adequate protection for borrowers and weakening constraints on this segment of the mortgage market.[331]

Unregulated and unmonitored compensation systems rewarded short-term gain without proper consideration of long-term consequences,[332] which is still a factor today. One example was AIG senior management's ignorance of the risks of the company's $79 billion derivatives exposure to mortgage-related securities.[333] Financial products salespeople earned multimillion-dollar bonuses by packaging and selling new kinds of investment products that claimed to be safe, but possessed

[325] FCIC Report, 101.
[326] FCIC Report, xviii.
[327] FCIC Report.
[328] FCIC Report.
[329] FCIC Report, xix.
[330] FCIC Report.
[331] FCIC Report, 126.
[332] FCIC Report, xix.
[333] FCIC Report.

complex and hidden risks.[334] Federal officials praised these "financial innovations" because they had been persuaded that they lowered borrowing costs and moved risks away from the biggest and most systemically important financial institutions.[335]

Regulators had ample warning of problems but ignored the representations of consumer advocacy and civil society groups. Consumer advocates and front-line local government officials raised concerns with the Federal Reserve and other banking regulators when homeowners began streaming into their offices to seek help in dealing with mortgages they could not afford to pay.[336] Officials in Cleveland and other Ohio cities reached out to the federal government for help and asked the Federal Reserve, as the entity with the authority to regulate risky lending practices, to use its power under the HOEPA to issue new mortgage lending rules.[337] Gail Burks, president and CEO of Nevada Fair Housing, Inc, a Las Vegas–based housing clinic, reports that she and other groups took their concerns directly to Greenspan, Chair of the Federal Reserve, in person describing to him "the metamorphosis in the lending industry: predatory lending practices such as flipping loans or misinforming seniors about reverse mortgages"; examples of growing sloppiness in paperwork, and not crediting payments appropriately or miscalculating accounts.[338] Consumer groups complained about predatory mortgage lending in the inner-city and asked the Federal Reserve to enforce the Truth in Lending Act, which prohibits granting credit without regard to the consumers' ability to pay, but the Federal Reserve refused to do so.[339] The concerns fell on un-listening ears. The Federal Reserve neglected its mission "to ensure the safety and soundness of the nation's banking and financial system and to protect the credit rights of consumers."[340]

The number of cases of reported mortgage fraud grew exponentially. Suspicious activity reports, also known as SAR, are reports filed to the Financial Crimes Enforcement Network (FinCEN), a bureau within the Treasury Department. FinCEN found a twentyfold increase in mortgage fraud reports between 1996 and 2005.[341] According to FinCEN, the figures likely represented a substantial underreporting because mortgage brokers who were not subject to any federal standard or oversight created and originated two-thirds of all the loans; and many lenders who were required to submit reports did not in fact do so.[342] To community activists and local officials, however, the lending practices were a matter of national economic concern.[343]

[334] FCIC Report, 6.
[335] FCIC Report.
[336] FCIC Report, 9.
[337] FCIC Report.
[338] FCIC Report, 11.
[339] Baradaran, *How the Other Half Banks*, 159.
[340] FCIC Report, xxiii.
[341] FCIC Report, 15.
[342] FCIC Report.
[343] FCIC Report.

The FCIC documented many unethical and illegal practices leading up to 2008. In Florida alone, 10,500 individuals with criminal records became mortgage brokers from 2000 to 2007, including 4,065 who had previously been convicted of such crimes as fraud, bank robbery, racketeering, and extortion.[344]

The FCIC heard testimony from Christopher Cruise, a Maryland-based corporate educator who trained loan officers for companies that were expanding mortgage originations. He coached 10,000 loan originators a year in auditoriums, including individuals working for Countrywide, Ameriquest, and Ditech, where most of their new hires were young, had no mortgage experience, and were fresh out of school; and he told them that the best of them could easily earn millions.[345]

The FCIC also found that financial insiders and other market participants who were not subject to regulatory oversight saw the meltdown coming and ignored the signs.[346] Individuals who spoke out were ignored, ridiculed, or fired.[347] Once the crisis hit, policy makers and regulators had no comprehensive strategic plan for containment of the financial crisis because they lacked a full understanding of the risks and interconnections in the financial markets.[348]

Also, of note is that the predominant players in the sub-prime market – mortgage brokers, independent mortgage companies, and Wall Street investment banks – were not subject to Community Reinvestment Act (CRA) requirements. "Only six percent of higher-priced loans, a proxy for sub-prime, were subject to the CRA, meaning that they were extended by CRA-obligated lenders to lower-income borrowers or neighbourhoods within their CRA assessment areas."[349] Yet Bocian et al, document that loans made to low- and moderate-income homebuyers as part of banks' efforts to meet their CRA obligations actually performed better than the rest of the sub-prime market.[350]

Lack of regulatory oversight created hugely inequitable outcomes. While millions lost their homes, executives profited from the sub-prime mortgage debacle. Taub cites examples of financial services executives who continued to push the selling of subprime mortgages but sold their shares in the lending companies on the eve of the meltdown for hundreds of millions of dollars.[351]

344 Rob Barry, Matthew Haggman, and Jack Dolan, "Ex-convicts active in mortgage fraud" *Miami Herald* (20 July 2008), www.miamiherald.com/news/special-reports/borrowers-betrayed/article 1931241.html. FCIC, 14.

345 FCIC Report, 8.

346 FDIC Report, 429.

347 See Charles L. Nier and Maureen R. St Cyr, "A Racial Financial Crisis: Rethinking the Theory of Reverse Redlining to Combat Predatory Lending Under the Fair Housing Act" (2011) 83 Temple L Rev, 941–77.

348 FCIC Report, xxi.

349 Bocian et al, "Lost Ground," 9.

350 Bocian et al, "Lost Ground."

351 Taub, *Other People's Houses*, 177.

Another lack of appropriate regulatory oversight is the Mortgage Electronic Registration Systems, Inc (MERS), a Delaware-registered corporation headquartered in Virginia, that masked the identities of the mortgagees of record.[352] Peterson documents how during the securitization process, loans were sold multiple times; so to speed up processing, the financial industry created MERS, an organization made up of 3,000 mortgage lenders.[353] MERS tracked changes in servicing rights and ownership interests in mortgage loans.

Peterson observed that when closing on home mortgages, mortgage lenders list MERS as the mortgagee of record on the paper mortgage rather than the lender that is the actual mortgagee.[354] The mortgage is then recorded with property registries under MERS' name rather than the lender's name even though MERS does not fund, service, or own any mortgage loans. MERS then purports to remain the mortgagee for the life of a mortgage loan even after loans are sold multiple times or securitized and sold to investors.[355] By 2010, 60 million mortgage loans were registered as held by MERS, which was 60 per cent of all mortgage loans in the United States at that time.[356]

The MERS electronic service thus masked the rapidness with which ownership of predatory mortgages were being pooled or sold, which was another contributing cause of the U.S. mortgage foreclosure crisis. Peterson observed that MERS facilitated predatory structured finance by decreasing the exit costs for originators: "As investment banks, hedge funds, institutional investors, and the credit rating agencies weighed the risks of dumping billions upon billions of dollars into mortgage securities drawn out of the balance sheets of thinly capitalized, bankruptcy-prone mortgage lenders, MERS provided an important additional inducement."[357] Companies could avoid paying registration fees each time a mortgage was sold and some local courts allowed the actual parties in interest to bring residential foreclosures under MERS' corporate identity instead of their own.[358]

Many of these financial practices continue in the market today, masking the degree to which securitization is occurring and the costs to millions of borrowers and to state revenue sources.

352 Christopher Lewis Peterson, "Foreclosure, Subprime Mortgage Lending, and the Mortgage Electronic Registration System" (2009) 78:4 *University of Cincinnati Law Review*, SSRN, https://ssrn.com/abstract=1469749. MERS operates a computer database designed to track servicing and ownership of mortgage loans anywhere in the United States.

353 FCIC Report, 407.

354 Peterson, "Predatory Structured," 1361.

355 Peterson, "Predatory Structured."

356 Peterson, "Predatory Structured," 1362.

357 Peterson, "Predatory Structured," 1398.

358 Peterson, "Predatory Structured," 1406.

However, in New York, the issue of whether MERS has standing to bring a foreclosure action, or whether MERS has the legal capacity to assign the note and the mortgage to a foreclosing plaintiff, has been the subject of considerable litigation., The Appellate Division of the Supreme Court of New York, Second Department held in *Bank of New York* v *Silverberg* that MERS only has standing to assign the right to foreclose when it holds or is assignee of the note and the mortgage at the commencement of the action.[359]

The next chapter examines how the financial products led to the targeting of African Americans in a concerted attempt to expand the market for sub-prime loans.

[359] *Bank of New York* v *Silverberg*, 86 AD 3d 274 (NY App Div 2011).

4

Predatory Lending Targeted African Americans

This chapter examines state, federal, and other studies that have documented how African Americans were particularly targeted for predatory and sub-prime lending even when they qualified for traditional mortgages. It examines the historical links between racism and limited access to traditional mortgage lenders and how this historical treatment fostered the sub-prime market. This chapter also explores the critically important question of why African Americans were targeted. No other community was targeted as aggressively as were black Americans. We explore why, concluding that as Professor Taunya Banks observed in commenting on this book, "the history of black economic exploitation is *sui generis*" (unique). The chapter concludes with a discussion of continued victimization and why African Americans harmed by predatory lending are not getting the help they need to begin to recover from the wealth drain that has damaged individuals, families, and entire communities.

I THE TARGETING OF AFRICAN AMERICANS

African Americans were four times as likely as similarly situated white Americans to pay sub-prime rates on their mortgages.[1] A study by the Center for Responsible Lending found that African-American and Latinx borrowers received higher-interest-rate sub-prime mortgages far more frequently than white borrowers, even when they were equally qualified for lower-cost loans.[2] Using data from 177,000

[1] Alan M. White, "Borrowing While Black: Applying Fair Lending Laws to Risk-Based Mortgage Pricing" (2009) 60:3 SCL Rev, 677. See also Monique W. Morris, "Discrimination and Mortgage Lending in America: A Summary of the Disparate Impact of Subprime Mortgage Lending on African Americans" (March 2009) National Association for the Advancement of Colored People.

[2] D. Gruenstein Bocian, K. S. Ernst and W. Li, "Unfair Lending, the Effect of Race and Ethnicity on the Price of Subprime Mortgages" (2006) Center for Responsible Lending, www.responsiblelending.org/research-publication/unfair-lending-effect-race-and-ethnicity-price-subprime-mortgages (hereafter Bocian et al, "Unfair Lending").

sub-prime loans, the study observed that while lenders claim they charged more because African-American and Latinx borrowers on average have shakier credit histories, the evidence demonstrates that this view is simply wrong.[3] African Americans and Latinx borrowers are commonly almost a third more likely to get a high-priced loan than white borrowers with the same credit scores.[4] The large dataset revealed that African-American and Latinx consumers received a disproportionate share of higher-interest-rate home loans even when controlling for factors such as borrower income and property location.[5]

The U.S. Center for Responsible Lending documented the following in 2011:

> Racial and ethnic differences in foreclosure rates persist even after accounting for differences in borrower incomes. Racial and ethnic disparities in foreclosure rates cannot be explained by income, since disparities persist even among higher-income groups. For example, approximately 10 percent of higher-income African-American borrowers and 15 percent of higher-income Latino borrowers have lost their home to foreclosure, compared with 4.6 percent of higher- income non-Hispanic white borrowers ... among borrowers with a FICO score of over 660 (indicating good credit), African Americans and Latinos received a high interest rate loan more than three times as often as white borrowers.[6]

Another issue for African-American borrowers at all levels of income was the proliferation of "no income no asset" loans that were approved based on the applicant's stated income and assets, with no requirement for documentation of employment income, assets, or credit worthiness.[7] "No income" did not mean that the borrower had no income, it referred to the mortgage broker not requiring or submitting documentation of the borrower's income. These loans were given to low income and middle-income borrowers even where they had documentation because the broker received higher fees for these higher interest sub-prime loans. Low-documentation mortgages were only a small fraction of the market in the 1990s, but by 2006, they represented more than 16 per cent of all new home loans.[8] The results were very harmful. By 2011, one in five homes in minority neighbourhoods in the United States that arranged mortgages from 2004 to 2008 were in foreclosure or loan payments were seriously delinquent.[9]

3 Bocian et al, "Unfair Lending."

4 Bocian et al, "Unfair Lending."

5 Bocian et al, "Unfair Lending," 3. The study used disclosures collected under the Home Mortgage Disclosure Act (HMDA).

6 Debbie Gruenstein Bocian, Wei Li, and Carolina Reid, "Lost Ground, 2011: Disparities in Mortgage Lending and Foreclosures" (2011) Center for Responsible Lending, 8, University of North Carolina, www.responsiblelending.org/mortgage-lending/research-analysis/Lost-Ground-2011.pdf (hereafter Bocian et al, "Lost Ground").

7 Kenneth Harney, "The Lowdown on Low-Doc Loans" *Washington Post* (25 November 2006), www.washingtonpost.com/archive/realestate/2006/11/25/the-lowdown-on-low-doc-loans/09d5f54a-7a01-43a4-b40e-3e2298bfbda0/ (hereafter Harney, "The Lowdown").

8 Harney, "The Lowdown."

9 Bocian et al, "Unfair Lending," 6.

What is now evident is that there are serious intergenerational effects of the sub-prime mortgage debacle. Millions used their life savings to pay for sub-prime mortgages, fees to refinance, fees to apply for modifications, and legal fees. Losing everything to foreclosure means economic insecurity for the borrowers; but it also results in losses to the next generation because the parents have no savings remaining to assist with their children's education or to help their children get a start in the housing market.[10] This profound loss of intergenerational wealth can be compared with figures that estimate that there will be a transfer of $24 trillion in intergenerational wealth in the United States in the next ten years for propertied (read white) families.[11]

1 *Qualified for Traditional Mortgages but Were Steered Inappropriately*

The Center for Responsible Lending study found that the effect of being an African-American borrower on the cost of credit was greatest for loans containing penalties for early payoff, which comprised over 60 per cent of the 177,000 mortgage loans examined.[12] African-American borrowers with prepayment penalties on their sub-prime home loans were 6 to 34 per cent more likely to receive a higher-rate loan than if they had been white American borrowers with similar qualifications.[13] One New York City study found that 33 per cent of borrowers under sub-prime loans qualified for less costly prime loans.[14]

Historically, bank mortgages were not available to African Americans, a legacy of years of racial segregation and racial discrimination. As a result, African Americans turned to less-regulated mortgage brokers.[15] They were therefore particularly vulnerable when mortgage brokers began to target borrowers for sub-prime loans. The availability of sub-prime loans, initially viewed as beneficial, became a macabre exercise in racism. For example, an affidavit by one Wells Fargo credit officer reported that African Americans were referred to internally as "mud people" and that she and her colleagues targeted African-American borrowers for sub-prime loans even when

[10] Bocian et al, "Unfair Lending," 5.

[11] Blackrock, "Larry Fink's 2019 Letter to CEOs: Purpose & Profit" (2019), www.blackrock.com/corporate/investor-relations/larry-fink-ceo-letter.

[12] Bocian et al, "Unfair Lending," 4.

[13] Bocian et al, "Unfair Lending." See also R. Marsico and J. Yoo, "Racial Disparities in Subprime Home Mortgage Lending in New York City: Meaning and Implications" (2008–2009) 53 NYL Sch L Rev 1011.

[14] Mehrsa Baradaran, *How the Other Half Banks: Exclusion, Exploitation, and the Threat to Democracy* (Cambridge, MA: Harvard University Press, 2015), 46–47 (hereafter Baradaran, *How the Other Half Banks*), citing Michael Powell and Janet Roberts, "Minorities Affected Most as New York Foreclosures Rise" *New York Times* (15 May 2009), www.nytimes.com/2009/05/16/nyregion/16foreclose.html.

[15] American Civil Liberties Union, "Justice Foreclosed: How Wall Street's Appetite for Subprime Mortgages Ended Up Hurting Black and Latino Communities" (October 2012), www.aclu.org/sites/default/files/field_document/justiceforclosed-singlepage-rel4.pdf (hereafter American Civil Liberties Union, "Justice Foreclosed"), 6.

they qualified for traditional mortgages.[16] Loan officers called black neighbourhoods slums and called the sub-prime loans they were aggressively marketing "ghetto loans."[17] A Wells Fargo credit manager testified that her district manager pressured its credit managers to conceal details of the predatory loans because African-American customers "could be talked into anything."[18] Another former Wells Fargo credit officer gave a sworn statement that Wells Fargo targeted African-American borrowers for high interest loans they could not afford because "the prevailing attitude was that African-American customers weren't savvy enough to know they were getting a bad loan."[19] An affidavit revealed that "Wells Fargo mortgage had an emerging-markets unit that specifically targeted black churches, because it figured church leaders had a lot of influence and could convince congregants to take out subprime loans."[20]

Fremont General Corporation was a Santa Monica, California-based holding company for Fremont Investment & Loan, a company that was one of the largest sub-prime mortgage lenders in the United States during the early and mid-2000s.[21] Fremont Investment & Loan was forced out of the sub-prime lending business in 2007 after regulators and the Federal Deposit Insurance Corporation (FDIC) filed a cease and desist notice against the company.[22] It had made ARM loans without considering the customers' ability to pay after the initial teaser rate had expired.

[16] Michael Powell, "Suit accuses Wells Fargo of steering blacks to subprime mortgages in Baltimore" *The New York Times* (7 June 2009), A16, www.nytimes.com/2009/06/07/us/07baltimore.html (hereafter Powell, "Suit Accuses").

[17] Declaration of Doris Dancy in *City of Memphis et al* v *Wells Fargo Bank, NA, et al*, No 09-2857 (STA), Document 29 First Amended Complaint (WD Tenn filed 7 April 2010), paras. 8, 67, 82, Civil Rights Litigation Clearinghouse, www.clearinghouse.net/chDocs/public/FH-TN-0002-0001.pdf (hereafter *Memphis* v *Wells Fargo*); Declaration of Elizabeth Jacobson and Tony Paschal in *City of Baltimore* v *Wells Fargo Bank*, No 8-062 (JFM), Document 133 Plaintiff Memorandum (D Md filed 16 October 2009), 9, Civil Rights Litigation Clearinghouse, www.clearinghouse.net/chDocs/public/FH-MD-0001-0009.pdf (hereafter *Baltimore* v *Wells Fargo*, Plaintiff Memorandum), 4, 17.

[18] Declaration of Doris Dancy in *Memphis* v *Wells Fargo*, cited in American Civil Liberties Union, "Justice Foreclosed," 8, 24.

[19] Thom Weidlich, "Foreclosures Prompt Cities to Sue Banks Over Mowing, Repairs" *Bloomberg* (11 May 2011), http://.bloomberg.com/news/2011-05-12/foreclosures-prompt-four-u-s-cities-to-sue-banks-for-mowing-home-repairs.html (hereafter Weidlich, "Foreclosures"). See also Cheryl L. Wade, "Fairness, Narrative, Empathy, and the US Racial Wealth Gap" in Janis P. Sarra, ed, *An Exploration of Fairness, Interdisciplinary Inquiries in Law, Science and the Humanities* (Toronto: Carswell, 2012) (hereafter Wade, "Fairness").

[20] Powell, "Suit Accuses," A16.

[21] *In re New Century TRS Holdings, Inc*, No 7-10416 (KJC), 465 BR 38, Final Report of the Bankruptcy Court Examiner (Bank D Del filed 29 February 2008), 37, FCIC, https://fcic-static.law.stanford.edu/cdn_media/fcic-docs/2008-02-29%20Missal%20-%20Final%20Report%20on%20the%20Bankruptcy%20of%20New%20Century.pdf, citing National Mortgage News Online data.

[22] Manisha Padi, "Consumer Protection Laws and the Mortgage Market: Evidence from Ohio" (2018) (Working Paper), 6, Manisha Padi, https://manishapadi.com/workingpapers/, referencing the National Low Income Housing Coalition, "Findings from the HB 4050 Predatory Lending Database Pilot Program" (1 April 2007), https://nlihc.org/resource/findings-hb-4050-predatory-lending-database-pilot-program (hereafter Padi, "Consumer Protection Ohio"), 4.

Other banks, brokerage firms, and investment firms engaged in the same practices. After the financial crisis, the Department of Justice brought actions against JP Morgan, Citigroup, Countrywide (Bank of America), Goldman Sachs, Morgan Stanley, Deutsche Bank, and Credit Suisse from 2013 to 2016.[23] These civil suits are discussed in Chapter 8.

Here is one first-hand story regarding Fremont's lending practices. "J" is a male from Queens, New York; he recounts his situation in September 2018:

> I am a construction worker. I have built bridges. I am unionized and make good wages. I am married with three children. My daughter is in college. It all started with the Fremont Mortgage loan. I applied for a loan for home ownership. Fremont offered $400,000. They asked me if I wanted some cash back and I said yes, but only if there was equity in the house to cover it. They added $100,000 to the mortgage and gave me $37,000 in cash. The loan was more than the value of the property, but they did not tell me that. I didn't have anyone who could look at the paperwork they had me sign.
>
> Something was fishy about the loan. When they brought the cheque, they met me on the street, in Brooklyn, near my house. They were two white people handing me the $37,000. They did not make it clear that the loan was for an additional $100,000 or that the payment amount would go up. My monthly payments went immediately from $3,200 a month to $5,000. When I found out about the additional $100,000, I was angry. The bills come in two different statements each month, the second is called an "equity line of credit" secured by the house.
>
> Construction work can get slow, and after a couple of months of not working, I fell behind in payments. My loan had been sold to another company, and now I was dealing with Wells Fargo. Now my work is steady and I can pay. Wells Fargo asked for two months' pay stubs and would not accept the employment gap, even though I have been working steady for three years now. I have been working with my lawyer Alice since 2012. They denied a modification of the mortgage loan because 27.48 percent of my income was going to my mortgage payment instead of the qualifying 31 percent threshold. Wells Fargo was paid the U.S. TARP money, icing on the cake of what it already made off me, to try to throw me out and get my home. My wife and I are earning $13,763 a month, my wife is disabled and they calculate our income to include her social security without looking at what our expenses are. They denied the modification to payments and now they want to auction off our home. I have worked all my life; I am not going backwards. My lawyer filed for bankruptcy for me, bankruptcy stops the foreclosure for a little while as my lawyer works on a loss mitigation program.

J's lawyer, Alice Nicholson, points out that her clients are frequently turned down for modifications. The reason often given is that the "investor" will not allow it.

23 National Credit Union Administration, "AME Allocations for Legal Recoveries, Fees and Expenses" (11 August 2017), www.ncua.gov/Legal/Documents/legal-recoveries-allocations.pdf (hereafter NCUA Settlements).

She believes that the investor is Fannie Mae, which has bragged about making more money during the financial crisis than any time in history.[24] She observes that Wells Fargo and JP Morgan Chase rarely grant modifications, and they do not give answers to applications, leaving thousands of applications pending so that their refusal statistics look low, thereby avoiding bad publicity.[25] Nicholson observes that at least bankruptcy gives mortgage borrowers a limited time to fight the foreclosure.[26]

Peterson documents many cases in which lenders ignored correspondence, telephone calls, and otherwise refused to provide account information, charged excessive and unnecessary attorney fees to borrowers in arrears, engineered servicing systems that encouraged foreclosure to generate fee revenue, and delayed and obstructed judicial, administrative, and consumer investigations.[27]

Even where individuals were well established in the home ownership market, they were steered to predatory loans with no accountability by the mortgage originators or servicers. Ten years after the height of the financial crisis, many borrowers are still fighting against foreclosure. Highly problematic was the huge drop in property values after the financial crisis commenced, many by 35 to 67 per cent.[28] This collapse in the value of homes has meant that the lenders' pressure to sell now means no recovery for the borrower because the collapsed market and resultant low prices erased the equity borrowers previously invested in the home or other property.

This narrative is from a woman living in Detroit:

> My parents, along with about 100,000 others, worked at Ford Rouge plant. That's how they were able to buy a home. The three big U.S. automakers made my parents middle class. Now, with the changes that technology has brought, only 7,000 workers work at the Ford Rouge plant—they make five times as many cars. These changes are good for Ford, but they are bad for workers. When it comes to foreclosure, Detroit was the hardest hit. 40 percent of homes owned since the 1930s were foreclosed on since the crisis started. Many say that Detroit is making a comeback but that's "a lie." The rising stock market benefits the rich only. Corporations are happy but workers are not. Water bills and taxes are so high—they get higher and higher. When we can't pay the taxes, the banks take our homes. When we can't pay the water bill, the water is shut off, and the banks take our homes. It's against the law to raise my children in a home with no water. They can take my children away because I have no water. Why is my water bill so high? I lived in a house with

[24] Alice Nicholson, lawyer specializing in foreclosures, interview, New York, September 2018 (on file with authors) (hereafter Nicholson, Interview).

[25] Nicholson, Interview.

[26] Nicholson, Interview.

[27] Christopher Peterson, "Predatory Structured Finance" (2007) 28:5 *Cardozo Law Review*, 2185-89, 2215–6, https://ssrn.com/abstract=929118 (hereafter Peterson, "Predatory Structured"); Celeste M. Hammond, "Predatory Lending: A Legal Definition and Update" (2005) 34 Real Est L J 176 (hereafter Hammond, "Predatory Lending").

[28] Jennifer S. Taub, *Other People's Houses* (New Haven, CT: Yale University Press, 2014) (hereafter Taub, *Other People's Houses*), 15.

> a $4,900 water bill; I couldn't pay it and the water was turned off for weeks. I lived in the house that belonged to my mom and dad. I have children but I couldn't live in a house that has no water with minor children. My parents didn't realize there were leaks in the basement. They transferred the home to me. They transferred the water bill to me too. Because of the leaks, the monthly water bill went from hundreds to thousands.
>
> After my parents paid off their mortgage and retired from Ford, the roof began to leak. They got the money to fix the leaky roof by taking a loan and using their home as collateral. They did not know it was a predatory loan. In the sixth month of the loan, they owed a balloon payment. They couldn't pay accrued interest. Mom became very ill and she had to go into a nursing home. Dad lived to 80 and died in the house. Then I lived in the house with the huge water bill. I took out a new mortgage to fix the roof. Then I had the house, but not a job at Ford. I went to court to tell the judge my story, but the judge said I have to get out.
>
> My home is boarded up now. Criminals trespass where I once lived, in the home I had to abandon. Developers have broken into my home and others in the neighborhood to steal hot water tanks, furnaces and fixtures. I have friends who committed suicide when they realized they couldn't live the way they used to before times got so hard. We had to walk away from our homes. Some went to live with relatives. I moved south. I remember my house with three bedrooms, a garage. I've brought my pictures with me along with my bible with notations that record my babies' births. I've taken the stuff with me along with the questions. What did I do wrong? What could I have done better? Am I the wrong race? Did I have the wrong spouse? The wrong career? I'm trying to make new friends but the pain never goes away.

Families who had lived for years in modest residences lost their homes. After they were evicted, many homes were ultimately abandoned, vandalized, and then stripped bare as scavengers ripped away copper pipes and aluminum siding to sell for scrap.[29]

Middle class African Americans who already had a solid amount of equity built up in their homes, and, in some instances, had fully paid off their mortgages, were also targeted for sub-prime mortgages. These sub-prime loans dramatically diminished the equity in their homes.

Steering borrowers who qualified for a traditional mortgage into financially untenable mortgage arrangements is fraudulent conduct. Yet the remedies that were provided as part of the settlements of the massive amount of litigation, as discussed in Chapter 8, did not make the borrowers "whole."[30]

As noted, African Americans were not the only people targeted. Latinx borrowers were also more likely to receive higher-rate loans than similarly situated white

[29] Taub, *Other People's Houses*, 9.

[30] Mindy Chen-Wishart, *Contract Law* (Oxford: Oxford University Press, 2015).

borrowers for mortgages used to purchase homes.[31] Latinx borrowers purchasing homes were 29 to 142 per cent more likely to receive a higher rate mortgage than if they had been non-Latinx and white, depending on the type of interest rate and whether the loan contained a prepayment penalty.[32]

2 *So-called "Liar Loans"*

Taub observes that a number of borrowers were falsely lured into buying homes they could not really afford.[33] There were also what the industry referred to as "liar loans," where the lender colluded with real estate appraisers, who appraised homes above their market value, and then steered borrowers to take out higher rate and higher risk mortgages than they were qualified for based on the false assessment of the value of the property.[34] The mortgages were called liar loans because mortgage originators encouraged borrowers to lie about their income or altered the borrowers' income after the borrowers applied to ensure that they qualified for the mortgage.[35] Some brokers and loan officers fraudulently altered the borrowers' financial information after it was submitted to the broker or loan officer to ensure that they would not qualify for traditional mortgages.[36] The collusion carried through to the independent mortgage brokers who were paid higher fees to sell these inflated mortgages to borrowers.

Millions of defrauded borrowers have been rendered invisible by the U.S. government's focus almost exclusively on banking reform, bail-in mechanisms, and investor protections. The pain and hardship continues more than ten years later.

Beatrice is a hairdresser living in Baltimore. Her story resonates with many who were given poor advice:

> Liberia was my home; I came to America 20 years ago to find my dream. A single mom, I wanted a home for my children. They said my credit was not that good. To buy a house, my friend and my daughter had to co-sign, I thought it was a blessing. I paid $1,600 a month, the family all together. Two years later, my friend asked me to refinance, she needed off the mortgage to finance her own home. She brought a mortgage man to me, he filled out papers, I signed at the library. It was a subprime mortgage, I did not know, no one explained what it was.

31 Bocian et al, "Unfair Lending," 4.
32 Bocian et al, "Unfair Lending," 4.
33 Taub, *Other People's Houses*, 126.
34 Taub, *Other People's Houses*, 261, noting the moral hazard resting with the lenders and their agents and employees.
35 Mechele Dickerson, *Homeownership and America's Financial Underclass: Flawed Premises, Broken Promises, New Prescriptions* (Cambridge: Cambridge University Press, 2014), 193 (hereafter Dickerson, *Homeownership*), 75.
36 Dickerson, *Homeownership*, 102.

The man sold my mortgage to Chase Bank, and suddenly I had to pay $2,000 a month, no one told me why the amount jumped. It was hard to keep up—that extra $40 was needed for the children in school, water, hydro, taxes. I had started my hairdressing business in 2008. When the financial crisis hit, I lost a lot of business—having your hair done is a luxury in a recession. Then someone came and said to me that there was government assistance to help with the mortgages, I paid them a fee of $350, then $350 again, then $350 again for their help in processing the papers to refinance; nothing happened. I sent thousands of pages of documents each year to Chase in 2009, 2010, 2011, and 2012—nothing changed, no relief, no one could give me answers. They sent me here, they sent me there, they asked for more fees, I paid—they gave me hope. Chase gave me a runaround for four years and then sold the mortgage on to Citifinance—I gave them more documents, more time lost, more fees paid. I fought for my home for nine years, I did everything asked of me, I paid more fees, they drained every cent from my savings.

I called everyone I could think of to help me, but legal clinics were swamped with work. Then the bank foreclosed. They came and took the keys from me and my children. I fought for my house, I even went to court, I lost. I could no longer afford a lawyer to continue to appeal. We had nowhere to live. They took money from us, they took every cent we had, they took every ounce of energy. There was no justice. They saw me as black, a woman, with an accent—no respect, no care—thoughtless. When I asked questions, they were mean to me. I feel crushed, hurt, taken advantage of.

My friend tells me that people with money control the economy and the government—they do not care about us. The program Obama put in place took money from us, we thought it was to help us, but the banks took our money and we never got the benefit of the program. It was a vicious cycle of running me around. It was so draining—they took our home, our emotional energy, our hopes. The stress affected my children deeply. My oldest daughter had to file for bankruptcy to get out from under the debt of co-signing the mortgage—we did not know. The children still have not recovered. These people have no compassion; they understood they were shattering our dreams, they did not care, they pulled me down, no matter how hard I tried. I do not know if I am recovering—I wish they knew the damage and pain they caused. I don't think they would care, but I wish they knew. That is my experience of the American dream.

Sandtown-Winchester, a Baltimore neighbourhood, provides a poignant example of the effects of the foreclosure crisis.[37] The Abell Foundation undertook an empirical study from 1990 to 2011 to capture the possible effects of rebuilding the community's housing stock and other reforms on the neighbourhood.[38] In 1990,

37 The Abell Foundation, "Sandtown-Winchester-Baltimore's Daring Experiment in Urban Renewal: 20 Years Later, What are the Lessons Learned?" (November 2013) 26:8 *The Abell Report*, www.abell.org/sites/default/files/publications/arn1113.pdf (hereafter Abell Foundation).

38 Abell Foundation, 2, 6.

Sandtown-Winchester was one of the poorest neighbourhoods in Baltimore, with four times the poverty rate. The residents were 98 per cent African American.[39] After the establishment of the Neighborhood Transformation Initiative, a public-private collaboration to transform the community, homeownership increased from 24 per cent to 31 per cent by 2000 and the poverty rates dropped significantly by more than 8 per cent.[40] Yet Sandtown-Winchester was hard hit with foreclosures from 2008 to 2010, resulting in a large increase in vacant and abandoned buildings.[41] By 2009, in the community around the neighbourhood, nearly one-third of the properties were vacant due to foreclosure.[42] There are still many streets with boarded up homes and apartments more than a decade later.

3 *Historical Context Helps Explain Why African Americans Were Targeted*

> It is obvious today that America has defaulted on this promissory note [of life, liberty and the pursuit of happiness], insofar as her citizens of color are concerned. Instead of honoring this sacred obligation, America has given the Negro people a bad check, a check which has come back marked 'insufficient funds'.
>
> Martin Luther King Jr, "I Have a Dream," 1963[43]

In the previous two sections of this chapter, we describe how African Americans were targeted for predatory home loans and include details about their continued victimization in this context. We also describe the impact of this exploitation on the lives of individuals, their families, and their communities. The American Civil Liberties Union observed in 2012 that the financial crisis has been a civil rights issue as much as it has been a financial issue.[44] Today's racial wealth gap is inextricably linked to the U.S. history of pervasive private and state-sanctioned discrimination and racism. For hundreds of years, African Americans were unable to bequeath to their children any wealth at all. The institution of slavery made it impossible. Decades after slavery was abolished, racism and discrimination in all areas of economic life made the accumulation of wealth impossible for African Americans.[45]

39 Abell Foundation, 3.

40 Abell Foundation.

41 Abell Foundation, 7.

42 Abell Foundation, 10.

43 Martin Luther King Jr, "I Have a Dream" (speech delivered at the Lincoln Memorial, Washington, DC, 28 August 1963), www.americanrhetoric.com/speeches/mlkihaveadream.htm (hereafter King, "Dream").

44 King, "I Have a Dream."

45 For example, Franklin D. Roosevelt's New Deal created the Federal Housing Administration to encourage homeownership among Americans, but explicitly excluded black Americans who could not get home loans. The Editorial Board, "How Segregation Destroys Black Wealth" *New York Times* (15 September 2015), www.nytimes.com/2015/09/15/opinion/how-segregation-destroys-black-wealth.html (hereafter Editorial Board).

Why were African Americans targeted for predatory home mortgages? We grapple with this salient but still unanswered question in this part. It is clear that profit in the form of lucrative bonuses and fees motivated lenders to steer borrowers into predatory loans even when they qualified for loans with a lower interest rate. But this monetary incentive does not explain why black Americans, and not white Americans, were targeted. Nor does it explain why black Americans were targeted more than Asian Americans and other people of colour, and why, when compared to Latinx borrowers, African Americans were targeted more aggressively.[46]

The reality of twenty-first century racial segregation provides one aspect of the explanation. Black Americans are relatively easy targets and easily identifiable as such because most live in exclusively or predominantly black neighbourhoods. But the locus of an equally pertinent explanation for the targeting of African Americans is in understanding the context of centuries-old anti-black bias in the United States. The devastation of the economic well-being of African Americans is best understood once it is placed in historical context, introduced in Chapter 2. The history of the economic exploitation of African Americans, its durability and ceaselessness, suggests that the exploitation will continue. It has, and we discuss this enduring exploitation in detail in Chapter 9.

The Great Migration, a pivotal part of American history that impacted the entire nation, was central to the existential evolution of blacks in the United States. Starting in the second decade of the twentieth century, more than six million African Americans migrated from southern states to northern cities. Some black southerners migrated north after labour agents sent by northern industrialists recruited them.[47] They were motivated by the possibility of finding dignified work that provided fair wages. The migration was a leaderless political act of the masses with macroeconomic consequences for African Americans and the nation. W. E. B. DuBois observed, "colored laborers [were]…determined to find a way for themselves."[48] The migration "led to higher earnings, an influential black electorate and a black middle class…"[49] DuBois defined the Great Migration as a "social evolution."[50]

46 See Powell, "Suit Accuses," regarding testimony from a Wells Fargo credit officer revealing that Wells Fargo employees called black people "mud people" and called the predatory loans into which black borrowers were steered "ghetto loans."

47 Joe William Trotter, Jr, "Introduction, Black Migration in Historical Perspective: A Review of the Literature" in Trotter, ed, *The Great Migration in Historical Perspective: New Dimensions of Race, Class, and Gender* (Bloomington and Indianapolis: Indiana University Press, 1991), 7, citing Emmett J. Scott, *Negro Migration during the War* (New York: Oxford University Press, 1920).

48 W. E. B. DuBois, "The Migration of Negroes" (June 1917) 14:2 *The Crisis* 63–66. The migration was "a mass movement and not a movement of the leaders."

49 Isabel Wilkerson, *The Warmth of Other Suns: The Epic Story of America's Great Migration* (New York City: Vintage Books, 2010), Epilogue, quoting sociologist Reynolds Farley (hereafter Wilkerson, *Warmth of Other Suns*).

50 W. E. B. DuBois, "The Economics of the Negro Problem" in Alexander Trachtenberg, ed, *The American Labor Yearbook 1917–18* (New York: Rand School of Social Science, 1918), 181.

This Great Migration began to wane during the 1960s and was essentially completed by the mid-1970s.[51]

During the six decades of the migration, African Americans fled the physical, existential, and economic brutality of the South. They escaped lynching, daily humiliation, threats to their physical safety, and a virulent racism based in industry and economics. They dodged the possibility of being arrested for debts they did not owe, crimes they did not commit, or crimes created to ensnare them.[52] For example, in the years after Reconstruction, selling one's crops after sundown became a felony offence. Once arrested and convicted, many African Americans were rented out to corporations in the steel and coal mining industries.[53] This newly emerging system of convict labour threatened African Americans' economic and physical well-being. The convicted, even those individuals unfairly or wrongly convicted, lived in forced labour camps where conditions were worse than conditions in which enslaved Africans had lived.[54] African Americans migrated also to escape other affronts to their economic and personal well-being. Some southern landowners simply seized African Americans and forced them into involuntary servitude.[55] Even though this servitude occurred after slavery's official abolition, individuals seized for forced labour had no legal recourse.

African-American migrants attempted to flee social degradation by finding work. But black migrants' dreams of an almost utopian existence in northern cities imploded in the face of the harsh reality of northern-style racism. "It was only during World War I that blacks had access to industrial jobs on a large scale ... when white soldiers began to return from duty overseas, blacks were often relegated to the most dangerous and demeaning jobs, usually earning a fraction of the wages paid to their white co-workers."[56] In almost every industry in which the migrants found work, the vestiges of slavery followed them. The narrative about ignorant, subhuman enslaved African Americans being especially suited for long, tedious labour in degrading conditions, followed the migrants. This narrative drove business leaders to place migrants in the lowest paying, and most dangerous, degrading jobs.

[51] Stewart E. Tolnay, "The African American 'Great Migration' and Beyond" (2003) 29 *Annual Review of Sociology* 209–32 at 210.

[52] See Douglas A. Blackmon, *Slavery by Another Name: The Re-Enslavement of Black Americans from the Civil War to World War II* (New York City: Anchor Books, 2008) (hereafter Blackmon, *Slavery by Another Name*).

[53] Blackmon, *Slavery by Another Name*

[54] Enslaved Africans, considered by their enslavers as property, were treated brutally but enslavers had an interest in preserving the physical well being of the human beings they considered property. The conditions in which convicts lived were worse because the convicts were not considered property. The convicted were beaten and tortured and if they were permanently maimed or killed, they were easily replaced by the ample supply of African Americans subject to arrest for minor offenses, or even for no offense at all. Blackmon, *Slavery by Another Name*.

[55] Blackmon, *Slavery by Another Name*.

[56] Leah Dickerman et al, *Jacob Lawrence: The Migration Series* (New York: The Museum of Modern Art and the Phillips Collection, 2015).

The tragedy of the Great Migration is that most of the migrants and their descendants failed to find peace, equality, and prosperity. In spite of the migrants' attempts to attain economic stability and something close to parity with white Americans, the racial wealth gap continues to widen 20 years into the twenty-first century. The story of the Great Migration reveals previously ignored truths about African Americans. They did the backbreaking work that many who already lived in the North refused to do. The migrants instilled in their children the traditional values of the South while encouraging them to thrive in their new home by conforming to the practices and mores of the North. In this way, the African American migrants resembled immigrants born outside of the United States who, unlike black Americans born in the United States, enjoyed a reputation for being ambitious and industrious.[57] Isabel Wilkerson interviewed many black migrants and discovered that almost all of them rejected the idea that they were immigrants because the notion invoked the pain of centuries-old rejection within their own nation where they could only be free by fleeing their southern roots.[58]

Most relevant to the thesis of this book, however, is the fact that the Great Migration provides important historical context that shapes understanding of the complexity, subtlety, and durability of the economic exploitation of African Americans. The migration story offers important insight into the relationship between African Americans and white businesses. Like the story of predatory lending practices that targeted African Americans, examining the migrants' relationships with private sector firms in the North is imperative to understanding the depth of the exploitation of black Americans.

An exploration of the contributions of three iconic private companies to the upward mobility of black Americans elucidates this complex relationship. Three companies, the Pullman Company, Pepsi-Cola, and the Ford Motor Company, illustrate how big business or private sector business organizations helped to move African-American families out of poverty and propelled them into the middle class. But the stories of these three businesses also illuminate the deep-rooted biases held by nineteenth and twentieth century business leaders about African Americans – biases that persist today.

The goal of African-American twentieth-century migrants was to share in the American Dream. They, like immigrants from all over the globe, sought prosperity and dignity through work. Finding employment with private companies in northern cities helped African Americans fight their way out of abject poverty and social subjugation. However, disparities in pay and treatment between black and white workers within those companies were salient impediments to equality between black and white Americans.

57 Wilkerson, *Warmth of Other Suns*.
58 Wilkerson, *Warmth of Other Suns*.

In the aftermath of the Civil War, George Pullman created The Pullman Company and recruited African Americans who were formerly enslaved in the South to work as porters, maids, waiters, and nannies. "In 1920, the Pullman Company was the single largest private employer of African-American men in the nation."[59] Pullman Company hired African-American men who had been maligned for centuries and had been described as lazy, unintelligent and subhuman. The creation of these myths justified their enslavement. Pullman Company's revolutionary decision to hire these formerly enslaved men seems like a significant step towards equality between black and white men until one peels back the layers and looks beneath the surface. "White men were hired as conductors; black men as Pullman porters. Black men would shine shoes, turn down beds on the sleeping cars ... change sheets and remake beds ... iron clothing ... but they never exchanged money or issued tickets, jobs reserved for conductors, all of whom were white."[60] The inequalities, degradation and isolation that African Americans tried to escape by leaving the South and migrating to the North followed them into the sleeping cars of the Pullman Company.

These formerly enslaved Americans provided cheap labour, and because of their subjugation during slavery, they had learned to be obsequious and compliant when dealing with white Americans. They were recruited by Pullman *because* they were obsequious and compliant. This remnant of slavery followed African Americans into the industrial age that blossomed in northern cities. The fulfilment of the expectation that African Americans perform their duties in a manner that was subservient was especially essential for the success of the porters hired by the Pullman Company.

These African-American workers moved themselves and their families into the middle class, but they did so by enduring "embarrassingly small salaries," being denied promotions, and working hours that were much longer with working conditions that were far more difficult than those endured by white Pullman workers.[61] In other words, the upward mobility of African-American Pullman workers cost more than that of non-black Americans. The Pullman employees and their families climbed to the middle class with all of the pathologies that attach to degradation and humiliation while working. They entered the middle class while earning far less than their white counterparts received for similar work.

Similar to the Pullman Company's nineteenth century practices, Henry Ford's Ford Motor Company ('FMC') was one of the first companies to adopt a hiring

59 Beth Tompkins Bates, *The Making of Black Detroit in the Age of Henry Ford* (Chapel Hill, NC: University of North Carolina Press, 2014), 2 (hereafter Bates, *Black Detroit*). See also Larry Tye, *Rising from The Rails: Pullman Porters and the Making of the Black Middle Class* (New York: Holt Paperbacks, 2004), 28.

60 Bates, *Black Detroit*, 2.

61 Bates, *Black Detroit*, 26.

policy that included black Americans in the twentieth century.[62] "After World War I, [Henry] Ford hired thousands of African-American men to work for the [Ford Motor Company], a policy decision that launched black workers on the road to modernity…".[63] FMC's practice of hiring African-American men and paying them the same wage that white men earned was revolutionary. This shift created a significant employment opportunity for African Americas who, in the decades following the abolition of slavery, had found work primarily on farms or in the service industry. Henry Ford "challenged the stereotype of the black man as servant" by being the first of the big three automakers to hire African Americans as skilled workers.[64] Ford's employment policies helped to propel African-American autoworkers and their families into solid middle-class life.[65]

"Ford claimed he hired black men, in part, because he thought it was the responsibility of the 'superior' race to open up jobs to African Americans."[66] Because Henry Ford thought that African Americans were inferior, he thought they were particularly well suited for monotonous assembly-line work that required little by way of intellectual acuity. Predictably, just as with the Pullman Company, racial inequities developed and festered at Ford. Black men received the same salary as their white counterparts, but eventually it became evident that black workers were willing to endure harsh labour conditions that white workers refused to accept.[67] African Americans accepted harsh workplace conditions at FMC because other companies were not as willing to hire them. Also, because they had far fewer available employment opportunities, educated black workers remained at FMC while their less educated counterparts found better labour conditions at other firms.[68] Just one or two generations away from slavery, the African-American migrants that Ford hired

[62] Ford was a raging, shameless anti-Semite, but he displayed atypical beneficence to African Americans. Curiously, he donated money to a trade school for African American children and enjoyed a close relationship with George Washington Carver that led to significant donations to the Tuskegee Institute, was founded by Carver. Douglas Brinkley, *Wheels for the World: Henry Ford, His Company, and a Century of Progress* (New York: Viking Press, 2003), 444–5 (hereafter Brinkley, *Wheels*). Henry Ford's legacy of workplace inclusion for African Americans drove the firm's hiring practices under Henry Ford II. Brinkley, *Wheels*, 645.

[63] Bates, *Black Detroit*, 154–6.

[64] Bates, *Black Detroit*.

[65] Bates, *Black Detroit*, 3.

[66] Bates, *Black Detroit*, 4.

[67] This situation was also true at the other auto manufacturers. The first African American autoworkers were hired for low-paying jobs as custodians and janitors, or they worked in positions that placed them in uncomfortable and hazardous conditions. Herb Boyd, *Black Detroit: A People's History of Self-Determination* (New York City: Amistad Press, 2017), 462–4 (hereafter Boyd, *Self-Determination*). "At the turn of the last century, emancipated black workers were the very vortex of the industrial age. Having migrated from the plantations of the South, many of them took on the most onerous tasks in the automobile plants, often being consigned to the most dangerous and lowest-paying jobs." Boyd, *Self-Determination*.

[68] Bates, *Black Detroit*.

were particularly vulnerable. Ford used the recently migrated black autoworkers to slow the strength and growth of unions.[69] Because it was next to impossible for the migrants to find work that paid as well as FMC did, black workers were easy recruits in Ford's battle against the autoworkers' union, and it left the workers without the protection and security that unions provided white autoworkers.

The creation of a special-markets sales staff at Pepsi-Cola provides another twentieth century example of the complicated relationship between private businesses and African Americans. Pepsi's decision to hire several black American salesmen in the 1940s had a systemic impact on black hiring that was different from that which occurred when the Pullman Company and FMC first hired black workers. Pepsi hired far fewer African Americans than Pullman and FMC, but the phenomenal success of the Pepsi salesmen provided an important testament to the mental acuity and work ethic of African Americans.[70] This success may have served to make access to business opportunities in corporate America attainable for other African Americans at other firms. But Pepsi's inclusiveness was not designed to level the playing field for African Americans. Pepsi hired black salesmen so that it could gain traction with black consumers. This strategy was successful. Pepsi outsold other soda companies in cities with large African-American populations.[71] But, while good for the company, the benefits of including African Americans in marketing decisions arguably did not extend to the consumers themselves when considering the potentially negative impact of Pepsi's product on consumer health. Moreover, the team of African-American salesmen was disbanded "without any meaningful plan for the continued hiring and promoting of minority applicants."[72]

Pullman, FMC, and Pepsi hired African Americans to further business interests, not to be socially responsible. Pullman needed cheap, pliable labour to cater to the elite class who travelled by train and to do the jobs no one else wanted. Ford hired African Americans because of labour shortages during the first and second world wars. He also hired African Americans as a union-busting strategy, and because he thought their lack of intellectual acuity made them especially suitable for assembly line work. Pepsi hired African Americans to market its products in black communities and expand its consumer base.

The stories of Pullman, FMC and Pepsi are, to some extent, success stories. African-American migrants who worked for these companies moved close to or into the middle class. But their disparate treatment is a story of the exploitation of African Americans for profit. Historical context provides a framework for understanding the exploitation of African Americans as employees and black American consumers

69 Bates, *Black Detroit*, 4.

70 Stephanie Capparell, *The Real Pepsi Challenge: How One Pioneering Company Broke Color Barriers in 1940s American Business* (New York: Simon & Schuster, 2007), xi (hereafter Capparell, *Pepsi Challenge*).

71 Capparell, *Pepsi Challenge*.

72 Capparell, *Pepsi Challenge*, xvii.

targeted by predatory lenders. False narratives about helping black Americans masked the exploitation in both contexts. The hiring of black workers provided jobs for individuals desperately seeking employment. The home mortgage loans ostensibly helped black consumers fulfil dreams of homeownership. African-American workers endured harsh working conditions after migrating north because they could not find work elsewhere. Predatory lenders easily targeted African-American consumers because they had been excluded from traditional lending sources. In both contexts, the exploitation impacted African Americans at all socio-economic levels.

The story of the Great Migration assists in developing more nuanced perceptions about the causes of the racial wealth gap. This history may help to dispel the perception 63 per cent of Americans have that African Americans, not racial discrimination, are responsible for the social and economic problems they endure.[73]

Long before the Great Migration, however, a distorted narrative of black inferiority that ignored the reality of black life emerged centuries ago, and analysis of this narrative is imperative in order to understand the economic exploitation of black Americans. The creation of the myth of black inferiority relied on untruths that had justified the brutal enslavement of men and women of African descent. These untruths – that blacks are lazy and subhuman – are the foundation of the myth that is sustained today by rewritten history that continues to displace factual historical accounts.

Bell Hooks analyzed the counter-narratives of enslaved men that precipitated negative stereotypes that have endured for centuries.[74] Hooks described the construction of black men in the 1800s and 1900s by using caricatures that depicted them as lazy and irresponsible, and the quick and thorough embedding of these images in public discourse and in the minds of white Americans. Hooks explained that in centuries past, black men were depicted as shiftless buffoons who cared only about good times and imbibing alcohol. These depictions created a racist narrative about black men that wiped out the invaluable contribution of their labour to building the U.S economy. In later decades, many white Americans used stereotypes of black men to justify their exclusion from meaningful employment. Hooks acknowledged that stereotypical distortions of the character of black men endured into the last decade of the twentieth century.[75] Tragically, these stereotypes have endured well into the twenty-first century.

[73] As found in one survey, see Claude Fischer, "It's the 50th Anniversary of the Civil Rights Act – Race Still Matters" *Boston Review* (2 July 2014), http://bostonreview.net/blog/claude-fischer-civil-rights-race (hereafter Fischer, "50th Anniversary"). Another survey revealed that even as late as 2012, half of all Americans believe that "blacks don't have the will" to seek better jobs and earn higher incomes. Fischer, "50th Anniversary."

[74] Bell Hooks, *Black Looks: Race and Representation* (Boston, MA: South End Press, 1992) (hereafter Hooks, *Black Looks*).

[75] Hooks, *Black Looks*, 90.

Even after slavery's abolition, the myth of black inferiority and the lack of intellectual acuity persisted. A Richmond businessman advocated for the social elevation of formerly enslaved Americans through desegregation.[76] But his advocacy derived from a desire to make African Americans assistants "in the production of wealth"[77] and was based on the common perception that stereotyped blacks as lazy and without ambition. Without the institution of slavery, the businessman wrote, "the black man was free only to be lazy and inefficient; for the whites lacked the slave-owner's power to compel labor, while the blacks lacked the incentive to hard work that comes from hope of reward and advancement."[78] In 1889, another author lamented the decline of the 'Negro race' in the years after slavery's abolishment.[79] "Such ideas soon became commonplace ... popularized ... in essays and novels ... [that] drew a sharp distinction between the 'old-time darkies' who were passing away and the 'new issue,' ... described as lazy, thriftless, intemperate, insolent, dishonest, and without the most rudimentary element of morality."[80] One clergyman expressed "a sense of disappointment that after the expenditure of millions and millions of dollars and hundreds of devoted lives, the typical negro is still lazy and shiftless ...".[81]

Explicit narratives of black inferiority continued into the first years of the twentieth century. Even well into the twenty-first century, an infamous Nevada rancher publicly suggested that black people were better off as slaves because during those times they were less idle.[82] These explicit articulations of modern-day stereotypes about African Americans have evolved in significant ways over the decades. Research conducted between 1932 and 2007 reveals the nature of this evolution. Samples of undergraduates spanning several decades were asked to choose from several adjectives that describe black Americans. In 1932, the participants used adjectives such as 'lazy, ignorant, and stupid'.[83] In 1950, study participants again described African

[76] George M. Fredrickson, *The Black Image in the White Mind: The Debate on Afro-American Character and Destiny, 1817–1914* (London and New York: Oxford University Press, 1971), 224 (hereafter Fredrickson, *Black Image*).

[77] We see a similar type of exploitation centuries later in the predatory lending context where African Americans assisted "in the production of wealth" accumulation for the predators who sold them the American Dream of homeownership by using deceptive and obfuscating lending practices. See Fredrickson, *Black Image*.

[78] Fredrickson, *Black Image*, 224.

[79] Fredrickson, *Black Image*, 259, citing Philip Alexander Bruce's "Influential Book," *The Plantation Negro as a Freeman* (New York and London: GP Putnam's Sons, 1889), 246–9 (Bruce, *Plantation Negro*)

[80] Bruce, *Plantation Negro*, 260.

[81] Bruce, *Plantation Negro*, 303.

[82] Mark Berman, "Cliven Bundy wonders if black people were 'better off as slaves'" *Washington Post* (24 April 2014), www.washingtonpost.com/news/post-nation/wp/2014/04/24/cliven-bundy-wonders-if-black-people-were-better-off-as-slaves/?utm_term=.91bb355681ae.

[83] Susan Fiske et al, "Images of Black Americans" (Spring 2009) 6:1 Du Bois Rev, National Center for Biotechnology Information, www.ncbi.nlm.nih.gov/pmc/articles/PMC3825175/ (hereafter Fiske et al, "Images").

Americans as 'lazy and ignorant' but they did not use the term 'stupid'. In 1967, participants said African Americans were 'lazy' but 'stupid and ignorant' were not part of that year's description. In the years 2000–2007, study participants dropped the terms 'lazy, stupid, and ignorant'. The adjectives used during this time period were: "loud; loyal to family ties; talkative; musical; very religious; aggressive; sportsmanlike; passionate; gregarious; and materialistic."[84]

This research shows how articulated stereotypes about African Americans have dramatically changed over the past decades. But the authors describing the research noted that while African Americans were not explicitly described as lazy or ignorant in recent studies as they had been in earlier research, the stereotypes evolved into what the authors called "warmth-related traits" like "passionate, gregarious, talkative, musical, very religious."[85] The authors call this "stereotyping-by-omission."[86] The twenty-first century study participants were more restrained by societal pressure to avoid revealing overt, explicit racist attitudes, so they chose positive adjectives to describe African Americans. But the adjectives chosen did not relate to competence or intellectual acuity. In other words, in the 2000s, "intelligent," "hardworking," "educated," or "savvy" did not replace the "lazy and ignorant" stereotypes explicitly articulated in earlier years.[87] Characteristics that would suggest that African Americans are competent enough to understand predatory mortgage documents, if relevant details were disclosed, were not included in the study participants' enumeration of African-American traits.

It is not farfetched to reason that many lenders hold perceptions about African Americans that are similar to those views held by the twenty-first century participants in the study described in the preceding paragraphs. Consider how stereotyping African Americans as "aggressive" or "materialistic" would operate for certain lenders. Such stereotyping supports the victim-blaming narrative that evolved in the Great Recession's aftermath.[88] African Americans, it could be argued, were just too

84 Fiske et al, "Images," Table 1. In 1932, 1950, and 1967 participants described African Americans as "superstitious," but this word was not used to describe blacks in the 2000–2007 studies. In 1932 and 1967, African Americans were described as "happy-go-lucky and ostentatious" but these descriptions were not used in 1950, and they were not used in the period from 2000 to 2007. In 1932 and 2000–2007, participants used "very religious, physically dirty, and naïve" but these descriptions were not used in 1950 or 1967. Participants said black Americans were "pleasure loving" in 1950 and 1967 but not in 1932 or in the years 2000–2007. In 1967 only, participants described African Americans as "sensitive." "Gregarious and talkative" were the stereotypes listed in 1967 and in 2000–2007. The additional adjectives that were used in 2000–2007 but not in earlier years to stereotype African Americans were "loud; loyal to family ties; aggressive; sportsmanlike; and materialistic." In each of the years the studies were untaken, African American stereotypes included the description "musical." Fiske et al, "Images."

85 Fiske et al, "Images."

86 Fiske et al, "Images."

87 Fiske et al, "Images."

88 Fiske et al, "Images," Table 1.

aggressive about pursuing *materialistic* goals like homeownership that they could not afford. Those individuals and groups that subscribe to these views may conclude that African Americans wanted homes for which they had not worked and saved, and this perspective easily allows observers to blame those individuals harmed by predatory lending rather than the predators themselves.

The twenty-first century study participants also chose adjectives that described African Americans as "talkative" or "musical." In another study, one researcher noted that "[w]hites are 10 times more likely to be seen as superior in artistic ability and abstract thinking ability; and African Americans were 10 times more likely to be seen as superior in athletic ability and rhythmic ability."[89] Being talkative, or musical, or having athletic and rhythmic ability are not traits that would discourage predatory lenders from targeting African Americans. In fact, predatory lenders who hold these stereotypes, even implicitly, may be encouraged to steer African Americans into predatory loans, because this over-generalization could create the presumption that they are not sophisticated consumers or that they would not be expected to understand home mortgage terms even if they were adequately explained. African Americans were perceived as easy targets for the type of fraud and obfuscation that lenders committed because lenders were likely to stereotype African Americans in the ways suggested by researchers. It is important to note that the targeting of African Americans for predatory loans is just as pernicious even when the stereotyping remains unarticulated, and even if lenders' beliefs in the stereotypes are implicitly held.

It is imperative that we acknowledge the connection between the stereotypes that supported the enslavement, subjugation, and, after slavery was abolished, segregation of African Americans on one hand, and modern-day stereotypes on the other. As late as the 1990s, research "revealed that 58.9 percent of black and white subjects endorsed at least one stereotypical difference in inborn ability."[90] The myth of black intellectual inferiority that was firmly established centuries ago, becoming an integral part of the fabric of American discourse and conviction, has not dissipated. That the myth endured throughout the twentieth century, and is alive and well in the twenty-first century, is beyond dispute. The book, *The Bell Curve*,[91] written in 1994, provides incontrovertible evidence of this fact.

The book presents data showing that in the United States, black people "score lower on average than white people" on tests that measure IQ (intelligence quotient).[92]

89 Laura Green, "Negative Racial Stereotypes and Their Effect on Attitudes Toward African-Americans" (2017) Jim Crow Museum, Ferris, https://ferris.edu/HTMLS/news/jimcrow/links/essays/vcu.htm (hereafter Green, "Negative Racial Stereotypes").

90 Green, "Negative Racial Stereotypes."

91 Richard J. Herrnstein and Charles A. Murray, *The Bell Curve: Intelligence and Class Structure in American Life* (New York: Free Press, 1994) (hereafter Hernstein and Murray, *Bell Curve*).

92 See Eric Siegel, "The Real Problem with Charles Murray and 'The Bell Curve'" *Scientific American* (12 April 2017), blogs.scientificamerican.com.

Arguments that black people are genetically inferior, particularly in terms of mental acuity, are based on pseudo-science that ignores the research of critical race theorists who have established, with the help of interdisciplinary research in the sciences, that race is not biological, but rather, a social construction.[93] These findings would negate genetics as a cause of racial disparities in IQ scores because, beyond phenotype, black people as a group (a group created by society) are not genetically alike, nor are they genetically different from white people.

There are a number of possible explanations for racial disparities in IQ scores. Developed in the early 1900s, these tests have undergone many iterations over the years and there has been criticism of their measurement bias, what is referred to as 'differential item functioning', due to embedded biases in the questions that disadvantage gender, race, and disability. In addition to the narrow construction of many of these tests, in terms of what types of intelligence they purport to measure, other factors contribute to lower scores among some African Americans. For example, a number of environmental factors such as segregated and inferior schools, inadequate medical care, and segregated neighbourhoods, have resulted in shrinking the life experiences of some black people in a way that contributes to lower IQ scores as measured by standardized tests. Even though race is a social construct, the racial differences that have been socially constructed in the United States result in real experiences. Black and white Americans experience life in the United States differently, but standardized tests are 'standard' in terms of the white, not the black, American experience. Yet the books' authors do not seem concerned with the causes of racial disparities in IQ scores. One commentator quoted *The Bell Curve* authors and offered the following observation:

> When suggesting a thought experiment in which the reader imagines IQ differences were known to originate entirely genetically, [the authors] suggest [readers ask themselves], 'If it were known that the black/white difference is genetic, would I treat individual blacks differently from the way I would treat them if the differences were environmental?' This plainly implies that one may already be treating individual black people differently in the first place.[94]

Critics of the book have gone "after its reasoning or its sources (or the authors' associations with the more notorious sources)."[95] For the most part, however, these critiques, for many, are unconvincing. The book has made a twenty-first century comeback. More than twenty years after it was first published in 1994, sales of *The Bell Curve* increased. The book's renewed popularity demonstrates the endurance of the narrative of black intellectual inferiority. It is a centuries-old narrative that was nurtured for hundreds of years and has significant twenty-first century presence.

93 Ian F. Haney-López, "The Social Construction of Race: Some Observations on Illusion, Fabrication, and Choice" (1994) 29 Harv Cr-CL L Rev 1, 27 (hereafter Haney-López, "Social Construction of Race").

94 Haney-López, "Social Construction of Race," quoting Bell Curve authors Hernstein and Murray, *Bell Curve*.

95 Haney-López, "Social Construction of Race."

The economic exploitation occurring in the form of predatory lending and the schemes created and still employed in its aftermath that entrench borrowers in debt and despair are not new. University of Virginia history and African-American studies professor Andrew Kahrl described several examples of twentieth-century theft of African Americans' land and property.[96] In a 2019 New York Times opinion piece, Kahrl acknowledged that the economic injustice of African-American enslavement and the failure to compensate African Americans even after emancipation were the initial causes of the racial wealth gap.[97] Kahrl then informed his readers of the remarkable fact that black Americans, in the face of threatened and real physical violence and virulent racism, amassed land, but "approximately 11 million acres" of that land was stolen by whites "through fraud, deception and outright theft…" in the twentieth and twenty-first centuries.[98]

Sometimes African Americans' property was destroyed in violent racist attacks such as the 1921 Tulsa, Oklahoma riot. At other times, the theft was subtle. White tax assessors routinely overvalued black-owned land, forcing black property owners to bear a heavier tax burden than whites, (to pay for services they didn't receive), and slowly draining families of earnings. If black-owned property became valuable or a black property owner challenged white supremacy, local officials could simply declare the property tax-delinquent and sell it at a tax sale.

Kahrl described another predatory practice – the forced partition sale. Because white Americans controlled the courts, black Americans who acquired property during Jim Crow (racial caste system) often opted to handle matters of inheritance informally, outside of the legal system. Instead of probating their wills, black property owners tended to bequeath their property to descendants in the form of undivided shares – an arrangement under which heirs become co-owners of a property, each with the right to sell his or her own interest. Predatory land speculators would search for a person who had inherited land this way and was willing to sell his or her share. Once the sale went through, the speculator – now a co-owner of the property – had the right to petition the courts to order a sale of the entire tract of land, against the wishes of those family members who lived on it, and would then buy it.

These partition sales invariably resulted in the land being sold at well below its market value, enriching the buyer while leaving the family with nothing. Speculators have used this legal trick to force the sale of millions of acres of black-owned land over the past several decades. Kahrl explained that the predatory practices of the twentieth and twenty-first centuries are just as important as slavery and post-slavery exploitation in explaining the wealth gap between white and black Americans.

[96] Andrew W. Kahrl, "Black People's Land Was Stolen" *The New York Times* (23 June 2019), SR 2 (hereafter Kahrl, "Black People's Land").

[97] Kahrl, "Black People's Land."

[98] Kahrl, "Black People's Land."

4 *Overt Racism Continues Today*

The story of City University of New York ('CUNY') philosophy professor Michael Levin provides another late twentieth-century example of the endurance of the myth of black inferiority. Levin wrote a letter in 1990 to the American Philosophical Association in which he asserted that black people have a lower level of intelligence on average, suggesting that it explained their underrepresentation in the field of philosophy.[99] Rather than confront the issue of racist comment, a CUNY Dean responded by establishing a parallel section of the required course he taught, scheduled at the same time as Levin's course, citing Levin's 'controversial views'.[100] The Philosophy Department chair opposed the action and the College's President twice requested that the Faculty Senate examine Levin's writing, but was twice refused.[101] The President eventually formed an *ad hoc* committee to determine whether Levin's perceptions affected his teaching, an initiative denounced by the Senate.[102] The committee failed to recommend that the administration take disciplinary action against Levin, but it supported the decision to hold alternatives to Levin's courses that ran concurrently with his.[103] The Committee concluded that Levin's racist assertions about the intellectual inferiority of African Americans potentially compromised the climate in his classrooms in a way that would impede his students' learning processes.[104]

Levin's story is an example of the durability of the myth of black intellectual inferiority. It is a myth held by too many individuals who hold positions of status and, in these contexts, especially dangerous because the ideas are widely disseminated.[105] In this regard, Levin's trial testimony in an action he brought against the City College President asserting an infringement of his First Amendment right to free speech[106] is illuminating. He claimed that the response of the college's President to his views endangered his tenure because Levin felt obliged to refuse *many* requests to express his views both in writing and in person."[107] The fact that Levin had many invitations to speak and write about his views about black intellectual inferiority speaks to the potential of easy dissemination of attacks on the intellectual ability of African Americans. As of July 2019, Levin remains on the CUNY faculty.

While qualitatively different than the attacks found in Murray and Herrnstein's book *The Bell Curve*, and iterated by Levin, there are other equally powerful

99 Michael Levin et al, "Letter to the Editor" (January 1990) 63:5 Proc & Addresses of the Am Phil Ass'n 61 at 62.
100 See Nathan Glazer, "Levin, Jeffries, and the Fate of Academic Autonomy" (1995) 36:2 Wm & Mary L Rev 703–12 (hereafter Glazer, "Fate of Academic Autonomy").
101 Glazer, "Fate of Academic Autonomy."
102 Glazer, "Fate of Academic Autonomy."
103 Glazer, "Fate of Academic Autonomy."
104 Glazer, "Fate of Academic Autonomy," 914.
105 Glazer, "Fate of Academic Autonomy," 912.
106 See *Levin* v *Harleston*, 770 F Supp 895 (SDNY 1991).
107 Glazer, "Fate of Academic Autonomy," 714.

examples of enduring beliefs about black intellectual inferiority. While Donald Trump has called many white Americans who disagree with him 'stupid', 'dumb', or 'low IQ', some observe that Trump disparages black Americans with whom he disagrees with attacks that focus more singularly on intellectual acuity.[108] His attacks on women – white and of colour – have similarly focused on intellect.[109] A New York Times columnist wrote, "I believe that the fact that he [Trump] so often attacks the intellectual capacity of women and minorities exposes a racial and gender bias, one that has a long history and a wide acceptance."[110] The idea that

[108] "Donald Trump has an endless and varied supply of insults and playground taunts to hurl at opponents but appears to have a one-track mind when it comes to African Americans and women… [While white Americans like] James Comey, John McCain and Mitt Romney receive a smorgasbord of… insults [other than being called "dumb"], the congresswoman Maxine Waters and TV host Don Lemon, both of whom are African American, appear to be denigrated for their intelligence alone." David Smith, "Trump's Tactic to Attack Black People and Women: Insult Their Intelligence" *The Guardian* (10 August 2018) (hereafter Smith, "Trump's Tactic"). "Trump has reportedly referred to Waters as 'low IQ' seven times" as of 10 August 2018, once calling her a "'seriously low-IQ person' before a cheering crowd [at a large rally]. He has had little to say about other aspects of Waters' personality or policies." Smith, "Trump's Tactic." The crowd's cheers in response to Trump's attack on Congresswoman Waters' intellectual acuity demonstrate how powerful individuals who adhere to stereotypes about black intelligence can impact the views of masses of people. Trump has called Don Lemon "dumb" at least three times while also attacking the intelligence of a black athlete. Trump tweeted that Lebron James, the African American basketball player "was just interviewed by the dumbest man on television, Don Lemon. He made Lebron look smart, which isn't easy to do." Smith, "Trump's Tactic." Trump also attacked African American April Ryan, a White House correspondent and political analyst for CNN, calling her "nasty" and a "loser" who "doesn't know what the hell she's doing." Brittany Britto, "Trump Calls Baltimore Native April Ryan a 'Loser,' Threatens to Revoke Press Credentials" *Baltimore Sun* (9 November 2018). Trump responded to a question from Abby Phillip, an African American reporter for CNN, by attacking her. "What a stupid question that is. What a stupid question. I watch you a lot, you ask a lot of stupid questions." Rose Minutaglio, "What Went Through CNN Reporter Abby Phillip's Head After Trump Called Her Question 'Stupid'" *Elle* (13 November 2018) (hereafter Minutaglio, "Abby Phillip"). Phillips had asked Trump whether he "wanted the acting attorney general… to 'rein in' special counsel Robert Mueller" who is investigating Trump's potential collusion with Russian operatives. Minutaglio, "Abby Phillip."

[109] Minutaglio, "Abby Phillip."

[110] Minutaglio, "Abby Phillip." See also Emily Jane Fox, "Michael Cohen Says Trump Repeatedly Used Racist Language Before His Presidency" *Vanity Fair* (2 November 2018), who reported: "Cohen [the president's former lawyer] recalled a discussion at Trump Tower, following the then-candidate's return from a campaign rally during the 2016 election cycle. Cohen had watched the rally on TV and noticed that the crowd was largely Caucasian. He offered this observation to his boss. "I told Trump that the rally looked vanilla on television. Trump responded, 'That's because black people are too stupid to vote for me.'" (The White House did not respond to multiple requests for comment.) This conversation, he noted, was reminiscent of an exchange that the two men had engaged in years earlier, after Nelson Mandela's death. "[Trump] said to me, 'Name one country run by a black person that's not a shithole,' and then he added, 'Name one city,'"… Cohen also recounted a conversation he had with Trump in the late 2000s, while they were traveling to Chicago for a Trump International Hotel board meeting. "We were going from the airport to the hotel, and we drove through what looked like a rougher neighborhood. Trump made a comment to me, saying that only the blacks could live like this."… "I truly thought the office would change him," he said. But it hasn't, Cohen continued. In fact, he said, it has exacerbated his rhetoric." See also Jamiles Lartey, "Michael Cohen Claims Trump Said 'Black People Are Too Stupid' to Vote for Him" *The Guardian* (2 November 2018).

Trump's use of terms that debase African Americans and their intellectual ability is widely accepted, at least among his base, is supported by the observations of a linguist and author:

> What's been interesting is to hear a mode of speech we associate with informal domestic or street exchange being used by someone in high office. That presumably is what made Trump so appealing to so many, avoiding the high oratory of his predecessor [former President Obama]. 'He talks like us,' I've heard people say.[111]

Consider also the January 2019 comment made by Steve King, who serves in the U.S. House of Representatives. "White nationalist, white supremacist, Western civilization – how did that language become offensive?"[112] Both Trump and King are political leaders whose opinions influence many Americans, making the stereotype of black intellectual inferiority and white intellectual supremacy a widely disseminated notion that helps illuminate why African Americans were targeted by lending predators.

The targeting of African Americans for predatory loans is itself evidence of the durability of the myth of black intellectual inferiority and its presence in the twenty-first century. The myth inspired lenders to target African Americans because of widely held perceptions that they are not intelligent. The pervasiveness of this perception among lenders is difficult to ascertain because lenders do not reveal these kinds of antisocial perspectives. But, the testimony of a Wells Fargo credit officer that the perception held by many at the firm was that African Americans are not "savvy" enough to realize the predatory nature of the loans they were offered provided rare and fortuitous concrete evidence that predatory lenders were not unaffected by the enduring myth of black intellectual inferiority. Wells Fargo's treatment of African-American consumers provides evidence that the stereotype endures.

Examining the reasons why African Americans were pressed into predatory loans is imperative. African Americans were targeted because of the centuries-old construction of African Americans as intellectually inferior. The salience of these stereotypes cannot be ignored. Clearly, the motives for predatory lending spring from greed – a desire to profit from bonuses and fees that are enhanced when a sub-prime loan is made. Systematic targeting of white Americans would have yielded the same kind of pecuniary gain for predatory lenders, yet whites were not steered into predatory sub-prime loans to the same extent that African Americans were, even when they were similarly situated in terms of background, experience, and educational attainment. Would white Americans or Asian Americans have fallen for the fraud and obfuscation perpetrated by predatory lenders? We cannot answer this question

[111] Smith, "Trump's Tactic," quoting an email from Professor David Crystal, author of The Cambridge Encyclopedia of Language.

[112] Trip Gabriel, "Steve King's White Supremacy Remark Is Rebuked by Iowa's Republican Senators" *New York Times* (11 January 2019).

in this context because white borrowers were not routinely placed in predatory loans anywhere to the extent that African Americans were. We can, however, surmise that white Americans were not methodically targeted in the way black Americans were because white Americans, as a group, are not burdened with stereotypes that construct them as lazy and intellectually inferior.

Our exploration of the deceptive lending practices that victimize African Americans illuminates the absurdity of the naively optimistic proclamations of post-racialism that followed President Obama's election. The targeting of African Americans for predatory loans in the years leading up to his election, and their continuing victimization as they attempt to hold on to their homes during and after his term, evidence the enduring nature of racialism and racism. The insights found in scholarly writing by critical race theorists for the last forty years[113] help to illuminate the racist underpinnings of predatory mortgage lending. We see in this context the relevance of constructing a racial category of black people. As Ian Haney-López explains, race is a social construct that creates racial groups in order to justify the subordination and victimization of the members of the group.[114] Creating the racial groups is only part of the social construction process. The creation of the group's attributes is also a social construct,[115] and for African Americans, the attributes assigned were grounded in stereotypes about black laziness and inferiority that justified enslavement, segregation, physical violence, and economic exploitation. Critical race theorist Derrick Bell's thesis about the permanence, indestructibility, and integral nature of racism in the United States helps

[113] See Richard Delgado and Jean Stefancic, "Critical Race Theory: Past, Present, and Future" (1998) 51:1 *Current Legal Problems* 467–91, https://doi.org/10.1093/clp/51.1.467 (hereafter Delgado and Stefancic, "Critical Race Theory"). "As a scholarly movement, Critical Race Theory … began in the early 1970s with the early writing of Derrick Bell, an African-American civil rights lawyer and the first black to teach at Harvard Law School." Delgado and Stefancic, "Critical Race Theory."

[114] Haney-López, "Social Construction of Race." "Race must be viewed as a social construction. … That is, human interaction rather than natural differentiation must be seen as the source and continued basis for racial categorization. The process by which racial meanings arise has been labeled racial formation. … In this formulation, race is not a determinant or a residue of some other social phenomenon, but rather stands on its own as an amalgamation of competing societal forces. Racial formation includes both the rise of racial groups and their constant reification in social thought." Haney-López, "Social Construction of Race," 27–8.

[115] Haney-López explores the social relationships between Mexicans and white Americans in order to explain why and how racial groups are constructed. "[T]he transformation of "Mexican" from a nationality to a race came about through the dynamic interplay of myriad social forces. … [T]he racialization of Mexicans did not occur in a vacuum, but in the context of a dominant ideology, perceived economic interests, and psychological necessity. … [T]he dominant Lockean ideology of the time, [was] an ideology that served to confirm the superiority of the industrialized Yankees and the inferiority of the pastoral Mexicans and Indians, and to justify the expropriation of their lands. … [T]he assertions regarding the racial character of these Mexicans reflected the psychological need to justify conquest: [Mexicans] were a race 'unfit' to govern their own land. … [R]acial fabrication must be viewed as a complex process subject to manifold social forces." Delgado and Stefancic, "Critical Race Theory," 30.

us to understand why stereotypes about black laziness and inferior intellect have not dissipated in modern times.[116] The stereotypes flourish and endure even in the twenty-first century.

The theft of land and property in recent decades drained wealth from African-American individuals and families, but it is imperative that we acknowledge an equally important fact – that theft enriched white American predators. The wealth gap widens not only because African Americans lose ground, but also because predators, mostly white Americans, are enriched by their predation. This observation not only explains why the wealth gap widens, it also explains why the predation occurs. Recognizing historical context and the systemic and institutionalized nature of economic predation as it relates to the homes and property of African Americans helps to avoid blaming African Americans for their own victimization. Kahrl ends his article insisting that we "work to dismantle the laws and policies that sanction the continued extraction of property and resources from black communities."[117] We participate in this work by examining the predatory practices we describe in our book.

II THE NARRATIVE THAT BLAMES THE INDIVIDUALS VICTIMIZED BY PREDATORY LENDING

Richard Delgado's work about the importance of narrative in delineating and exploring racial oppression is saliently relevant to thesis of this book.[118] By telling the stories of black Americans harmed by predatory lending, we provide the narratives that counter one predominant account of the predatory lending debacle that places blame on the individuals victimized. We explore this victim-blaming narrative in the section that follows.

African Americans who lost homes to foreclosure are still in crisis. "... [E]ven those African Americans who have avoided foreclosure remain locked in high-cost subprime loans that impede their ability to accumulate wealth."[119] Entire communities continue to suffer the repercussions of discriminatory sub-prime lending. It is imperative to explore the reasons why the disproportionately harsh impact of the crisis on the economic well-being of African Americans persists more than a decade after the financial crisis began. This understanding and exploration is possible only if the pervasiveness and depth of the victim blaming in this context is acknowledged.

116 Derrick Bell, *Faces at the Bottom of the Well: The Permanence of Racism* (New York: Basic Books, 1992) (hereafter Bell, *Faces at the Bottom of the Well*).

117 Kahrl, "Black People's Land."

118 Richard Delgado, "Storytelling for Oppositionists and Others: A Plea for Narrative" (1989) 87:8 Michigan L Rev, 2411.

119 Charles L. Nier and Maureen R. St Cyr, "A Racial Financial Crisis: Rethinking the Theory of Reverse Redlining to Combat Predatory Lending Under the Fair Housing Act" (2011) 83:4 Temple L Rev 941–77.

Anti-black stereotypes also explain the emergence of a victim-blaming narrative about the African Americans who were predatory lending targets. "Predominant modern stereotypes … [include] the lazy African-American female—the Welfare Mother."[120] The stereotypical image of African-American women as welfare mother endorses the perception that they try to get something for nothing and do not deserve to own a home for which they have not worked and saved. This type of misrepresentation helps to undergird the notion that African Americans are too lazy to save for a home, or too lazy to educate themselves enough to understand the terms of a proffered mortgage.

On 24 September 2015, then Republican presidential candidate Jeb Bush answered a question posed to him about how he would win African-American support for his candidacy for U.S. President. "Our message is one of hope and aspiration," he said. "It isn't one of division and get in line and we'll take care of you with free stuff. Our message … says you can achieve earned success."[121] Jeb Bush's statement reflects the implicit, frequently unconscious, attitude that some white Americans have about African Americans. The attitude derives from the centuries-old narrative that African-American laziness prevents them from sharing the same aspirations as other Americans. African Americans are 'waiting in line' for 'free stuff'. The successes they have, the property they own, are not 'earned'. Like the stereotype of black intellectual inferiority, the stereotype about African-American laziness has endured for centuries.[122]

The national discourse about predatory lending in the aftermath of the 2008 recession reveals attitudes about African Americans that derive from these misconceptions. The stereotypes about laziness and intellectual inferiority allow those individuals who hold them to ignore lenders' predation while focusing on the notion that African Americans want something for free. Some conservative commentators captured much of the discussion about sub-prime borrowers in the aftermath of the housing market collapse and subsequent rise in foreclosures. Borrowers were labelled greedy and irresponsible.[123] Some commentators placed blame for predatory lending, and even for

[120] Green, "Negative Racial Stereotypes."

[121] See Philip Bump, "Why Jeb Bush's 'Free Stuff' Argument about Black Voters Is So Off-the-Mark" *The Washington Post* (25 September 2015) (hereafter Bump, "Jeb Bush's 'Free Stuff'").

[122] Bump, "Jeb Bush's 'Free Stuff'."

[123] See Gretchen Morgenson, "Blame the Borrowers? Not So Fast" *New York Times* (25 November 2007) S 3 at 1 ("It has become fashionable of late to say that America's subprime borrowers themselves deserve a good part of the blame for the mortgage mess. They were either greedy … or irresponsible. …"). One observer quoted Congressman Jim Sensenbrenner's reference to sub-prime mortgagors as "happy-go-lucky borrowers" and "cagey borrowers." See Dean Starkman, "No, Americans Are Not All to Blame for the Financial Crisis" *New Republic* (9 March 2014), https://newrepublic.com/article/116919/big-lie-haunts-post-crash-conomy. In 2010, Mort Zuckerman, the chairman and editor-in-chief of U.S. News & World Report and publisher of the New York Daily News, in describing the causes of the financial crisis, observed that U.S. homeowners, borrowers, and consumers were as much to blame as mortgage lenders and bankers. Mortimer B. Zuckerman, "Who to Blame for the Financial Crisis" *U.S. News* (29 January 2010), www.usnews.com/opinion/mzuckerman/articles/2010/01/29/mort-zuckerman-who-to-blame-for-the-financial-crisis- (hereafter Zuckerman, "Who to Blame." Homeowners, he opined, "purchased homes they couldn't pay for with mortgages they couldn't afford." Zuckerman, "Who to Blame").

the recession itself, squarely on minority and low-income borrowers, while ignoring the deceptive lending practices that precipitated a high number of foreclosures.[124]

Baradaran observes that many pundits and politicians have "made the completely unsupported claim that the financial crisis was caused by poor people borrowing money to buy homes they could not afford."[125] She reports that economist Thomas DiLorenzo wrote that the financial crisis was the "direct result of thirty years of government policy that has forced banks to make bad loans to uncreditworthy borrowers."[126] Baradaran notes that even though banks' high debts crippled the U.S. economy, "our collective moral outrage is still reserved for the poor and underwater mortgage owners."[127]

In a blog post for the New York Times, a business writer lamented the lack of personal responsibility on the part of borrowers.[128] Commenting on then Professor Elizabeth Warren's work in helping to create the Consumer Financial Protection Bureau (CFPB), the author opined that Warren focused blamed for the foreclosure crisis on inadequate regulation of consumer financial products and ignored the consumers' failure to exercise the due diligence that would have enlightened them about the transactions to which they committed.[129] He then suggested that the CFPB's creation provided an excuse for all consumers that eclipses personal responsibility for predicaments in which consumers find themselves after agreeing to enter into certain financial arrangements. He expressed concern about a lack of prudence among consumers in general when borrowing money and signing documents without carefully reading them. He asserted that consumers are irresponsible when they attempt to live beyond their means and suggested that the CFPB's creation would allow them to blame others for their irresponsibility.[130]

The New York Times blogger acknowledged that some consumers lost their homes because they were victimized by predatory mortgage brokers and lenders, but he then asserted that the overwhelming majority of foreclosure victims completely understood the transactions to which they agreed.[131] He observed that a majority of homeowners

[124] See for example, Larry Keller, "Minority Meltdown: Immigrants Blamed for Mortgage Crisis" (Spring 2009) 133 S Poverty L Ctr, www.splcenter.org/get-informed/intelligence-report/browse-all-issues/2009/spring/minority-meltdown (explaining that many commentators blamed the Community Reinvestment Act, Pub L 95–128, enacted 12 October 1977, which encouraged lending to people living in lower-income communities).

[125] Baradaran, *How the Other Half Banks*, 120.

[126] Baradaran, *How the Other Half Banks*, 156, citing E. Laderman and C. Reid, "CRA Lending During the Subprime Meltdown" (February 2009) Federal Reserve Bank of San Francisco, www.frbsf.org/community-development/file/cra_lending_during_subprime_meltdown.pdf.

[127] Baradaran, *How the Other Half Banks*, 120.

[128] See William D. Cohan, "The Elizabeth Warren Fallacy" *New York Times* (30 September 2010) (hereafter Cohan, "Elizabeth Warren Fallacy").

[129] Cohan, "Elizabeth Warren Fallacy."

[130] Cohan, "Elizabeth Warren Fallacy."

[131] Cohan, "Elizabeth Warren Fallacy."

signed mortgage documents that were replete with false information about the borrower's income, assets, wealth, and ability to repay the loan. He questioned why these consumers would sign documents that contained glaring inaccuracies while knowing that they could not repay the loans.[132] This commentator failed to acknowledge the fact that the inaccurate information was supplied by lenders and typically was based on deceptively high real estate appraisals solicited by the lenders to steer borrowers into high interest rate loans that were based on appraisers' lies about property values.[133] These liar loans, as discussed in Section 4.1.2 of this chapter, were created by the lenders and brokers, but many, like the New York Times blogger, described them in a way that made it appear that the liars were the borrowers rather than the lenders.

The New York Times blogger never mentioned race and the disproportionately high numbers of people of colour who were steered into liar loans, but we are left to wonder whether the narrative would have unfolded in the same way if white Americans had been systematically victimized in the same way. Other pundits, however, were more explicit about the relevance of race in their critiques. Neil Cavuto of Fox News said that "[l]oaning to minorities and risky folks is a disaster."[134]

Some observers blamed the financial crisis of 2008 on the enactment of the Community Reinvestment Act (CRA).[135] The victim-blaming discourse and its racial implications become obvious when considering that the CRA was enacted to require banks covered by the FDIC to refrain from the discriminatory practice of redlining.[136] As discussed earlier, the CRA was enacted to combat the practice of denying credit to individuals and businesses in minority neighbourhoods without

[132] Cohan, "Elizabeth Warren Fallacy."

[133] See Cohan, "Elizabeth Warren Fallacy." In the documentary *American Casino*, an investigative journalist interviewed defectors from financial institutions and mortgage lenders and other industry insiders who revealed that the lenders, not the borrowers, lied about the borrower's income. *American Casino*, directed by Leslie Cockburn (Baltimore: Table Rock Films, 2009); see American Casino, "Synopsis" (2019), www.americancasinothemovie.com/synopsis (hereafter *American Casino* Documentary). Even when borrowers did not qualify for a loan and could not repay it, predatory lenders inflated borrowers' income to receive the high fees that are typically earned when originating sub-prime loans. Stephen Holden, "Meltdown on Wall Street, and Homeowners Left in the Lurch on Main Street" *New York Times* (1 September 2009), C5. When the borrower defaulted on a loan, the borrower lost the home, but lenders did not lose the fees they "earned" from originating the loan. *American Casino* Documentary.

[134] Jeremy Holden, "Cavuto Suggests Congress Should Have Warned that '[l]oaning to minorities and risky folks is a disaster'" *Media Matters For America* (19 September 2008), http://mediamatters.org/mmtv/200809190021.

[135] Robert Gordon, "Did Liberals Cause the Sub-Prime Crisis?" *The American Prospect* (7 April 2008), www.prospect.org/cs/articles?article=did_liberals_cause_the_subprime_crisis (detailing how the "Blame-CRA theme" was discussed in many conservative forums such as Freerepublic.com and The Cato Institute).

[136] See e.g. Randall Kroszner, "The Community Reinvestment Act and the Recent Mortgage Crisis" in Eric Rosengren et al, *Revisiting the CRA: Perspectives on the Future of the Community Reinvestment Act* (San Francisco, CA: Federal Reserve Bank of San Francisco, 2009), 8, www.frbsf.org/community-development/files/revisiting_cra.pdf ("The act required the banking regulators to encourage depository institutions ... to help meet the credit needs of their entire community. ...").

regard to their creditworthiness.[137] The CRA was aimed at mitigating the effects of redlining. Ignoring the racial segregation that the law was aimed at remedying, some argued that the quest for increasing home ownership among minorities and working-class Americans caused the 2008 economic crisis. Larry Kudlow commented: "The Community Reinvestment Act… literally pushed these lenders to make low-income loans… [Members of Congress's] [l]iberal, guilt[y] consciences forced banks and lenders to make lousy, substandard loans."[138]

One scholar described the discourse:

> As the subprime mortgage meltdown has spurred the wider financial crisis, some commentators have blamed the CRA, passed in 1977, for the events that began to unfold twenty-five years later. According to the theory, the CRA forced banks to engage in risky loans to risky borrowers in risky neighbourhoods—predominantly in low-income and minority communities. If it were not for this decades-old law and aggressive efforts by community advocates promoting compliance with it, commentators posit that events in the earlier part of this decade, where questionable loans were extended on unfavorable terms to borrowers that could not afford them, might have turned out differently. Were it not for this law and the power of community-based groups that championed it, the argument goes, long-standing underwriting principles would not have given way to exotic loans made to borrowers who had no business owning a home.[139]

Consider also the following 2017 observation regarding a prevalent narrative about blameworthy-constituencies.

> One story of the housing crisis goes like this: Government programs that helped low-income households purchase houses led to widespread defaults on the subprime loans they held, sparking the entire financial meltdown. For example, Lawrence Kudlow and Stephen Moore, both of whom have been named as economic advisors to Donald Trump, argue that the financial crisis and recession were caused by policies… that were designed to stop discrimination in housing loans, known as 'redlining,' in poor areas.[140]

[137] Financial Crisis Inquiry Commission, *Final Report of the National Commission on the Causes of the Financial and Economic Crisis in the United States, Submitted Pursuant to Public Law 111–21* (Washington, DC: FCIC, January 2011), xv, https://fcic-static.law.stanford.edu/cdn_media/fcic-reports/fcic_final_report_full.pdf (hereafter FCIC Report), xxvii. The CRA requires banks and savings and loans to lend, invest, and provide services to the communities from which they take deposits, consistent with bank safety and soundness. The FCIC concluded the CRA was not a significant factor in sub-prime lending or the crisis because many sub-prime lenders were not subject to the CRA.

[138] John McCain, interview with Joe Scarborough, *Morning Joe* (MSNBC television broadcast, 24 February 2008).

[139] Raymond H. Brescia, "Part of the Disease of Part of the Cure: The Financial Crisis and The Community Reinvestment Act" (2009) S C L Rev, 617,t 618–19.

[140] Mark Thomas, "Here's what really caused the housing crisis" *CBS* (10 January 2017), www.cbsnews.com/news/heres-what-really-caused-housing-crisis/. See also Barry Ritholtz, "Lending to Poor People Didn't Cause the Financial Crisis" *Bloomberg* (22 June 2016).

The narrative by Kudlow and Moore made tacit references to black borrowers in carefully coded language. Words like "low-income" and "former redlining victims" made clear that much of the narrative was about black Americans without explicitly saying so.

The account by Kudlow and Moore of the causes of the financial crisis has been disproven, but the fact that the narrative existed is powerful. Stephen Moore is a former contributor for CNN and Fox News, and Lawrence Kudlow is a former talk show host on CNBC and WABC who has served as Director of the National Economic Council under Donald Trump since 2018. Both Kudlow and Moore are mired in an unsophisticated approach to economics that is not part of mainstream analysis or reporting. Yet their connection to the Trump administration makes their observations potently credible for some. At least one commentator attributed the ineffectiveness of the Home Affordable Modification Program (HAMP) in helping borrowers (discussed in Chapter 7) to the victim-blaming messages embedded in the discourse we describe here.[141]

We acknowledge that the substance of the dominant narrative about who to blame for the financial crisis was varied and nuanced. The narrative unfolded differently in more sophisticated accounts in business and financial sources like Ben Bernanke's 2010 testimony, "Causes of the Recent Financial and Economic Crisis,"[142] and in the 2011 Financial Crisis Inquiry Report.[143] These accounts do not include borrower-centered arguments that place most of the blame on predatory lending victims. Also enlightening is the fact that in a University of Chicago survey of 74 economists who were asked to choose from a list of 12 possible factors that contributed to the crisis, the borrower's blameworthiness was not included among the enumerated choices from which the economists were asked to select.[144]

It is imperative that we note a subtle but important distinction between blaming borrowers (along with other contributing factors) for the financial crisis, and blaming borrowers for their own victimization by predatory lenders. This borrower-centered narrative is salient in our work. We are writing about the causes of the predatory practices that targeted black Americans, rather than the causes of the financial crisis. The focus of some of the discourse in the years immediately following the crisis seemed to blame borrowers for the predation itself. It was somewhat analogous to blaming a sexual assault victim for jogging at midnight or for being scantily clad without focusing on the conduct of the sexual predator.

[141] See Dean Starkman, "The Big Lie that Hounds the Post-Crash Economy" *New Lie* (9 March 2014), https://newrepublic.com/article/116919/big-lie-haunts-post-crash-conomy.

[142] Chairman Ben Bernanke, "Causes of the Recent Financial and Economic Crisis" (2 September 2010) Board of Governors of the Federal Reserve, www.federalreserve.gov/newsevents/testimony/bernanke20100902a.htm.

[143] FCIC Report.

[144] Chicago Booth Media Relations and Communications, "What economists think caused the financial crisis" (20 October 2017), http://news.chicagobooth.edu/newsroom/what-economists-think-caused-financial-crisis.

1 *Judicial Contributions to "Victim-blaming"*

It is important to examine the victim-blaming discourse of politicians, pundits, and commentators, but it is equally important to acknowledge the instances when jurists engage in such discourse. A look into the procedural history of litigation brought by the city of Baltimore seeking to hold Wells Fargo accountable for the impact of its predatory lending practices on predominantly black neighbourhoods is illustrative.

Wells Fargo provides one-fourth of all mortgages in the United States.[145] Baltimore's mayor and city council filed a claim against Wells Fargo in 2008, claiming that Wells Fargo's predatory lending practices increased urban blight in the black communities that the bank targeted. The city sought compensation from Wells Fargo for the costs of maintaining vacant homes that were lost in foreclosure and abandoned. After foreclosing on the homes, Wells Fargo did nothing to maintain them. Squatters moved into some of the homes. Others were plagued with criminal activity. The city of Baltimore incurred significant expenditures when police officers and firefighters were called to the abandoned homes to address and resolve the problems that foreseeably arise when buildings are left vacant.

A United States District Judge, J. Frederick Motz, dismissed Baltimore's initial claim because he concluded that the causal connection between Wells Fargo's predation and Baltimore's harm was "implausible when considered against the background of other factors leading to the deterioration of the inner city, such as… irresponsible parenting, disrespect for the law, widespread drug use, and violence."[146] Motz seemed to place all of the blame for deteriorating neighbourhoods on the individuals victimized by predatory lending. He explained urban blight by focusing solely on the alleged lawlessness, violence, and poor parenting of the African-American residents of communities targeted by Wells Fargo's predation. Motz also mentioned unemployment and lack of educational opportunity as additional factors that contributed to the deterioration of the Baltimore communities that predatory lenders targeted. He did not, however, discuss the impact that lack of education or employment has on increasing homelessness and criminal activity in communities such as the ones Wells Fargo targeted.

It is clear that, as Motz suggested, drug use and other lawless activity destroy communities. But he ignored the predatory bank practices that drastically exacerbated difficult circumstances in already vulnerable communities. The problems that, in fact, plague some inner-city residents eclipsed Motz's ability to see a causal connection between neighbourhood deterioration and the predatory lending practices that contributed to high foreclosure rates and abandoned homes. The judge's victim blaming is explicit even in the context of what could have been a rational argument

145 hereafter Baradaran, *How the Other Half Banks*, 58.

146 *City of Baltimore* v *Wells Fargo Bank*, 677 F Supp 2d 847, No 8-062 (JFM), Opinion (D Md 2010), *850, Civil Rights Litigation Clearinghouse, www.clearinghouse.net/chDocs/public/FH-MD-0001-0002.pdf (hereafter *Baltimore* v *Wells Fargo* Opinion).

about proximate causation. Motz joined with some politicians and commentators to embrace stereotypes about African Americans as violent individuals who are irresponsible parents and have no respect for the law, while failing to acknowledge Wells Fargo's role in contributing to the blight in black communities.

Motz seemed to blame individuals harmed by predatory lending for living in troubled neighbourhoods. He states in his opinion:

> The severe problems faced by the inner city preexisted the making of Wells Fargo's loans. That is not to say, however, that improper lending activities are actionable only where loans are made in stable communities. Conceivably, there might be situations in which a significant amount of improper lending activity in a particular neighborhood caused then ongoing rehabilitation efforts by other homeowners in that neighborhood to fail or caused a deteriorating neighborhood to become dramatically worse.

One of this book's authors, Cheryl Wade, visited East Baltimore, Maryland in June 2011 to prepare for a symposium that focused on efforts to reform the secondary mortgage market in the aftermath of the 2008 recession.[147] East Baltimore was, and still is, an inner-city community where impoverished African Americans share the neighbourhood with working-class African Americans. The community was not economically stable before the height of the sub-prime lending and foreclosure crisis and, at the time of her visit, it had deteriorated even more. The windows of some houses were boarded. Some buildings were just empty shells. On one block, a small attached home with beautiful red flowers thriving in two small window flower boxes was nestled between several abandoned houses. This neighbourhood was the type that Judge Motz was likely to have pictured when writing his opinion.

Wade observed:

> I had many questions for the residents of this blighted neighborhood. What is it like to live among so many abandoned homes? How do you feel when you see your children playing next door to vacant, boarded-up structures? What does it do to your sense of security, and your sense of self-worth? When I spotted several people cooking, serving, and eating food prepared on barbeque grills set up on a sidewalk, I stopped to talk to them. I was in front of a church, Restoration Christian Ecclesia at 1249 East North Avenue. The wife of the church's minister greeted me and when I told her that I had questions about the impact of subprime lending on her community, she invited me inside to talk to another woman who served as one of the church's deacons. Both women were married with children. The deacon had just completed her degree in early-child education. Her plans to expand her small family daycare center into a preschool were stalled because she and her husband were in the middle of foreclosure proceedings. The realtor who sold them their home recommended ASC Lending, a nonbank mortgage originator, and the deacon and

[147] See Cheryl L. Wade, "How Predatory Mortgage Lending Changed African American Communities and Families" (2012) 35 Hamline L Rev 437 (hereafter Wade, "Predatory Mortgage Lending").

her husband took out a sub-prime mortgage. The minister's wife revealed that her family had used the same lender and they also had taken out a sub-prime mortgage. The minister, her husband and their two young children were living in a small apartment after having lost their home.

After spending more than an hour with them, the women told me that the barbeque in front of the church was for 'less fortunate' neighbourhood residents. They used their family's money to buy most of the food they served in order to help their neighbours who had no jobs, no income, and no food.

When he wrote about the neighbourhoods that Wells Fargo targeted, Judge Motz attributed the communities' problems to poor parenting, drug use, violence, and lawlessness without acknowledging the impact of predatory lending on lawful, responsible residents in black neighbourhoods. His perspective was uninformed by the stories of predatory lending victims like the women Wade interviewed in Baltimore. Without their narratives, Judge Motz, jurists, and policymakers in general, cannot understand communities targeted by Wells Fargo for predatory loans. African-American communities like East Baltimore are racially homogenous, but they are diverse in terms of the socio-economic status, educational background, and value systems of their residents. It may be true that some residents have little respect for the law, use drugs, are neglectful parents, and even violent. But typically, the aspirations of this segment of the community would not include homeownership. These residents were not predatory lending victims. Wells Fargo targeted residents like the women Wade met. When Judge Motz wrote that, "there might be situations in which a significant amount of improper lending activity in a particular neighborhood caused then ongoing rehabilitation efforts by other homeowners in that neighborhood to fail. …", he unknowingly described a significant segment of every black neighbourhood where working class and low-income residents live among residents with different value systems. Predatory lending destroys neighbourhoods by destroying the economic lives of the people who work hard to rehabilitate their communities.

Citizens like the ones that Wade interviewed in East Baltimore who bring stability to the communities targeted by predatory lenders appeared invisible to Judge Motz when he wrote the opinion dismissing Baltimore's early case against Wells Fargo. Engaging with their narratives would assist decision makers like Judge Motz in understanding the socio-economic diversity and complexity of African-American communities. Without these narratives, race essentialism will impact the decisions of individuals like Motz who live outside these communities. "Essentialism is the view that certain categories (e.g. women, racial groups, dinosaurs, etc.) have an underlying reality or true nature. …"[148] Essentialism explains the judge's sweeping statements about the residents of the communities that predatory lenders targeted because it obscures the ways that race and class intersect in individuals and in

[148] Susan A. Gelman, PhD, "Essentialism in Everyday Thought" (May 2005) Psychological Science Agenda, www.apa.org/science/about/psa/2005/05/gelman.

neighbourhoods. Essentialist analysis constructs neighbourhoods like those targeted by Wells Fargo as a monolith and ignores the fact that different socio-economic circumstances come together in these communities.[149]

Judge Motz did not explicitly mention race. He implicitly discussed class, specifically the underclass, and ignored the socio-economic differences that exist even in struggling African-American communities. His reasoning erased differences among the residents of African-American communities. Judge Motz failed to understand that in troubled African-American Baltimore neighbourhoods such as the ones that Wells Fargo targeted, some of the residents are working class, others are low income, and some belong to the lawless, violent, and careless underclass that he described. Invisible to Judge Motz were the inner-city residents who respect the law and are not violent, drug users, or irresponsible parents. He wrote that his decision may have been different if the predatory lending caused "ongoing rehabilitation efforts by" others in the community to fail,[150] but his essentialist approach eclipsed the efforts of predatory lending victims like the minister's wife and deacon in East Baltimore.

It is not surprising that Judge Motz failed to understand the socio-economic diversity of black communities. Motz, like many other white Americans, is not likely to interact closely with working class and low-income black Americans. Hyper-segregation precludes meaningful interaction between working class or low-income black Americans and their white counterparts.[151] This *de facto* racial segregation of American neighbourhoods made black Americans particularly vulnerable targets for predatory lenders because black communities are so easily identified.[152] Potential interactions that the judge may have with working-class African Americans in the workplace will probably not be deep and frequent enough to reveal anything meaningful about their personal lives or turbulent financial circumstances.

The anatomy of Baltimore's litigation against Wells Fargo after Judge Motz's 2010 dismissal of the city's case is illuminating. After the city amended its complaint several times, Motz allowed the case to go forward by denying the bank's motion to dismiss on the grounds that Baltimore lacked standing to bring the suit because the city had failed to establish Wells Fargo's lending practices caused harm to the city.[153] The city's litigation was allowed to proceed because it "plausibly alleged that the

[149] Recognizing race and class intersections is imperative. "Discussing race without including class analysis is like watching a bird fly without looking at the sky: it's possible, but it misses the larger context. Intersections of race and class are complicated … and they need to be acknowledged." Rhonda Soto, "Race and Class: Taking Action at the Intersections" (Fall 2008) 11:3 *Diversity & Democracy*, www.aacu.org/diversitydemocracy/2008/fall/soto.

[150] *Baltimore* v *Wells Fargo* Opinion *851.

[151] See Jacob S. Rugh and Douglas S. Massey, "Racial Segregation and the American Foreclosure Crisis" (2010) 75 Am Soc Rev, 629 (hereafter Rugh and Massey, "Racial Segregation").

[152] Rugh and Massey, "Racial Segregation," 632.

[153] *City of Baltimore* v *Wells Fargo Bank*, No 8-062 (JFM), Document 185 Memorandum (D Md filed 22 April 2011), 11, Civil Rights Litigation Clearinghouse, www.clearinghouse.net/chDocs/public/FH-MD-0001-0012.pdf (hereafter *Baltimore* v *Wells Fargo* Memorandum).

properties in question would not have become vacant but for the allegedly improper loans made by Wells Fargo."[154] Judge Motz described the allegations that enabled the city of Baltimore to avoid the dismissal of its case.

> The City states that Wells Fargo deliberately steered African-American borrowers who qualified for prime loans into more onerous sub-prime loans. As a result, says the City, borrowers who would have been able to keep up with mortgage payments under the terms of a less expensive prime loan became unable to make the more demanding payments required by sub-prime loans. The City asserts that this practice caused foreclosures and eventual vacancies in properties that otherwise would have remained occupied had the borrowers been given prime loans.[155]

Motz described the second type of Wells Fargo's alleged predation.

> The City also alleges that Wells Fargo approved unqualified African-American borrowers for refinance or home equity loans when Wells Fargo knew or should have known that these borrowers would be unable to make the required monthly payments. According to the City, these unqualified borrowers then defaulted on their mortgage payments, causing additional foreclosures and vacancies. Importantly, refinance and home equity loans are given to borrowers who already own and occupy their homes, and the City asserts that the borrowers in this case owned their houses subject to modest, 'comfortably afford[able]' mortgages—or no mortgage at all—prior to taking on these allegedly improper loans. Consequently, the City maintains that if not for these refinance and home equity loans, 'the subject properties would not have become vacant and would have remained occupied during the period for which the City claims damages.'
>
> By limiting its allegations to those situations involving borrowers who were already owning and occupying their homes, the City… successfully fills in the gap between its claimed injuries and Wells Fargo's alleged conduct. Presumably, absent Wells Fargo's allegedly unaffordable refinance and home equity loans, these homeowners would have continued to make their monthly mortgage payments and occupy their properties. It is therefore plausible that any injuries arising from these vacant Wells Fargo foreclosure properties are fairly traceable to Wells Fargo's alleged predatory lending to unqualified borrowers.[156]

The city of Baltimore, according to Motz, established plausible causation that linked the bank's predatory practices to vacant, abandoned homes that would have been occupied but for the bank's predation. Motz also concluded that the city provided "hard data" showing that Wells Fargo's predatory practices impacted former homeowners of "properties located in Baltimore's African-American neighborhoods which are the subject of this law suit."[157] In his 2011 opinion, Motz referred back to his

[154] *Baltimore* v *Wells Fargo* Memorandum, 5.
[155] *Baltimore* v *Wells Fargo* Memorandum, 5–6.
[156] *Baltimore* v *Wells Fargo* Memorandum, 6–7.
[157] *Baltimore* v *Wells Fargo* Memorandum, 8.

language we critiqued previously about the alleged lawlessness, violence, neglectful parenting, and drug use prevalent in African-American neighbourhoods.[158] He acknowledged that Wells Fargo pressed the same argument that the city's expenditures related to a "complex weave of social and economic factors" that broke the chain of causation between the bank's lending practices and the city's damages.[159] In the 2011 litigation, Motz retreats from this position.

Judge Motz's 2011 change in position on the causal relation between Wells Fargo's predation and the city's harm seemed to have been inspired by the city's amended complaint in which it identified "190 properties on which subprime loans had been made, resulting in foreclosures."[160] Motz may have been persuaded also by the sworn testimony of the former Wells Fargo loan officer, which he cited in the 2011 opinion. The former bank employee "described watching loan officers comb through heavily African-American areas such as Baltimore and Prince George's County, forging relationships with churches and community groups to sell their members shoddy mortgages."[161] She described how the predatory loans were marketed to black churches and at so-called wealth building seminars in black communities, and revealed her belief that the mortgages were intentionally designed to be unaffordable to borrowers.[162]

The former employee testified that she became Wells Fargo's most prolific subprime loan officer by processing "loans for homeowners with sterling credit ratings with higher interest rates than they needed to pay."[163] She testified that she gave "millions of dollars in mortgages to people with no paperwork and low incomes."[164] In a written affidavit, the former loan officer described her experience of Wells Fargo's predation.

> The quickest and most profitable way to make loans was to steer borrowers into the new breed of subprime mortgages. It didn't matter if they couldn't afford the mortgage in the long run. All loan officers were paid by the number of loans they approved, not whether they succeeded.
>
> Subprime loans were so lucrative … that many of [the loan officer's] counterparts selling traditional mortgages realized they could make more money by referring borrowers to her than by making their own loans. That meant customers were offered subprime mortgages even if they qualified for better interest rates. Other

[158] *Baltimore* v *Wells Fargo* Memorandum, 8–9, referring to *Baltimore* v *Wells Fargo* Opinion, *850.

[159] *Baltimore* v *Wells Fargo* Memorandum, 9.

[160] Brendan Kearney, "Baltimore Can Proceed with Suit against Wells Fargo" *The Daily Record* (25 April 2011), https://thedailyrecord.com/2011/04/25/baltimore-can-proceed-with-suit-against-wells-fargo/.

[161] Yian Q. Mui, "Ex-loan Officer Claims Wells Fargo Targeted Black Communities for Shoddy Loans" *The Washington Post* (12 June 2012) (hereafter Mui, "Ex-loan Officer").

[162] Mui, "Ex-loan Officer."

[163] Mui, "Ex-loan Officer."

[164] Mui, "Ex-loan Officer."

times, brokers encouraged buyers not to provide a down payment or income document, automatically funneling them into the more profitable subprime division.[165]

It is important that we acknowledge two points. First, Wells Fargo vehemently denied the predatory lending allegations.[166] Second, we offer no opinion as to whether Judge Motz was correct when he dismissed the city of Baltimore's 2010 case for failing to establish "a plausible causal connection" between the city's damages and the bank's lending practices.[167] Our quarrel with the judge relates only to his sweeping indictment of residents of the neighbourhoods targeted by predatory lenders like Wells Fargo by attributing the community's blight to the residents whom he described as irresponsible parents, drug users, or violent with no respect for the law.[168] By doing so, he ignored the fact that irresponsible, lawless, and violent residents were not predatory lending victims, but they shared the community with people victimized by predatory lending who lived peacefully, respected the law, and diligently parented their children. The implicit message in the portion of Judge Motz's opinion where he provided the reasoning for his decision to dismiss Baltimore's case for lack of plausible proof of causation is that all of the blame for the victimized individual's financial decline appropriately fell on them.

In 2012, Baltimore and Wells Fargo settled the litigation and the District Court dismissed the city's case.[169] Judge Motz signed the settlement order. The settlement allowed the city to recover $7.5 million.[170] Portions of the settlement amount will be devoted to programs aimed at improving the community, along with foreclosure prevention programs and plans devoted to housing issues in troubled neighbourhoods.[171]

The national discourse that blamed predatory lending on the borrowers contributed to their shame and reticence about disclosing their stories.[172] The discourse questioned the personal responsibility of borrowers, while ignoring the greed and

[165] Mui, "Ex-loan Officer." Another former Wells Fargo loan officer, Tony Paschal, provided details in an affidavit claiming that black consumers in Baltimore, Prince George's County, Maryland, and southeast Washington were targeted for unfair refinancing loans. See Powell, "Suit Accuses." Paschal alleged that Wells Fargo employees referred to minority borrowers as people with bad credit and who do not pay their bills. See also *Baltimore* v *Wells Fargo* Plaintiff Memorandum, 26.

[166] Mui, "Ex-loan Officer."

[167] *Baltimore* v *Wells Fargo* Opinion, *850–1, FN2.

[168] *Baltimore* v *Wells Fargo* Opinion.

[169] *City of Baltimore* v *Wells Fargo Bank*, No 8-062 (JFM), Document 222 Settlement Order (D Md filed 7 August 2012), Civil Rights Litigation Clearinghouse, www.clearinghouse.net/chDocs/public/FH-MD-0001-0013.pdf (hereafter *Baltimore* v *Wells Fargo* Settlement Order).

[170] See Gary Haber, "Wells Fargo to Pay Baltimore $7.5 M in Discrimination Deal" *Baltimore Business Journal* (12 July 2012) (hereafter Haber, "Wells Fargo to Pay $7.5 M").

[171] Haber, "Wells Fargo to Pay $7.5 M."

[172] In an interview with Mike Stanley, a community organizer who works for Equal, part of the non-profit organization Industrial Areas Foundation, he spoke about the shame that haunts predatory lending victims. Stanley worked with New York City ministers who attempted to get more information about predatory sub-prime lending. Two pastors with hundreds of congregants in neighbourhoods that were targeted for sub-prime loans and in which foreclosures were extremely high invited

criminality of mortgage lenders and the failure of major banks to perform basic due diligence with respect to the loans they securitized. There was little to no discussion about successful and responsible low-income borrowers in the discourse that took place in the immediate aftermath of the predatory lending crisis. For example, one non-profit organization, Neighborhood Housing Services of Orange County, assists first-time homebuyers by connecting them with banks that make CRA loans.[173] "In its 14-year history, the non-profit has helped 1,200 families buy their first homes. Score so far: No foreclosures and a delinquency rate under 1 percent."[174] Another company, the Nehemiah Project, in the business of building and selling homes to the working poor of New York City since the 1980s, reports extremely high repayment rates on loans made to almost four thousand borrowers, with only a few defaults.[175]

In Chapter 9, we describe predatory lending schemes that replicate the structure, if not the form, of the predatory sub-prime loans that are the subject of this book. We describe the ordeal of a consumer, Zachary Anderson, who entered into a contract-for-deed arrangement. Also called rent-to-own deals, these arrangements have onerous terms that are designed to cheat would-be homebuyers. Years after he moved in and had completed extensive repairs, he realized that he did not own the home.[176] The owner was a limited partnership that had targeted Anderson and other African Americans with high interest rates and other unfair terms that are similar to those seen in predatory sub-prime home loans.[177] In this chapter about the victim-blaming discourse that ignores African Americans victimized by predatory lending who work hard to attempt to meet the terms of predatory arrangements, we foretell Anderson's story. While half of the individuals exploited by contracts for deed who were tracked over a period of twenty-one years defaulted on their contracts, 20 per cent of the borrowers met the exceedingly burdensome terms of the contract, eventually receiving the deed and becoming property owners.[178] Anderson does not yet

parishioners to come forward with their stories. No one came forward in one of the churches. In the other church, Shiloh Baptist, a survey of senior citizens was distributed. Two hundred fifty-two seniors responded to the survey with only five admitting that they had faced foreclosure. (The survey protected their privacy by allowing participants to respond anonymously.) But fifty percent said they knew someone in foreclosure or in danger of foreclosure. See Wade, "Predatory Mortgage Lending."

173 See Ronald Campbell, "Most Subprime Lenders Weren't Subject to Federal Lending Law" *Orange County Register* (16 November 2008), www.ocregister.com/2008/11/16/most-subprime-lenders-werent-subject-to-federal-lending-law/ (hereafter Campbell, "Most Subprime Lenders").

174 Campbell, "Most Subprime Lenders."

175 Jim Zarroli, "Low-Cost Brooklyn Housing Sees Few Foreclosures" *NPR* (20 October 2009), www.npr.org/templates/story/story.php?storyId=113931948.

176 Alana Semuels, "A House You Can Buy, But Never Own" *The Atlantic Magazine* (10 April 2018), NCRC, https://ncrc.org/the-atlantic-a-house-you-can-buy-but-never-own/ (hereafter Semuels, "Buy, But Never Own."

177 Semuels, "Buy, But Never Own."

178 Semuels, "Buy, But Never Own."

own the property, but he continues to make timely payments, even after the limited partnership threatened to evict him when he missed one payment while he was hospitalized.[179]

III POST-RACIALISM

The relevance of racist stereotypes about African Americans cannot be ignored as an important contributor to lenders' decisions to target African Americans for predatory sub-prime loans. Explicit evidence of the significance of anti-black stereotypes in lending decisions was discussed earlier in this chapter in the testimony of former Wells Fargo loan officers.[180] Many Americans, however, were unaware or unconcerned about the targeting of African Americans and the victim-blaming narrative that emerged. We posit that post-racial ideology eclipsed widespread understanding or knowledge regarding the impact of predatory lending on African Americans, their families, and communities. Post-racialism is "a twenty-first century ideology that reflects a belief that due to the significant racial progress that has been made, the state need not engage in race-based decision-making or adopt race-based remedies, and that civil society should eschew race as a central organizing principle of social action".[181] Scholar Cynthia Lee describes our "not yet post-racial society":

> Post-racialists believe 'race does not matter, and should not be taken into account or even noticed.' Central to post-racialism is the idea that 'racial thinking and racial remedies are no longer needed because the nation has… transcended racial divisions of past generations.' Post-racialists think we should stop obsessing over race and recognize that we have come a long way from the days when bigotry and racially discriminatory acts were accepted. Many post-racialists think we currently live in a meritocratic color-blind society.[182]

Scholars and observers cite to President Obama's election as the impetus for post-racial ideology.[183] President Obama's election provided evidence for some Americans

179 Semuels, "Buy, But Never Own."

180 See the discussion in Chapter 4, Part I, Section 1, referencing *Baltimore* v *Wells Fargo*, Plaintiff Memorandum, *Memphis* v *Wells Fargo*, and Powell, "Suit Accuses."

181 Sumi Cho, "Post-Racialism" (2009) 94 Iowa L Rev, 1589–94 (hereafter Cho, "Post-Racialism"). See also Taunya Lovell Banks, "A Darker Shade of Pale Revisited: Light-Skinned Negroes, New-Mulattoes and Colorism in the 'Post-Racial' Obama Era" (13 August 2010) (unpublished), SSRN, dx.doi.org/10.2139/ssrn.2529264 (exploring the depth, complexity and relevance of skin colour as opposed to traditional racial constructs after the 2008 election).

182 Cynthia Lee, "Making Race Salient: Trayvon Martin and Implicit Bias in a Not Yet Post-Racial Society" (2013) 91 NC L Rev, 1555–65, (hereafter Lee, "Making Race Salient").

183 See e.g. Ian F. Haney-López, "Is the Post in Post-Racial the Blind in Colorblind" (2010) 32 Cardozo L Rev 807 (hereafter Haney-López, "Post in Post-Racial"); Lee, "Making Race Salient"; Michael C. Dawson and Lawrence D. Bobo, "One Year Later and the Myth of a Post-racial Society" (2009) 6:2 *Du Bois Review: Social Science Research on Race*, 247, Harvard, http://nrs.harvard.edu/urn-3:HUL.InstRepos:10347165 (introducing a volume of *The Du Bois Review* contributing "substantial social

that racial discrimination is no longer an issue in twenty-first century America. One of these scholars, Ian Haney-López, confronts post-racial ideology by examining "racialized mass incarceration. Because race seems so central to the contemporary administration of criminal justice, it constitutes a particular challenge to the post-racial narrative."[184] Haney-López points to a 2009 report, the interpretation of which challenges the accuracy of post-racialism: "... [O]ne in every eleven African Americans, one in every twenty-seven Latinos, and one in every forty-five whites" is "in prison or on parole or probation ..."[185]

Cynthia Lee confronts post-racialism, using the shooting of seventeen-year-old African American, Trayvon Martin, by a Hispanic neighbourhood watch captain, to explain why the United States is far from being post-racial:

> The shooting of Trayvon Martin belies [the] claim of post-racial triumph. It is unlikely that he [the watch captain] would have thought Martin was 'real suspicious', 'up to no good,' and 'on drugs or something' if Martin had been White. Race likely influenced the watch captain's perception that Martin posed a threat of criminality, whether he was aware of this or not.[186]

Lee goes on to note the likelihood that race influenced the government's decision not to arrest the watch captain. "Had [he] been an African American man who followed and then shot an unarmed Caucasian teenager during a fist-fight, it is unlikely that police would have released [the watchman] without any charges. When there is a dead victim and police know who killed the victim, they usually arrest the obvious perpetrator of the homicide and then investigate."[187]

Lee then points to the deep racial division in the national discourse about whether the watchman's shooting and killing of Martin was justified.[188] "Eighty percent of

science evidence that the racial order—while evolving—continues to shape American life, society, and politics"). "Many commentators, both conservative and liberal, have celebrated the election of Barack Obama as president of the United States, claiming the election signified America has truly become a "post-racial" society. It is not just Lou Dobbs who argues the United States in the "21st century [is a] post-partisan, post-racial society." This view is consistent with beliefs the majority of White Americans have held for well over a decade: that African Americans have achieved, or will soon achieve, racial equality in the United States despite substantial evidence to the contrary. Indeed, this view is consistent with opinions found in the *Boston Globe, Wall Street Journal, New York Times*, and elsewhere...."

184 Haney-López, "Post in Post-Racial."

185 Haney-López, "Post in Post-Racial," 807–8. In addition to indicating the inaccuracy of post-racialism, Haney-López assesses post-racialism's predecessor theory – the quest for a colorblind society. He then goes on to explain how colorblindness and post-racialism facilitated "racialized mass incarceration."

186 Lee, "Making Race Salient," 1565–6.

187 Lee, "Making Race Salient," 1566. "Florida's "Stand Your Ground" law, which prohibits Florida law enforcement personnel from arresting a person for using force unless they first determine that there is probable cause to believe that the force used was unlawful, should not have prevented an arrest in this case. Arguably, there was probable cause to believe that [the watch captain's] use of deadly force was unlawful. Martin was at least twenty pounds lighter than [the watch captain]. Moreover, [the watch captain] used a gun against Martin, who was unarmed." Lee, "Making Race Salient," 1566–7.

188 Lee, "Making Race Salient." 1567.

Blacks surveyed said they thought the killing of Martin was unjustified, while only thirty-eight percent of Whites surveyed felt the same way."[189] She observes that this kind of division along racial lines occurred only because post-racialism is a myth and race still matters very much in the United States. [190] Providing additional evidence that U.S. post-racialism remains unrealized, Lee examines public reaction to President Obama's comment after Martin's shooting. "I can only imagine what these parents are going through. ... If I had a son, he'd look like Trayvon."[191] Lee describes criticism of the President's reaction by two white conservative political leaders as acerbic, and cites a Newsweek poll reporting that most white Americans did not support the way President Obama responded to the teenager's shooting.[192] She discusses the diametrically opposite reaction of prominent African Americans to the President's reaction to Martin's death as further proof that post-racialism remains unachieved.[193]

After establishing the fallacy of post-racial ideology, Lee explains how post-racialism impedes the ability to uncover and acknowledge implicit bias. "Implicit bias is unintended bias that operates without our conscious awareness."[194] Lee then discusses the interaction between the kinds of negative anti-black stereotypes we describe earlier and the way implicit bias operates:

> Many, if not most, Americans sincerely believe in equal treatment for Blacks and Whites. Yet despite these egalitarian beliefs, Americans are constantly exposed to negative stereotypes about Blacks. These stereotypes include the idea that Blacks are lazy people who would rather live on or cheat welfare than work ...[195]

Lee explains that Americans who embrace notions of racial equality may be undermined by implicit biases that are nurtured by negative racial stereotypes.[196] Racial stereotypes foment implicit bias.

It is Lee's observation about post-racialism's impact on implicit bias that is particularly relevant in understanding the role of race and racism in the predatory lending debacle. "The effects of implicit bias are particularly likely to operate under the radar in a society like ours that views itself as post-racial."[197] Post-racialism obscures implicit bias. Implicit biases go unnoticed among those individuals who believe that race is no longer relevant. The consequences of post-racialism are relevant also to Haney-López, as discussed previously.[198] Some of the targeting of African Americans for predatory lending may have resulted from implicit bias, and

189 Lee, "Making Race Salient."
190 Lee, "Making Race Salient."
191 Lee, "Making Race Salient."
192 Lee, "Making Race Salient," 1567–8.
193 Lee, "Making Race Salient," 1568.
194 Lee, "Making Race Salient," 1559.
195 Lee, "Making Race Salient," 560–1.
196 Lee, "Making Race Salient," 1560.
197 Lee, "Making Race Salient."
198 Haney-López, "Post in Post-Racial," 808.

Lee's premise about post-racialism obscuring implicit bias is helpful. But we know that much of the bias that drove the victimization of African Americans was not implicit. It was conscious and explicit. For example, as we discussed earlier in this chapter, former Wells Fargo loan officers testified about shocking examples of overt racism in determining that African Americans would be steered into sub-prime loans even when they qualified for prime loans.[199]

Post-racial ideology becomes even more problematic when bias is explicit rather than implicit. Post-racialists are likely to more vehemently deny explicit and overt racism because they believe that it was eradicated during and immediately after the Civil Rights era.[200] Post-racialists point to the decades-long evolution and improvement in the lives, status, and rights of African Americans. They offer the progress that resulted from the militancy of the 1960s Black Power Movement, and the advent of race-based affirmative action as evidence of post-racialism. They believe that to the extent explicit racism persists, it exists only at the margins of civil society – among Ku Klux Klan members, Neo-Nazis, white nationalists, and white supremacists – and not in the offices of Wells Fargo and other lenders. Yet twenty-first century predatory lending is a poignant example that illustrates that the United States is not post-racial, but post-racial ideology obscures the reality of persisting explicit bias, especially when it concerns the decision-making of mainstream business leaders.

Around the same time that post-racial ideology reached its height after President Obama's election near the end of 2008, Bear Stearns and Merrill Lynch collapsed and Lehman Brothers suffered huge losses.[201] The possibility of a financial meltdown presaged the victim-blaming narrative that placed much of the onus of the economic unravelling on the shoulders of the mostly black and brown predatory lending targets. It never occurred to some Americans that the predicament in which individuals victimized by predatory lending found themselves could be the result of racial discrimination. The nation had, after all, just elected a black President.

IV CONTINUED VICTIMIZATION: WHY NO HELP FOR PREDATORY LENDING TARGETS?

Earlier in this chapter, we explored the reasons why African Americans were targeted for predatory loans. We now turn to an equally salient question. Why are African Americans victimized by predatory lending, including the individuals we

199 See the discussion at Chapter 4, Part I, Section 1, referencing *Baltimore* v *Wells Fargo* Plaintiff Memorandum, *Memphis* v *Wells Fargo*, and Powell, "Suit Accuses."

200 See e.g. *Brown* v *Board of Education*; The Civil Rights Act of 1964, Pub L No 88–352, 78 Stat 241 (1964) (hereafter Civil Rights Act); The Voting Rights Act of 1965, Pub L No 89–110, 79 Stat 437 (1965).

201 See generally Greg Farrell, *Crash of the Titans: Greed, Hubris, the Fall of Merrill Lynch, and the Near-Collapse of Bank of America* (New York: Crown Publishing Group, 2010); Andrew Ross Sorking, *Too Big To Fail* (New York: Viking Press, 2009); Paul Muolo and Mathew Padilla, *Chain of Blame: How Wall Street Caused the Mortgage and Credit Crisis* (Hoboken, NJ: Wiley, 2008).

interviewed, not getting the help they need to begin to recover from the wealth drain that has damaged individuals, families, and entire communities? Our description of the victims' narratives includes details about the unwillingness of lenders to help borrowers with loan modifications. Even after the passage of the Dodd-Frank Act[202] and the creation of the CFPB,[203] and in spite of already-existing legislation prohibiting lending discrimination and consumer fraud, the financial position of victimized borrowers continues to deteriorate. Many borrowers are victimized by new schemes when they ask lenders to modify the predatory loans.[204] As we explain in Chapter 9, new iterations of exploitation arise when borrowers cannot meet the predatory terms of their mortgages.[205] The impact of foreclosures on children around the country has also been enormously destabilizing.[206] One-third of the children who experienced homelessness after the financial crisis did so because of foreclosures of the housing that their parents owned or were renting, according to a recent study.[207]

The continued victimization of African-American borrowers over a decade after the recession's end may be best explained by focusing on persisting racist attitudes that are unrevealed and, therefore, left undisturbed. It is safe to say that the post-racialism myth has been debunked.[208] The death knell for post-racial ideology and its predecessor, the theory of colour-blindness, was resolutely delivered with the election of Donald Trump.[209] Post-racialism obscured the salience of race in the United States, and in its aftermath, we are left with a nation that is acutely racial but reticent about its significance. Post-racialism allowed Americans to grow accustomed to denying racism. This denial is why so many Americans are impervious to the

202 Dodd-Frank Wall Street Reform and Consumer Protection Act of 2010, Pub L No 111–203, effective 21 July 2010 (hereafter Dodd-Frank Act 2010). The Act was amended in 2018; see the discussion in Chapter 7.

203 The Dodd-Frank Act transferred Home Mortgage Disclosure Act rulemaking authority from the Federal Reserve Board to the CFPB; CFPB, "Consumer Financial Protection Bureau Proposes Changes to *HMDA* Rules" (2 May 2019), www.consumerfinance.gov/about-us/newsroom/bureau-proposes-changes-hmda-rules/.

204 See Dodd-Frank Act 2010, Chapter 9, Part III.

205 See Dodd-Frank Act 2010, Chapter 9, Part IV.

206 Baradaran, *How the Other Half Banks*, 409.

207 Baradaran, *How the Other Half Banks*, 409, citing National Association for the Education of Homeless Children and Youth (NAEHCY) and First Focus, "A Critical Moment: Child and Youth Homelessness in Our Nation's Schools" (July 2010), 2. In early 2010, NAEHCY and First Focus conducted a survey of 2,200 school districts. When they were asked the reasons for the increased enrollment of students experiencing homelessness, 62 per cent cited the economic downturn, 40 per cent attributed it to greater school and community awareness of homelessness, and 38 per cent cited problems stemming from the foreclosure crisis.

208 Nikole Hannah-Jones, "The End of the Postracial Myth" *The New York Times Magazine* (15 November 2016) (hereafter Hannah-Jones, "End of Postracial Myth"); Ta-Nehisi Coates, "There Is No Post-Racial America" *The Atlantic Magazine* (July/August 2015), www.theatlantic.com/magazine/archive/2015/07/post-racial-society-distant-dream/395255/.

209 Hannah-Jones, "End of Postracial Myth."

plight of African Americans victimized by predatory lending even as they attempt to navigate the emergence of new schemes that drain wealth, including modification scams. In the aftermath of post-racialism's obfuscation, unsympathetic courts fail to recognize the discrimination that continues to threaten financial stability and the very homes in which the victims live.

Understanding the nature of the racism that underlies predatory lending and the continued victimization of the individuals who were targeted is imperative. In the contexts of predatory lending and scam modifications, we see the conflation of the racism of individuals with structural, institutional, and systemic racism. It is important to understand that addressing the problems predatory lending victims continue to face requires confronting both the racism of individuals like the former Wells Fargo officers, along with racial inequities that are systemic in nature.

Related to the analysis of racism in commerce that infects not only individuals, but also U.S. systems such as housing and lending markets, is the concept of structural racism:

> Structural racism is a complex, dynamic system of conferring social benefits on some groups and imposing burdens on others that results in segregation, poverty, and denial of opportunity for millions of people of color. It comprises cultural beliefs, historical legacies, and institutional policies within and among public and private organizations that interweave to create drastic racial disparities in life outcomes.[210]

The structural nature of the racism undergirding the predatory lending scams in the 2000s, along with the inertia that precludes help for victims over a decade later, is evident. Institutional policies in private organizations such as banks and other lenders, and the institutional policies of public bodies such as court systems, provide no redress for predatory lending victims who continue to be scammed.

The complexity of the structural racism that supports the continuing victimization of African-American borrowers is in the fact that it is embedded, profitable, and largely invisible. "Structural racism is invisible and operates behind the illusion of colorblindness and neutrality."[211] William Wiecek comments on the invisibility of structural racism – "… though the racism-based impoverishment of some African-American, Latino, and Native American communities is apparent, its causes are not, nor are the structural processes that created and maintain it."[212]

210 William M. Wiecek, "Structural Racism and the Law in America Today: An Introduction" (2011) 100 Kentucky L J, 1, 5, 17 (hereafter Wiecek, "Structural Racism").

211 Wiecek, "Structural Racism," 6. Wiecek provides an example of the invisibility of structural racism. "… [T]hough the racism-based impoverishment of some African American, Latinx, and Native American communities is apparent, its causes are not, nor are the structural processes that created and maintain it." Wiecek, "Structural Racism," 13.

212 Wiecek, "Structural Racism," 13.

The impact of the fallacies of colour-blindness and racial neutrality has been exacerbated by years of post-racialism discourse that further obscured and rendered invisible the mortgage lending predation. Moreover, the fact that lenders and investors, the overwhelming majority of whom are white, profited from the system of predatory lending is profoundly important. The harm that results from systemic and structural racism cannot be mitigated without understanding how white Americans benefited. This understanding is just as important as acknowledging the ways that black borrowers were disadvantaged. In other words, in parsing the structural nature of predatory lending, "White advantage is just as important an outcome as black subordination, if not more so."[213]

By focusing not only on the ways predatory lending disadvantaged black borrowers, but also on its profitability for lenders and investors, we find important insight about the phenomenon of white privilege.

> When legal analysis ignores [white privilege], it reinforces what sociologists call 'white normativity.' Whites unthinkingly assume that their privileged situation is the norm, and that all others could experience it too, were it not for those others' deficiencies (originally taken to be racial/biological, now assumed to be cultural and social).[214]

In the context of predatory lending, many white Americans do not think about the financial advantage they enjoy when compared to many African Americans. They assume that the racial wealth gap exists because of the deficiencies of African Americans, and these assumptions are reinforced by the racial stereotypes we describe earlier in this chapter. The contemporary structural and systemic racism inherent in the predatory lending context is rooted in the perhaps unconscious desire to maintain the systems that privilege whiteness. It is a privilege that is largely invisible and the resistance to levelling the playing field may be unconscious.

Wiecek notes that, "structural racism is dynamic" and that it "operates automatically."[215] This observation may explain the almost automatic evolution of predatory schemes and the emergence of new scams. We write this book to shed light on one profoundly important cause of the racial wealth gap. Unlike the atrocities faced by civil rights protesters in the 1950s United States, and the African-American deaths at the hands of criminally aggressive police officers, there are no cameras recording the victimization of black borrowers in America.

[213] Wiecek, "Structural Racism," 6.
[214] Wiecek, "Structural Racism," 11–12.
[215] Wiecek, "Structural Racism," 7.

5

The Implications of the Collapse of the Mortgage-backed Securities Market for Consumer Borrowers

Much has already been written on the causes and consequences of the collapse of the mortgage-backed securities market, and this book does not intend to repeat those analyses.[1] However, it is important to understand the impact the collapse had on consumer borrowers who had predatory sub-prime mortgages. This chapter briefly discusses the financial failures of several companies and measures to bail out businesses and banks. These massive bailouts for the financial sector juxtaposed with ineffective government efforts to assist African Americans facing foreclosure illustrate the antithesis of fairness principles discussed in Chapter 2. The system that responded immediately to the crises of large financial institutions was not responsive to the plight of millions of mortgage borrowers at risk. The disadvantage and unfairness were exacerbated because African Americans had little or no access to traditional banking services to secure bridge financing to survive the financial crisis.

Bear Stearns, the first firm that failed in 2008, had invested heavily in sub-prime mortgages and other mortgage-linked securities including CDO that were dependent on cash flows derived from borrowers making their monthly payments on high-risk mortgages.[2] Once investors lost confidence in the market, Bear Stearns did not have the capital or liquidity needed to meet its payment requirements. The Federal Reserve of New York observed that repo lenders, who rolled over funding on a daily basis, began to refuse to roll over the loans, and Bear Stearns needed to sell off some of the securities or other assets or find another lender.[3] This scenario repeated itself over and over again across the market in 2008 and 2009. At the outset of the crisis, large investment banks had billions of dollars tied up in their securities portfolios

[1] See for example, William Cohan, *House of Cards: A Tale of Hubris and Wretched Excess on Wall Street* (New York: Doubleday, 2009), 283–330 (hereafter Cohan, *House of Cards*); Kathleen Engel and Patricia McCoy, *The Subprime Virus: Reckless Credit, Regulatory Failure, and Next Steps* (New York: Oxford University Press, 2011), 232 (hereafter Engel and McCoy, *The Subprime Virus*).

[2] Jennifer S. Taub, *Other People's Houses* (New Haven, CT: Yale University Press, 2014) (hereafter Taub, *Other People's Houses*), 189–90.

[3] Cohan, *House of Cards*, 283–330.

in the repo market, which the Federal Reserve Bank of New York estimated to be a market of between $2.8 trillion and $4.5 trillion in 2008.[4]

Bear Stearns did not have to file for bankruptcy because the Secretary of the U.S. Department of the Treasury brokered a rescue package in which the firm was bought by JP Morgan Chase at a severely discounted price, backed by the Federal Reserve lending $30 billion to JP Morgan Chase as bail-out support.[5] Jonathan Macey has criticized the Federal Reserve for the bailout of the investment bank. Macey observed that JP Morgan Chase secured the $30 billion loan promise from the Federal Reserve at an interest rate substantially lower than market in exchange for assuming Bear Stearns' liabilities. Then JP Morgan Chase used the CDO on other deeply troubled assets on Bear Stearns' books as collateral for the loan. The federal government bore all the risk beyond the first billion in losses resulting in a total of $29 billion in contingent liability for taxpayers.[6] The Bear Stearns' situation was only the tip of the massive sub-prime iceberg.

In September 2008, Lehman Brothers Holdings Inc filed for bankruptcy with $613 billion in debt and over 100,000 creditors, which was a tipping point for the financial meltdown. Investors fled the market, causing a run in money markets and revealing that investment banks and many other companies did not have anywhere near sufficient capital or liquidity to meet their short-term obligations. Lehman Brothers was highly complicit in the sub-prime predatory mortgage market. Insurers that sold mortgage insurance, such as AIG, began to experience financial distress because they did not have the capital to pay out to policyholders the value of insured mortgages upon default.[7] In the week of 15 September 2008, over $300 billion was

4 Adam Copeland, Antoine Martin, and Michael Walker, "The Tri-Party Repo Market before the 2010 Reforms" (November 2010) Federal Reserve Bank of New York Staff Report No 477, www.newyorkfed.org/research/staff_reports/sr477.html and Michael Fleming, Warren Hrung, and Frank Keane, "Repo Market Effects of the Term Securities Lending Facility" (16 December 2008) Federal Reserve Bank of New York Staff Report No 426, discussed in Michael J. Fleming, "Federal Reserve Liquidity Provision during the Financial Crisis of 2007–2009" (October 2012) 4 *Annual Review of Financial Economics* 161–77, www.annualreviews.org/doi/10.1146/annurev-financial-110311-101735.

5 Jonathan Macey, "Brave New Fed" (31 March 2008) *Wall Street Journal*, Hoover Daily Report, www.hoover.org/research/brave-new-fed (hereafter Macey, "Brave New Fed"). Macey also observed that: "The flawed process employed by the Fed (Federal Reserve) in that unprecedented move violated the spirit of an important law—the Federal Deposit Insurance Corporation Improvement Act (FDICIA). The FDICIA was passed specifically to establish procedures to be used by regulators when dealing with failed financial institutions. But FDICIA applies only to federally insured depository institutions such as banks and savings and loan associations. When the statute was passed nobody in their wildest dreams thought that government bailouts would extend beyond federally insured deposit institutions to include investment banks—which unlike commercial banks have no small creditors and no federally insured deposits to protect."

6 Macey, "Brave New Fed."

7 AIG started to fail when it could not meet counterparty demands to settle CDS and interest swaps that it had sold on a cash-settled basis as counterparties experience credit events. For a discussion, see Sarra, "Embedding Fairness."

withdrawn from prime money market funds.[8] Credit default swaps (CDS) that related to tranches of securitized mortgages were not transparent with respect to the underlying value of the mortgages on which they were written and there had been no regulatory requirement of counterparties to set aside capital reserves to cover future commitments.[9] Short-term credit markets froze, and financial institutions and operating companies were unable to effectively fund their daily operations.[10]

Then began a series of measures by the U.S. Department of the Treasury to slow the run on capital through temporary guarantees of net asset value in money market fund shares. The U.S. government used emergency powers to lend money at low rates to commercial banks, and directly bailed out businesses and banks by agreeing to directly purchase up to $1.8 trillion in commercial paper.[11] The U.S. government bailed out AIG by using its emergency authority under the Federal Reserve Act to provide it with $85 billion, $62 billion of which was used to pay off its CDS counterparties at full value of the claims. The U.S. government justified the bailout on the basis that AIG's failure would be more systemically devastating than Lehman Brothers failure.[12]

All of these initiatives were aimed at protecting financial institutions and their investors. The system that responded immediately to the crises in the large financial institutions was not so responsive to the plight of millions of mortgage borrowers at risk. For these individuals, the lack of financial relief from their mortgage obligations meant millions of foreclosures. Note that the amount of public dollars directly expended on paying out commercial counterparties, $85 billion, could have been directed to prevent millions of foreclosures. Instead, the public dollars were directed towards saving the financial institutions that precipitated the crisis.

The lack of relationship between the lenders and the borrowers, given securitization, meant that lenders were not willing to negotiate forbearance on payment schedules or negotiate some debt relief. The U.S. government, however, could have attached conditions to the large bailouts that would have forced the financial institutions to give immediate relief to residential mortgage borrowers.

In many cases, a mortgage had been sold so often that it was unclear who held the mortgage. In many states, foreclosures were allowed to proceed without the party foreclosing establishing its ownership of the mortgage. In other cases, courts

8 U.S. Securities and Exchange Commission, "Statement of SEC Chairman Mary Schapiro on Money Market Fund Reform" (22 August 2012), www.sec.gov/news/press-release/2012-2012-166htm (hereafter SEC, "Chair Shapiro Statement.").

9 For a discussion, see Gillian Tett, *Fool's Gold: The Inside Story of JP Morgan and How Wall St Greed Corrupted Its Bold Dream and created a Financial Catastrophe* (New York: Penguin Press, 2009). For a discussion of how purchases of CDS did not have any financial interest or "skin in the game" regarding the assets that they were purchasing CDS for and the incentive effects, see Sarra, "Embedding Fairness."

10 SEC, "Chair Shapiro Statement."

11 Taub, *Other People's Houses*, 249.

12 Taub, *Other People's Houses*, 250.

questioned ownership. Porter cites federal courts in Ohio dismissing dozens of foreclosure lawsuits because the plaintiff lenders could not prove they were the record owners of the mortgage.[13] The Honourable L. Priscilla Hall, retired Judge of the New York Supreme Court, Appellate Division, observed that there were so many foreclosure applications before the court that had proffered no evidence of who held the mortgages that the Court had to implement new evidentiary rules before parties were able to bring applications before the court.[14] To bring a foreclosure action in New York, the plaintiff must own both the mortgage and note at the inception of the action.[15] A legal or equitable interest in the mortgage is required to foreclose.[16] For an assignee of a mortgage loan to have standing to foreclose, the assignment must be complete when the action is commenced.[17] The new pleading requirements for high cost and sub-prime loans are that the plaintiff must plead that it is the owner of the mortgage and note or has been delegated the authority to institute a foreclosure action by the owner of the mortgage.[18] In October 2010, New York State Unified Court System instituted a new filing requirement for residential foreclosure cases to "protect the integrity of the foreclosure process and prevent wrongful foreclosures."[19] The rule promotes the court's ability to consider standing and the *prima facie* case contemporaneously in determining the merits of a foreclosure action, which is also viewed as means to avoid wasting court time and resources.[20] According to the requirements, counsel must affirm that counsel has taken "reasonable steps—including inquiry to banks and lenders and careful review of the papers filed in the case—to verify the accuracy of the documents filed in support…"[21]

This situation is echoed elsewhere. Porter cites Judge Keith Lundin of the U.S. Bankruptcy Court for the Middle District of Tennessee who found mortgage servicers were filing claims against mortgage borrowers with incomplete records, with claims bloated with illegal and fraudulent fees sometimes totalling several

13 Katherine Porter, "Misbehavior and Mistake in Bankruptcy Mortgage Claims" (2008) 87 Tex L Rev 121–79 (hereafter Porter, "Misbehavior."), citing *In re Foreclosure Cases*, 521 F Supp 2d 650, 654 (SD Ohio 2007); *In re Foreclosure Cases*, No 07-2282, 2007 WL 3232430 (ND Ohio 2007), *3.

14 Cited with permission, on file with authors.

15 Legal Services NYC, "Standing and Capacity to Sue in New York Foreclosure Actions" (August 2012), Empire Justice, http://empirejustice.org/wp-content/uploads/2018/02/AGHOPPWebinar_WhereDoWeStandOnStanding_Guidelines.pdf (hereafter Legal Services NYC, "Standing."), citing *Deutsche Bank National Trust Company* v *Barnett*, 88 AD3d 636, 931 NYS2d 630 (2d Dep't 2011).

16 Legal Services NYC, "Standing," citing *Katz* v *Eastville Realty Co*, 249 AD2d 243, 672 NYS2d 308 (NY App Div 1998).

17 Legal Services NYC, "Standing," 2.

18 Legal Services NYC, "Standing," 8.

19 Legal Services NYC, "Standing," 17, citing State of New York, Unified Court System, "New York Courts First in Country to Institute Filing Requirement to Preserve Integrity of Foreclosure Process" (20 October 2010).

20 Legal Services NYC, "Standing," 17.

21 Legal Services NYC, "Standing."

thousand dollars, with irreconcilable and unexplained balances that appeared on amended proofs of claim, and with servicers refusing to provide loan payment histories.[22]

The market collapse disproportionately harmed African-American sub-prime and traditional mortgage holders. The costs of their individual losses were obviously smaller in dollar value than the investors and lenders, but as a percentage of their income and personal wealth, the losses were devastatingly high. Millions struggled to hold on to their homes, but they did not have the power, time, energy, or resources to lobby federal and state governments to help in a meaningful way, unlike the lenders who were aggressive in their lobbying efforts and who managed to ensure that even programs aimed at helping individual homeowners were really programs that lined their own pockets.

I THE WIDENING WEALTH GAP

Increasingly evident is the widening wealth gap between African Americans and white Americans as a result of the sub-prime mortgages market meltdown. One study using U.S. government data found that between 2005 and 2009, median net worth for white households fell 16 per cent, whereas for African-American households and Latinx households median net worth fell 53 per cent and 66 per cent, respectively. The end result is that median wealth for white households is now twenty times that of black households.[23] As a result of these declines, in 2009, the typical African-American household had just $5,677 in wealth (assets minus debts), the typical Hispanic household $6,325, and the typical white household $113,149.[24]

Another study found that from 2009 to 2011, white wealth levels, excluding home equity, began to show signs of recovery, whereas African-American households continued to experience severe declines, with the typical African-American household losing 40 per cent of non-home-equity wealth.[25] When including home equity, the typical white family's losses slowed to zero in this period, while the typical black family lost an additional 13 per cent of its wealth.[26] A study by the American Civil Liberties Union observed:

[22] Porter, "Misbehavior," 135. See also *In re Schuessler*, 386 BR 458 (Bankr SD NY 2008); *Jones* v *Wells Fargo Home Mortgage*, 366 BR 584 (Bankr ED La 2007); *In re Parsley*, 384 BR 138 (Bankr SD Tex 2008) slip op, 1.

[23] Rakesh Kochhar et al, "Twenty to One: Wealth Gaps Rise to Record Highs between Whites, Blacks and Hispanics" (2011), Pew Research Center, www.pewresearch.org/wp-content/uploads/sites/3/2011/07/SDT-Wealth-Report_7-26-11_FINAL.pdf (hereafter Kochhar et al, "Twenty to One").

[24] Kochhar et al, "Twenty to One."

[25] Sarah Burd-Sharps and Rebecca Rasch, "Impact of the US Housing Crisis on the Racial Wealth Gap Across Generations: An Independent Report Commissioned by the American Civil Liberties Union," Social Science Research Council (June 2015), 2, www.aclu.org/files/field_document/discrimlend_final.pdf (hereafter Burd-Sharps and Rasch, "Impact").

[26] Burd-Sharps and Rasch, "Impact," 2.

> Unequal opportunity to rebuild wealth coming out of the crisis is leading to widening racial disparities. The racial wealth gap, in other words, is now on track to compound over time. This trend has urgent implications for the future of racial justice in America, and it should inform policymaking strategies aimed at guaranteeing fair economic opportunities in the coming years ... Without policy actions to remedy it, the racial wealth gap will be significantly greater in the next generation because of the differential impact of the Great Recession.[27]

The authors of a 2018 report from the Center for American Progress described the dramatic widening of the racial wealth gap after the 2008 recession.[28] "The Great Recession did greater damage to black wealth than it did to white wealth, widening the racial wealth gap even further" in the ten years since the recession ended.[29] William Wiecek observed in 2011: "Since the crisis, 'the median net worth for white households had fallen 24 percent to $97,860.' In striking contrast, black household net worth had fallen 83 percent to $2,170, or, as an economist ... put it, 'for every dollar of wealth the average white household had, black households only had two cents.'"[30]

The authors of the 2018 report enumerated several factors that contributed to the racial wealth gap, including the fact that "blacks are much less likely to become homeowners due to systematic housing and mortgage discrimination,"[31] an issue we canvassed at length in Chapter 3. The report's authors also acknowledge that, "... black families are more likely to face predatory lending practices. ..."[32] The report concludes with an observation about the wealth gap in general as "a product of intentional systematic policy choices," concluding that the "only way to correct this wrong is to make intentional systematic changes in response."[33]

II LACK OF RELATIONSHIP WITH LENDERS EXACERBATES FINANCIAL HARDSHIP

Another issue for African-American consumer borrowers is that banks are not located in their communities such that there is an ongoing relationship between the lender and the community. The result is that lenders are unlikely to forebear on

[27] Burd-Sharps and Rasch, "Impact."

[28] Angela Hanks, Danyelle Solomon, and Christian E. Weller, "Systematic Inequality: How America's Structural Racism Helped Create the Black-White Wealth Gap" (21 February 2018) Center for American Progress, www.americanprogress.org/issues/race/reports/2018/02/21/447051/systematic-inequality/ (hereafter Hanks et al, "Systematic Inequality"). "In 2016, median black wealth stood at ... about half of the median black wealth recorded just before the Great Recession. ... At the same time, median white wealth was only one-quarter less than it was prior to the Great Recession. ..." Hanks et al, "Systematic Inequality."

[29] Hanks et al, "Systematic Inequality."

[30] William M. Wiecek, "Structural Racism and the Law in America Today: An Introduction" (2011) 100 Kentucky L J 1, 5, 17 (hereafter Wiecek, "Structural Racism").

[31] Hanks et al, "Systematic Inequality."

[32] Hanks et al, "Systematic Inequality."

[33] Hanks et al, "Systematic Inequality."

enforcement of in-default mortgages or to negotiate new more affordable loan terms when borrowers encounter temporary financial setbacks from job loss or medical expenses.

Mehrsa Baradaran's research on the "unbanked" and the "underbanked" offers another important insight that underpins the sub-prime mortgage debacle.[34] She observes that part of the precariousness in black communities is the number of people who are unbanked. Once community banks exited poor neighbourhoods, fringe lenders, such as payday loan businesses, filled the void.[35] Baradaran documents how the high cost of credit exacerbates the already-strained lives of the poor, ensuring they remain in poverty.[36] Credit at a reasonable price and on reasonable terms is important to achieving income security and acquiring a home. Millions of Americans benefit from credit to bridge over financial trouble or establish a business, but many African Americans do not have access to these benefits.[37]

Baradaran also observes that banks benefit tremendously from the U.S. government. The U.S. central bank, the Federal Reserve, uses four main tools to control monetary supply in support of the economy: the federal fund rate (the rate at which banks lend to one another), the discount rate (liquidity – cheap loans – from the government that allow banks to remain in business during a short-term credit crunch), the reserve requirement (requiring banks to keep a specified amount of capital in reserve), and quantitative easing (the Federal Reserve purchasing large quantities of securities to get a slow economy moving).[38] An example of the latter is that the Federal Reserve bought over $1.25 trillion in mortgage-backed securities from banks in 2008. Baradaran reports that this purchase was made on the theory that banks would use this money to lend. Instead, the banks used most of the money to triple their stock prices by issuing dividends and buying back stock.[39]

Baradaran notes that the U.S. government relied on banks to disseminate the bailout funds to the public without making sure they would do so. The Troubled Asset Relief Program was "sold" to Congress and the American public on the basis that it would relieve mortgage debts through modifications and direct relief, yet it failed to achieve any meaningful relief.[40] After the taxpayer bailouts, firms paid hefty bonuses to executives – the same individuals who caused the crisis – and the U.S. government claimed its hands were tied and it could not prevent the bonuses from being paid.[41]

[34] Mehrsa Baradaran, *How the Other Half Banks: Exclusion, Exploitation, and the Threat to Democracy* (Cambridge, MA: Harvard University Press, 2015), 8 (hereafter Baradaran, *How the Other Half Banks*).

[35] Baradaran, *How the Other Half Banks*, 8.

[36] Baradaran, *How the Other Half Banks*, 9.

[37] Baradaran, *How the Other Half Banks*, 10.

[38] Baradaran, *How the Other Half Banks*, 14–16.

[39] Baradaran, *How the Other Half Banks*, 16.

[40] Baradaran, *How the Other Half Banks*, 23–4. See the discussion in Chapter 8.

[41] Baradaran, *How the Other Half Banks*, 57.

As competition in capital markets increased, banks increasingly exited low-income neighbourhoods, which was a rebirth of the redlining that was discussed in Chapter 2.[42] The growing number of unbanked individuals is large, approximately 70 million Americans do not have a bank account or access to traditional financial services.[43] Families that do not have a bank account pay 10 per cent or more of their income to make bill payments, get money orders, and make other money arrangements, because they do not have access to basic banking services.[44] Baradaran observes that the line between illiquidity and insolvency is often not clear. The reality is that the poor teeter on the edge of insolvency because they have no financial cushion; but the current market for lending to low and middle-income individuals does not distinguish between the two.[45]

Deregulation resulted in rejection of the idea that banks had unique public responsibilities, and laws protecting consumers were weakened.[46] The unbanked are forced to resort to payday loans for short-term credit, which can quickly become a revolving door nightmare. Studies show payday loans are for food and rent, or to cover medical emergencies, and that many of the poor understand how these debts work, but have no other options.[47] Many states do not regulate payday loans or have set maximum interest rates at 300 per cent APR to 1,900 per cent APR.[48] The few states that have banned payday loans have allowed "title loans," where the combination of fees and penalties that the borrowers pay amount to the same prohibitively expensive costs as payday loans.[49]

Referring back to the discussion of fairness in Chapter 2, it is clear that regulators and market participants did not accord equal concern to the interests of all stakeholders affected by the financial crisis. Financial firms, mortgage originators, and servicers profited directly and personally on the profits made from African-American mortgage borrowers, and African Americans were disproportionately harmed compared to white borrowers. There was absolutely no consideration of a Rawlsian approach of trying to place one's self in the position of the millions facing foreclosure. Even the judiciary failed to be empathetic in some of their deliberations. As noted in Chapter 2, having one's interests accorded equal concern in the choice of mortgage law principles does not equate to being given identical treatment. In fact, historical disadvantage and racism require a reconceptualization of how we approach foreclosure, which is discussed further in Chapter 10.

42 Baradaran, *How the Other Half Banks*, 50.
43 Baradaran, *How the Other Half Banks*, 138–9.
44 Baradaran, *How the Other Half Banks*.
45 Baradaran, *How the Other Half Banks*, 134–5.
46 Baradaran, *How the Other Half Banks*, 56.
47 Baradaran, *How the Other Half Banks*, 116.
48 Baradaran, *How the Other Half Banks*, 124.
49 Baradaran, *How the Other Half Banks*, 125.

6

A Missed Opportunity

> For the master's tools will never dismantle the master's house. They may allow us temporarily to beat him at his own game, but they will never enable us to bring about genuine change.
>
> Audre Lord, 1984[1]

It has become increasingly evident that the "master's mortgage tools" – the mortgage products and financial services that precipitated the crisis, many of which continue today – and the abusive conduct underpinning sub-prime lending are an integral part of the story of racism in the United States. Predatory lending resulted in massive destruction of the dream of home ownership for many African Americans that will take decades, if not longer, to repair. An entire generation of African Americans is unlikely to recover from the economic harms associated with losing their homes. Yet financial and policy responses to the crisis continue to use the same financial structures, the same market tools, and the same market players. As long as reform only includes regulatory change that "tinkers" at the edges of the structural problems, it is unlikely that there will be any systematic relief from inappropriate exercise of power or any meaningful justice for the millions of African Americans and other individuals harmed by predatory lending. In the language quoted in this chapter's epigraph, Audre Lord poignantly observes that using the master's tools will never bring about meaningful change.

This chapter discusses how lobbying by mortgage lenders and servicers in the U.S. Senate resulted in a vitally important missed opportunity to give a lifeline through bankruptcy reform to millions of Americans facing foreclosure. Bankruptcy forgiveness could have been an immediate and highly effective strategy to deal with the millions of threatened home foreclosures at the height of the crisis.

[1] Audre Lord, "The Master's Tools Will Never Dismantle the Master's House" in Audre Lorde, ed, *Sister Outsider: Essays and Speeches* (Berkeley, CA: Crossing Press, 1984), 2, https://collectiveliberation.org/wp-content/uploads/2013/01/Lorde_The_Masters_Tools.pdf.

I BANKRUPTCY REFORM COULD HAVE PROVIDED A VITALLY IMPORTANT SAFETY NET

The U.S. government could have enacted changes to bankruptcy legislation requiring mortgage lenders and servicers to negotiate reductions to the principal on home mortgages, which would have been a sustainable strategy to prevent millions of foreclosures and grant relief to mortgagors harmed by predatory lending practices. The U.S. government failed to do so.

Bankruptcy filings under the United States Bankruptcy Code are aimed at a "fresh start" for overindebted consumer or business borrowers ("debtors").[2] For individual consumer debtors, there are two options. The first is to file under Chapter 7 of the Bankruptcy Code, which results in liquidation of all the debtor's assets with the exception of a few protected assets and collateral already subject to secured loans.[3] The bankruptcy trustee then distributes the realized value to creditors on a *pro rata* basis based on the payment priorities set out in the Bankruptcy Code. In such cases, the home is lost to the debtor, but the individual has shed most or all the debt load. Another option is to file under Chapter 13 of the Bankruptcy Code, a proceeding in which the debtor keeps control of the assets and works with the trustee to develop a plan that sets out compromised debts or extended time for payment terms, allowing debtors and their families to stay in their home and continue to pay their debts over a three- to five-year period, but on a modified and more manageable basis.[4] A debtor can attempt to cure arrearage under a Chapter 13 repayment plan as long as bankruptcy has been filed prior to their property being sold at a foreclosure sale.[5] However, the process is expensive because the debtor has to pay substantial fees to the government and trustee. Yet it may be the only realistic way to try to keep the home.

It is under amended use of Chapter 13 of the Bankruptcy Code that the U.S. government could have provided meaningful relief to the financial stress experienced by millions of mortgage borrowers. However, as discussed herein, the U.S. government failed to enact amendments that would assist financially distressed or insolvent mortgage borrowers.

Both options under the Bankruptcy Code provide consumer debtors with an opportunity for a fresh start. The option to file under Chapter 13 provides a chance

2 United States Bankruptcy Code, 11 USC (1978), as amended (hereafter *Bankruptcy Code*).

3 Jean Braucher, "Humpty Dumpty and the Foreclosure Crisis: Lessons from the Lackluster First Year of the Home Affordable Modification Program (HAMP)" (2010) 52 *Ariz L Rev*, 782 (hereafter Braucher, "Humpty Dumpty").

4 Braucher, "Humpty Dumpty," 783–4, noting that in either Chapter 7 or Chapter 13, a debtor can surrender collateral to a secured lender and ultimately discharge personal liability for any deficiency in whole or part, citing Bankruptcy Code, §§ 521(a)(2)(A), 521(a)(6), 524(a), 1325(a)(5)(C), 1325(b), 1328(a). See also Elizabeth Warren and Jay Westbrook, *The Law of Debtors and Creditors*, 5th ed. (The Hague: Wolters Kluwer, 2006).

5 Bankruptcy Code, § 1322(e).

for debtors to remain in their homes. There are about 800,000 consumer bankruptcy filings annually in the United States.[6] The decision of individuals to commence bankruptcy proceedings is difficult because it affects their credit ratings for an extended period, thus reducing their ability to borrow and increasing the costs of any borrowing. There also continues to be social stigma attached to bankruptcy.

Katherine Porter notes that the greatest fear of many families in serious financial trouble is that they will lose their homes.[7] "Hundreds of thousands of Americans file Chapter 13 bankruptcy each year hoping to save their homes from foreclosure."[8] Her predictions about the financial crisis could not have been more apt. She writes at the start of the crisis:

> Bankruptcy offers a last chance for families to save their homes by halting a foreclosure and by repaying any default on their mortgage loans over a period of years. Mortgage companies participate in bankruptcy by filing proofs of claim with the court for the amount of the mortgage debt. To retain their homes, bankruptcy debtors must pay these claims.[9]

However, the bankruptcy system has its imperfections in terms of lender conduct. Using original data from 1,700 Chapter 13 bankruptcy cases, Porter concludes that mortgage companies frequently do not comply with bankruptcy law.[10] Most mortgage claims are missing one or more of the required pieces of documentation regarding the mortgage. Fees and charges on claims are often poorly identified, which makes it impossible to verify whether such fees are legally permissible or accurate. Moreover, in nearly all cases, debtors and mortgage companies disagree on the amount of outstanding mortgage debt.[11] However, as bankruptcy is a court-supervised process, bankruptcy judges can ensure the interests are better balanced in the bankruptcy proceeding, as compared with situations where consumer borrowers are trying to deal with lenders on a private contractual basis.

[6] United States Courts, "Just the Facts: Consumer Bankruptcy Filings, 2006–2017" (7 March 2018), Table 1 Nonbusiness Bankruptcy Filings by Year, www.uscourts.gov/news/2018/03/07/just-facts-consumer-bankruptcy-filings-2006-2017. In 2007, there were a total of 775,344 nonbusiness bankruptcies; the total grew from just over 1 million in 2008 to as high as over 1.5 million in 2010 and has steadily declined since then to 767,721 in 2017. The percentage of those filings under a Chapter 13 repayment plan, which provides for a debtor to save their home from foreclosure, experienced an inverse correlation during that time; the greatest proportion of liquidations occurred in 2010 with only 28 per cent of the 1,538,033 bankruptcies filed under Chapter 13.

[7] Katherine Porter, "Misbehavior and Mistake in Bankruptcy Mortgage Claims" (2008) 87 *Tex L Rev.*, 147 (hereafter Porter, "Misbehavior").

[8] Porter, "Misbehavior," 181.

[9] Porter, "Misbehavior."

[10] Porter's Mortgage Study sample contains 1,733 Chapter 13 bankruptcy cases filed by homeowners. The sample includes cases from forty-four judicial districts in twenty-three states and the District of Columbia, which represented 61 per cent of all Chapter 13 cases filed in 2006; Porter, "Misbehavior," 141.

[11] Porter, "Misbehavior."

Yet a major weakness in the U.S. bankruptcy system is the inability to compromise on home mortgages, even when the debtor has negative equity (i.e. when the outstanding mortgage amount is higher than the value of the home). There was a previous practice of forgiving some principal on mortgages held by underwater debtors. However, in 1993, the U.S. Supreme Court in *Nobelman* v *American Savings Bank* ended this relief for debtors.[12] The judgment prevented home mortgage modification through bankruptcy. The Court rejected the argument that Section 506 of the Bankruptcy Code, which addresses creditors whose collateral is valued at less than the value of the secured loan, allows the court to bifurcate the claim into a secured loan for the actual value and a second unsecured loan for the remaining amount.[13] As a result of the case, the homeowners lost their home: it was auctioned on the steps of the courthouse, and the mortgage holder company foreclosed and then purchased the home for itself at a greatly reduced market value.[14] This practice was common. Often there were few or no bidders when homes were auctioned off on the steps of the courthouse and the mortgage holder made a bid and acquired title to the property at a reduced price.[15] *Nobelman* v *American Savings Bank* halted the practice of banks foregoing some of the principal amount of the mortgage as a fresh start tool for consumer debtors in financial distress.

Yet bankruptcy forgiveness could have been an immediate and highly effective strategy to deal with the millions of home foreclosures at the height of the crisis. The bankruptcy process to address threatened foreclosure could have offered the timeliness, transparency, fairness, and accountability discussed in Chapter 2. Strong financial disclosure requirements placed upon debtors filing for bankruptcy protect the integrity of the process, which is designed to balance the interests of creditors and honest, but unfortunate, borrowers who cannot pay their debts as they become due.[16] The bankruptcy courts are well equipped and experienced in hearing such cases and granting remedies appropriate to encouraging a fresh start. Repayment terms are geared to budget needs and availability of any surplus income must be directed towards debts. Courts balance the interests of debtors and creditors in sanctioning modification of debt levels or terms of payment.[17] Debtors are monitored for up to five years on their repayment plans. Debtors cannot increase their debts, their income is monitored, and adjustments are made when surplus income becomes available.

[12] *Nobelman* v *American Savings Bank*, 508 U.S. 324 (1993).

[13] See also the discussion in Braucher, "Humpty Dumpty." The Court held that there was no way, as a practical matter, to avoid modifying the secured mortgage lenders' rights if the mortgage payments were to end before the full thirty-year term.

[14] Steve McGonigle, "Pair Lose Court Fight Over Condo" *Dallas Morning News* (2 June 1993).

[15] Jennifer S. Taub, *Other People's Houses* (New Haven, CT: Yale University Press, 2014), 119 (hereafter Taub, *Other People's Houses*).

[16] Lloyd Houlden, Geoffrey Morawetz, and Janis P. Sarra, *Annotated Bankruptcy and Insolvency Act, 2019* (Toronto: Carswell, 2019) (hereafter Houlden et al, *Annotated*).

[17] Houlden et al, *Annotated*.

This careful supervision by the bankruptcy courts means that opportunities for misuse of the provisions are slim.[18]

The stay of proceedings on filing under the Bankruptcy Code grants temporary relief from foreclosure and other creditor pressure to pay debts as they become due. A stay essentially stops creditors for a period from moving to enforce their claims by foreclosing against the borrower, and is aimed at giving the borrower "breathing space" to see if there are other options to meet debt obligations. But it is only a temporary reprieve. Section 1322(b)(2) specifies that the court can approve a plan that can "modify the rights of holders of secured claims, other than a claim secured only by a security interest in real property that is the debtor's principal residence, or of holders of unsecured claims, or leave unaffected the rights of holders of any class of claims."[19]

Often a bankruptcy filing is the only way to "stop the clock" for a short period. Texas, for example, is a non-judicial foreclosure state, which means that, absent a bankruptcy filing, a home can be taken based on the words of the trust deed – a mortgage type document – without appearance before a judge, after mailing notice to the borrower and posting a notice on the property.[20] The home then can be auctioned on the county courthouse steps, literally.[21] There is no transparency, fairness or due process prior to the auction.

What was the missed opportunity? There was an effort to amend the treatment of mortgages under bankruptcy through the proposed Helping Families Save Their Home Act of 2009.[22] Senator Dick Durbin (D-IL) sought an amendment dealing with bankruptcy modifications, which would have allowed homeowners at risk of foreclosure to modify their primary mortgage loan in bankruptcy court if they had not received a reasonable offer from their mortgage servicer to modify the loan.[23] The proposed legislation was aimed at creating an incentive for servicers to voluntarily restructure failing mortgages in an effort to keep families in their homes. The Center for Responsible Lending estimated that the amendments would have

[18] Center for Responsible Lending, "The Helping Families Save Their Homes in Bankruptcy Act of 2009 (S 61 and HR 200)" (23 January 2009), www.responsiblelending.org/research-publication/reducing-foreclosures-without-cost-taxpayers.

[19] Bankruptcy Code, § 1322(b)(2). Bankruptcy Code, § 101(13) specifies that the term "debtor's principal residence (A) means a residential structure if used as the principal residence by the debtor, including incidental property, without regard to whether that structure is attached to real property; and (B) includes an individual condominium or cooperative unit, a mobile or manufactured home, or trailer if used as the principal residence by the debtor."

[20] Taub, *Other People's Houses*, 15.

[21] Taub, *Other People's Houses*, 5.

[22] Helping Families Save Their Homes Act of 2009, Pub Law No. 111–22, 111th Congress, online: www.congress.gov/bill/111th-congress/senate-bill/896/text?overview.

[23] The Durbin Amendment (SA 1014). Durbin highlighted that aggressive and fair foreclosure prevention is a necessary step in our nation's effort to stabilize families, neighborhoods, banks, and the broader economy. Democratic Policy Committee, "S 896, the Helping Families Save Their Homes Act of 2009" (30 April 2009), United States Senate www.dpc.senate.gov/dpcdoc.cfm?doc_name=lb-111-1-63.

prevented 1.7 million mortgage foreclosures in 2009 alone and would have preserved over $300 billion in home equity for neighbouring homeowners.[24] However, large banks and financial companies fought against the proposed Bankruptcy Code amendment, spending $42 million in lobbying to block this reform and arguing that the reform would create a moral hazard and a "flood of filings" in the bankruptcy courts,[25] even though studies show that mortgage modification does not result in such negative effects.[26] The bank lobby was too powerful. The proposed Durbin amendment failed in the Senate vote in April 2009.[27]

In September 2008, then-presidential candidate Barack Obama announced at a rally that he would change the *Bankruptcy Code* to allow use of bankruptcy proceedings to help underwater homeowners reduce the principal on their loans.[28] One week later, the Troubled Asset Relief Program (TARP) was announced. Congress approved it and President George W. Bush signed it into force thereby creating the Emergency Economic Stabilization Act (EESA) in October 2008. The $700 billion TARP was enacted to bail out the banks, and in early 2009, the American Recovery and Reinvestment Act of 2009 (ARRA) was enacted to stimulate the weakening economy, thus costing another $787 billion in tax cuts and government spending.[29]

While the high cost of the bailout was being debated in Congress, President Obama changed his position on mortgage principal reduction. Taub noted that "nominee Obama had just given away their (mortgage borrowers') chance at leverage" in terms of negotiating in the shadow of bankruptcy.[30] Even after his election, President Obama did not champion the call for bankruptcy reform advocated by many economics and bankruptcy specialists and consumer advocates.[31]

Referring back to the discussion about framing principles in Chapter 2, there was no fairness in either the costly and powerful lobbying by mortgage interests or in the failure of Congress to take seriously the plight of millions of families facing

[24] Center for Responsible Lending, "Bankers Win, Homeowners Lose in Senate's Bankruptcy Vote" (30 April 2009), www.responsiblelending.org/media/bankers-win-homeowners-lose-senate-s-bankruptcy-vote. Center for Responsible Lending, "Senate Ignores Help for Homeowners, Bankruptcy Change the Most Effective Solution" (2 April 2008), www.responsiblelending.org/media/senate-ignores-help-homeowners-bankruptcy-change-most-effective-solution.

[25] Taub, *Other People's Houses*, 257.

[26] Adam Levitin has observed that permitting modification of mortgages has little or no impact on mortgage credit cost or availability, and the losses are smaller from modification than from foreclosure. Adam Levitin, "Resolving the Foreclosure Crisis: Modification of Mortgages in Bankruptcy" (2009) *Wis L Rev*, 566–577, The Congressional Budget Office.

[27] Taub, *Other People's Houses*, 262.

[28] Taub, *Other People's Houses*, 251, citing S. Davis, "Obama's Remarks on Economic Crisis" *Wall Street Journal* (16 September 2008).

[29] Financial Crisis Inquiry Commission, *Final Report of the National Commission on the Causes of the Financial and Economic Crisis in the United States, Submitted Pursuant to Public Law 111–21* (Washington, DC: FCIC, January 2011), 400, https://fcic-static.law.stanford.edu/cdn_media/fcic-reports/fcic_final_report_full.pdf (hereafter FCIC Report).

[30] Taub, *Other People's Houses*, 252, citing a press briefing on 24 September.

[31] Taub, *Other People's Houses*, 253.

foreclosure. There was no effort to consider the interests and perspectives of consumer borrowers to achieve more equitable outcomes. There were no timely and effective processes for the resolution of issues in respect of pending foreclosures, including legal ways for individuals to remain in their homes during the period that they challenged the foreclosure notice. Creditors had the ability to prematurely foreclose on them. As noted in Chapter 2, perspective taking alone will not allow a retooling of the system of mortgage lending to embed a fairness norm when privileged and wealthy financial firms wield their political power to prevent meaningful reform. Here, the law continued to sanction favourable treatment of the propertied and neglected to address the inequitable impact that the failure to amend the *Bankruptcy Code* would have on African Americans and many other borrowers. Acting in good faith and according equal concern to the interests of borrowers and other stakeholders were ignored.

7

Financial Crisis Reforms Woefully Inadequate

This chapter builds on the previous chapter and explores a host of other reforms implemented after the height of the financial crisis. The U.S. government's efforts to protect homeowners were well intentioned but ineffective for millions of home borrowers, and some strategies placed individuals and families in even graver and more precarious financial situations. While there are new standards for documenting and underwriting mortgage transactions, aimed at verifying that consumer borrowers can meet their mortgage obligations, the reforms do not prohibit predatory lending.

I AN INADEQUATE LEGISLATIVE AGENDA TO ADDRESS PREDATORY LENDING

The pain experienced by the people who we interviewed in Detroit, Baltimore, and New York is palpable. The frustration of their lawyers in dealing with an unresponsive legal, financial, and judicial system is evident. The post-crisis reforms aimed ostensibly at relieving hardship for home borrowers created a new set of incentives for lenders and brokers to exploit mortgage holders.

Ultimately, consumer mortgage borrowers paid dearly financially, socially, emotionally, and physically for the decision by legislators to bail out banks and other financial institutions rather than direct some of those substantial resources to millions of borrowers whose homes were lost. The measures introduced by the Bush administration and carried on by the following administration essentially put the "foxes in charge of the hen house," in that they relied on the same market participants who had engaged in unethical practices to roll out their mortgage modification programs. The statute that was ultimately enacted did not assist families in saving their homes. It encouraged, but did not require, lenders to modify loan terms, and did not require them to reduce any principal owing.[1] Taub observes that by 2014, the same reckless banks still engaged in high-risk practices, and lax regulators who overlooked fraud and abuse are now housed in new institutions with the same laxness and failure to protect the public interest.[2]

1 Home Affordable Modification Program Created Incentives for Further Egregious Behaviour

The U.S. government's attempts to protect homeowners through mortgage modification programs were well intentioned, but ineffectual. The U.S. government issued statements committing $75 billion of the Troubled Assests Relief Program (TARP) funds, which it announced was aimed at helping three to four million struggling homeowners avoid foreclosure and reduce the spillover effects of the foreclosure crisis on the economy.

One of the first efforts was the "Hope Now Alliance" in 2007, a voluntary initiative encouraging servicers to work with borrowers on potential modifications. By all accounts, it was completely ineffective. One study found that 63 per cent of the modifications added the overdue payments to the mortgage principal, and very few had any payments reduced.[3]

In early 2009, a U.S. government-sponsored program, Making Home Affordable (MHA), was established pursuant to the Emergency Economic Stabilization Act (EESA) of 2008, aimed at providing alternatives to foreclosure for homeowners impacted by the financial crisis.[4] The Home Affordable Modification Program (HAMP), the largest program under MHA, was established to provide permanent mortgage modifications to struggling homeowners with mortgage liens originated on or before 1 January 2009.[5] Congress enacted the HAMP in March 2009, a comparatively small carve-out of more than a trillion dollars of relief to the financial sector. The funds were intended to go through the banks to provide relief to struggling homeowners. Instead, the money was largely directed to returning banks to profitability.[6]

1 Jennifer S. Taub, *Other People's Houses* (New Haven, CT: Yale University Press, 2014), 263 (hereafter Taub, *Other People's Houses*).

2 Taub, *Other People's Houses*, 5.

3 Congressional Oversight Panel Report, *The Foreclosure Crisis: Working Towards a Solution* (Washington, DC: Congress, 6 March 2009), 31; Brian Grow, Keith Epstein, and Robert Berner, "How Banks are Worsening the Foreclosure Crisis" *Bloomberg BusinessWeek* (11 February 2009).

4 Emergency Economic Stabilization Act of 2008, Pub L No 110–343, 110th Congress; Department of Treasury, "Treasury, HUD and FHFA White Paper on the Future of Foreclosure Prevention" (25 July 2016), U.S. Treasury, www.treasury.gov/press-center/press-releases/Pages/jl0527.aspx (hereafter Treasury, "White Paper").

5 Treasury, "White Paper," 5.

6 Mehrsa Baradaran, *How the Other Half Banks: Exclusion, Exploitation, and the Threat to Democracy* (Cambridge, MA: Harvard University Press, 2015), 24–5 (hereafter Baradaran, *How the Other Half Banks*).

The HAMP program had many problems, most important of which was that it relied on the voluntary participation of the loan servicers.[7] It was not designed to require or even request that lenders forgive any of the balance remaining on a mortgage, but was only a request to restructure by extending the period of the loan.[8] The incentives under HAMP were skewed and rewarded the very people who engaged in misconduct. For example, Countrywide's servicing arm was eligible to earn over $5 billion in incentives through HAMP; and one study found that 21 of 25 firms receiving HAMP money had strong connections to the sub-prime mortgage industry.[9]

Another 2009 program, the Home Affordable Refinance Program (HARP), was aimed at allowing borrowers to restructure and repay their mortgages but failed for many of the same reasons that HAMP failed. HARP's goal was to lower monthly loan payments for creditworthy borrowers who had underwater mortgages insured or owned by Fannie Mae and Freddie Mac.[10] The voluntary nature, plus no requirement of any loan forgiveness, rendered the program ineffective in alleviating the financial hardship of the borrowers.

The Federal Housing Finance Administration (FHFA) and the U.S. government-sponsored enterprises, Fannie Mae and Freddie Mac, then introduced the Servicing Alignment Initiative (SAI) to assist struggling homeowners and to mitigate government-sponsored enterprise (GSE) losses.[11] The U.S. Department of Housing and Urban Development (HUD) expanded options for mortgages insured by the FHA. The stated aim was to create additional assistance to struggling homeowners and try to create common standards across mortgage servicers.[12]

The first option for which most homeowners were evaluated was a traditional HAMP modification, referred to as HAMP Tier 1 for non-GSE loans and GSE HAMP for GSE loans.[13] HAMP Tier 1 and GSE HAMP targeted a housing debt-to-income (DTI) ratio of 31 per cent and were only offered on loans secured by principal residences.[14] In 2012, additional modification options were aimed at increasing the number of homeowners eligible for assistance with the standard modification for GSE loans and HAMP Tier 2 for non-GSE loans introduced to help homeowners ineligible for assistance under GSE HAMP or HAMP Tier 1.[15]

7 Mechele Dickerson, *Homeownership and America's Financial Underclass: Flawed Premises, Broken Promises, New Prescriptions* (Cambridge: Cambridge University Press, 2014), 111 (hereafter Dickerson, *Homeownership*).

8 Dickerson, *Homeownership*.

9 John Dunbar, "You Broke It, You Fix It? Subprime Players Get Tax Money to Fix Subprime Mess" (26 August 2009) The Center for Public Integrity (hereafter Dunbar, "You Broke It").

10 Dunbar, "You Broke It."

11 Treasury, "White Paper, " 5.

12 Treasury, "White Paper," 2.

13 Treasury, "White Paper," 6.

14 Treasury, "White Paper," 6.

15 Treasury, "White Paper."

These modifications were aimed at providing a target post-modification housing DTI ratio equal to or greater than 10 per cent and less than 55 per cent, and opened the program to loans secured by a non-owner occupied property.[16] Over time, the U.S. government tried to introduce streamlined modification options for GSE (GSE Streamlined Modification) and non-GSE (Streamlined HAMP) loans under which an eligible homeowner who was 90 or more days delinquent was proactively offered a loan modification without being required to submit an application.[17] However, if a complete borrower application package was received, then a borrower would be evaluated for a HAMP modification of Tier 1, Tier 2, or GSE HAMP, as applicable. HUD also introduced a "Loss Mitigation Home Retention Priority Waterfall for FHA-insured Mortgages" aimed at a targeted payment reduction of 20 per cent for FHA-HAMP modifications with a resulting housing DTI ratio equal to or greater than 25 per cent and less than or equal to 31 per cent.[18]

One can easily see how all of these compartmentalized requirements facilitated gaps in coverage and thus excluded many borrowers from eligibility. The U.S. Department of the Treasury HAMP program failed to address foreclosures in a timely manner.[19] After HAMP was implemented, foreclosure filings increased to 2.8 million in 2009, up from 2.3 million in 2008.[20] One year after it was implemented, only about 230,000 borrowers had entered into permanent HAMP modifications, and even these modifications were not necessarily truly permanent.[21] Even borrowers who

[16] Treasury, "White Paper."

[17] Treasury, "White Paper," 6, and the program stated that the servicer was not required to verify income or underwrite to a targeted housing DTI.

[18] Treasury, "White Paper," 7.

[19] U.S. Department of the Treasury, "Home Affordable Modification Program Guidelines" (4 March 2009), www.treasury.gov/press-center/press-releases/Documents/modification_program_guidelines.pdf and Making Home Affordable, "Home Affordable Modification Program Supplemental Directive 09-01" (6 April 2009). Per HAMP guidelines, borrowers' eligibility during the program was based on numerous factors: the property had to be owner-occupied and the borrower's primary residence; the property had to be a single-family (one- to four-unit) property, with a maximum unpaid principal balance on the unmodified first-lien mortgage equal to or less than $729,750 for a one-unit property; the loans had to have been originated on or before 1 January 2009; the first-lien mortgage payment had to be more than 31 per cent of the homeowner's gross monthly income for the program to reduce the household monthly debt burden to a target of 31 per cent. In addition, the borrower application for modification had to pass the Net Present Value (NPV) test obtaining a positive value in the test, implying that providing a permanent HAMP modification would yield higher expected payments to the lenders/investors relative to the case of no modification and potential foreclosure. Finally, the program rules required the servicers to offer a trial modification first, which may be subsequently converted into a permanent modification only if the modification was successful during the trial period (i.e. borrowers make payments per the changed contract that was offered on a trial basis, which typically took about six months). Sumit Agarwal et al, "Policy Intervention in Debt Renegotiation: Evidence from the Home Affordable Modification Program" (2017) 125:6 *J Polit Econ* 654–658 (hereafter Agarwal et al, "Policy Intervention").

[20] Taub, *Other People's Houses*, 264.

[21] Jean Braucher, "Humpty Dumpty and the Foreclosure Crisis: Lessons from the Lackluster First Year of the Home Affordable Modification Program (HAMP)" (2010) 52 *Ariz L Rev* (hereafter Braucher, "Humpty Dumpty").

were the beneficiaries of HAMP modifications typically ended up owing more on their homes than the home's value, with high and difficult to sustain debt burdens overall.[22] Although HAMP modifications reduced monthly mortgage payments to 31 per cent of gross monthly income, borrowers were left with high overall debt-to-income ratios because lenders did not have to offer any reduction in loan principal even for those borrowers owing much more than the value of their homes.[23]

The HAMP calculation only focused on first mortgage expense in relation to income, it did not look at affordability in terms of the debtor's overall household budget requirements, which created a high risk of redefault because the modification terms were often not affordable.[24] The primarily temporary interest rate breaks resulted in a high risk of redefault.[25] Redefault rates continued to be high. The Oversight Congressional Council found that over half of modifications in the first half of 2008 had redefaulted.[26]

HAMP fell far short of the 3 to 4 million families targeted for help by the end of 2012.[27] As of December 2010, HAMP had resulted in the permanent modification of only 520,000 mortgages.[28] Although banks reported that they had independently approved 3.4 million loan alterations of various kinds, many of these modifications simply rolled missed payments into a new mortgage with the interest added to the principal, thus resulting in higher monthly payments.[29] Borrowers who had been paying down mortgages for years and had built up substantial equity were especially susceptible to being turned down for loan modifications because the lender would prefer that they simply sell their homes.[30] Competing incentives encouraged banks to view

[22] The program produced only 230,801 permanent modifications in the first year of operations: Making Home Affordable Program, "Servicer Performance Report through March 2010" (2010) Federal Reserve Bank of St Louis, 4, https://fraser.stlouisfed.org/files/docs/historical/fct/treasury/treasury_hamp_report_201003.pdf.

[23] Only at the end of the first year did HAMP announce plans to add incentives to reduce principal, applicable when LTV ratio exceeded 115 per cent, but participating servicers were not required to write the loan down: Braucher, "Humpty Dumpty," 732–3.

[24] Braucher, "Humpty Dumpty," 741.

[25] Braucher, "Humpty Dumpty," 729, reports that by the end of the first year the U.S. government was predicting a 40 per cent redefault rate.

[26] Ruth Simon, "Easing Mortgages Isn't a Panacea" *Wall Street Journal* (9 December 2008).

[27] Financial Crisis Inquiry Commission, *Final Report of the National Commission on the Causes of the Financial and Economic Crisis in the United States, Submitted Pursuant to Public Law 111–21* (Washington, DC: FCIC, January 2011), 405, https://fcic-static.law.stanford.edu/cdn_media/fcic-reports/fcic_final_report_full.pdf (hereafter FCIC Report).

[28] FCIC Report, 405, citing Congressional Oversight Panel, *December Oversight Report: A Review of Treasury's Foreclosure Prevention Programs* (Washington, DC: Congress, 14 December 2010), 4, 7, 18.

[29] FCIC Report, 405, citing HOPE NOW, "Industry Extrapolations and Metrics (October 2010)" (6 December 2010), 3.

[30] FCIC Report, 405, citing Kirsten Keefe, a senior staff attorney with the Empire Justice Center in Albany, New York, and Diane Thompson, National Consumer Law Center, who testified to the United States Senate Committee on Banking, Housing, and Urban Affairs: "only a very few of the potentially eligible borrowers have been able to obtain permanent modifications."

foreclosure as quicker, easier, and often cheaper than modifying the terms of existing mortgages.[31]

A number of other obstacles made modifications difficult, including tensions between various interests. For example, there were competing interests among various investors in a mortgage-backed security. Proceeds from a foreclosure may be enough to pay off the investors holding the highest rated tranches of securities, while the holders of the lower tranches would likely have their interests wiped out.[32] As a result, the holders of the lower-rated tranches might prefer a modification that extends the mortgage period for a long time, if it produced more cash flow than a foreclosure.[33]

By 2014, only $3 billion of the $75 billion allocated for borrower relief had been used, but millions and millions of homes had been foreclosed during the program's operation.[34] Banks ensured the failure of HAMP by stringing along homeowners on their modification applications, saying that the applications were still being considered while they continued foreclosure proceedings against them. Court-filed sworn statements in which Bank of America employees gave evidence confirmed that they frequently lied to homeowners and were paid bonuses to force them into foreclosure by denying modification applications *en masse*, up to 1,500 applications at a time.[35] One former senior debt collector's sworn statement said: "We were told to lie to customers and claim that Bank of America had not received documents it had requested … collectors 'who placed ten or more accounts into foreclosure in a given month received a $500 bonus.'"[36] Placing the very mortgage lenders who had caused the problem in control of administering the modifications had the exact opposite effect intended. They had every incentive to delay processing applications and foreclose on people's homes.

The following first-hand account from a man in Brooklyn, New York illustrates what was occurring with the modification program:

> I owned a mixed-use commercial use building that I purchased in 1998, which I refinanced in 2006. Everything was going well, but in 2012, I was struck by a car crossing the street and could not work for six months. Nationstar offered me modifications on my mortgage—they gave me $25,000 lump sum, with payments of $500 for 18 months. I sent payments in on time each month. Then I found it was Ocwen Financial holding my mortgage. It had been sold.

31 FCIC Report, 405, citing also the National Consumer Law Center, "Why Servicers Foreclose When They Should Modify and Other Puzzles of Servicer Behavior" (October 2009).

32 FCIC Report, 406.

33 FCIC Report.

34 Taub, *Other People's Houses*, 254, 263. Agarwal et al found that a few large lenders offered HAMP modifications at only half the rate of other institutions, and this meant that about 70 per cent more permanent modifications were not approved; Agarwal et al, "Policy Intervention."

35 Paul Kiel, "Bank of America Lied to Homeowners and Rewarded Foreclosures, Former Employees Say" *ProPublica* (14 June 2013), www.propublica.org/article/bank-of-america-lied-to-homeowners-and-rewarded-foreclosures (hereafter Kiel, "Bank of America"), writing about sworn statements filed in Federal Court in Boston as part of a multi-state class action suit brought on behalf of homeowners who sought to avoid foreclosure through the HAMP program, 2011.

36 Kiel, "Bank of America."

After 12 months, I was just a few months away from paying off my 18-month loan, when Ocwen Financial called me and said they had miscalculated and that I needed to make a payment of $5,000 right away for arrears they had just calculated or they would cancel the financing arrangement. I couldn't raise the money. Ocwen put me in default without giving me a chance. I had only six months to go before the entire loan was paid off. Once they cancelled, they would not accept any more monthly payments. They were misapplying my payments to pay their legal costs and penalties instead of putting it towards my interest and principal payments of the loan. I hired a lawyer, and only then did they agree to discuss modification—said I was to give them all my documents. I gave them all the documents and three months later, Ocwen came back and said there was a problem with the deed. I said I had owned the building for 20 years and there was no problem with the deed when they first lent to me. Ocwen said I had to start the loan process all over again. I paid for another appraisal and more fees with the loan application. Six more months passed and they said I did not qualify to pay a modified rate.

Over 18 months, they took $80,000 from me in fees and charges. I was paying $5,000 a month. The principal on the entire loan was only $165,000, but all of that $80,000 went to fees, none to my payments. For example, they charged $5,000 for that new appraisal of a building I had owned for 20 years, but never showed up to appraise the building. Then they told me to find another finance company. They pressured me to sell when property prices were at an all-time low. Instead of foreclosure, I agreed to a 3-month bridge loan at 9 percent interest, where I was paying only interest, bridging me to find new financing. If I did not find refinancing, it would go up to 14 percent in three months. I now owed $242,000 to them.

I feel violated in every sense. I drive a cab now, I used to be a substitute teacher. I can no longer afford a lawyer, my previous lawyer used up all my savings. My lawyer said the time in court would be too expensive and costlier than the cost of refinancing. I was less than five years away from paying off the entire property. I went to five institutions for financing, they refused to give me rejection letters, only two would. They do not want their stats to suffer, so they leave you in their system without giving an answer on your application. I am hoping charges against Ocwen Financial will help me—they have been charged by state attorneys in many states.

Even where consumers had built up equity savings, predatory lenders took advantage of them. The following first-hand account from "D," a single mother in Queens, New York, illustrates not only the lenders' conflicts of interest, but how they manipulated and lied to borrowers seeking mortgage modifications:

I got my loan in 2007 and had planned to buy four homes—new construction. I had purchased my first home years before when I was 26 for myself and my son, but my relationship with my partner didn't work out and I sold the house when I became a single mom. I bought an investment property in Pennsylvania and moved with my two boys to my mom's three-bedroom apartment where several of my siblings and their children lived. Eventually, my mom got custody of several nieces and nephews and there were lots of us in a little space. Then I saw four two-family homes under construction in Queens and I went into a contract on all four. I work for an insurance wholesaler and I don't make a lot of money, but the builder had representatives who made the purchase very easy. I PUT $1,000 down on each home. The real estate office I was dealing with connected me to the builders.

I had prepaid legal services available to me, but the builder encouraged me to hire a lawyer it knew for the closing. The builder's representatives told me that this attorney would make the transaction go quickly, that this lawyer doesn't work for the builder, and the builder could build the cost of the lawyer into the mortgage. I did as they suggested because I was living in a situation where I needed to move. My mom and I signed the contracts in late spring 2007. For some reason, the builder did not sign until late fall. I closed in December 2007, right at the end of the housing bubble. But only one house closed instead of all four, the one with the highest loan note. I thought that everything would be okay once I got the rental income from the downstairs apartment in the house.

After I closed on the one house, the other mortgage offers were retracted. I moved into the house with my two sons and planned to rent out downstairs, but the builders did not obtain a certificate of occupancy so I couldn't open the day care centre I had planned to operate in the house. So, I contacted Wells Fargo, which was servicing my loan, right away to say that because I couldn't get the rental income and could not open the day care centre, I would not be able to make future payments. The Wells Fargo representative said because I *WAS NOT* in arrears, I could not get a mortgage modification. While this was happening, my 11-year-old niece who was living with my mom was approached by a sexual predator, and I moved my mom and nieces into the downstairs apartment of my house. After all, my mom's name was on the deed. I fell behind. I called the bank for a mortgage modification and the Wells Fargo rep said that because I *WAS* in arrears I can't get a modification. I took money out of my 401K to catch up, called Wells Fargo and the rep said, I couldn't get a modification because I *WAS NOT* in arrears.

I went to court to seek a modification, but the bonuses I get at work bumped up my salary so I did not qualify. I'm not guaranteed a bonus; I may not get one at all some years, or the amount may change. I read the terms and conditions for the modification program. Wells Fargo could have overlooked the bonuses; they did not have to be included in the calculation for my modification payments. The lawyer representing Wells Fargo said, "my client has a right to include your bonuses and they will exercise that right." Eventually I got the certificate of occupancy, and then Hurricane Sandy hit and I'm still not able to rent out the apartment or open the day care center business. My house was about to be auctioned so I filed for bankruptcy. I feel like I failed my family. I look at my son and feel I failed him. I didn't look at myself as a victim. I look at myself as a failure. I was overly ambitious. Maybe I should not have rushed.

D's lawyer points out that Wells Fargo was offering clients like D interest-only mortgages at 7 per cent, so that they would never be able to pay off any principal. In D's case, interest and taxes amount to $5,000 per month. Some damage to D's home from the hurricane is still not fixed because builders under the city's program post-hurricane will not fix the roof unless she gets a modification, and the modification issue continues to be unresolved. Her lawyer also observes that Rushmore is one of the servicers under the TARP program; that it has been buying up notes on a discounted basis, and even though it was paid 40 cents on the dollar, it is coming after the borrowers for the full amount of the loan plus interest, exacerbating what is already an unacceptable system of exploiting mortgage borrowers.[37] Almost two years after meeting with her lawyer, we were shocked to learn that the mortgage servicer for D refused her offer to pay $100,000 on the outstanding mortgage, a large part of that drawn from her retirement fund, in order to keep her home. She offered to pay the remaining principal of $475,000 at 7 per cent for a loan term of 40 years, the principal and interest amounting to $2,951 plus taxes and insurance; and even though her lawyer submitted the evidence of her ability to pay, the servicer refused the modification.

D's lawyer notes that many people are still struggling with lenders about loans from 2008, and that in September 2018, there were more than 10,000 foreclosures pending at that moment in New York City alone. She also notes the profound toll on families, some family units splitting from the pressure, entire blocks of Queens' neighbourhoods boarded up, and the toll on her clients' health from ten years of fighting disclosure has been profound.[38]

Jean Braucher observes that a significant amount of taxpayer-paid incentives went into the pockets of servicers and investors who were not required to write down principal of the predatory and sub-prime mortgages.[39] Essentially, borrowers were given temporary relief, the benefit going directly to lenders and their investors, and even then, there was no enforcement of the conduct of servicers.[40] HAMP modifications in the first year did not reduce negative equity and actually increased it slightly in most cases.[41] Many HAMP participants were left with very high total debt-to-income ratios, which meant they were unable to afford their modified loans in the event of reductions in their incomes or increases in their expenses. With negative equity, they would be unable to sell their homes to pay off their loans before moving to cheaper housing.[42] Modification relief was not available at all if the person was unemployed, as it was based on income.

Servicers were often not responsive to requests for information or trial modifications, so that borrowers suffered long wait times on the telephone, received misinformation, experienced long delays in getting responses to requests for information or trial plan offers, and were frequently denied without explanation,[43] which

37 Alice Nicholson, lawyer specializing in foreclosures, interview, New York, September 2018 (on file with authors) (hereafter Nicholson, Interview).

38 Nicholson, Interview.

39 Braucher, "Humpty Dumpty," 740.

40 Braucher, "Humpty Dumpty," 742.

41 Braucher, "Humpty Dumpty," 742.

42 Braucher, "Humpty Dumpty," 777.

43 U.S. Senate, *The Worsening Foreclosure Crisis: Is It Time to Reconsider Bankruptcy Reform?: Written Testimony Before the Subcommittee on Administrative Oversight and the Courts of the Committee on the Judiciary*, 111th Cong 4, 28, 30, 45 (23 July 2009), 71 (written testimony of Alys Cohen, National Consumer Law Center) (hereafter U.S. Senate, Cohen Testimony), www.judiciary.senate.gov/imo/media/doc/07-23-09CohenTestimony.pdf (concerning borrowers' difficulties in getting information and timely and accurate processing of requests for modifications). See also the discussion in Braucher, "Humpty Dumpty," 777.

confirms the experience of the first-hand accounts we collected. The Congressional Oversight Panel found that servicers falsely reported that they had made trial modification offers when they had not.[44]

Braucher also documents cases where the trial plans required higher payments or limited modifications for five years and servicers routinely refused to accept requests for modifications despite having signed up for HAMP.[45] She also documents cases of servicers charging fees to consider requests for modifications in violation of HAMP rules and conducting foreclosure sales while a review or trial plan was in progress but keeping payments made in the meantime.[46] In the first year, only 7 per cent of modifications successfully made the transition from trial to permanent status. Then after compliance reviews, the U.S. Department of the Treasury discovered missing documents and the possibility that servicers were at fault.[47] Its conversion drive succeeded in producing closer to 25 per cent of permanent modifications, an improvement, but clearly still an inappropriately small number.[48] Braucher notes that a "striking finding of the Congressional Oversight Panel was that more than three-quarters of permanent modifications (76 percent) under HAMP left the borrower underwater, with a median (mean) loan to value ratio of 126 (143) percent."[49]

A judgment of the Supreme Court of the State of New York in March 2018 found that Wells Fargo was engaging in manipulation of value for the express purpose of stating that a property had equity and therefore that a request for modification failed the net present value test under HAMP.[50] The Court held:

> The Court notes that this case is symptomatic of a larger problem that has arisen in the post-HAMP landscape ... Wells Fargo's modification program forgives all of the interest and balloons the arrears. Affordability and net-present-value (NPV) are then calculated utilizing the unpaid principal balance (UPB). Here, as in most of this Court's cases subject to this analysis, the modification was denied based on NPV (that is, the amount that the bank could expect to collect at foreclosure auction—taking into account the delay in doing so and the amount of equity in the property—exceeded the current value of what it would collect under a modification). This case is particularly egregious, however, in that the parties agree that the premises is actually underwater (that is, that the amount owed exceeds the value of the property)—and yet, Plaintiff has denied Defendant's modification request based on NPV (utilizing the much lower UPB rather than the entire debt).

The judgment illustrates that this problem of manipulating value for purposes of denying modifications is a growing problem.

44 U.S. Senate, Cohen Testimony, 71, 217.
45 Braucher, "Humpty Dumpty," 777.
46 Braucher, "Humpty Dumpty," 777.
47 Braucher, "Humpty Dumpty," 779–80.
48 Braucher, "Humpty Dumpty."
49 Braucher, "Humpty Dumpty," 767.
50 *U.S. Bank* v *Anuola Austin et al*, No 13-504967, Decision and Order of Judge Noach dear (NY Sup Ct filed 13 March 2018).

2 Short Sales and Transfers of Deed in Lieu of Foreclosure Exacerbated Inappropriate Incentives

The U.S. government's aid program was amended also to promote short sales and transfers of a deed in lieu of foreclosure, both of which also proved highly problematic for sub-prime mortgage borrowers.

A short sale is a sale to a willing buyer, with the deficiency in the negative equity in a home forgiven. A deed in lieu of foreclosure means the borrower voluntarily gives up the home to the servicer, with the debt cancelled.[51] Although both involve some debt forgiveness for borrowers, neither allows the borrowers to stay in their homes and neither addresses the equity value lost by homeowners in terms of savings originally invested. Arguably, the programs created incentives for lenders to push homeowners out of their homes to replace them with people they thought were a better credit risk. Alice, the lawyer for the couple in New York, recounts how Wells Fargo and JP Morgan Chase launched a huge campaign to have borrowers come to centres, ostensibly to discuss modifications, but then pressured them into transferring the deed of their home in lieu of foreclosure. They offered them $5,000 to move, then they took the house away from them.[52] The Obama administration's decision to allow short sales and transfers of deeds in lieu considerably heightened lender incentives to force people out of their homes.

3 Reform Measures Not Sufficient

There has been some consumer protection law enacted in the United States since the financial crisis, including the creation of the Consumer Financial Protection Bureau (CFPB) after the passage of the Dodd-Frank Wall Street Reform and Consumer Protection Act of 2010 (Dodd-Frank Act).[53] However, in the eight years since that legislation, little empirical evidence exists about the benefits or costs of these statutory protections.[54] Congress missed an opportunity to abolish the issuer-pays credit rating system, to require rating agencies to regularly update their rating of financial products and other securities, and to enact liabilities for parties holding mortgages that have been sold instead of just remedies against the originators for illegal or fraudulent loans.

[51] Braucher, "Humpty Dumpty," 743.

[52] Nicholson, Interview.

[53] Dodd-Frank Wall Street Reform and Consumer Protection Act of 2010, Pub L No 111-203, 124 Stat 1376.

[54] Manisha Padi, "Consumer Protection Laws and the Mortgage Market: Evidence from Ohio" (2018) (Working Paper), 1, Manisha Padi, https://manishapadi.com/workingpapers/, referencing the National Low Income Housing Coalition, "Findings from the HB 4050 Predatory Lending Database Pilot Program" (1 April 2007), https://nlihc.org/resource/findings-hb-4050-predatory-lending-database-pilot-program (hereafter Padi, "Consumer Protection Ohio"). She compares loans in Ohio to loans across state borders in Pennsylvania, West Virginia, Indiana, and Kentucky, relative to the difference across state borders prior to the 2007 introduction of the law.

The Dodd-Frank Act was enacted in 2010 ostensibly to overhaul the financial regulatory system in the United States. While detailed examination of the Dodd-Frank Act is beyond the scope of this book, of note is that disclosure to investors was enhanced,[55] including more information during sales of collateralized debt obligations (CDO); however, the underlying rational for having such financial products in the market was never examined. Congress missed an important opportunity to prohibit the sale of particular kinds of high-risk structured financial products to retail investors. It did not take measures to address the speculative market, such as taxing transactions by volume of sales, which would have slowed the market.[56] Underwriting standards with respect to products sold were not strengthened sufficiently.

Several Dodd-Frank Act measures important to consumers are discussed in this section. However, there was considerable pressure from the outset to repeal some or all of the reforms, driven largely by political lobbying of both parties. On 9 June 2017, The Financial Choice Act, aimed at repealing significant parts of the Dodd-Frank Act, passed the House with a vote of 233 to 186.[57] On 14 March 2018, the Senate passed the Economic Growth, Regulatory Relief, and Consumer Protection Act that exempted dozens of U.S. banks from the Dodd-Frank Act banking regulations.[58] On 22 May 2018, the law passed in the House of Representatives and President Trump signed it in to law on 24 May 2018.[59] The result of this rolling back of regulatory oversight of a number of banks and other financial institutions is beyond the scope of this book, but merits serious consideration going forward. For the most part, the CFPB provisions were untouched in the 2018 bill; however, in March 2018, the director of the CFPB announced a review of the "usefulness" of the agency's consumer complaint gathering and reporting, which includes a consumer complaint database available to the public.[60]

55 See, for example, 17 CFR §§ 229.1111; 17 CFR § 230.424; 17 CFR § 239.45; and 79 Fed Reg 57184, 57259.

56 Janis Sarra, "Embedding Fairness as a Fundamental Norm in Financial Markets" in Janis P. Sarra, ed, *An Exploration of Fairness, Interdisciplinary Inquiries in Law, Science and the Humanities* (Toronto: Carswell, 2012) (hereafter Sarra, "Embedding Fairness").

57 Alan Rappeport and Emily Flitter, "Congress Approves First Big Dodd-Frank Rollback" *New York Times* (22 May 2018), www.nytimes.com/2018/05/22/business/congress-passes-dodd-frank-rollback-for-smaller-banks.html. Alan Rappeport, "Bill to Erase Some Dodd-Frank Banking Rules Passes in House" *The New York Times* (8 June 2017). Bob Bryan, "The House Quietly Voted to Destroy Post-Financial-Crisis Wall Street Regulations" *Business Insider* (9 June 2017).

58 Economic Growth, Regulatory Relief and Consumer Protection Act, S 2155, Pub L 115–174, enacted 24 May 2018. See also Sylvan Lane, "Senate Passes Bipartisan Bill to Roll Back Dodd-Frank" *The Hill* (14 March 2018), http://thehill.com/policy/finance/378491-senate-passes-bipartisan-bill-to-rollback-dodd-frank.

59 Erik Sherman, "Congress Just Approved a Bill to Dismantle Parts of the Dodd-Frank Banking Rule" *NBC News* (23 May 2018), www.nbcnews.com/business/economy/congress-just-approved-bill-dismantle-parts-dodd-frank-banking-rule-n876516; Sylvan Lane, "Trump signs Dodd-Frank rollback" *The Hill* (24 May 2018), http://thehill.com/policy/finance/389212-trump-signs-dodd-frank-rollback.

60 Shen Lu, "How the GOP's Dodd-Frank Act Overhaul Could Impact You" *KGW* (15 March 2018), www.kgw.com/article/money/magnify-money/how-the-gops-dodd-frank-act-overhaul-could-impact-you/507-528947709 (hereafter Lu, "Dodd-Frank Overhaul").

A number of new regulations were created under the Dodd-Frank Act. Some protected consumer borrowers, but most protected investors. One positive requirement is that no creditor may make a residential mortgage loan unless the creditor makes a reasonable and good faith determination, based on verified and documented information, that the consumer has a reasonable ability to repay the loan, based on the terms offered. The creditor must assess the borrower's current and expected income and credit rating as well as other factors.[61] It must determine the ability of the consumer to repay using a payment schedule that fully amortizes the loan over the term of the loan.[62] This requirement is likely to halt the pre-crisis practice of brokers arranging "no document" loans so that they could receive higher fees, even where the mortgage borrower's documents were available.

Both the Dodd-Frank Act and the CFPB regulations designate "qualified mortgages,"[63] which are mortgages that have substantially equal periodic payments; limits on fees,[64] maximum 30-year terms, are underwritten to the maximum interest rate in the first five years; and where the borrower's verified debt-to-income ratio does not exceed 43 per cent.[65] The qualified mortgage is significant because it creates a safe harbour for the lender in terms of the borrower's ability to repay.[66] It also prohibits pre-payment penalties on non-qualified mortgages and adjustable-rate mortgages and restricts the amount of prepayment penalties for some qualified mortgage loans.[67] The Dodd-Frank Act also requires property appraisals to be independent, specifying that the appraisal must be performed by a certified or licensed appraiser who conducts a physical property visit. This provision is aimed at protecting investors in the securitization market by ensuring properties are underwritten at loan-to-value ratios that are realistic.[68] While the regulations may assist consumer borrowers by creating standards of conduct for mortgage lenders, many of the provisions protect investors in capital markets. Moreover, the complex language of the regulations makes them largely incomprehensible for the average borrower who, therefore, will be unable to determine whether or not their mortgage lender is in fact complying. The provisions do not address many of the other structural problems in the mortgage lender market that have been identified throughout this book.

[61] Dodd-Frank Act, 15 USC § 1639c(a)1 and 3.

[62] Dodd-Frank Act, 15 USC § 1639c(a)3.

[63] Dodd-Frank Act, 15 USC § 1639c(b)3(A) and Minimum standards for transactions secured by a dwelling, (e) Qualified mortgages, 12 CFR § 1206.43(e)(2) (hereafter 12 CFR § 1206.43).

[64] "Except for the effect that any interest rate change after consummation has on the payment in the case of an adjustable-rate or step-rate mortgage, that do not (A) Result in an increase of the principal balance; (B) Allow the consumer to defer repayment of principal, except as provided in paragraph (f) of this section; or (C) Result in a balloon payment, as defined in § 1026.18(s)(5)(i), except as provided in paragraph (f) of this section," 12 CFR § 1206.43€(2).

[65] 12 CFR § 1206.43(e)(2). See the entire section for detailed requirements.

[66] 12 CFR § 1206.43(e)(1).

[67] Dodd-Frank Act, 15 USC § 1639(b) and (c).

[68] Dodd-Frank Act, 15 USC § 1639(h), Property appraisal requirements.

Also of note is the fact that the 5 per cent "skin-in-the-game" requirement under the Dodd-Frank Act does not apply to securitization of "qualified residential mortgages," defined as "qualified mortgages" under the CFPB regulations,[69] discussed further in Chapter 9.

It also warrants mention that the CFPB enacted servicing regulations in 2013 that prohibit servicers from commencing a foreclosure before a loan is 120 days delinquent and require the servicer to be in contact with the borrower within 36 days of delinquency to inform the borrower about the availability of loss mitigation options.[70] It specifies that a "servicer shall not evade the requirement to evaluate a complete loss mitigation application for all loss mitigation options available."[71] Here again, the requirements are very detailed, with a few time-limited exemptions. They do not appear to be particularly helpful, given our discussion in Chapter 9 about how current loss mitigation strategies and oversight are geared to protecting investors not mortgage borrowers. The regulation provides that "nothing in § 1024.41 imposes a duty on a servicer to provide any borrower with any specific loss mitigation option."[72] That means that principal forgiveness does not need to be offered. That can be contrasted with businesses in financial distress, where lenders frequently compromise the level of principal debt owing to allow the business to continue.

One positive reform coming out of the Dodd-Frank Act in 2010, the Consumer Financial Protection Bureau, was aimed at giving it supervisory and enforcement authority over the origination and servicing of mortgages, including the ability to issue rules and protect consumers.[73] The Dodd-Frank Act grants the CFPB the authority to promulgate rules aimed at preventing unfair, deceptive, or abusive practices in markets for consumer financial products and services.[74] Section 1031(a) specifies:

> The Bureau may take any action authorized under subtitle E [enforcement powers] to prevent a covered person or service provider from committing or engaging in an unfair, deceptive, or abusive act or practice under Federal law in connection with any transaction with a consumer for a consumer financial product or service, or the offering of a consumer financial product or service.

The CFPB is given rulemaking powers in this respect.[75] The Dodd-Frank Act then qualifies this authority by stating that the CFPB has no authority to declare an act or practice in connection with an offering or transaction with a consumer for a

69 Dodd-Frank Act, 15 USC 78o-11(B) Credit risk retention and 12 CFR § 1234.13(a) Exemption for qualified residential mortgages.

70 12 CFR § 1024.39 Early intervention requirements for certain borrowers; 12 CFR § 1024.40 Continuity of contact; and 12 CFR § 1024.41 Loss mitigation procedures (hereafter 12 CFR § 1024.41).

71 12 CFR § 1024.41(a)(B)(2).

72 12 CFR § 1024.41(a).

73 Dodd-Frank Wall Street Reform and Consumer Protection Act, Pub L 111–203, as amended through Pub Law 115–174, enacted 24 May 2018, § 1041 (hereafter Dodd-Frank Act 2018).

74 Dodd-Frank Act 2018, § 1031.

75 Dodd-Frank Act 2018, § 1031(b).

consumer financial product or service to be unlawful on the grounds of *unfairness* unless the CFPB has a reasonable basis to conclude that "the act or practice causes or is likely to cause substantial injury to consumers which is not reasonably avoidable by consumers;" and "such substantial injury is not outweighed by countervailing benefits to consumers or to competition."[76] "In determining whether an act or practice is unfair, the Bureau may consider established public policies as evidence to be considered with all other evidence. Such public policy considerations may not serve as a primary basis for such determination."[77]

Let's pause at "unfairness." Not only is the authority of the CFPB limited to "substantial injury," it is qualified by two additional factors, whether the consumer could have reasonably avoided the injury and weighing the injury against benefits to competition. Moreover, the public policy of preventing harm to consumers cannot serve as the primary basis for finding unfairness. The language sets up hurdles to the effectiveness of the CFPB as the oversight regulator of fairness in the consumer mortgage market, thus limiting the scope of its powers and ability to provide meaningful remedies.

In determining "abusive," the Dodd-Frank Act specifies that:

> the Bureau shall have no authority to declare an act or practice abusive in connection with the provision of a consumer financial product or service, unless the act or practice (1) materially interferes with the ability of a consumer to understand a term or condition of a consumer financial product or service; or (2) takes unreasonable advantage of—(A) a lack of understanding on the part of the consumer of the material risks, costs, or conditions of the product or service; (B) the inability of the consumer to protect the interests of the consumer in selecting or using a consumer financial product or service; or (C) the reasonable reliance by the consumer on a covered person to act in the interests of the consumer.[78]

This language may allow for some relief but is tied to 'materially interfering' with the ability of the consumer to understand a term or condition or 'takes unreasonable advantage' of a lack of understanding, thus placing the onus on the consumer to meet this threshold.

Ostensibly, the statute prohibits lenders from giving mortgages unless they make a reasonable and good faith determination based on verified and documented information that the consumer has a reasonable ability to repay the loan.[79] It specifies:

> §129C. Minimum standards for residential mortgage loans "(a) ABILITY TO REPAY.—"(1) IN GENERAL.—In accordance with regulations prescribed by the Board, no creditor may make a residential mortgage loan unless the creditor makes a reasonable and good faith determination based on verified and documented

76 Dodd-Frank Act 2018, § 1031(c)(1)(B).
77 Dodd-Frank Act 2018.
78 Dodd-Frank Act 2018, § 1031(d).
79 Dodd-Frank Act 2018, TITLE XIV § 1411 Ability to Repay.

> information that, at the time the loan is consummated, the consumer has a reasonable ability to repay the loan, according to its terms, and all applicable taxes, insurance (including mortgage guarantee insurance), and assessments.[80]

If there is more than one mortgage on a residential property, the creditor is to make a reasonable and good faith determination based on verified and documented information that the consumer has a reasonable ability to repay the combined payments of all loans on the same dwelling according to the terms of those loans and all applicable taxes, insurance (including mortgage guarantee insurance), and assessments.[81]

Factors specified in the statute to determine ability to repay include consideration of the consumer's credit history, current income, expected income the consumer is reasonably assured of receiving, current obligations, debt-to-income ratio, or the residual income the consumer will have after paying non-mortgage debt and mortgage-related obligations, employment status, and other financial resources other than the consumer's equity in the dwelling or real property that secures repayment of the loan.[82] A creditor is to determine the ability of the consumer to repay using a payment schedule that fully amortizes the loan over the term of the loan.[83] It gives direction on how to calculate the costs of loan payments, thus requiring lenders to assess the affordability of mortgages including adjustable rate mortgages (ARM) and interest-only mortgages based on the maximum interest rate a borrower would have to pay in the first five years of the loan.[84] This five-year period provides some protection for consumer borrowers in the first five years of the mortgage, but leaves open the possibility of a rapid ramp up of interest rates at the five-year mark that leaves mortgagors with price shock at that time. Moreover, mortgagors will be hit with a large tax bill at the end of five years, which could result in a wave of tax-related foreclosures.

The Dodd-Frank Act also requires loan originators to consider taxes and insurance when calculating whether the mortgage borrower can afford the loan, and it originally required the lender to escrow taxes and insurance for the first five years.[85] However, the 2018 reforms expand an exemption that allows mortgage lenders to avoid escrowing taxes and insurance on some high-cost mortgages, even though the rule was enacted to make sure that homebuyers could afford their loans and additional costs. Joe Valenti, director of Consumer Finance at the Center for American Progress observed:

> …25 of the biggest 38 U.S. banks—which together hold about one-sixth of the assets in the entire financial sector—wouldn't be subjected to [*Dodd*-Frank's] stricter rules,…
>
> Potential homebuyers may not know exactly what they are getting into price-wise once you factor in taxes and insurance. Once they are in a home, without an

[80] Dodd-Frank Act 2018.
[81] Dodd-Frank Act 2018.
[82] Dodd-Frank Act 2018.
[83] Dodd-Frank Act 2018, § 1411.
[84] Dodd-Frank Act 2018, § 1411.
[85] Dodd-Frank Act 2018, § 1411.

escrow, people may find it difficult to come up with the money for a property tax bill or for homeowners insurance. In extreme cases, a homeowner could potentially lose his/her house or have to deal with forced placed insurance, which means the lender picks the homeowner's insurance policy for the homeowner, which can typically be expensive and not very helpful to the buyer.[86]

The Dodd-Frank Act also requires that mortgagors with hybrid ARM receive notice six months prior to any rate adjustment.[87] Here again was a missed opportunity to simply place a maximum cap on interest rate adjustments, either over specified periods or over the life of the loan. It also missed the opportunity to require a defined level of adequate capitalization of all originators and brokers. Hence, it did not address the problem of incentives created when mortgage market participants are thinly capitalized.

The Dodd-Frank Act limited the size and duration of prepayment penalties,[88] which, as discussed in Chapter 3, can be devastating for borrowers locked into predatory mortgages. ARM are not to have prepayment penalties at all and for fixed-rate loans prepayment penalties are only allowed in qualified loans, as defined by statute, and cannot exceed 3 per cent in the first year and must expire by the end of the third year.[89] The Dodd-Frank Act also banned the practice of yield spreads premiums such that loan originators are now not supposed to be compensated based on any term of a loan other than the size of the loan.[90]

One option not adopted by the U.S. government was to require all mortgage originators and brokers always to offer consumer borrowers a fixed-rate mortgage with no prepayment penalties or hidden fees. Such an option would allow consumer borrowers to compare the price with other mortgage products. Although Congress briefly considered such a provision, the lending institutions strenuously lobbied against such a provision and it was never adopted.

Manisha Padi observes that non-depository bank mortgage lenders like Quicken Loans and mortgage brokers were exempt from many Dodd-Frank Act regulations and have expanded to take over more than half the mortgage market.[91] Kim et al, have observed that the reform focus on banks imposed costs on banks but provided fertile ground for non-bank consumer mortgage lenders to proliferate, essentially continuing the risks to borrowers, but in entities not as regulated as banks.[92]

86 Joe Valenti, as quoted in Lu, "Dodd-Frank Overhaul."
87 Dodd-Frank Act 2018, § 1418.
88 Dodd-Frank Act 2018, § 1414.
89 Dodd-Frank Act 2018, § 1414.
90 Dodd-Frank Act 2018, § 1403.
91 Y. S. Kim, S. M. Laufer, K. Pence, R. Stanton, and N. Wallace, "Liquidity Crises in the Mortgage Market" (2018) *Finance and Economics Discussion Series* 2018-016, Board of Governors of the Federal Reserve System, https://doi.org/10.17016/FEDS.2018.016r1 (hereafter Kim et al, "Liquidity Crises").
92 Kim et al, "Liquidity Crises."

Some state governments have enacted laws to try to fill the gap in consumer mortgage protection at the federal level. Padi undertook an empirical study of consumer mortgage protection in Ohio after it enacted the Homebuyers' Protection Act (HPA) in 2007.[93] The HPA imposed potential liability on state banks, brokers, and non-bank lenders for unfair acts and new standards of care, including potential liability for unconscionable lender actions. The law authorized the state Attorney General and local prosecutors to sue brokers and lenders who violate the state's Consumer Sales Practices Act and brokers who fail to fulfil their duties to their clients, thus giving them authority to prosecute mortgage lenders for unfair or deceptive practices and mortgage brokers for violating their duties towards borrowers.[94] The HPA defines certain actions as unconscionable, which, if proved, allows the contract to be unwound at any time.[95] Consumers can claim that their mortgage originator engaged in unconscionable acts as an affirmative defence against foreclosure.[96]

State laws cannot affect federal law with respect to national banks, their subsidiaries, and third parties that act as their exclusive agents.[97] However, they are enforceable against local banks and local third-party originators, including originators who act as non-exclusive brokers for national banks, located within a state that has enacted legislation.[98] This latter point is critically important as they impose standards on non-bank mortgage lenders that are growing in market share and are largely unregulated players.[99]

Ohio law requires lenders and brokers to provide disclosure to consumers getting a mortgage with a loan-to-value (LTV) ratio above 90 per cent that states their mortgage is particularly at risk of default and may not be refinanced.[100] But Padi observes that the law relies on consumers to understand the disclosure; thus the impact of the requirements are mediated by consumers' behavioural biases.[101] Padi found:

93 Padi, "Consumer Protection Ohio," 2; effective 1 January 2007.

94 Padi reports that "more than 50 residential mortgage disputes have been brought in Ohio since 2007 pursuant to the Act, none have been resolved on the basis of the Homebuyers' Act language." Padi, "Consumer Protection Ohio," 2, 7.

95 For example, standard includes contracts that are "based predominantly on the supplier's realization of the foreclosure or liquidation value of the consumer's collateral without regard to the consumer's ability to repay the loan in accordance with its terms"; for other examples of unconscionable contracts, see Ohio Rev Code § 1345.031 Unconscionable acts by supplier prohibited – unconscionable provisions.

96 Padi, "Consumer Protection Ohio," 8. "Remedies include injunctive relief against foreclosure or debt collection, and monetary penalties between $5,000 and $25,000 [Ohio Rev Code § 1345.07(A)(2)(b) and (D)]. It also provides for a private right of action, through which consumers can recover three times their actual economic damages, as well as attorney's fees"; referring to Ohio Rev Code § 1345.09(B), Padi suggests that standards of care must be enforced by the regulator, the attorney general, or the borrower after a harm has been done, Padi, "Consumer Protection Ohio," 8.

97 *State Farm Bank* v *Reardon*, 539 F3d 336 (6th Cir 2008).

98 Kim et al, "Liquidity Crises."

99 Kim et al, "Liquidity Crises."

100 Padi, "Consumer Protection Ohio," 2.

101 Padi, "Consumer Protection Ohio," 2.

> Results demonstrate that standards of care decrease foreclosure rates and consumer bankruptcy filings. Standards of care changed the composition of loans shifting away from risky features such ARMs, balloon payments, and prepayment penalties. They also contracted the size of the market for loans overall. The evidence suggests that standards of care work by changing lenders' post-origination behavior, by encouraging leniency towards borrowers, and by eliminating the sale of some risky loan types. In addition, mandated disclosures result in smaller loans being taken, and conditional on loan characteristics, lowers delinquency rates. In contrast to the standards that target firms, disclosures encourage responsible consumer behavior.[102]

Padi measured the primary outcome by measuring consumer well being in bankruptcy and found the rate of bankruptcy filings is about 9 per cent lower after the Ohio law was enacted relative to change in comparable loans across state borders and that "prior to 2007, bankruptcy filings were becoming increasingly more common in Ohio and the law reversed that trend and caused Ohio's bankruptcy rates to fall into line with neighboring states."[103] She found a drop in foreclosure after the introduction of the HPA of nearly 20 per cent relative to the baseline, and while foreclosure rates were increasing in Ohio prior to 2007, after the law was introduced, foreclosures dropped below the level of comparable states.[104]

Significantly, she found that loans originated in Ohio after the 2007 legislation have been less likely to have adjustable interest rates, less likely to require balloon payments at the end of the mortgage term, less likely to have prepayment penalties, and more likely to be a purchase loan rather than a refinancing transaction.[105] Padi observes that disclosure under the Ohio law appears to target borrower behaviour, rather than lender behaviour; and that mandated disclosure seems to incentivize borrowers to take smaller loans.[106] She saw no effect on the Ohio disclosure of the number of originations above 90 per cent LTV threshold, but did see an effect on the delinquency rate of those loans and other characteristics.[107]

This research illustrates that imposing standards of care on financial lenders can reduce the rate of foreclosures and enhance the well being of consumer mortgage borrowers. However, this lesson has not yet permeated federal regulatory policy.

Chapter 9 explores how predatory lending has had a resurgence in new forms and under new names, largely because Congress failed to squarely address predatory lending in the post-crisis period. While deposit-taking banks have largely exited the sub-prime mortgage market, less regulated non-bank lenders now dominate

102 Padi, "Consumer Protection Ohio," 3.
103 Padi, "Consumer Protection Ohio," 14.
104 Padi, "Consumer Protection Ohio."
105 Padi, "Consumer Protection Ohio," 14, 17; she observes that "the primary effect of the mandated disclosure appears to be the drop in loan amounts."
106 Padi, "Consumer Protection Ohio," 17.
107 Padi, "Consumer Protection Ohio," 17.

the market, with traditional banks still providing warehouse lines of credit to these thinly capitalized companies. The next chapter examines the settlements of a large number of lawsuits arising out of predatory lending in the mortgage market. As you read, observe where the penalties and settlement amounts are being directed – it raises serious questions as to whether these lawsuits have acted as deterrents to future misconduct, particularly given the weak legislative reform post-crisis.

8

Incomplete Justice: Legal Actions against Predatory Lenders

This chapter analyzes in detail the billions of dollars paid by financial firms to settle the lawsuits arising out of the sub-prime mortgage debacle. As a global amount, the settlement figures – approximately $119.7 billion, of which $74 billion went to investors and state authorities as penalties, and the remainder was credit to be earned through consumer relief – appear extraordinary. While the settlements reference accountability to investors, they are remarkably silent on accountability to African Americans and others intentionally targeted for, and victimized by, predatory sub-prime mortgages. Recall from Chapter 2 that accountability is required in a democracy when consumer borrowers' interests have been harmed; yet no one has been held accountable for the predatory lending practices that led to millions of families losing their homes. This lack of accountability incentivizes further misconduct in respect of mortgage lending and servicing in the future.

While the settlement amounts are huge, one study has placed the losses resulting from fraud on mortgage loans made between 2005 and 2007 at $112 billion,[1] and that was losses only in the two years prior to the massive foreclosures during the ten-year period that this book covers. Moreover, careful analysis reveals that the majority of the money went to the investors of the financial firms, to the U.S. Securities and Exchange Commission (SEC), and to other parties, rather than borrowers who suffered foreclosure. Research for this chapter has revealed that the litigation was incredibly important, but that in the end, the settlements were like shell games, the money on paper being moved around so much that it is hard to discern what mortgage borrowers received as compensation, if anything.

1 Financial Crisis Inquiry Commission, *Final Report of the National Commission on the Causes of the Financial and Economic Crisis in the United States, Submitted Pursuant to Public Law 111–21* (Washington, DC: FCIC, January 2011), xxi, https://fcic-static.law.stanford.edu/cdn_media/fcic-reports/fcic_final_report_full.pdf (hereafter FCIC Report). The FCIC was established as part of the Fraud Enforcement and Recovery Act.

The chapter commences with a brief overview of the types of settlements negotiated, and then turns to the specific financial firms that issued or serviced predatory mortgages and residential mortgage-backed securities (RMBS). It unpacks, to the extent that public disclosures have allowed us to research, how the money, intended in part for consumers, was used. The chapter analyzes how the money from the settlements could have been more equitably distributed, which would have offered different signals to the mortgage industry going forward in such a way as to prevent the most recent forms of predatory lending. For the most part, investors in these banks, brokerage, and servicing firms appear to have recouped a sizable amount of their losses. Consumer borrowers were not as fortunate.

Parts I and II briefly summarize the results of allegations of fraud and violation of various federal and state securities and financial services law by looking at suits against a number of firms that issued RMBS based on predatory mortgages. The sheer volume of dollars being directed to settlements highlights the devastating effects that predatory lending had on the U.S. economy. There does not yet appear to be comprehensive data on the amount of relief that has flowed to mortgage borrowers. Given the structure of the settlements, there may never be clarity on the actual relief given. Part III then discusses cases brought against predatory sub-prime lenders alleging violation of anti-discrimination law.

I SETTLEMENTS OF LAWSUITS FOR PREDATORY LENDING BROUGHT BY THE U.S. DEPARTMENT OF JUSTICE AND STATE ATTORNEYS GENERAL

The U.S. Department of Justice (DOJ) and 49 of the nation's State Attorneys General banded together in the fall of 2010 to investigate foreclosure irregularities and explore potential redress for investors and borrowers who were harmed by improper foreclosures.[2] In 2014, the DOJ stated that the settlements were part of the ongoing efforts of President Obama's Financial Fraud Enforcement Task Force and its Residential Mortgage-Backed Securities Working Group, which had "recovered $36.65 billion to date for American consumers and investors."[3]

The Financial Crisis Inquiry Commission (FCIC) concluded that firms securitizing mortgages failed to perform adequate due diligence on the mortgages they purchased and at times knowingly waived compliance with underwriting standards.[4] Large investment banks, bank holding companies, and insurance companies, including Merrill Lynch, Citigroup, and AIG, had significant corporate governance

2 FCIC Report, 407.

3 Department of Justice, "Bank of America to Pay $16.65 Billion in Historic Justice Department Settlement for Financial Fraud Leading up to and During the Financial Crisis" (21 August 2014), www.justice.gov/opa/pr/bank-america-pay-1665-billion-historic-justice-department-settlement-financial-fraud-leading (hereafter DOJ, "Bank of America to Pay $16.65 Billion").

4 FCIC Report, 187.

and risk management failures.[5] Executive and employee compensation systems at these institutions disproportionally rewarded short-term risk taking.[6] Potential investors were not fully informed or were misled about the poor quality of the mortgages contained in mortgage-related securities.[7]

Note, as you read below, the type of conduct at which the lawsuits were directed. The list of misconduct is almost too egregious to comprehend. It includes fraud, violation of federal loan statutes, securities law violations, misrepresentation, and other unlawful conduct. Fraudulent conduct identified included invalid notarizations, forged signatures, backdated mortgage paperwork, and changing applicants' income amounts after they submitted applications for mortgages.[8] A number of firms failed to demonstrate having legal standing to foreclose on many homes, in other words, they failed to establish that they held the legal right to repossess a home.[9] The problem of legal standing arose because the massive amount of mortgage securitization meant that ownership of the loan was hard to discern. Securitization had outpaced the ability of the legal and financial system to accurately record who owned the mortgage.[10]

Some lenders relied on "robo-signers" that substituted speed for accuracy by signing, and sometimes backdating, hundreds of affidavits claiming personal knowledge of facts about mortgages that they did not actually know to be true.[11] One such robo-signer, Jeffrey Stephan of General Motors Acceptance Corporation (GMAC), said that he signed 10,000 affidavits per month, roughly one per minute, making it highly unlikely that he verified payment histories in each individual case of foreclosure.[12]

For the settlements with the DOJ and the State Attorneys General, there were monetary penalties, payments to investors misled by representations of the firms, and consumer relief provisions.

Figure 8.1 is a visual representation of the $12.6 billion settlement between Royal Bank of Scotland (RBS) and the DOJ and other members of Obama's Financial Fraud Enforcement Task Force's RMBS Working Group, specifically, where the settlement dollars were allocated. The details of the settlement are set out in Tables A.22 and A.23 of the Appendix.[13] Of the $12.6 billion, only $400 million

5 FCIC Report, 279.
6 FCIC Report, 279.
7 FCIC Report, 187.
8 FCIC Report, 407.
9 FCIC Report, 407.
10 FCIC Report, 407.
11 FCIC Report, 407.
12 FCIC Report, 407.
13 RBS Settlement Agreement Recitals (14 August 2018), para. 1, Department of Justice, www.justice.gov/opa/press-release/file/1087146/download (hereafter RBS DOJ Settlement). Department of Justice, "Royal Bank of Scotland Agrees to Pay $4.9 Billion for Financial Crisis-Era Misconduct" (14 August 2018), United States Government, www.justice.gov/opa/pr/royal-bank-scotland-agrees-pay-49-billion-financial-crisis-era-misconduct. Jonathan Stempel, "RBS to Pay $44 Million to Settle

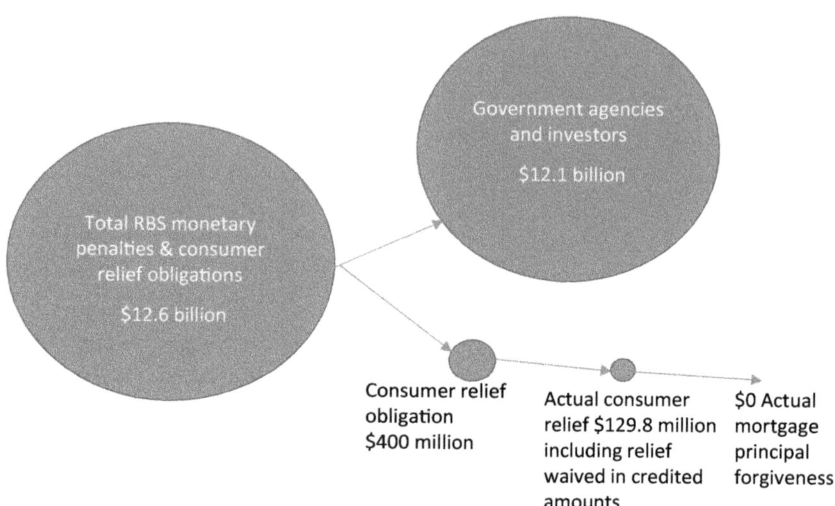

FIGURE 8.1. RBS settlement with the U.S. Department of Justice and State Attorneys General

from the State of New York settlement was allocated to relief to aid consumers harmed by RBS' allegedly unlawful conduct. This relief included community reinvestment, neighbourhood stabilization, and affordable rental housing, but also gave "credited amounts" for being timely, so that the actual amount of relief was less than $400 million.[14]

US Charges It Defrauded Customers", *Reuters* (26 October 2017), www.reuters.com/article/us-rbs-settlement/rbs-to-pay-44-million-to-settle-u-s-charges-it-defrauded-customers-idUSKBN1CV2QD (hereafter Stempel, "RBS to Pay $44 Million"). National Credit Union Administration, "AME Allocations for Legal Recoveries, Fees and Expenses" (11 August 2017), www.ncua.gov/Legal/Documents/legal-recoveries-allocations.pdf (hereafter NCUA Settlements). Federal Deposit Insurance Corporation Settlement and Release Agreement (26 May 2016), para. 1, FDIC, www.fdic.gov/about/freedom/plsa/colonialbankreditsuissesecuritiesubssecurities.pdf (hereafter FDIC Settlement). RBS Federal Housing Finance Agency Settlement Agreement (12 July 2017), para. 2, www.fhfa.gov/Media/PublicAffairs/PublicAffairsDocuments/FHFA-RBS-Settlement-Agreement.pdf (hereafter RBS FHFA Settlement). U.S. Securities and Exchange Commission, "SEC Charges Royal Bank of Scotland Subsidiary with Misleading Investors in Subprime RMBS Offering" (7 November 2013), www.sec.gov/news/press-release/2013-239 (hereafter RBS SEC Settlement). RBS Financial Products Settlement Agreement (6 March 2018), para. 2, RBS Monitor, https://rbs.mortgage-settlementmonitor.com/Settlement-Agreement-Documents/RBS-Settlement-Agreement-3-6-18.pdf (hereafter RBS New York Settlement). California Attorney General Pressroom, "Attorney General Xavier Becerra Announces $125 Million Settlement against Royal Bank of Scotland for Misleading California's Pension Funds" (22 December 2017), California Attorney General, https://oag.ca.gov/news/press-releases/attorney-general-xavier-becerra-announces-125-million-settlement-against-royal (hereafter RBS California Settlement). Nate Raymond, "RBS to Pay $120 Million to Resolve Connecticut Mortgage Bond Probe", *Reuters* (3 October 2016), www.reuters.com/article/us-royal-bank-scot-settlement/rbs-to-pay-120-million-to-resolve-connecticut-mortgage-bond-probe-idUSKCN1231PQ (hereafter RBS Connecticut Settlement).

[14] RBS New York Settlement, para. 3.

As will become evident in this chapter, the other settlements had larger and much more complex consumer relief, complex in the sense that huge amounts were credited for timeliness and type of relief, meaning that the firm had a reduction in the amount of settlement money paid. The reporting of relief does not separate out first mortgage or second-lien forgiveness from amounts that likely were to be written off for tax reasons already. There are also complex formulas for calculating actual versus credited relief, as is evident in the following discussion about Bank of America and the tables in the Appendix.

1 *National Mortgage Settlements*

In 2012, the largest U.S. mortgage servicers entered into settlements with state and federal authorities. Settlements were made between various State Attorneys General, regulators, and federal agencies and the five largest mortgage servicers: Ally/ResCap, Bank of America, Citigroup, JP Morgan Chase, and Wells Fargo. These settlements were intended to resolve the harms caused by alleged abusive mortgage servicing practices and the processing of foreclosures without properly reviewing the materials associated with the loans.[15] The $25 billion settlement was supposed to provide relief to affected borrowers and to address the lack of consumer protections relating to mortgage servicing.[16]

There are two primary settlement categories: the National Mortgage Settlement (NMS), a joint settlement by all five servicers, comprised of a $5.9 billion direct payment to state and federal governments, and regulators for consumer/state relief; and $19.1 billion aimed at consumer relief to borrowers.[17] The second type of settlements were the RMBS or Origination Settlements (DOJ Settlements) in which the servicers other than Ally Financial, Inc, and additionally a number of smaller servicers, came to independent settlements with the same parties for related issues. In some instances, monitors were appointed to determine compliance with the consumer relief terms of the settlement.[18]

[15] Laurie Goodman and Maia Woluchem, "National Mortgage Settlement: Lessons Learned" (15 April 2014) Urban Institute, www.urban.org/research/publication/national-mortgage-settlement-lessons-learned (hereafter Goodman and Woluchem, "National Mortgage Settlement").

[16] Goodman and Woluchem, "National Mortgage Settlement," 1.

[17] Goodman and Woluchem, "National Mortgage Settlement."

[18] Specifically, Joseph A. Smith of Poyner Spruill LLP was monitor for the NMS and JP Morgan Chase DOJ Settlement, HSBC, Ocwen, and SunTrust; Eric Green of Resolutions LLC was monitor for the Bank of America DOJ Settlement, as well as monitor for Goldman Sachs, Morgan Stanley, and Royal Bank of Scotland; Thomas J. Perrelli of Jenner & Block LLP was monitor for the Citigroup DOJ Settlement; Neil Barofsky of Jenner & Block LLP was the monitor for Credit Suisse; and Michael J. Bresnick of Venable LLP was the monitor for Deutsche Bank. NMS Digital Archive, "Consent Judgments" (2012–2016), NMS, https://scholarship.law.unc.edu/mortgage-settlements/servicing/consent-judgments/ (hereafter NMS Consent Judgments); note that the links to the Wells

2 Understanding the Terms of Settlement

The terminology used in all the settlements is opaque and thus careful attention to terminology is important. For example, the term "actuals" in the representative table in this chapter (Bank of America) and in all the settlements listed in the Appendix are the U.S. dollars that benefited the litigants. In most categories, the actuals are the actual dollars paid out by the bank to the litigants. In some categories, actuals are an estimated future value based on a formula; for example, the "gross relief" provided under a rate reduction is calculated by multiplying the reduction of the interest rate by the unpaid principal balance by the average period in which the reduced interest rate will be in effect (usually around 8 years).[19]

In some categories, actual relief is not actual dollars paid because the credit is entirely a *bonus*. The banks received a flat amount of credit ($10,000 credit) for each loan that they sold to borrowers who would not have qualified for refinancing, but the borrower must repay the loan according to "reasonable terms," so the actual monetary relief to the consumer borrower is $0 even though the loan may be $500,000.

i National Mortgage Settlements – Overview

The NMS Consent Judgment was issued on 4 April 2012 (NMS Consent Judgment), and the settlement was completed by 18 March 2014.[20] The Office of Mortgage Settlement Oversight released a report summarizing the relief actions.[21] According to that report, $50 billion in relief or the equivalent was given to 600,000 families.[22] While significant, the report does not specify what principal forgiveness, as opposed to modifications, were given.

Fargo and Ally judgments are mislabelled in the NMS Digital Archive; and that the terms of the Consent Judgments are identical, including the Exhibits, with the exception of two unique payment amounts: the direct payment at para 3 and the consumer relief requirement at para. 5. NMS Digital Archive, "Final Crediting Report" (18 March 2014), NMS, https://scholarship.law.unc.edu/mortgage-settlements/servicing/publications/30/ (hereafter NMS Final Report). JP Morgan Chase Bank et al, Settlement Agreement Recitals (19 November 2013), paras. 1–2, United States Department of Justice, www.justice.gov/iso/opa/resources/69520131119191246941958.pdf (hereafter JP Morgan Chase DOJ Settlement). Bank of America Settlement Agreement Recitals (21 August 2014), paras. 1–2, Department of Justice, www.justice.gov/iso/opa/resources/3392014829141150385241.pdf (hereafter Bank of America DOJ Settlement). Citigroup Settlement Agreement Recitals (14 July 2014), Department of Justice, www.justice.gov/iso/opa/resources/471201471413656848428.pdf (hereafter Citigroup DOJ Settlement).

[19] Per the NMS Final Report, 9 and the JP Morgan Chase Bank et al, Settlement Agreement Annex 2 Consumer Relief (19 November 2013), Department of Justice, www.justice.gov/iso/opa/resources/6442013111916475916 3425.pdf (hereafter JP Morgan Chase DOJ Settlement, Annex 2).

[20] NMS Consent Judgments and NMS Final Report.

[21] Goodman and Woluchem, "National Mortgage Settlement," 1.

[22] NMS Final Report, 2.

The NMS was divided into two components: relief to the states and borrowers, and a "new regime of servicing standards to be implemented by the servicers."[23] Relief under the NMS was broken into $19.1 billion of financial relief that was to be provided to borrowers by servicers, including short sales, principal reductions, "anti-blight loss mitigation," and refinancing programs for underwater borrowers. Of $5.9 billion in payments to state and federal governments under the NMS, $1.5 billion was to be directed towards cash payments to borrowers who lost their homes through foreclosure.[24]

ii Direct Payment under the NMS Settlement

Details of the NMS direct payment, including terms and breakdown of contributions by category and servicer, can be found in Table 8.1 and in the tables in the Appendix. The only aspect of these settlements that may have benefited consumer borrowers directly is under the category "borrower payments," pursuant to the NMS Consent Judgment.[25] The cumulative total distributed was $1,489,813,925; however, the actual benefit derived by consumers is not available, even from the appointed monitors.[26]

The term "borrower payments" refers to remedial payments that servicers were required to make to certain eligible borrowers pursuant to the NMS Consent Judgment.[27] Primary terms of eligibility for remedial payments were that (1) their homes were finally sold or foreclosed between 1 January 2008 and 31 December 2011, inclusive, and (2) they met the criteria for "covered conduct," where the servicer made certain actions, errors, or omissions relating to residential mortgage loan servicing, foreclosure services, and loan origination services.[28] Both of these conditions had to be established before borrowers could receive any remedial payments.

iii Consumer Relief

There were three categories of consumer relief: mortgage modification, various other creditable items, and the refinancing program.[29] The same mortgage companies that originated and/or serviced the sub-prime loans were entrusted with administering the settlement funds, including determining who was entitled to relief. The firms could write down or write off defaulted mortgages and credit that amount towards the settlement of the litigation. It appears that many of these

23 Goodman and Woluchem, "National Mortgage Settlement," 1.
24 Goodman and Woluchem, "National Mortgage Settlement."
25 NMS Consent Judgments, Exhibit B, para. 2(a).
26 NMS Consent Judgments, para. 4. Several monitors advised us that the precise benefit to consumers could not be accurately calculated, but declined our request to be quoted by name.
27 NMS Consent Judgments Exhibits C and G.
28 NMS Consent Judgments, Exhibit G.
29 NMS Consent Judgments, Exhibit D.

defaulted mortgages would have been written down or written off anyway, in part for the tax benefits. Yet under the terms of the settlement, the firms could claim the dollar value of credit towards the amount they were required to pay. Thus, they could claim substantial portions of the relief by writing off loans that had no value to them. None of this credit provided a benefit to consumer borrowers. Moreover, since the firms in some instances still held interests in the value of the foreclosed homes and the land on which they were situated, they accrued that benefit as well. The financial firms also could write off the loans owned by investors in the securitized portfolios, which meant no financial cost to the mortgage lender or servicer, yet it was credited with the value in terms of the settlement.[30] They did receive credit at a lower rate for non-performing and investor owned loans.

The Urban Institute reports that all of the servicers in the NMS settlement focused at least 30 per cent of their consumer relief on first-lien modifications, as required under the settlement.[31] For all the servicers except Citigroup, the second highest amount of relief was "other creditable items," specifically, short sales and deeds in lieu,[32] which of course, did not prevent any losses of the borrowers' homes.

The settlements have been controversial. Despite the large dollar value, the amounts directed to relief of persons fails to compensate for the harms caused. Only 600,000 families received any compensation, and these people were primarily borrowers still trying to save their homes. There was little for the 17 million families who suffered foreclosure of their home. Since the administrative costs came out of the settlement amount, the amount of relief is even smaller. Investors also were unhappy because 24 per cent of all the crediting came from loans owned by the investors instead of the servicers themselves. For example, Bank of America earned 39 per cent of its credits through this mechanism and JP Morgan Chase earned 29 per cent.[33] Offloading that amount of the settlement costs on to investors does little to sanction the servicers for their misconduct or to create incentives for better conduct going forward.

Second-lien modifications also comprised a sizable amount of relief. Here the Urban Institute observes that all five servicers were credited with writing off seriously delinquent loans, which they would have written off anyway.[34] Significantly, it noted that Citigroup was the only servicer of the five to earn credits from forgiveness in lieu of foreclosure, which was 4.61 per cent of its total credited relief.[35] Since forgiveness of mortgage debt instead of foreclosure is the best strategy for the consumer borrowers, it speaks volumes that the servicers offered so little in this respect.

[30] Goodman and Woluchem, "National Mortgage Settlement," 4.
[31] Goodman and Woluchem, "National Mortgage Settlement," 3.
[32] Goodman and Woluchem, "National Mortgage Settlement."
[33] Goodman and Woluchem, "National Mortgage Settlement," 4.
[34] Goodman and Woluchem, "National Mortgage Settlement," 5.
[35] Goodman and Woluchem, "National Mortgage Settlement."

TABLE 8.1. *Minimum credit requirements, National Mortgage settlement*

	Modification and Other Creditable Items	Refinancing Program	Totals
Ally et al	$185,000,000	$15,000,000	$200,000,000
Bank of America	$7,626,200,000	$948,000,000	$8,574,200,000
Citigroup	$1,411,000,000	$378,000,000	$1,789,000,000
JP Morgan Chase	$3,675,400,000	$537,000,000	$4,212,400,000
Well Fargo	$3,434,000,000	$903,000,000	$4,337,000,000
TOTAL	$16,331,600,000	$2,781,000,000	$19,112,600,000

Note: NMS Final Report, 5; see also NMS Consent Judgments, para. 5, with details of the categories at Exhibit D.

Some complaints about the effectiveness of the settlements include that the consulting firms selected to pay claims took too long to tell borrowers what relief they were entitled to; some of the cheques to these people bounced; some borrowers received cheques in the wrong amounts; some cheques went to incorrect addresses; and some cheques went to people that were already deceased.[36] Moreover, the states received money to direct relief to people who had been foreclosed on, but some states did not direct the monies to that relief and instead used the funds to close budget gaps.[37]

The minimum credit requirements were a negotiated apportioning of the consumer relief under various categories. Table 8.1 sets out the agreements, pulled from the various court documents, followed by discussion of what minimum credit, modification, and "other creditable items" mean.

All relief was subject to certain requirements. For mortgage modifications, the settlement specified that a minimum of 60 per cent of the amount of the settlement had to be directed towards mortgage modifications, a minimum of 30 per cent of the overall amount had to be directed towards first-lien principal forgiveness, and a maximum of 12.5 per cent could be directed towards forbearance forgiveness. In terms of other creditable items, a maximum of 5 per cent could be directed towards "enhanced borrower transitional funds," a maximum of 10 per cent directed towards "foreclosure sale deficiency waivers," and a maximum of 12 per cent towards "anti-blight provisions."[38]

36 Mechele Dickerson, *Homeownership and America's Financial Underclass: Flawed Premises, Broken Promises, New Prescriptions* (Cambridge: *Cambridge University Press*, 2014), 103 (hereafter Dickerson, *Homeownership*).

37 Dickerson, *Homeownership*, 104.

38 NMS Consent Judgments, Exhibits D1-1 through D1-3.

The settlements built in timing incentives, whereby a percentage of the settlement amounts were forgiven if the financial firm complied in a timely manner. For example, the firm received 25 per cent bonus credit off the settlement amount for first- or second-lien principal reduction and refinancing program contributions within twelve months, if it completed 75 per cent of the settlement within two years. Not having to pay one quarter of the settlement was an enormous incentive to move quickly. On the other side, the settlement agreements specified that there would be a 140 per cent penalty for failure to complete the first- or second-lien principal reduction and refinancing program after three years and a 125 per cent penalty for failure to complete the remaining portion after three years. No doubt the threat of penalty also motivated firms to act. Given that the monitors' reports indicate that all the settlement commitments were completed in 2014, the result is that at least 60 per cent of the total credited amounts in the chart, and all the refinancing program, are 25 per cent less than listed.

Mortgage modifications under the settlements were generally in a form that reduced future payments, rather than providing immediate relief, and they often failed to prevent the borrower from losing their home, as seen with short sales, in which the financial firm purchased the house for less than the loan price, with the deficiency in the amount of mortgages forgiven.[39] While the borrower gets relief from the mortgage debt outstanding, the borrower loses her or his home and receives no value for any equity she or he had built up. The settlement allowed the firms to count the entire amount of the mortgage as credit towards the settlement, and the firms also received the income from the short sale to a willing new buyer. The settlement created incentives for lenders to push homeowners out to replace them with people they thought a better credit risk. The lenders then received the credit in the settlement and the purchase price from the new buyer.

Other creditable items were primarily in the form of short sales/deeds in lieu and enhanced borrower transitional funds. "Borrower transitional funds" is funding provided to homeowners affected by short sales and deeds in lieu, facilitating their "exit" from their home. Deficiency waivers were credited where the servicer had the "ability to pursue" a deficiency against a borrower after completion of a foreclosure sale and did not. Ability to pursue did not mean any ability to pay, so written off loans also qualified as credit in the settlement.

Other creditable items included payment to an unrelated second-lien holder, payments of cash for demolition of property, real estate owned (REO) properties donated,[40]

39 NMS Consent Judgments, 4–5 (types of relief are described followed by amounts per lender), 11 (Bank of America), 13 (JP Morgan Chase), 15 (Citigroup), 17 (Ally), and 19 (Wells Fargo).

40 REO refers to credit that is earned for the development of programs that facilitate discount sale or donation of low-value REO properties so that they can be demolished or salvaged for productive use; NMS Consent Judgments, A-25.

and contribution to the borrower HOPE loan portal.[41] "Refinancing" relief was essentially the reduction of the interest rate on underwater performing first- and second-lien loans, as explained by the Settlement Monitor.[42] These loans were granted according to certain guidelines[43] e.g. the Home Affordable Modification Program (HAMP), and borrower eligibility was subject to a number of conditions. These conditions included that:

- Mortgages must be first lien, originated prior to 1 January 2009, with no delinquencies in the past 12 months, no modifications/foreclosure in the past 24 months, and no borrower bankruptcy in the past 24 months.
- The loan must have a minimum loan to value (LTV) of 100 per cent, minimum interest greater of 5.252 per cent or PMMS+100 basis points; and if fixed, adjustable rate mortgage (ARM) or interest only (I/O) mortgage, minimum initial period of five years.[44]
- Mortgages must not be Federal Housing Administration (FHA) or Veterans Administration (VA) mortgages on property outside the United States and Puerto Rico, or on manufactured homes.
- Post-modification, the mortgage must have a maximum unpaid principal balance according to applicable limits, and a minimum difference between pre- and post-interest rate must be either 25 basis points or a $100/month payment reduction.

The complex formula was aimed at setting criteria for eligibility and how relief was to be allocated, but the terms are not easily comprehensible to consumer borrowers. Absent effective legal and financial advice, they would be unlikely to understand their entitlement to any relief and the accuracy of any calculation. The monitors were not implementing the settlement, but only providing general monitoring of the financial firm's implementation.

Different firms adopted different strategies to minimize their losses. Across the five servicers in the NMS, 24 per cent were modifications to investor-owned mortgages, resulting in no costs to the company.[45] While investors were assured that

41 NMS Consent Judgments, Exhibits D and D1. Hope LoanPort is credit earned for the development and implementation of a neutral, nationwide loan portal system to be linked to the bank's primary servicing system to enhance communications with housing counsellors; NMS Consent Judgments, A-25.

42 NMS Final Report, 4–9; see especially page 9 for a general explanation of how the reduction was calculated.

43 Pursuant to the NMS Consent Judgments, Exhibit D.

44 NMS Consent Judgments, I-7. PMMS refers to the Primary Mortgage Market Survey promulgated by the Federal Home Loan Mortgage Corporation to facilitate the reduction of interest rates through loan modification programs.

45 Goodman and Woluchem, "National Mortgage Settlement," 4.

all modifications would pass a net-present-value test, to ensure the modification means less return than a foreclosure, investors have complained that the tests on these proprietary modifications are not transparent and so they cannot assess the reasonableness.[46] The Urban Institute concluded that Bank of America, JP Morgan Chase, and Ally/Recscap disproportionately wrote down investor loans, thus reducing the firm's own costs.[47] It also noted that all five servicers provided a number of second-lien modifications in meeting their obligations, much of which would have been written off anyway, observing that crediting rates may have contributed to this misalignment of incentives.[48]

II THE BANK OF AMERICA SETTLEMENTS

This part describes the Bank of America settlements in detail to give the reader a sense of the complexity of the settlements. The other settlements are summarized in Tables A.1–A.28 in the Appendix.

Between 2014 and 2018, Bank of America and its former and current subsidiaries, including Countrywide Financial Corporation and Merrill Lynch, reached a $34.6 billion settlement to resolve state and federal claims regarding misconduct.[49] Of that amount, almost $16 billion was to be paid to settle federal and state civil claims by various entities related to RMBS, collateralized debt obligations (CDO), and other types of fraud.[50]

1 *The Conduct of Bank of America, Countrywide Financial and Merrill Lynch*

The settlement also resolved the complaint filed against Bank of America in August 2013 by the U.S. Attorney's Office for the Western District of North Carolina concerning an $850 million securitization.[51] Bank of America acknowledged in the settlement that it marketed this securitization as being backed by bank-originated prime mortgages that were underwritten in accordance with its underwriting guidelines, yet Bank of America knew that a significant number of loans in the security were "wholesale" mortgages originated through mortgage brokers.[52] Bank of America acknowledged that based on its internal reporting, such loans were experiencing a marked increase in underwriting defects and a noticeable decrease in performance.[53] Notwithstanding these red flags, the bank sold these RMBS to federally

[46] Goodman and Woluchem, "National Mortgage Settlement."
[47] Goodman and Woluchem, "National Mortgage Settlement," 6.
[48] Goodman and Woluchem, "National Mortgage Settlement," 8.
[49] DOJ, "Bank of America to Pay $16.65 Billion." Bank of America DOJ Settlement, paras. 1–2.
[50] Bank of America DOJ Settlement. See the following discussion for figures on the NMS settlement.
[51] Bank of America DOJ Settlement.
[52] Bank of America DOJ Settlement, Annex 1, 1.
[53] Bank of America DOJ Settlement, 1.

backed financial institutions without conducting any third-party due diligence on the securitized loans and without disclosing key facts to investors in the offering documents filed with the SEC.[54]

A related case concerning the same securitization was filed by the SEC against Bank of America and was resolved as part of this settlement. The settlement also resolved civil investigations related to the packaging, marketing, sale, structuring, and issuance of RMBS, CDO, and the bank's practices concerning the underwriting and origination of mortgage loans.[55] The settlement included a statement of facts in which the bank acknowledged that it sold billions of dollars of RMBS without disclosing to investors the key facts about the quality of the securitized loans. When the RMBS market collapsed, investors, including federally-insured financial institutions, lost billions of dollars. Bank of America also conceded that it originated risky mortgage loans and made misrepresentations about the quality of those loans to Fannie Mae, Freddie Mac, and the FHA.[56] In addition, Countrywide and Bank of America made admissions that they were aware that many of the residential mortgage loans they had made to borrowers were defective, that many of the representations and warranties they made to the government-sponsored entity (GSE) about the quality of the loans were inaccurate, and that they did not self-report to the GSE the mortgage loans they had internally identified as defective.[57]

Countrywide, a subsidiary of Bank of America, represented to investors that it originated loans based on underwriting standards that were designed to ensure that borrowers could repay their loans, although Countrywide had information that certain borrowers had a high probability of defaulting on their loans. Countrywide also admitted concealing from RMBS investors its use of "shadow guidelines" that permitted loans to riskier borrowers than Countrywide's underwriting guidelines would otherwise permit.[58] Countrywide's origination arm was motivated by the "saleability" of loans and Countrywide was willing to originate "exception loans" (i.e. loans that fell outside of its underwriting guidelines) so long as the loans, and the attendant risk, could be sold. Countrywide admitted that it expanded its loan offerings to include "extreme Alt-A" loans, which one Countrywide executive described as a hazardous product, but it failed to tell RMBS investors that these loans were being originated outside of Countrywide's underwriting guidelines.[59] Countrywide knew that these exception loans were performing far worse than loans originated

[54] Bank of America DOJ Settlement, 2.

[55] DOJ, "Bank of America to Pay $16.65 Billion."

[56] This conduct was also subject to a settlement of another proceeding brought by the FHFA against Bank of America: Federal Housing Finance Agency, "FHFA Announces $9.3 Billion Settlement With Bank of America Corporation" (26 March 2014), www.fhfa.gov/Media/PublicAffairs/Pages/FHFA-Announces-$9-3-Billion-Settlement-With-Bank-of-America-Corporation.aspx.

[57] DOJ, "Bank of America to Pay $16.65 Billion."

[58] Bank of America DOJ Settlement, Annex 1, 7.

[59] Bank of America DOJ Settlement, Annex 1, 11.

without exceptions, although it never disclosed this fact to investors. "For years, Countrywide and Bank of America unloaded toxic mortgage loans on the government sponsored enterprises Fannie Mae and Freddie Mac with false representations that the loans were quality investments," said U.S. Attorney Preet Bharara for the Southern District of New York in announcing the settlement.[60]

Investigation into misrepresentations made by Merrill Lynch to investors in 72 RMBS throughout 2006 and 2007 found that Merrill Lynch regularly told investors that the loans it was securitizing were made to borrowers who were able and likely to repay their debts.[61] Merrill Lynch made these representations even though it knew that a significant number of the loans had material underwriting and compliance defects, including as many as 55 per cent in a single pool.[62] Merrill Lynch also disregarded its own due diligence and securitized loans that the due diligence vendors had identified as defective and rarely reviewed loans to ensure that the defects observed in the samples were not present throughout the remainder of the pools.[63] In the period prior to the financial crisis, Merrill Lynch bought more and more mortgage loans, packaged them together, and sold them as securities, even when the bank knew a substantial number of those loans were defective.[64] U.S. Attorney Anne M. Tompkins for the Western District of North Carolina said "Even reputable institutions like Bank of America caved to the pernicious forces of greed and cut corners, putting profits ahead of their customers."[65]

As part of the settlement, Bank of America agreed to pay $15.6 billion to resolve federal and state civil claims by various entities related to RMBS, including $5 billion civil penalty under the Financial Institutions Reform, Recovery, and Enforcement Act (FIRREA) and $2.05 billion for federal fraud claims related to origination and sale of mortgages.[66] The amount of $1.03 billion was to be paid to settle federal and state securities claims by the Federal Deposit Insurance Corporation (FDIC), and $135.84 million was to be paid to settle claims by the SEC.[67]

The U.S. Attorney's Office for the Eastern District of New York, together with the U.S. Department of Housing and Urban Development (HUD) found that Bank of America knowingly caused the FHA to insure loans that were not eligible for FHA mortgage insurance, and as a result, HUD incurred hundreds of millions of dollars of losses.[68] "Bank of America failed to make accurate and complete disclosure to

60 DOJ, "Bank of America to Pay $16.65 Billion."
61 Bank of America DOJ Settlement, Annex 1, 2.
62 Bank of America DOJ Settlement, Annex 1, 4.
63 Bank of America DOJ Settlement, Annex 1, 4.
64 Bank of America DOJ Settlement, Annex 1, 4.
65 DOJ, "Bank of America to Pay $16.65 Billion."
66 DOJ, "Bank of America to Pay $16.65 Billion" and Bank of America DOJ Settlement, para. 1.
67 Bank of America DOJ Settlement, paras. C-D and 1–2.
68 DOJ, "Bank of America to Pay $16.65 Billion."

investors and its illegal conduct kept investors in the dark."[69] Rhea Kemble Dignam, Regional Director of the SEC's Atlanta office observed: "Requiring an admission of wrongdoing as part of Bank of America's agreement to resolve the SEC charges filed today provides an additional level of accountability for its violation of the federal securities laws."[70]

Notice the language in Bank of America's statement of facts, and in the settlements and the statements by the DOJ and the State Attorneys General. The conduct denounced is the misrepresentation to capital markets investors and state authorities. While Bank of America agreed to relief for mortgage borrowers, there was no admission of culpability in its predatory lending activities. Where Bank of America's statement of facts suggests misconduct in giving the mortgages, the language is decidedly designed to make it sound as if the borrowers were the problem. Examples include the following:

> During the period May 1, 2009 through March 31, 2012, Bank of America underwrote and insured FHA insurance loans to borrowers who did not qualify for loans under the criteria set by HUD. In certain cases, Bank of America, *inter alia*, did not properly verify borrowers' income, did not adequately verify the source of gift funds borrowers used to make the statutory minimum down payment, and approved borrowers that may have lacked the ability to make monthly mortgage payments.[71]
>
> ...
>
> When using the CLUES [Countrywide Loan Underwriting Expert System] system,[72] Bank of America sometimes changed an applicant's financial information and then re-submitted the loan multiple times in an effort to get a CLUES "accept." For example, in at least one instance, Bank of America's underwriter attempted to get a CLUES accept rating more than forty times and in other cases underwriters regularly changed the relevant data and re-submitted the loans through CLUES more than twenty times. In a case note, one underwriter characterized what she was doing as trying to "trick" the CLUES system into giving an "accept" rating.[73]

There are no admissions of fraud or misrepresentation to consumer borrowers in the statements of fact for the settlement of litigation. There is no mention of targeting African Americans.

[69] DOJ, "Bank of America to Pay $16.65 Billion."
[70] DOJ, "Bank of America to Pay $16.65 Billion."
[71] Bank of America DOJ Settlement, Annex 1, 16.
[72] Bank of America used an automated underwriting system referred to as the Countrywide Loan Underwriting Expert System. Bank of America DOJ Settlement, Annex 1, 26.
[73] Bank of America DOJ Settlement, Annex 1, 27.

2 *Relief to Bank of America's Consumer Borrowers*

Under the terms of the DOJ settlement, Bank of America agreed to earn $7 billion credit in the form of consumer relief. That relief was to include principal reduction loan modifications that result in numerous homeowners no longer being underwater on their mortgages, new loans to credit worthy borrowers struggling to get a loan, donations to assist communities in recovering from the financial crisis, and financing for affordable rental housing.[74]

An independent monitor was appointed to determine whether Bank of America was satisfying its obligations.[75] The Monitor of the Bank of America Settlement filed his Final Consumer Relief Report and Certificate of Compliance on 17 June 2014. The settlements with Bank of America are set out in Tables 8.2–8.4 below; but they require considerable explanation, which follows.

Slightly easier might be the visual in Figure 8.2. It gives a visual representation of all the settlements and how the money was allocated, although some figures were not publicly disclosed, such as the extent to which first-lien forgiveness was actual forgiveness as opposed to a form of modification. In some instances, the public disclosures reveal that there was no value to mortgage borrowers. Figure 8.2 visually shows how most went to penalties, investors, and "credit towards" consumer relief rather than giving a detailed breakdown of all relief.

The Monitor for the Bank of America settlement was quoted by *Marketplace* as follows:

> "As big as this program was, and this was the largest program of its kind, in a sense it's still insufficient for the harm caused by the mortgage crisis and the bursting of the housing bubble," Green said, reflecting of the settlement's impact.
>
> He estimates about 150,000 people may have received some form of aid through the settlement. "What's more," he added. "This settlement happened in 2014 and the bank completed its consumer relief obligations in two years instead of the four years it had. It did it very fast, but it was still too late for too many people."[76]

[74] DOJ, "Bank of America to Pay $16.65 Billion." For the terms of consumer relief, see Bank of America Settlement Agreement Annex 2 Consumer Relief (21 August 2014), Department of Justice, www.justice.gov/iso/opa/resources/8492014829141239967961.pdf (hereafter Bank of America DOJ Settlement, Annex 2).

[75] Bank of America DOJ Settlement.

[76] Tracey Samuelson, "Following the Money: What Happened to a Nearly $17 Billion Bank Settlement?" *Marketplace* (19 September 2018), www.marketplace.org/2018/09/19/17-billion-bank-settlement-where-did-money-go/ (hereafter Samuelson, "Following the Money").

TABLE 8.2. *Monetary penalties and consumer relief credit, Bank of America settlements*

MONETARY PENALTIES – Actual Payments by Bank	
U.S Department of Justice (DOJ) and Independent Settlements[1]	
U.S. Treasury General Fund, pursuant to the FIRREA	$5,000,000,000
National Credit Union Administration (NCUA)	$165,000,000
Federal Deposit Insurance Corporation (FDIC)	$1,031,000,000
Federal Housing Finance Agency (FHFA)	$5,828,883,292
Federal Housing Administration (FHA)	$2,050,000,000
U.S Securities Exchange Commission (SEC)	$135,840,000
State of New York	$300,000,000
State of California	$300,000,000
State of Illinois	$200,000,000
State of Delaware	$45,000,000
State of Maryland	$75,000,000
Commonwealth of Kentucky	$23,000,000
Tax Relief	$490,160,000
Subtotal – DOJ Settlement Monetary Penalties	$15,643,883,292
National Mortgage Settlement (NMS)[2]	
Subtotal – NMS Monetary Penalties	$2,382,415,075
TOTAL MONETARY PENALTIES – ACTUALS	$18,026,298,367
CONSUMER RELIEF OBLIGATIONS – Credit Adjusted Per Settlement Terms	
DOJ Credit Earned	$7,005,373,353
NMS Credit Earned	$9,610,418,492
TOTAL CONSUMER RELIEF CREDIT EARNED	$16,615,791,845
TOTAL SETTLEMENT (Monetary Penalties + Consumer Relief Credit)	$34,642,090,212

1 Bank of America DOJ Settlement, para. 3 (complete breakdown of monetary penalties paid to the listed litigants). See also NCUA Settlements; Federal Housing Finance Agency, "Fact Sheet: FHFA Final Update on Private Label Securities Actions" (17 September 2018), FHFA, www.fhfa.gov/Media/PublicAffairs/Pages/FHFA-Final-Update-on-Private-Label-Securities-Actions-9172018.aspx (hereafter FHFA Private Label Securities Actions).

2 *United States of America, et al* v *Bank of America Corp, et al*, No 12-0361 (RMC), Document 11 Consent Judgment (DDC filed 4 April 2012), para. 3, National Mortgage Settlements, https://scholarship.law.unc.edu/cgi/viewcontent.cgi?article=1000&context=mortgage-settlements (hereafter Bank of America NMS Consent Judgment).

TABLE 8.3. *Bank of America – U.S. Department of Justice settlement – consumer relief*

Type of Relief	Credit Earned[1]	Actual Relief
First-Lien Principal Forgiveness	$3,031,552,456	$1,253,550,146
Principal Forgiveness of Forbearance	$565,181,334	$444,444,974
First-Lien Forbearance	$170,422,953	$675,515,566
Second-Lien Extinguishment	$76,521,480	$67,274,425
Junior Liens – Unsecured Principal Forgiveness Extinguishment	$1,534,521,483	$3,402,660,476
Subtotal – Modifications/Forgiveness	$5,378,199,706	$5,843,445,587
Subtotal – Low- to Moderate-Income Lending and Other Lending	$416,999,000	$0[2]
Principal Extinguishment	$296,594,622	$258,040,915
Donations of Mortgages and REO Properties	$68,703,427	$60,507,316
Donations for Rehabilitation/Maintenance of Donated Property	$14,094,058	$6,150,188
Donations to Community Development Funds and HUD Approved Housing Counselling Agencies	$156,283,564	$70,000,000
Donations for Legal Assistance	$69,000,000	$30,000,000
Subtotal – Community Reinvestment and Neighbourhood Stabilization	$604,675,671	$424,698,419
Subtotal – Affordable Rental Housing	$441,865,938	$109,565,000
Subtotal – Additional Credit for Exceeding Minimum	$163,633,038	$0
Total Consumer Relief	$7,005,373,353	$6,377,709,006

1 Eric D. Green, Monitor, "Bank of America DOJ Final Report" (17 March 2017) (on file with author), 43 (hereafter Bank of America DOJ Final Report).

2 The bank earned $417 billion credit at a rate of $10,000 credit, plus incentive credit, for each purchase money loan sold to credit worthy borrowers in hardest hit areas, who lost a primary residence to foreclosure or short sale or who were first time LMI homebuyers with an income at or below the area median income. The value of the loans is not included as actual relief because the borrowers were required to repay the loans with interest. See Bank of America DOJ Settlement, Annex 2, 6.

TABLE 8.4. *Bank of America National Mortgage settlement – consumer relief*

Type of Relief	Credit Earned	Actual Relief
First-Lien Mortgage Modifications	$3,365,196,272	$4,869,347,311
Second-Lien Portfolio Modifications	$2,210,934,257	$9,655,705,939
Subtotal – Modifications/Forgiveness	$5,576,130,529	$14,525,053,250
Subtotal – Refinancing Program	$1,013,769,682	$811,006,154
Enhanced Borrower Transitional Funds	$68,349,672	$162,354,522
Short Sales/Deeds in Lieu	$2,952,168,609	$11,846,419,147
Subtotal – Other Creditable Items	$3,020,518,281	$12,008,773,669
Total Consumer Relief	$9,610,418,492	$27,344,833,073

Note: NMS Final Report, 11.

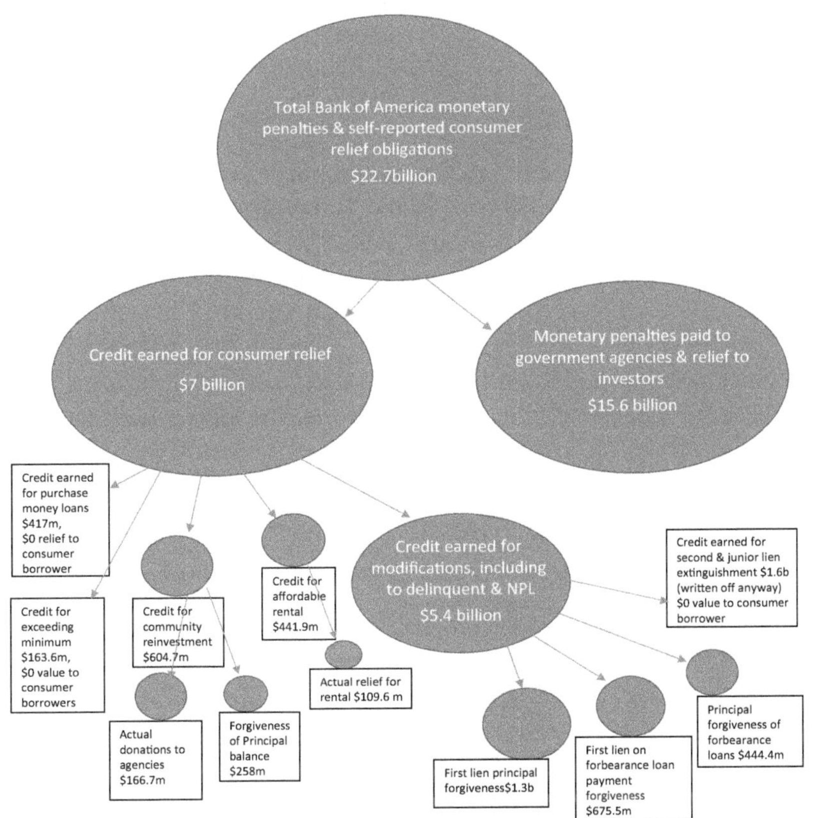

FIGURE 8.2. Bank of America settlements with the U.S. Department of Justice and States Attorneys General, as of July 2019 (not including NMS)

The monetary penalties were actual dollars paid directly to the litigants pursuant to the terms of each settlement.[77] Bank of America paid a total of $18 billion in monetary penalties under its settlement with the DOJ.

The National Mortgage Settlement was a cumulative settlement between the five largest mortgage servicers: Ally, Bank of America, Citigroup, JP Morgan Chase, and Wells Fargo.[78] For the monetary penalties, each bank paid an amount into escrow; Bank of America contributed $2.38 billion.[79] The total $5 billion[80] paid by the five firms was divided among the recipients as follows:

- Federal Payment Settlement Amounts: $684.1 million was distributed to the FHA Capital Reserve, Veterans Housing Benefit Program Fund, or otherwise as directed by the DOJ;[81] and $227.7 million was to resolve five civil settlements.[82]
- State Payment Settlement Amounts: $2.54 billion was distributed among states that were parties to the settlement.[83]
- Other Payments: $1.49 billion, including the cost of distribution, was distributed as remedial payment to borrowers whose homes were finally sold or foreclosed between 1 January 2008 and 31 December 2011, inclusive.[84] This distribution included borrowers who were eligible to submit claims for harm allegedly arising under Covered Conduct;[85] and borrowers who otherwise met certain criteria set forth by the State members of the Monitoring Committee.[86] An amount of $15 million was provided to the Financial Services and Consumer Protection Enforcement, Education and Training Fund, to be administered by the National Association of Attorneys General.[87] $10 million was provided to the Ameriquest Financial Services Fund for reimbursement of costs and fees during the investigation of the case.[88] $65 million was provided to the Conference of State Bank Supervisors, including $15 million to establish the State Financial Regulation Fund, and $1 million to each state financial regulator of the States party to the agreement.[89] Finally, interest earned on funds while they were held

77 Bank of America DOJ Settlement, para. 3.

78 Joseph A. Smith, Monitor, "Initial Report" (29 August 2012), 3, National Mortgage Settlements, https://scholarship.law.unc.edu/cgi/viewcontent.cgi?article=1034&context=mortgage-settlements (hereafter NMS Initial Report).

79 Bank of America NMS Consent Judgment, para. 3.

80 NMS Initial Report, 2.

81 Bank of America NMS Consent Judgment, Exhibit B, para. 1(a)(i).

82 Bank of America NMS Consent Judgment, Exhibit B, para. 1(a)(ii).

83 Bank of America NMS Consent Judgment, Exhibit B, para. 1(b), Exhibit B-1 (complete breakdown of state payments), Exhibit B-2 (breakdown described).

84 Bank of America NMS Consent Judgment, para. 4, Exhibit B, para. 2(a), and Exhibit C.

85 Bank of America NMS Consent Judgment, para. 4 and Exhibit G.

86 Bank of America NMS Consent Judgment, para. 4.

87 Bank of America NMS Consent Judgment, Exhibit B, para. 2(b).

88 Bank of America NMS Consent Judgment, Exhibit B, para. I(c).

89 Bank of America NMS Consent Judgment, Exhibit B, para. 2(d).

by the escrow agent were to be used for administrative costs and expenses, or for any other housing related purpose, at the discretion of the State members of the Monitoring Committee.[90]

The credited amount for consumer relief was derived from the actual relief the bank provided to borrowers; the Monitor took each dollar of actual relief and made various upward and downward adjustments to determine how much of each dollar would be counted towards the total consumer relief credit according to the terms of the settlement as outlined below.[91]

The terms placed minimum and maximum relief obligations on certain categories of relief:[92]

- Minimum $2.15 billion credit earned in first-lien principal forgiveness.
- Minimum 50 per cent of modifications earned in hardest hit areas.[93]
- Minimum $50 million credit earned in donations to community development funds.
- Minimum $30 million credit earned in donations for legal assistance.
- Minimum $20 million credit earned in donations to HUD approved housing counselling agencies.
- Credit equivalent of minimum $100 million lost on loans for affordable rental housing.
- Maximum $2.5 billion credit earned in second-lien extinguishment and junior liens.
- Maximum $2.5 billion credit earned in principal extinguishment.
- Maximum $3 billion credit earned cumulatively in principal and second-lien extinguishment and junior liens.
- Minimum $500 million credit earned in each of California and New York.
- Minimum $150 million credit earned in Delaware, Maryland, and Kentucky, cumulatively.
- Minimum $100 million credit earned in Illinois.

These minimums and maximums make calculating the relief and tracking the dollars and credits very difficult. Credit in this context is essentially dollars off the settlement amounts for offering relief. For example, Bank of America earned $3 billion credit for $1.3 billion actual relief in the form of first-lien principal forgiveness, due to the addition of 150 per cent early incentive credit for forgiveness completed by 31 May 2015, 115 per cent early incentive credit for forgiveness completed by 31 August 2015, 115 per cent bonus credit for amounts in excess of state minimums for each participating state, 115–125 per cent bonus credit depending on the amount of incremental LTV

90 Bank of America NMS Consent Judgment, Exhibit B, para. 3.

91 For detail on the adjustments applied, see Bank of America DOJ Settlement, Annex 2.

92 Bank of America DOJ Final Report, 17–18, and 19 (with additional minimums in California and New York); see also Bank of America DOJ Final Report, 9.

93 Bank of America DOJ Settlement, Annex 2, 3.

reduction, and 115 per cent bonus credit for relief in hardest hit areas for amounts in excess of the minimum requirement (earned cumulatively).[94]

Settlement terms also provided various ways for Bank of America to earn credit (dollars subtracted from settlement amounts) for modifications. The complex formula was aimed at granting more credit for certain types of relief:

- $1,253,550,146 actual relief provided to consumers in first-lien principal forgiveness, earned $3,031,552,456 credit.[95] Subject to certain eligibility requirements to ensure the necessity and sufficiency of relief, credit was earned as follows:[96]
    - $1 forgiveness = $1 credit, or
    - $1 forgiveness = $1.75 credit on FHA-insured or VA-guaranteed loans, or
    - $1 forgiveness = $0.50 credit on loans serviced by Bank of America but owned by other investors, or
    - $1 investor incentive payments = $1 credit when paid consistently with those in the HAMP; and
    - 150 per cent credit for forgiveness completed by 31 May 2015, and
    - 115 per cent credit for incremental LTV reduction between 90 and 100 per cent, and
    - 120 per cent credit for incremental LTV reduction between 76 and 90 per cent, and
    - 125 per cent credit for entire amount of principal forgiven if post-modification LTV equal to or less than 75 per cent, and
    - 115 per cent credit for the incremental relief in hardest hit areas beyond the first 50 per cent of modifications in those areas
- $444,444,974 actual relief provided to consumers in principal forgiveness of forbearance, earned $565,181,334 credit.[97] Subject to certain eligibility requirements to ensure the necessity and sufficiency of relief, credit was earned as follows:[98]
    - $1 forgiveness = $1 credit, or
    - $1 forgiveness = $0.50 credit on loans serviced by Bank of America but owned by other investors, or
    - $1 investor incentive payments = $1 credit when paid consistently with those in HAMP; and
    - 115 per cent credit for incremental LTV reduction below 100 per cent, and

[94] Bank of America DOJ Settlement, Annex 2, 2–4, 9. Bank of America DOJ Final Report, 16–18, 51; in the report, "forgiveness" is the equivalent of actual relief: "Forgiveness is the amount prior to any adjustments required to determine credit," according to Thomas Cooper of BDO USA LLP, email message to MaryGrace Johnstone, 16 May 2019.

[95] Bank of America DOJ Final Report, 51.

[96] Bank of America DOJ Settlement, Annex 2, 2–4.

[97] Bank of America DOJ Final Report, 57.

[98] Bank of America DOJ Settlement, Annex 2, 2–4.

  - 115 per cent credit for the incremental relief in hardest hit areas beyond the first 50 per cent of modifications in those areas

- $675,515,566 actual relief provided to consumers in payment forgiveness of first-lien forbearance, earned $170,422,953 credit.[99] Subject to certain eligibility requirements to ensure the necessity and sufficiency of relief, credit was earned as follows:[100]

  - Actual relief calculated as a product of the loan's pre-modification rate, forborne unpaid principal balance, and an average life of 8 years; or
  - $1 forgiveness = $0.50 credit on loans serviced by Bank of America but owned by other investors, or
  - $1 investor incentive payments = $1 credit when paid consistently with those in HAMP; and
  - 115 per cent credit for the incremental relief in hardest hit areas beyond the first 50 per cent of modifications in those areas.

- $67,274,425 actual relief provided to consumers in second-lien extinguishments, earned $76,521,480 credit.[101] Subject to certain eligibility requirements to ensure the necessity and sufficiency of relief, credit was earned as follows:[102]

  - 115 per cent credit for the incremental relief in hardest hit areas beyond the first 50 per cent of modifications in those areas, and
  - $1 investor incentive payments = $1 credit when paid consistently with those in HAMP; or
  - For performing loans (90 days or less past due):
    i. $1 forgiveness = $1 credit, or
    ii. $1 forgiveness = $0.50 credit on loans serviced by Bank of America but owned by other investors, or
  - For seriously delinquent and non-performing loans (more than 90 days past due) $1 forgiveness = $0.40 credit.

- $3,402,660,476 in relief provided to consumers in junior liens and outstanding unsecured mortgage debt principal forgiveness and extinguishment, earned $1,534,521,483 credit.[103] Subject to certain eligibility requirements to ensure the necessity and sufficiency of relief, credit was earned as follows:[104]

  - $1 forgiveness = $0.40 credit, and
  - 115 per cent credit for the incremental relief in hardest hit areas beyond the first 50 per cent of modifications in those areas.

99 Bank of America DOJ Final Report, 71.
100 Bank of America DOJ Settlement, Annex 2, 2–4.
101 Bank of America DOJ Final Report, 72.
102 Bank of America DOJ Settlement, Annex 2, 4–5.
103 Bank of America DOJ Final Report, 76.
104 Bank of America DOJ Settlement, Annex 2, 5–6.

Still with us? The settlement is profoundly lacking in transparency, and is really beyond the capacity of many professionals, let alone individuals victimized by the predatory lending. Moreover, the bank earned $416,999,000 credit for selling loans to eligible borrowers;[105] that is almost $417 million knocked off the settlement costs to Bank of America for one measure. A $10,000 credit was earned for each purchase money loan to credit worthy borrowers in hardest hit areas who lost a primary residence to foreclosure or short sale, or who were first time low-to-moderate-income (LMI) homebuyers with an income at or below the area median income.[106]

Similarly, the part of the settlement Bank of America agreed to for "Community Reinvestment and Neighborhood Stabilization" is less than transparent in terms of the actual relief given and the amount of dollars forgiven off the settlement amount. An amount of $258,040,915 in actual relief was to be provided to consumers in forgiveness of principal associated with a property where foreclosure was not pursued and the liens released, earning $296,594,622 credit at a rate of $1 forgiveness = $1 credit.[107] $60,507,316 actual relief was to be provided in donations of REO properties to accepting municipalities, land banks or non-profits, or to servicemembers with disabilities or relatives of deceased servicemembers, earning $68,703,427 credit at a rate of $1 property value or reasonable rehabilitation costs = $1 credit.[108] $6,150,188 actual relief was to be provided in donations to non-profits to facilitate the reduction, rehabilitation, or maintenance of abandoned and uninhabitable residential properties donated under the previous category, earning $14,094,058 credit at a rate of $1 payment = $2 credit.[109] An amount of $70 million in relief was to be provided in donations to capitalize certified Community Development Financial Institutions, land banks subject to state or local regulation, or community development funds administered by non-profits or local governments, and HUD approved housing counselling agencies, earning $156,283,564 credit at a rate of $1 payment = $2 credit.[110] $30 million actual relief was to be provided to consumers in donations for legal assistance, earning $69 million credit at a rate of $1 payment = $2 credit.[111]

Community investment may benefit African Americans and other people of colour. For example, an apartment building under construction in the Bronx that will rent units at below-market rates received $4 million through the Bank of America settlement, which helped to close a funding gap, and for its contribution, the bank was able to claim nearly $15 million of settlement credit, more than three times what it actually gave.[112]

Then there were settlement amounts to be provided to consumers for affordable rental housing (not ownership). It included $109,565,000 actual relief to be provided

[105] Bank of America DOJ Final Report, 93.
[106] Bank of America DOJ Settlement, Annex 2, 6.
[107] Bank of America DOJ Final Report 104; Bank of America DOJ Settlement, Annex 2, 6.
[108] Bank of America DOJ Final Report, 115; Bank of America DOJ Settlement, Annex 2, 6.
[109] Bank of America DOJ Final Report, 116; Bank of America DOJ Settlement, Annex 2, 7.
[110] Bank of America DOJ Final Report, 120; Bank of America DOJ Settlement, Annex 2, 7.
[111] Bank of America DOJ Final Report, 121; Bank of America DOJ Settlement, Annex 2, 7.
[112] Samuelson, "Following the Money."

to consumers in affordable rental housing, earning Bank of America $441,865,938 credit towards the settlement amount,[113] according to the following terms:[114] $1 loss = $3.25 credit, or $1 loss = $3.75 credit for critical need family housing developments, subject to certain requirements to ensure that size and affordability meet a reasonable standard.[115] The bank earned $163,633,038 bonus credit for exceeding its overall minimum requirement, and $490,160,000 for payment of consumer tax liability.[116]

The staggering accounting continues.

Bank of America's NMS settlement included a consumer relief component. The bank was required to earn a minimum of $7.6 billion in consumer relief credit, as well as $948 million in refinancing relief credit.[117] The credit was earned according to another set of terms that placed maximum and minimum relief obligations on certain categories of relief:[118]

- At least 30 per cent of credited consumer relief was to come from first-lien principal forgiveness, and at least 60 per cent was to come from a combination of first- and second-lien modifications.
- Maximum 12.5 per cent for forgiveness of forbearance amounts on existing modifications.
- Maximum 5 per cent for enhanced borrower transitional funds.

Overall Bank of America received 25 per cent credit for any first- or second-lien principal reduction and amounts credited pursuant to the refinancing program within 12 months of the start date.[119] Then there was credit by category. For first-lien mortgage modifications: $4,869,347,311 actual relief was provided to consumers, earning $3,365,196,272 credit. First-lien principal forgiveness modification, earned subject to certain eligibility requirements to ensure the necessity and sufficiency of relief, at a rate of $1 write-down = $1 credit on loans with LTV at or below 175 per cent, or $1 write-down = $0.50 credit for the portion of principal forgiven over LTV 175 per cent.[120] First-lien principal forgiveness modification on investor loans (forgiveness by an investor, not the bank) was provided at a rate of $1 write-down = $0.45 credit.

113 Bank of America DOJ Final Report, 122.

114 Bank of America DOJ Settlement, Annex 2, 8.

115 Bank of America DOJ Final Report, 8, 33; and Bank of America DOJ Settlement, para. 2 (pursuant to the terms at Annex 3).

116 Bank of America DOJ Final Report, 8, 33 and Bank of America DOJ Settlement, para. 2, (pursuant to the terms at Annex 3).

117 Bank of America NMS Consent Judgment, para. 5.

118 Bank of America NMS Consent Judgment, Exhibits D1-1 through D1-3.

119 Bank of America NMS Consent Judgment, Exhibit D-11.

120 Bank of America NMS Consent Judgment, Exhibits D1-1, D1-2. Forgiveness of forbearance amounts on existing modifications at a rate of $1 write-down = $0.40 credit. Earned forgiveness over a period of no greater than three years, provided consistent with PRA, at a rate of: $1 write-down = $0.85 credit on loans with LTV at or below 175 per cent, or $1 write-down = $0.45 credit for the portion of principal forgiven over LTV 175 per cent.

Then there was "Earned forgiveness over a period of no greater than 3 years on investor loans, provided it was consistent with PRA."[121]

Ultimately, Bank of America reported that 39 per cent of its consumer relief was first-lien modifications.[122] These modifications largely took the form of reducing monthly payments to 31 per cent debt to income ratio. It reported that 26 per cent of its consumer relief was second-lien modifications.[123] For second-lien portfolio modifications – $9,655,705,939 relief was provided to consumers in second-lien portfolio modifications, which earned $2,210,934,257 credit in different ways, as set out in the footnote.[124]

Under the refinancing program, $811,006,154 actual relief was to be provided to eligible borrowers, subject to certain conditions to ensure the necessity of relief, which earned Bank of America $1,013,769,682 credit, calculated as the difference between the pre-existing rate and the offered interest rate times the unpaid principal balance times a multiplier based on the life of the loan (5 or 8 years).[125]

At this point, the court-appointed monitor is likely reeling, let alone the average reader or person seeking relief under this settlement. But there is more.

Bank of America agreed to pay $162,354,522 in actual relief to consumers in transitional funds to homeowners in connection with a short sale or deed in lieu of foreclosure to homeowners,[126] which earned the bank $68,349,672 credit.[127] Finally, Bank of America agreed to an amount of $11,846,419,147 in respect of short sales and deeds in lieu of foreclosure, which also earned the Bank $2,952,168,609 in credit towards the settlement.[128]

[121] Bank of America NMS Consent Judgment, Exhibit D1-2, at a rate of: $1 write-down = $0.40 credit on loans with LTV at or below 175 per cent, or $1 write-down = $0.20 credit for the portion of principal forgiven over LTV 175 per cent.

[122] Goodman and Woluchem, "National Mortgage Settlement," 3.

[123] Goodman and Woluchem, "National Mortgage Settlement."

[124] Bank of America NMS Consent Judgment, Exhibits D1-2, D1-3. Earned credit for (1) performing second liens (0–90 days delinquent), at a rate of 1. $1 write-down = $0.90 credit, (2) seriously delinquent second liens (91–179 days delinquent), at a rate of $1 write-down = $0.50 credit, and (3) non-performing second liens (180+ days delinquent), at a rate of $1 write-down = $0.10 credit.

[125] Bank of America NMS Consent Judgment, Exhibits D-9 through D-11.

[126] Bank of America NMS Consent Judgment, Exhibit D-6.

[127] Bank of America NMS Consent Judgment, Exhibit D1-3. Earned credit for (1) payments by the bank, at a rate of $1 payment = $1 credit for amounts over $1,500 and (2) non-GSE payments by investors, at a rate of $1 payment = $0.45 credit for amounts of $1,500.

[128] Bank of America NMS Consent Judgment, Exhibits D-6, D-7. Recall that both these exit strategies leave the borrower without their home. The payment was subject to certain conditions to ensure the necessity and sufficiency of relief, earned credit for (1) payments by the bank to unrelated second-lien holders for the release of the lien at a rate of $1 payment = $1 credit, (2) forgiveness of deficiency and release on first-lien portfolio loans by the bank at a rate of $1 write-down = $0.45 credit, (3) forgiveness of deficiency and release on first-lien portfolio loans by investors at a rate of $1 write-down = $0.20 credit, (4) forgiveness of deficiency and release on performing second-lien portfolio loans at a rate of $1 write-down = $0.90 credit, (5) forgiveness of deficiency and release on seriously delinquent second-lien portfolio loans at a rate of $1 write-down = $0.50 credit, and (6) forgiveness of deficiency and release on non-performing second-lien portfolio loans at a rate of $1 write-down = $0.10 credit. Bank of America NMS Consent Judgment, Exhibits D1-3, D1-4.

Dickerson reports that Bank of America agreed to the settlement, but then resisted efforts to pay borrowers for improperly foreclosing on their homes.[129] Bank of America also resisted paying by requiring victimized borrowers to provide documentation that was not required by the terms of the settlement, and by failing to compile a list of borrowers entitled to be paid out more than a year after the settlement.[130]

Significantly, Bank of America earned 39 per cent of its credits by modifying investor-owned loans instead of mortgages it held, thus passing off the costs directly to investors.[131]

We purposely set out the Bank of America settlement in detail, so that the reader could appreciate how the actual relief to consumer borrowers and the amounts actually paid by the bank have been obfuscated, which resulted in little accountability. Even the court-appointed monitor could not advise on the actual amount of principal forgiveness that was given, if any, or actual dollars that went directly to harmed consumer borrowers. That said, it is evident that some relief flowed to mortgage borrowers, particularly individuals still fighting to stay in their homes, in the form of interest relief, on average reduced from 5.4 per cent to 2.1 per cent for Bank of America borrowers.[132] What is not at all clear is whether, and how much, relief was given to the millions who had already lost their homes. The Monitor's final report is more than 1,400 pages, and while it provides details by region and type of credited consumer relief, it obfuscates amounts that Bank of America would have written off for tax reasons, which were amounts the bank would have loaned anyway in a continuing market, and amounts of relief, if any, to foreclosed on homeowners.

Next, we very briefly summarize some of the other settlements, including the conduct to which the defendant stipulated, without the same detail as the Bank of America settlement. However, for the tenacious reader, that detail can be found in the Appendix tables.

III THE CITIGROUP SETTLEMENTS

Citigroup settled lawsuits for $9.3 billion with the DOJ and the Attorneys General of the states of California, Delaware, Illinois, New York, and Massachusetts, for violations of federal laws in connection with Citigroup RMBS and CDO.[133]

[129] Dickerson, *Homeownership*, 103.

[130] Dickerson, *Homeownership*.

[131] Goodman and Woluchem, "National Mortgage Settlement," 4.

[132] Goodman and Woluchem, "National Mortgage Settlement."

[133] Citigroup DOJ Settlement, paras. 1–2. Department of Justice, "Justice Department, Federal and State Partners Secure Record $7 Billion Global Settlement with Citigroup for Misleading Investors about Securities Containing Toxic Mortgages" (14 July 2014), www.justice.gov/opa/pr/justice-department-federal-and-state-partners-secure-record-7-billion-global-settlement (hereafter DOJ, "Record $7 Billion Global Settlement with Citigroup"). NCUA Settlements. FHFA Private Label Securities Actions. U.S. Securities and Exchange Commission, "Financial Crisis Enforcement Actions: SEC Monetary Recoveries" (19 October 2011), SEC, www.sec.gov/news/press/2011/2011-214-chart-recoveries.pdf (hereafter SEC Monetary Recoveries).

The settlements came after 50 subpoenas to Citigroup, trustees, servicers, providers, and their employees, and after collecting nearly 25 million documents relating to RMBS issued or underwritten by Citigroup.[134] The breakdown of the settlements is set out in the Appendix, Tables A.6 and A.7, and the NMS settlement with Citigroup is in Table A.8.

1 *The Conduct of Citigroup*

The federal and state civil claims related to Citigroup's conduct in the packaging, securitization, marketing, and issuance of RMBS prior to January 2009. The resolution included a $4 billion civil penalty under the FIRREA.[135]

The settlement includes an agreed upon statement of facts in which Citigroup acknowledged that it made serious misrepresentations to RMBS investors about the quality of the mortgage loans it securitized and sold to investors.[136] Citigroup securitized and sold RMBS with underlying mortgage loans that it knew had material defects. Despite internal emails expressing concerns about the quality of the loans, Citigroup nevertheless securitized the loan pools containing defective loans and sold the resulting RMBS to investors for billions of dollars.[137] "This conduct, along with similar conduct by other banks that bundled defective and toxic loans into securities and misled investors who purchased those securities, contributed to the financial crisis."[138]

2 *Relief to Citigroup's Consumer Borrowers*

The consumer relief Citigroup was to pay was to be directed towards: loan modification for underwater homeowners, refinancing for distressed borrowers, down payment and closing cost assistance to homebuyers, and donations to organizations assisting communities in redevelopment and affordable rental housing for low-income families in high-cost areas.[139] Although the settlement agreement and its Annex are not particularly transparent, it appears that whether consumer borrowers

[134] DOJ, "Record $7 Billion Global Settlement with Citigroup."

[135] DOJ, "Record $7 Billion Global Settlement with Citigroup." For a breakdown, see Table A.6 of the Appendix.

[136] Citigroup DOJ Settlement Agreement Annex 1 Statement of Facts (14 July 2014), Department of Justice, www.justice.gov/iso/opa/resources/558201471413645397758.pdf (hereafter Citigroup DOJ Settlement Annex 1).

[137] Citigroup DOJ Settlement Annex 1.

[138] DOJ, "Record $7 Billion Global Settlement with Citigroup."

[139] Citigroup DOJ Settlement Agreement Annex 2 Consumer Relief (14 July 2014), 2, Department of Justice, www.justice.gov/iso/opa/resources/649201471413721380969.pdf (hereafter Citigroup DOJ Settlement, Annex 2).

received relief still depended on them going through the modification procedures that have all the problems discussed previously.[140]

The consumer relief under the settlement agreement between Citigroup and the DOJ is ongoing and merits tracking going forward. As reported by the monitor in its tenth report, by May 2019, Citigroup has made $1.2 billion in modifications and other relief, for a credit of $1.9 billion;[141] the actual amount excludes rate reductions, which were not included in the monitor's reports.[142] Citigroup has given $729.5 million in mortgage modifications and forgiveness, although the breakdown of modification versus forgiveness is not available.[143]

The monitor reported that an additional $241.8 million was given in principal forgiveness without foreclosure, which is very important because it meant consumer borrowers could stay in their homes, unlike a considerable amount of deficiency forgiveness where the borrowers lost their homes.[144] An amount of $50 million was given in donations, earning Citigroup a credit of $115 million.[145] Citigroup had also given $194 million in rental housing, earning it credit towards the settlement of $759.7 million.[146] Citigroup thus gave $486 million in community investment and neighbourhood stabilization for a credit towards the settlement of $1.15 billion. All the breakdown is available in Table A.7 of Appendix.

IV THE GOLDMAN SACHS SETTLEMENT

Goldman, Sachs & Co, through certain of its affiliates, securitized thousands of prime, Alt-A, and sub-prime mortgage loans and sold the resulting RMBS for tens of billions of dollars to investors.[147] In 2016, the DOJ, along with federal and

140 Monitor was Thomas J. Perrelli, with any costs associated with the monitor borne by Citigroup. Citigroup DOJ Settlement, Annex 2, para. 2.

141 Thomas J. Perrelli, Monitor, "Citi Monitorship: Tenth Report" (May 2019), 14, Citigroup Monitorship, www.citigroupmonitorship.com/wp-content/uploads/2019/05/CitigroupMonitor_10thReport.pdf (hereafter Citigroup DOJ Tenth Report).

142 Thomas J. Perrelli, Monitor, "Citi Monitorship: Seventh Report" (June 2017), 3–8, Citigroup Monitorship, www.citigroupmonitorship.com/wp-content/uploads/2017/06/Citi_Monitorship_seventh_report_6-15-2017.pdf (hereafter Citigroup DOJ Seventh Report).

143 Citigroup DOJ Tenth Report, 9. Thomas J. Perrelli, Monitor, "Citi Monitorship: Eighth Report" (April 2018), 11–12, Citigroup Monitorship, www.citigroupmonitorship.com/wp-content/uploads/2018/04/CitigroupMonitor_8thReport_FINAL-3-red.pdf (hereafter Citigroup DOJ Eighth Report). Thomas J. Perrelli, Monitor, "Citi Monitorship: Ninth Report" (November 2018), 25–6, Citigroup Monitorship, www.citigroupmonitorship.com/wp-content/uploads/2018/11/citigroupmonitor_9threport_final.pdf (hereafter Citigroup DOJ Ninth Report).

144 Citigroup DOJ Ninth Report, 19–21.

145 Thomas J. Perrelli, Monitor, "Citi Monitorship: Fifth Report" (June 2016), 11, Citigroup Monitorship, www.citigroupmonitorship.com/wp-content/uploads/2016/06/Citi_Monitorship_fifth_report_6-27-2016.pdf (hereafter Citigroup DOJ Fifth Report).

146 Citigroup DOJ Seventh Report.

147 Goldman Sachs Settlement Agreement Annex 1 Statement of Facts (11 April 2016), Department of Justice, www.justice.gov/opa/file/839901/download (hereafter Goldman Sachs DOJ Settlement, Annex 1).

state partners, reached a $6.3 billion settlement with Goldman Sachs related to the firm's conduct in the packaging, securitization, marketing, sale, and issuance of RMBS between 2005 and 2007.[148] The settlement required Goldman Sachs to pay almost $2.4 billion in a civil penalty under the FIRREA.[149] Goldman was also to pay $875 million to resolve claims by other federal entities and state claims.[150] Goldman Sachs was also required to earn a minimum of $1.8 billion in consumer relief credit,[151] according to the terms of the settlement in Tables A.12 and A.13 of the Appendix.

Goldman Sachs engaged in serious misconduct in falsely assuring investors that securities it sold were backed by sound mortgages when it knew that they were full of mortgages that were likely to fail.[152] The agreed-upon statement of facts describes how Goldman Sachs made false and misleading representations to prospective investors about the characteristics of the loans it securitized and the ways in which Goldman would protect investors in its RMBS from harm.[153] Goldman admitted that it "received information indicating that, for certain loan pools, significant percentages of the loans reviewed did not conform to the representations made to investors about the pools of loans to be securitized."[154] Goldman admitted that even when its due diligence on samples of loans from those pools revealed significant problems, it failed to identify and eliminate loans with credit exceptions, thus issuing sub-prime RMBS that included loans originated with "extremely aggressive underwriting."[155] Goldman admitted that it "received certain negative information regarding the originators' business practices," most of which was not disclosed to investors.[156]

[148] Department of Justice, "Goldman Sachs Agrees to Pay More than $5 Billion in Connection with Its Sale of Residential Mortgage Backed Securities" (11 April 2016), www.justice.gov/opa/pr/goldman-sachs-agrees-pay-more-5-billion-connection-its-sale-residential-mortgage-backed (hereafter DOJ, "Goldman Sachs Agrees to Pay More than $5 Billion"). Goldman Sachs additionally came to independent settlements with the FHFA for $1.2 billion and the SEC for $550 million. FHFA Private Label Securities Actions. SEC Monetary Recoveries. *Securities and Exchange Commission* v *Goldman, Sachs & Co and Fabrice Tourre*, No 10-3229 Consent Judgment (SDNY filed 15 July 2010), para. 2, SEC, www.sec.gov/litigation/litreleases/2010/consent-pr2010-123.pdf (hereafter Goldman Sachs SEC Consent Judgment).

[149] Goldman Sachs SEC Consent Judgment.

[150] Goldman Sachs SEC Consent Judgment.

[151] Goldman Sachs Settlement Agreement Recitals (11 April 2016), para. 2, Department of Justice, www.justice.gov/opa/file/839891/download (hereafter Goldman Sachs DOJ Settlement). For the terms of consumer relief, see Goldman Sachs Settlement Agreement Annex 2 Consumer Relief (11 April 2016), Department of Justice, www.justice.gov/opa/file/839906/download (hereafter Goldman Sachs DOJ Settlement, Annex 2).

[152] Goldman Sachs DOJ Settlement, Annex 2.

[153] Goldman Sachs DOJ Settlement, Annex 1.

[154] Goldman Sachs DOJ Settlement, Annex 1, 1.

[155] Goldman Sachs DOJ Settlement, Annex 1, 6, 9.

[156] Goldman Sachs DOJ Settlement, Annex 1, 9.

Goldman further admitted that Fremont was viewed by Goldman Sachs as a key originator and top priority client; and that while it recognized in mid-2006 that Fremont's level of early payment defaults was increasing, and while there were early indicators of fraud, Goldman Sachs continued to purchase loan pools from Fremont.[157]

The DOJ observed:

> [Goldman Sachs] knowingly put investors at risk and in so doing contributed significantly to the financial crisis.... Goldman took $10 billion in TARP [Troubled Asset Relief Program] bailout funds knowing that it had fraudulently misrepresented to investors the quality of residential mortgages bundled into mortgage backed securities," said Special Inspector General Christy Goldsmith Romero for TARP. "Many of these toxic securities were traded in a taxpayer funded bailout program that was designed to unlock frozen credit markets during the crisis. While crisis investigations take time, SIGTARP [Special Inspector General for the Troubled Asset Relief Program] is committed to working with our law enforcement partners to protect taxpayers and bring accountability and justice."[158]

V THE JP MORGAN CHASE & CO SETTLEMENTS

JP Morgan Chase & Co settled with the DOJ, federal, and state authorities for $18.8 billion to resolve civil claims arising out of the packaging, marketing, sale, and issuance of RMBS by JP Morgan, Bear Stearns, and Washington Mutual prior to January 2009.[159]

JP Morgan Chase admitted in the settlement statement of facts that it regularly represented to RMBS investors that the mortgage loans in various securities complied with underwriting guidelines, even though its employees knew they did not, and that it allowed the loans to be securitized and sold without disclosing this information to investors.[160] JP Morgan Chase sold securities knowing that many of the loans backing those certificates were toxic; the settlement announcement observing that credit unions, banks, and other investors victimized by the firm continue to struggle with losses they suffered as a result.

157 Goldman Sachs DOJ Settlement, Annex 1, 9–10.

158 DOJ, "Goldman Sachs Agrees to Pay More than $5 Billion."

159 Department of Justice, "Justice Department, Federal and State Partners Secure Record $13 Billion Global Settlement with JPMorgan for Misleading Investors about Securities Containing Toxic Mortgages" (19 November 2013), www.justice.gov/opa/pr/justice-department-federal-and-state-partners-secure-record-13-billion-global-settlement (hereafter DOJ, "Record Settlement with JPMorgan").

160 JP Morgan Chase et al, Settlement Agreement Annex 1 Statement of Facts (19 November 2013), Department of Justice, www.justice.gov/iso/opa/resources/94320131119151031990622.pdf (hereafter JP Morgan Chase DOJ Settlement, Annex 1).

Of the $9.2 billion in monetary penalties, JP Morgan was to pay $2 billion as a civil penalty to settle DOJ claims under FIRREA, $1.4 billion to settle securities claims by the National Credit Union Administration, $4 billion to settle federal and state claims by FHFA, $298.9 million to settle claims by the State of California, $19.7 million to settle claims by the State of Delaware, $100 million to settle claims by the State of Illinois, $34.4 million to settle claims by the Commonwealth of Massachusetts, and $613 million to settle claims by the State of New York.[161] JP Morgan Chase had profited by giving California's pension funds incomplete information about mortgage investments, and "the settlement returns the money to California's pension funds that JP Morgan wrongfully took from them."[162] $515.4 million of the amount settled was to provide a significant recovery for six FDIC receiverships, thus securing the funds for return to the Deposit Insurance Fund, uninsured depositors, and creditors of failed banks.[163]

1 *Relief to JP Morgan Chase & Co Mortgage Borrowers*

JP Morgan agreed to pay a credited amount of $4 billion in the form of relief to aid consumers harmed by the unlawful conduct of JP Morgan Chase, Bear Stearns, and Washington Mutual.[164] The relief was to include principal forgiveness, loan modification, targeted originations, and efforts to reduce blight. Table A.17 in the Appendix indicates that JP Morgan gave $1.28 billion in first-lien principal forgiveness, including $231.48 million in principal forgiveness or forbearance, $1.08 billion in first-lien forbearance, $737 million in second-lien principal forgiveness and extinguishment; $1.1 billion in rate reduction, and $15.77 billion credit in purchase money loans sold to credit worthy, low to moderate income borrowers in disaster areas.[165] The $15.77 billion is not actual relief and can be quite misleading as JP Morgan Chase received $10,000 credit for each purchase money loan sold, plus 125 per cent credit for hardest hit areas and 115 per cent early incentive credit, an example of a category where the actual relief is effectively $0.

2 *Consumer Relief under the NMS*

JP Morgan Chase's NMS settlement also included a consumer relief component, as set out in Table A.18 of the Appendix. The bank was required to earn a minimum

[161] DOJ, "Record Settlement with JP Morgan."
[162] DOJ, "Record Settlement with JP Morgan."
[163] DOJ, "Record Settlement with JP Morgan."
[164] DOJ, "Record Settlement with JP Morgan."
[165] Joseph A. Smith Jr, Monitor, "Chase RMBS Settlement: Consumer Relief through March 31, 2016" (2016), 3, 8, National Mortgage Settlements, https://scholarship.law.unc.edu/cgi/viewcontent.cgi?article=1178&context=mortgage-settlements (hereafter JP Morgan Chase DOJ Final Report).

of $3,675,400,000 in consumer relief credit, as well as $537 million in refinancing relief.[166] JP Morgan reported providing $2.9 billion actual relief to consumers in first-lien mortgage modifications,[167] and $2.2 billion in second-lien portfolio modification.[168] An amount of $492,247,276 in actual relief was provided to eligible borrowers under the refinancing program, subject to certain conditions.[169] There was also $170 million in "enhanced borrower transitional funds" provided to borrowers in connection with a short sale or deed in lieu of foreclosure to borrowers.[170] Note in each of these figures in Table A.18 of the Appendix the amount credit that was given as opposed to actual payments. So, for example, of the $5.6 billion in relief for short sale or deed in lieu transactions, what is referred to as "dignified exit from a property,"[171] the bank got $1.5 billion in settlement credit.[172]

Another category allocated $15.9 million in relief to consumers in payments to unrelated second-lien holders to facilitate short sales or deeds in lieu of foreclosure and releases of liens for which JP Morgan Chase earned $9.8 million in credit towards the settlement.[173] The rate at which credit was provided is not available.

VI THE WELLS FARGO SETTLEMENTS

Wells Fargo & Company and its wholly owned subsidiary, Wells Fargo Bank, NA, and that subsidiary's wholly owned subsidiary, Wells Fargo Asset Securities Corporation, and its mortgage division, Wells Fargo Home Mortgage, settled civil

166 *United States of America, et al* v *Bank of America Corp, et al*, No 12-0361 (RMC), Consent Judgment (DDC filed 4 April 2012), para. 5, National Mortgage Settlements, https://scholarship.law.unc.edu/cgi/viewcontent.cgi?article=1001&context=mortgage-settlements (hereafter JP Morgan Chase NMS Consent Judgment). NMS Final Report, 5.

167 NMS Final Report, 13, earning $1,851,496,721 credit as set out in Table A.18 of the Appendix and per the terms in JP Morgan Chase NMS Consent Judgment, Exhibits D1-1, D1-2.

168 NMS Final Report, 13, earning $308,672,792 credit as per the terms in JP Morgan Chase NMS Consent Judgment, Exhibits D1-2, D1-3.

169 NMS Final Report, 13, earning $623,424,705 credit as per the terms in JP Morgan Chase NMS Consent Judgment, Exhibits D-9 through D-11. Subject to certain conditions to ensure the necessity and sufficiency of relief; credit was calculated as the difference between the pre-existing rate and the offered interest rate, times the unpaid principal balance, times a multiplier based on the life of the loan (5 or 8 years).

170 NMS Final Report, 13, earning $136,957,159 credit.

171 NMS Final Report, 13 as per the terms in JP Morgan Chase NMS Consent Judgment, Exhibits D-6, D-7, D1-3, D1-4, earning $1,495,692,789 credit, subject to certain conditions to ensure the necessity and sufficiency of relief.

172 NMS Final Report.

173 NMS Final Report, 13 as per the terms in JP Morgan Chase NMS Consent Judgment, Exhibit D1-3. There was also an Anti-Blight Provision of $37,499,126 actual relief provided to consumers and credit earned in REO properties donated at a rate of $1 payment = $1 credit. NMS Final Report, 13 as per the terms in JP Morgan Chase NMS Consent Judgment, Exhibits D1-4, D1-5.

lawsuits alleging misconduct related to mortgage lending and securitization.[174] The mortgage division was the second largest originator of residential mortgage loans in the United States.[175] The Wells Fargo settlements amounted to $9.26 billion.[176] As will be discussed in part III of this chapter, in 2012, Wells Fargo also settled a case prosecuted by the Fair Lending Unit in the Civil Rights Division's Housing and Civil Enforcement Section, U.S. Attorney's Office for the District of Columbia, and the DOJ for its targeting of African Americans for sub-prime loans.[177]

1 *Wells Fargo's Conduct*

In 2018, the DOJ announced that Wells Fargo Bank, NA and its affiliates would pay a civil penalty of $2.09 billion under the FIRREA based on the bank's alleged origination and sale of residential mortgage loans that it knew contained misstated income information.[178] It noted that investors, including federally insured financial institutions, suffered billions of dollars in losses from investing in RMBS containing loans originated by Wells Fargo.[179]

The settlement recitals stated that from 2005 to 2007 Wells Fargo engaged in the following conduct:

1. As Wells Fargo saw its retail market share of loan origination decrease, it aimed to double its production of subprime and Alt-A loans from 2005 to 2006. Towards that end, Wells Fargo took a number of steps. First, it instituted a campaign in 2005 called "Courageous Underwriting," a philosophy that encouraged Wells Fargo's underwriters to take more chances and be more aggressive in approving loans that were outside of Wells Fargo's underwriting guidelines. Also, in 2005, Wells Fargo changed the way that certain of its credit risk professionals were compensated, adding new categories of compensation for "Market Share Growth" and "Competitive Positioning to Drive Volume."

[174] Wells Fargo Settlement Agreement Recitals (1 August 2018), para. 1, Department of Justice, www.justice.gov/opa/press-release/file/1084371/download (hereafter Wells Fargo DOJ Settlement).

[175] Wells Fargo DOJ Settlement, para. B.

[176] The DOJ, along with other members of Obama's Financial Fraud Enforcement Task Force's RMBS Working Group. The figures are set out in Table A.27 of the Appendix.

[177] Department of Justice, "Justice Department Reaches Settlement with Wells Fargo Resulting in More Than $175 Million in Relief for Homeowners to Resolve Fair Lending Claims" (12 July 2012), www.justice.gov/opa/pr/justice-department-reaches-settlement-wells-fargo-resulting-more-175-million-relief (hereafter DOJ, "Wells Fargo Fair Lending Claims").

[178] Department of Justice, "Wells Fargo Agrees to Pay $2.09 Billion Penalty for Allegedly Misrepresenting Quality of Loans Used in Residential Mortgage-Backed Securities" (1 August 2018), www.justice.gov/opa/pr/wells-fargo-agrees-pay-209-billion-penalty-allegedly-misrepresenting-quality-loans-used (hereafter DOJ, "Wells Fargo Agrees to Pay $2.09 Billion").

[179] DOJ, "Wells Fargo Agrees to Pay $2.09 Billion."

2. Wells Fargo then sought to and did expand its stated income loan programs and loosened requirements for these loans, including allowing less money down, lower credit scores, blemished credit histories, higher debt-to-income ratios, and lower asset and reserve requirements, as well as offering an interest-only payment option.[180]

Despite its knowledge that a substantial portion of its stated income loans contained misstated income, Wells Fargo failed to disclose this information and instead reported to investors false debt-to-income ratios in connection with the loans it sold.[181] Wells Fargo also took steps to protect itself from losses by screening out many of its stated income loans from its own portfolio of loans that it held for investment and selling them on to other investors.[182] There was no admission of fraud in the 2018 settlement.

2 *Wells Fargo's Relief to Mortgage Borrowers*

Wells Fargo sold at least 73,539 stated-income loans that were included in RMBS between 2005 to 2007, and nearly half of those loans had defaulted at the time of the settlement, resulting in billions of dollars in losses to investors,[183] but also massive losses to the homeowners, a figure not included in the DOJ settlement.

According to the court-appointed monitor, Wells Fargo gave actual relief as follows: $1.76 billion in first-lien mortgage modifications; $1.6 billion in second-lien portfolio modifications; $1.1 billion refinancing; $12.68 million in enhanced borrower transition funds; $3.0 billion in short sales and deed in lieu; $9.13 million in payments to unrelated second-lien holders; $82,463 in cash payments for demolition of property; $393 million in deficiency waivers;[184] and $4 million in REO properties donated.[185] Under the NMS, Wells Fargo reported that it paid $7.9 billion in consumer relief, thus earning $4.57 billion credit off the settlement.[186] As with the other files, relief included first- and second-lien mortgage modifications, short sale or deed in lieu of foreclosure, and refinancing.

180 Wells Fargo DOJ Settlement, 3.
181 Wells Fargo DOJ Settlement, 5.
182 Wells Fargo DOJ Settlement, 6.
183 DOJ, "Wells Fargo Agrees to Pay $2.09 Billion."
184 Where the bank could have pursued the deficiency but did not after completion of the foreclosure sale; NMS Final Report, 19, as set out in Table A.28 of the Appendix and per the terms in *United States of America et al* v *Bank of America Corp et al*, No 12-0361 (RMC), Document 14 Consent Judgment (DDC filed 4 April 2012), Exhibits D-7, D1-4, D1-5, National Mortgage Settlement Digital Archive, www.nationalmortgagesettlement.com/files/Consent_Judgment_WellsFargo-4-11-12.pdf (hereafter Wells Fargo NMS Consent Judgment).
185 Wells Fargo DOJ Settlement, 19.
186 NMS Final Report, 9. Figures in Table A.28 of the Appendix.

VII THE OCWEN FINANCIAL CORPORATION SETTLEMENT

Ocwen Financial Corporation settled civil law enforcement lawsuits for $2.2 billion in a Joint State-Federal Settlement with 49 U.S. states and the Consumer Financial Protection Bureau in December 2013.[187] The settlement addressed mortgage servicing misconduct by Atlanta-based Ocwen and two companies it acquired – Homeward Residential Inc and Litton Home Servicing LP. The misconduct resulted in premature and unauthorized foreclosures, violations of homeowners' rights and protections, and the use of false and deceptive documents and affidavits, including robo-signing. An independent monitor was appointed to observe implementation of the settlement to ensure compliance. However, the agreement specifies that because of the complexity of the mortgage market and the agreement, which would span a three-year period, Ocwen was to contact borrowers directly regarding principal reductions. A settlement administrator was to contact qualified borrowers associated with foreclosed loans regarding cash payments. Here again, it seems counterintuitive that the firm that caused the harms to mortgage borrowers would be left to contact them again to determine relief.

In 2017, Ocwen settled two more class action suits regarding its disclosure misconduct in the way that it valued and recorded financial transactions.[188] The SEC had prohibited Ocwen from acquiring any new residential mortgage servicing rights until 30 April 2018, but lifted the cease and desist orders when the suits were settled. In July 2017, Ocwen announced it would pay $49 million to settle a class action lawsuit claiming that the company misstated its net income in 2013 and 2014, including agreeing to give $7 million in company stock (2.5 million shares) to the plaintiffs.[189] Note that the conduct was occurring well after the financial meltdown and well after the implementation of the Dodd-Frank Act, yet another indicator that regulatory oversight of misconduct is still ineffective.

According to the consumer relief component of the settlement, Ocwen was required to earn a minimum of $2 billion credit in first-lien principal reduction

[187] *Consumer Financial Protection Bureau et al* v *Ocwen Financial Corporation and Ocwen Loan Servicing, LLC*, No 13-02025 (RMC), Document 12 Consent Judgment (DDC filed 26 February 2014), paras. 4–5, Department of Justice, Ocwen Consent Judgment (26 February 2014), paras. 4–5, National Ocwen Settlement, www.nationalocwensettlement.com/Portals/0/Documents/ConsentJudgement.pdf (hereafter Ocwen Consent Judgment). See also Illinois Attorney General, "$2.1 Billion Settlement with Sixth Mortgage Servicer over Foreclosure Abuses" (19 December 2013), http://illinoisattorneygeneral.gov/pressroom/2013_12/20131219.html.

[188] Ben Lane, "Ocwen reaches mortgage servicing settlements with two more states" *Housing Wire* (27 December 2017), www.housingwire.com/articles/42155-ocwen-reaches-mortgage-servicing-settlements-with-two-more-states.

[189] Ben Lane, "Ocwen to pay $49 million to settle class action lawsuit over restated financials" *Housing Wire* (20 July 2017), www.housingwire.com/articles/40735-ocwen-to-pay-49-million-to-settle-class-action-lawsuit-over-restated-financials (hereafter Lane, "Ocwen to pay $49 million").

and $127 million credit relief associated with 183,984 foreclosed loans.[190] The credited amount was derived from the actual relief the bank provided to borrowers. According to the terms of the settlement, the monitor took each dollar of actual relief and made various upward and downward adjustments to determine how much of each dollar would be counted towards the total consumer relief credit.[191] Actuals are not available for this settlement.[192] As with Bank of America, the complex formula determining actual relief to be paid is in the Appendix.

The Urban Institute observed that investors who had Ocwen's RMBS carried the vast majority of Ocwen's settlement financial burden, as it primarily modified the loans owned by investors.[193]

VIII THE DEUTSCHE BANK SETTLEMENTS

Deutsche Bank settled lawsuits for $7.6 billion with the DOJ and the Obama Task Force with payments to the U.S Department of the Treasury, FDIC, SEC, and other organizations as set out in Table A.11 of the Appendix.[194] The settlement

190 Lane, "Ocwen to pay $49 million", para. 5. Table A.21 of the Appendix. See also Montana Department of Justice, "Attorney General Fox Announces $2.1 Billion Joint State-Federal Settlement with Ocwen Mortgage" (20 December 2013), https://dojmt.gov/attorney-general-fox-announces-2-1-billion-joint-state-federal-settlement-with-ocwen-mortgage/#more-30699. The Ocwen settlement does not grant immunity from criminal offenses and would not affect criminal prosecutions. The agreement does not prevent homeowners or investors from pursuing individual, institutional, or class action civil cases. The agreement also preserves the authority of state attorneys general and federal agencies to investigate and pursue other aspects of the mortgage crisis, including securities cases.

191 For detail on the adjustments applied, see *Consumer Financial Protection Bureau et al* v *Ocwen Financial Corporation and Ocwen Loan Servicing, LLC*, No 13-02025 (RMC), Documents 1–6 Exhibits D and D1 (DDC filed 19 December 2013), Court Listener, www.courtlistener.com/recap/gov.uscourts.dcd.163745.1.6.pdf (hereafter Ocwen Consent Judgment, Exhibits D and D1).

192 *Consumer Financial Protection Bureau, et al* v *Ocwen Financial Corporation and Ocwen Loan Servicing, LLC*, No 13-02025 (RMC), Document 38 Final Consumer Relief Report (DDC filed 28 April 2016), Schedule Y, National Mortgage Settlements, https://scholarship.law.unc.edu/cgi/viewcontent.cgi?article=1118&context=mortgage-settlements (hereafter Ocwen Final Report). Schedule Y is not in the public record.

193 Goodman and Woluchem, "National Mortgage Settlement," 7.

194 Deutsche Bank Settlement Agreement Recitals (17 January 2017), paras 1–2, United States Department of Justice, www.justice.gov/opa/press-release/file/928096/download (hereafter Deutsche Bank DOJ Settlement). NCUA Settlements. FDIC Settlement. Deutsche Bank FHFA Settlement Agreement (19 December 2013), 2, FHFA, www.fhfa.gov/Media/PublicAffairs/Documents/FHFADeutscheBankSettlementAgreement122013.pdf (hereafter Deutsche Bank FHFA Settlement). Deutsche Bank Multi-State Settlement Agreement (25 October 2017), para. 71, NY Government, https://ag.ny.gov/sites/default/files/db_settlement_agreement_signed.pdf (hereafter Deutsche Bank State Settlement). *In the Matter of Deutsche Bank Securities Inc and Benjamin Solomon*, No 3-18367, Order (SEC filed 12 February 2018), para 22, SEC, www.sec.gov/litigation/admin/2018/34-82686.pdf (hereafter Deutsche Bank SEC Settlement). Department of Justice, "Deutsche Bank Agrees to

resolved federal civil claims that Deutsche Bank misled investors in the packaging, securitization, marketing, sale, and issuance of RMBS. Deutsche Bank securitized over 400,000 sub-prime and Alt-A residential mortgages in RMBS between 2006 and 2007.

In the Statement of Facts accompanying the settlement, Deutsche Bank admitted misconduct that ran 73 pages of the document, including intentionally making false representations and omitting material information from disclosures to investors about key characteristics of mortgage loans that it securitized in certain RMBS. The bank also concealed from investors that it knew that the value of the properties securing the loans was far below the value reflected by the originator's appraisal.[195] Deutsche Bank's due diligence reports from 2006 to 2007 revealed poor and fraudulent underwriting practices of mortgage loan originators, which it did not disclose to investors. Deutsche Bank admitted that it tolerated misrepresentation from mortgage loan originators with "misdirected lending practices," such as "marking out" borrowers' pay stubs in order to state, often fraudulently, that the borrowers had higher incomes.[196] Deutsche Bank often allowed large originators, such as Countrywide, to add or substitute significant numbers of loans to the pool after it had completed its due diligence, many of which Deutsche Bank knew would not meet its representations to investors.[197] Deutsche Bank admitted that despite its knowledge of pervasive appraisal fraud in the mortgage industry, it generally conducted no valuation diligence whatsoever for RMBS when it did not retain any risk of its own.[198]

$2.2 billion credit was earned for consumer relief and the remaining $5.4 billion went to investors and monetary penalties.

IX THE CREDIT SUISSE SETTLEMENTS

The DOJ settled with Credit Suisse in the amount of $5.28 billion related to Credit Suisse's conduct in the packaging, securitization, issuance, marketing, and sale of RMBS between 2005 and 2007.[199] The settlement requires Credit Suisse

Pay $7.2 Billion for Misleading Investors in its Sale of Residential Mortgage-Backed Securities" (11 February 2016), www.justice.gov/opa/pr/deutsche-bank-agrees-pay-72-billion-misleading-investors-its-sale-residential-mortgage-backed (hereafter DOJ, "Deutsche Bank Agrees to Pay $7.2 Billion").

195 Deutsche Bank Statement of Facts (17 January 2017), United States Department of Justice, www.justice.gov/opa/press-release/file/927271/download (hereafter Deutsche Bank State of Facts).

196 Deutsche Bank State of Facts, 11.

197 Deutsche Bank State of Facts, 21.

198 Deutsche Bank State of Facts, 31.

199 Department of Justice, "Credit Suisse Agrees to Pay $5.28 Billion in Connection with its Sale of Residential Mortgage-Backed Securities" (18 January 2017), www.justice.gov/opa/pr/credit-suisse-agrees-pay-528-billion-connection-its-sale-residential-mortgage-backed (hereafter DOJ, "Credit Suisse Agrees to Pay $5.28 Billion"). Credit Suisse Settlement Agreement Annex 1 Statement of Facts (18 January 2017), www.justice.gov/opa/press-release/file/928496/download.

to pay $2.48 billion as a civil penalty under the FIRREA, in addition to paying $1.5 billion to other members of Obama's Financial Fraud Enforcement Task Force's RMBS Working Group under independent settlements.[200]

1 *Credit Suisse's Conduct*

In the settlement, the bank conceded that it knew it was peddling investments containing loans that were likely to fail. The settlement includes a statement of facts to which Credit Suisse agreed:[201]

> Credit Suisse repeatedly received information indicating that many of the loans reviewed did not conform to the representations that would be made by Credit Suisse to investors about the loans to be securitized. It has acknowledged that in many cases, it purchased and securitized loans into its RMBS that "did not comply with applicable underwriting guidelines and lacked sufficient factors" and/or "w[ere] not originated in compliance with applicable laws and regulations." Credit Suisse employees even referred to some loans they securitized as "bad loans," "complete crap" and "utter complete garbage".
>
> Credit Suisse acquired some of the mortgage loans it securitized by buying, from other loan originators, "Bulk" packages containing numerous loans. For example, in December 2006, Credit Suisse purchased a "Bulk" pool of approximately 10,000 loans originated by Countrywide Home Loans. Credit Suisse selected fewer than 10 percent of these loans for due diligence review. "Reports from Credit Suisse's due diligence vendors showed that approximately 85 percent of the loans in this sample violated Countrywide's underwriting guidelines and/or applicable law," but "Credit Suisse securitized over half of the loans into various RMBS it then sold to investors." Credit Suisse did not review the remaining unsampled 90 percent of the pool to determine whether those loans had similar problems. Instead, it "securitized an additional $1.5 billion worth of unsampled—and therefore unreviewed—loans from this pool into various RMBS it then sold to investors."...
>
> Credit Suisse has acknowledged that it also "received reports from vendors that it might have been acquiring and securitizing loans with inflated appraisals" and that its approach for reviewing the property values associated with the mortgage loans "could lead to the acceptance of inflated appraisals." In August 2006, a Credit Suisse manager wrote to two senior traders, "How would investors react if we say

[200] DOJ, "Credit Suisse Agrees to Pay $5.28 Billion." Credit Suisse Settlement Agreement Recitals (18 January 2017), para 1–2, United States Department of Justice, www.justice.gov/opa/press-release/file/928521/download (hereafter Credit Suisse DOJ Settlement). NCUA Settlements. FDIC Settlement. FHFA Private Label Securities Actions; see also Credit Suisse FHFA Settlement Agreement (21 March 2014), www.fhfa.gov/Media/PublicAffairs/PublicAffairsDocuments/CORRECTEDCreditSuisseSettlement032114F.pdf. *In the Matter of Credit Suisse Securities et al*, No 3-15098, Order (SEC filed 16 November 2012), IV(c) and (d), SEC, www.sec.gov/litigation/admin/2012/33-9368.pdf (hereafter Credit Suisse SEC Settlement). See Table A.9 in the Appendix.

[201] DOJ, "Credit Suisse Agrees to Pay $5.28 Billion."

that 20 percent of the pool have values off by 15 percent? If we are comfortable buying these loans, we should be comfortable telling investors."

The FDIC, as receiver for five failed banks, in 2016 announced a $190 million settlement of RMBS claims with Credit Suisse Securities (USA) LLC, Barclays Capital Inc, BNP Paribas Securities Corporation, Deutsche Bank Securities Inc, Edward D. Jones & Co, Goldman, Sachs & Co, RBS Securities Inc, and UBS Securities LLC.[202] The settlement resolved securities law claims based on misrepresentations in the offering documents for 21 Countrywide RMBS purchased by the five failed banks, with the settlement funds to be distributed to creditors of the bank receiverships.[203]

2 *Relief to Credit Suisse's Mortgage Borrowers*

Credit Suisse's settlement with the DOJ included a consumer relief component. The bank was required to earn a minimum of $2.8 billion in consumer relief "credit."[204] Specifically, Credit Suisse agreed to provide loan modifications, including loan forgiveness and forbearance, to distressed and underwater homeowners and to provide financing for affordable rental and for-sale housing. As of February 2019, Credit Suisse had given $143 million in consumer relief and earned $73.4 million in credit.[205]

X THE ALLY FINANCIAL, RESCAP, AND GMAC SETTLEMENTS

In 2016, Ally Financial Inc, generally known as Residential Capital, LLC (ResCap), agreed to pay the DOJ and other authorities $52 million to settle allegations that its subsidiaries acted improperly in relation to ten sub-prime RMBS in 2006 and 2007, including pooling of 40,000 sub-prime mortgages, packaging, securitization, marketing, sale, and issuance of the RMBS.[206] In 2006, ResCap subsidiaries

[202] FDIC Settlement.

[203] FDIC Settlement Colonial Bank of Montgomery, Alabama, which failed on 14 August 2009; Franklin Bank, S.S.B. of Houston, Texas, which failed on 7 November 2008; Guaranty Bank of Austin, Texas, which failed on 21 August 2009; Security Savings Bank of Henderson, Nevada, which failed on 27 February 2009; and Strategic Capital Bank of Champaign, Illinois, which failed on 22 May 2009.

[204] Credit Suisse DOJ Settlement, para. 2.

[205] The credited amount was derived from the actual relief the bank provided to borrowers as set out in in Table A.10 of the Appendix.

[206] Department of Justice, "Ally Financial Agrees to Pay $52 Million to Resolve Investigation into Improper Conduct Related to Issuance of Mortgage-Backed Securities" (21 November 2016), United States Department of Justice, www.justice.gov/usao-cdca/pr/ally-financial-agrees-pay-52-million-resolve-investigation-improper-conduct-related; Ally Settlement Agreement (21 November 2016), United States Department of Justice, www.justice.gov/usao-cdca/case-document/file/912531/download (hereafter Ally DOJ Settlement).

ranked amongst the largest mortgage warehouse lenders, RMBS issuers, and servicers in the country.[207]

In addition to paying the $52 million civil penalty, Ally agreed to immediately discontinue operations of, wind-down, and de-register its registered broker-dealer, Ally Securities, LLC. As the lead underwriter, Ally Securities LLC recognized in 2006 that there was a consistent trend of deterioration in the quality of the mortgage loan pool stemming from deficiencies in mortgage underwriting guidelines and diligence prior to securitization but failed to disclose this information to investors. All the securities sustained losses as a result of underlying mortgage loans falling delinquent. Yet Ally received substantial Troubled Asset Relief Program (TARP) bailout funds.

As noted, Ally also settled under the NMS, which was a cumulative settlement between the five largest mortgage servicers and Ally contributed $109,628,425.[208]

XI THE MORGAN STANLEY SETTLEMENTS

Morgan Stanley reached settlements totalling $5 billion with the DOJ and federal and state regulators, as set out in Table A.19 of the Appendix.[209] Of the settlement amount, approximately $401 million was directed in relief aid to consumers in New York harmed by Morgan Stanley's allegedly unlawful conduct, including loan modification, refinancing for distressed borrowers, down payment and closing cost assistance to homebuyers, and donations to organizations assisting communities in redevelopment and affordable rental housing for low-income families in high-cost areas.[210]

207 Ally Settlement Agreement, Annex A (21 November 2016), www.justice.gov/usao-cdca/case-document/file/912536/download. ResCap encompassed several entities dedicated to the acquisition and securitization of non-conforming residential mortgage loans, including Ally Securities LLC, also known as GMAC.

208 *United States of America, et al* v *Bank of America Corp, et al*, No 12-0361 (RMC), Document 13 Consent Judgment (DDC filed 4 April 2012), para. 3, National Mortgage Settlements, https://scholarship.law.unc.edu/cgi/viewcontent.cgi?article=1003&context=mortgage-settlements (hereafter Ally NMS Consent Judgment). See Table A.1, Appendix.

209 Department of Justice, "Morgan Stanley Agrees to Pay $2.6 Billion Penalty in Connection with Its Sale of Residential Mortgage Backed Securities" (11 February 2016), www.justice.gov/opa/pr/morgan-stanley-agrees-pay-26-billion-penalty-connection-its-sale-residential-mortgage-backed (hereafter DOJ, "Morgan Stanley Agrees to Pay RMBS Penalty").

210 The breakdown of that relief is set out in Table A.20, Appendix. Morgan Stanley Settlement Agreement (11 February 2016), paras. 1-2, New York Attorney General, https://ag.ny.gov/pdfs/Final_NYAG_Settlement_Agreement.pdf (hereafter Morgan Stanley New York Settlement). In addition to $150 million cash provided to the State of New York, consumer credited relief provided by Morgan Stanley included $205,012,079 financing for critical-need housing developments; $126,672,501 financing acquisition and remediation of non-performing loans

In the settlement Statement of Facts, Morgan Stanley admitted telling investors that it did not securitize loans that exceeded the value of the property, when it had expanded its "risk tolerance" in evaluating loans in 2006 to purchase and securitize "everything possible." Morgan Stanley ignored information indicating that thousands of securitized loans were underwater and has now acknowledged that it "did not disclose to securitization investors that employees of Morgan Stanley received information that, in certain instances, loans that did not comply with underwriting guidelines and lacked adequate compensating factors ... were included in the RMBS sold and marketed to investors."[211] Morgan Stanley increased the percentage of mortgage loans it purchased for its RMBS, notwithstanding its awareness of "deteriorating appraisal quality" and "sloppy underwriting."[212]

XII THE SUNTRUST SETTLEMENT

In 2014, the DOJ, HUD, and the Consumer Financial Protection Bureau, 49 State Attorneys General and the District of Columbia's Attorney General reached a $970 million agreement with SunTrust Mortgage, Inc to address mortgage origination, servicing, and foreclosure abuses.[213] Of that amount, $418 million plus interest was to resolve its claims under the federal False Claims Act for originating and underwriting loans that violated its obligations as a participant in the FHA insurance program.[214]

or making grants for certified community land banks or housing quality improvement and enforcement programs; $70,005,583 forgiveness of first-lien and second-lien loan balances owed by individual homeowners. Eric Green, "Monitor: Morgan Stanley Completes Consumer-Relief Obligations under NY Mortgage Settlement that Targeted Blight, Struggling Communities" *PR Newswire* (20 December 2017), www.prnewswire.com/news-releases/monitor-morgan-stanley-completes-consumer-relief-obligations-under-ny-mortgage-settlement-that-targeted-blight-struggling-communities-300574165.html. Will Astor, "NY to get $150 million from settlement with Morgan Stanley" *Rochester Business Journal* (11 February 2016), RBJ, https://rbj.net/2016/02/11/n-y-to-get-150-million-from-settlement-with-morgan-stanley/.

[211] Morgan Stanley Settlement Agreement and Statement of Facts (11 February 2016), United States Department of Justice, www.justice.gov/opa/file/823671/download (hereafter Morgan Stanley DOJ Settlement).

[212] Morgan Stanley DOJ Settlement.

[213] Department of Justice, "Federal Government and State Attorneys General Reach Nearly $1 Billion Agreement with SunTrust to Address Mortgage Loan Origination as Well as Servicing and Foreclosure Abuses: Agreement Provides Homeowner Relief and New Protections, Stops Abuses" (17 June 2014), www.justice.gov/opa/pr/federal-government-and-state-attorneys-general-reach-nearly-1-billion-agreement-suntrust. See also *United States of America, et al v SunTrust Mortgage, Inc*, No 14-01028 (RMC), Document 65 Consent Judgment (DDC filed 30 September 2014), paras 3–5, Department of Justice, www.justice.gov/opa/file/831121/download (hereafter SunTrust Consent Judgment).

[214] Tables A.24 and A.25 in the Appendix.

1 *SunTrust's Conduct*

SunTrust admitted that between January 2006 and March 2012, it originated and underwrote FHA-insured mortgages that did not meet FHA requirements, that it failed to carry out an effective quality control program to identify non-compliant loans, and that it failed to self-report to HUD even the defective loans it did identify. SunTrust also admitted that numerous audits and other reports to its management between 2009 and 2012 described significant flaws and inadequacies in SunTrust's origination, underwriting, and quality control processes, and notified SunTrust management that as many as 50 per cent or more of SunTrust's FHA-insured mortgages did not comply with FHA requirements. Other reports received by SunTrust management described its quality control program as "severely flawed" and "ineffective." Observe again that the conduct was continuing well after the 2008 market meltdown.

2 *Relief to SunTrust's Mortgage Borrowers*

Relief to borrowers and homeowners was to include, among other things, reducing the principal on mortgages for borrowers at risk of default, and reducing mortgage interest rates for homeowners underwater on their mortgages. According to the consumer relief component of the settlement, SunTrust was required to earn a minimum of $500 million in consumer relief credit, in addition to $40 million of the escrow account distributed to borrowers through the NMS Borrower Payment Fund.[215] Similar to the other settlements, the credited amount was derived from the actual relief the bank provided to borrowers; the monitor took each dollar of actual relief and made various upward and downward adjustments to determine how much of each dollar would be counted towards the total consumer relief credit.[216] Actual relief given to borrowers is not available for this settlement.[217]

3 *SunTrust Misconduct Regarding Home Affordable Modification Program*

A DOJ notice of settlement in 2014[218] resolved a criminal investigation of SunTrust's administration of the HAMP. SunTrust misled numerous mortgage servicing customers who sought mortgage relief through HAMP. It made material

215 SunTrust Consent Judgment, paras. 4–5.

216 *United States of America, et al* v *SunTrust Mortgage, Inc*, No 14-01028 (RMC), Document 74 Final Consumer Relief Report (DDC filed 10 August 2017), Exhibits D and D1, National Mortgage Settlements, https://scholarship.law.unc.edu/cgi/viewcontent.cgi?article=1182&context=mortgage-settlements (hereafter SunTrust Final Report).

217 SunTrust Final Report, II(D) Consumer Relief and V Total Consumer Relief, referring to actual relief data in Schedule Y. Schedule Y is not in the public record.

218 Department of Justice, "SunTrust Mortgage Agrees to $320 Million Settlement: Money Will Provide Relief to Harmed Borrowers and Establish Prevention Fund" (3 July 2014), www.justice.gov/opa/pr/suntrust-mortgage-agrees-320-million-settlement (hereafter DOJ, "SunTrust Mortgage Agrees to $320 Million Settlement").

misrepresentations and omissions to borrowers in HAMP solicitations, and failed to process HAMP applications in a timely fashion. As a result, thousands of homeowners who applied for a HAMP modification with SunTrust suffered serious financial harm. SunTrust agreed to pay $320 million to resolve the criminal investigation:

> SunTrust will pay $179 million in restitution to compensate borrowers for damage caused by its mismanagement of HAMP. That money will be distributed to borrowers in eight pre-determined categories of harm. If more than $179 million is needed, the bank will also guarantee an additional $95 million for additional restitution. SunTrust will also pay $10 million in restitution directly to Fannie Mae and Freddie Mac.

SunTrust was also to provide $16 million to law enforcement agencies working on mortgage fraud and other matters related to the misuse of TARP funds. Further, SunTrust was required to allocate $20 million to establish a fund for distribution to organizations providing counselling and other services to distressed homeowners.[219]

This case, as others, revealed that misconduct continued even after the financial meltdown occurred, with firms engaging in illegal conduct in respect of the government's programs to assist the foreclosure crisis.

XIII THE HSBC SETTLEMENTS

HSBC paid $1.79 billion to settle lawsuits, as set out in Table A.14 of the Appendix. HSBC did not admit to the conduct, but the settlement statement issued by DOJ indicates why all the settlement went to civil penalties:

> Over a one-and-a-half year period, between January 2006 and June 2007, HSBC's primary due diligence vendor flagged over 7,400 loans as having low grades—more than one out of every four loans the vendor reviewed for HSBC during that time. When HSBC employees saw loans with low grades, they sometimes "waived" those loans through or recategorized the grades to make the due diligence "percentages look better." They also expressed views about the deals they were issuing. For example, in 2007, an HSBC trader said, in reference to an RMBS that HSBC was about to issue, "it will suck."
>
> For a loan pool HSBC purchased in 2006, HSBC learned of what employees referred to as an "abnormally large" and "alarmingly" high number of payment defaults. HSBC had purchased the loan pool but had not securitized it yet. Early payment defaults (EPDs)—when a borrower fails to make one of the first few payments on a mortgage—could be, in the words of HSBC's co-head of RMBS, "an indicator of higher expected loss on the pool." In an internal email, HSBC's head of risk management for RMBS wrote that the high EPD rate could be a sign of systemic problems with the pool. Others within HSBC's risk management group

219 DOJ, "SunTrust Mortgage Agrees to $320 Million Settlement.

expressed concern that the pool "may be contaminated" and asked whether "they should hold back on the securitization launch until there is further clarity on all the issues…." The next day, the head of HSBC's whole loan trading risk management group stated that he was "comfortable that we need not make any further disclosures to investors…." HSBC issued the securitization a few days later. A later post-close quality control review indicated that loans that "appear to have fraud or misrep" went into the securitization. HSBC went on to buy and securitize more loans from the same originator, even after the head of HSBC's due diligence team concluded that the originator had offered "bad collateral."[220]

As part of the overall settlements, in October 2018, HSBC settled a lawsuit and agreed to pay $765 million to settle claims related to its packaging, securitization, issuance, marketing, and sale of RMBS to be paid as a civil penalty pursuant to the FIRREA.[221] In an earlier settlement with the DOJ and 49 state attorneys general, HSBC Bank USA NA and its affiliates agreed to pay $470 million to address mortgage origination, servicing, and foreclosure abuses, which included $371 million in creditable consumer relief and required HSBC to reform its servicing standards.[222] Here again, much of the relief is credit towards measures that do not prevent further foreclosures and do not compensate for the loss of consumer borrowers' homes.

At the outset of this chapter, we noted how the settlements have been a shell game. To our knowledge no one has been able to say with any precision what real relief consumer borrowers received, but what is clear is that very few of the dollars towards relief actually kept borrowers in their homes.

XIV THE UBS SETTLEMENTS

UBS paid $1.45 billion to settle lawsuits with federal and state regulators, as set out in Table A.26 of the Appendix.[223] The settlement with the State of New York additionally requires that by the end of 2019, UBS must earn a minimum of $189 million

[220] DOJ, "SunTrust Mortgage Agrees to $320 Million Settlement.

[221] Department of Justice, "HSBC Agrees to Pay $765 Million in Connection with Its Sale of Residential Mortgage-Backed Securities" (9 October 2018), www.justice.gov/usao-co/pr/hsbc-agrees-pay-765-million-connection-its-sale-residential-mortgage-backed-securities.

[222] Department of Justice, "Justice Department Reaches $470 Million Joint State-Federal Settlement with HSBC to Address Mortgage Loan Origination, Servicing and Foreclosure Abuses" (5 February 2016), www.justice.gov/opa/pr/justice-department-reaches-470-million-joint-state-federal-settlement-hsbc-address-mortgage; *United States of America, et al* v *HSBC North America Holdings, et al*, No 16-00199 (RJL), Document 8 Consent Judgment (DDC filed 14 March 2016), para. 3, National Mortgage Settlements, https://scholarship.law.unc.edu/cgi/viewcontent.cgi?article=1116&context=mortgage-settlements (hereafter HSBC Consent Judgment).

[223] NCUA Settlements; FHFA Private Label Securities Actions; New York Attorney General UBS Settlement Agreement (20 March 2018), New York Attorney General, https://ag.ny.gov/sites/default/files/ubs_settlement.pdf (hereafter UBS New York Settlement).

credit in donations to certain eligible housing programs.[224] The DOJ is pursuing a settlement, which has not yet been resolved.[225]

The agreed statement of facts for the settlement with the Attorney General of New York acknowledged that in 2006–2007, UBS Real Estate Securities Inc and UBS Securities LLC (UBS) participated in the process of securitizing tens of thousands of residential mortgage loans and selling the resulting $10 billion RMBS to investors.[226] UBS misrepresented in its prospectus offerings of the RMBS that the mortgages met its underwriting guidelines and also failed to disclose that a third-party vendor assessing the qualities of the mortgages reported that many did not comply with underwriting guidelines or applicable laws and regulation.[227]

The lawsuit by the FHFA as conservator of Fannie Mae and Freddie Mac alleged that UBS Americas made numerous material misstatements and omissions about the mortgage loans underlying the private-label RMBS, including the creditworthiness of the borrowers and the quality of the origination and underwriting practices used to evaluate and approve such loans.[228] The settlement between the FHFA and UBS involved an $885 million settlement payable to Freddie Mac and Fannie Mae.[229] The agreement expressly states that the settlement does not constitute an admission by any of the UBS defendants of any liability or wrongdoing.[230]

XV NO WAY TO TELL IF CONSUMER BORROWERS RECEIVED ANY PRINCIPAL FORGIVENESS

As noted throughout this chapter, forms of relief included first and second mortgage and lien modifications, short sales, deeds in lieu, benefits for servicemembers, enhanced borrower transitional funds, anti-blight loss mitigation activities, deficiency waivers, and refinancing.[231] It is clear that some relief has been granted across

224 UBS New York Settlement, para. 3.

225 *United States* v *UBS Securities LLC*, No 18-06369 (MKB), Document 1 Complaint (EDNY filed 8 November 2018), Court Listener, www.courtlistener.com/docket/8161829/united-states-v-ubs-securities-llc/ (hereafter UBS DOJ Settlement).

226 UBS New York Settlement, Appendix A Statement of Facts, paras. 1–2.

227 UBS New York Settlement, paras. 12–19.

228 FHFA, "FHFA Sues UBS to Recover Losses to Fannie Mae and Freddie Mac" (27 July 2011), www.fhfa.gov/Media/PublicAffairs/Pages/FHFA-Sues-UBS-to-Recover-Losses-to-Fannie-Mae-and-Freddie-Mac.aspx.

229 FHFA as conservator of Fannie Mae and Freddie Mac and UBS Americas, Inc, UBS Real Estate Securities Inc, UBS Securities et al, Settlement Agreement (25 July 2013), FHFA, www.fhfa.gov/Media/PublicAffairs/Documents/UBSSettlement072513.pdf (hereafter UBS Settlement Agreement).

230 UBS Settlement Agreement, 4.

231 Joseph A. Smith Jr, Monitor under *United States of America et al* v *Bank of America Corp et al*, No 12-0361 (RMC), Document 145 Monitor's Final Consumer Relief Report Regarding Defendant CitiMortgage, Inc (DDC filed 18 March 2014), 5–6, National Mortgage Settlement, https://scholarship.law.unc.edu/cgi/viewcontent.cgi?article=1018&context=mortgage-settlements (hereafter

the country, but it is not clear who received the relief and whether or not African Americans were once again inequitably treated in the giving of any relief.

While the definition of modification does allow for some debt forgiveness, hidden in a footnote to the report among a series of measures that make up "modification," there is a reference to principal forgiveness as one of six possible modifications.[232] Principal forgiveness, however, is not required, and is not measured specifically, which is very telling. For example, short sales, really aimed at forcing consumers to walk away from their homes with none of the equity they invested, is measured as consumer relief, and it is not clear how much of the total of so-called consumer relief were short sales, as they are reported in with other creditor relief.

Interestingly, to incent the servicers to grant consumer relief promptly, they were to receive additional credit for meeting their obligations; for the NMS, this amount was 25 per cent of the actual credits earned on relief activities completed before 28 February 2013.[233] Although there was a penalty for unmet consumer relief requirements within three years,[234] the incentives really allowed the servicers to essentially complete only 75 per cent of what they were ordered to do and receive full credit for credit relief.

1 *Professionals within the Banks, Brokerages, and Servicing Companies Test Their Own Compliance with the Lawsuit Settlement*

There were also many provisions detailing percentages for certain kinds of relief.[235] To ascertain compliance, there was sample testing drawn from the three testing populations. The testing was undertaken by the servicer or other entity against which the lawsuit was brought; its internal review group (IRG), which was an internal quality control group established by the servicer. The IRG was supposed to be "independent from [the] Servicer's mortgage servicing operations."[236] The IRG conducted an independent review to determine whether the loan was eligible for credit and whether the amount of credit reported by servicers was calculated correctly.[237]

Bank of America Final Consumer Relief Report). "*Servicer* means CitiMortgage, Inc, and *Servicers* mean the following: (1) JP Morgan Chase Bank, N.A., (2) Ocwen Loan Servicing, LLC and Green Tree Servicing LLC, successors by assignment to Residential Capital, LLC and GMAC Mortgage, LLC, (3) Bank of America, N.A., (4) CitiMortgage, Inc, and (5) Wells Fargo & Company and Wells Fargo Bank, N.A." Bank of America Final Consumer Relief Report, 4.

232 Bank of America Final Consumer Relief Report, 5.

233 Bank of America Final Consumer Relief Report, 6.

234 Bank of America Final Consumer Relief Report.

235 Bank of America Final Consumer Relief Report.

236 Bank of America Final Consumer Relief Report, 3.

237 Bank of America Final Consumer Relief Report, 14.

In other words, another arm of the financial firm that caused the harms has the mandate to test whether the relief agreed to is being implemented. While we are not in a position to assess the statistical reliability of this method of monitoring, it does strike us that the monitor relies entirely on the data provided by the servicer to assess whether it has passed the Satisfaction Review without any contact with the borrowers themselves to document their experiences.

At the monitor's direction, the primary professional firm (PPF) conducted an extensive review of the testing conducted by the IRG relative to consumer relief crediting for the Second Testing Period.[238] The monitor then reviewed their results.

Another salient point is that the independent monitors were paid directly by the banks that they were monitoring; and although the settlement recitals specify that the monitor is to be fully independent of the bank, all the costs for fees and disbursements of the monitor were paid by the bank without any intermediary considering the incentive effects. This arrangement arguably created some risk of the monitors being favourably disposed to approving the self-reporting that settlement terms had been met.[239] Only in very few instances did the monitors ask for any adjustment to the credit figures reported.

XVI LAWSUITS AGAINST PREDATORY LENDERS BROUGHT UNDER ANTI-DISCRIMINATION LAW

In an earlier settlement of litigation with Wells Fargo in 2012, the DOJ announced that, "African-American and Hispanic Borrowers who qualified for loans and were charged higher fees or rates or were improperly placed into sub-prime loans are eligible for compensation."[240] The DOJ alleged that, between 2004 and 2009, Wells Fargo discriminated by charging approximately 30,000 African-American and Hispanic wholesale borrowers higher fees and rates than non-Hispanic white borrowers based on their race or national origin, rather than on the borrowers' credit worthiness or other objective criteria related to borrower risk.[241] The DOJ also alleged that in the same period, Wells Fargo discriminated by steering approximately 4,000 African-American and Hispanic wholesale borrowers, as well as additional retail borrowers, into sub-prime mortgages when non-African-American and non-Hispanic borrowers with similar credit profiles received prime loans.

The complaint also alleged that, as a result of Wells Fargo's policies and practices, African-American and Hispanic wholesale borrowers who qualified for prime loans were placed in sub-prime loans rather than prime loans even when similarly qualified

238 Bank of America Final Consumer Relief Report, 17, 3.
239 Bank of America DOJ Settlement, 8–9.
240 DOJ, "Wells Fargo Fair Lending Claims."
241 DOJ, "Wells Fargo Fair Lending Claims."

white borrowers were placed in prime loans. The discriminatory placement of wholesale borrowers in sub-prime loans, also known as "steering," occurred because it was the bank's business practice to allow mortgage brokers and employees to place a loan applicant in a sub-prime loan even when the applicant qualified for a prime loan.

The Wells Fargo settlement provided $184.3 million in compensation for wholesale borrowers who were steered into sub-prime mortgages or who paid higher fees and rates than white borrowers because of their race or national origin.[242] Wells Fargo was to provide $50 million in direct down payment assistance to borrowers in communities that were hard hit by the housing crisis.

Wells Fargo also settled a lawsuit with the City of Memphis, agreeing to invest $400 million in loans to generate economic activity.[243] As noted, affidavit evidence given by Wells Fargo loan officers revealed that Wells Fargo systematically steered African-American and Latinx borrowers to sub-prime mortgages and sub-prime cash-out refinancing loans. Loan officers were told that their commissions and bonuses would be higher if they steered borrowers who qualified for traditional mortgages into sub-prime mortgages.[244] The loan officers were actively encouraged to misrepresent the risks associated with ARM mortgages and other sub-prime financial products, including failing to tell them when the interest rate would reset after the teaser rate expired or how much higher payments were then going to be, or that they faced severe prepayment penalties if they attempted to prepay their sub-prime mortgage, or even that the mortgages were much more expensive overall.[245]

The Wells Fargo affidavits also revealed "affinity fraud" conduct by its loan officers. Affinity fraud occurs when African-American loan officers or mortgage brokers target other African Americans to induce them into sub-prime or other harmful financial transactions, sometimes going door-to-door or frequently accessing community meeting places such as churches to steer multiple members into fraudulent sub-prime transactions.[246] Sometimes loan officers would offer to make a donation to the church after a borrower's sub-prime loan was approved.[247] The evidence in the Wells Fargo lawsuit revealed that elderly borrowers and first-time buyers were the most vulnerable to this predation.[248] Under the terms of the settlement, Wells Fargo was to offer financial assistance and new loans for borrowers with low and moderate incomes, plus pay the city for economic development.[249] Wells Fargo made no admission of racial bias in any of its settlements.

242 DOJ, "Wells Fargo Fair Lending Claims."
243 Dickerson, *Homeownership*, 169.
244 Dickerson, *Homeownership*, 170.
245 Dickerson, *Homeownership*.
246 Dickerson, *Homeownership*, 172.
247 Dickerson, *Homeownership*.
248 Dickerson, *Homeownership*.
249 Dickerson, *Homeownership*.

As discussed previously, given that some African Americans have less access to highly regulated financial institutions because they are unbanked or underbanked, they are more likely to rely on information provided through churches or other organizations in the community and more likely to rely on mortgage brokers who offer services at these local meeting places and during unsolicited visits to homes. Lack of access to mainstream financial institutions makes these borrowers particularly vulnerable.

In 2007, the FDIC filed a cease and desist notice against Fremont for issuing subprime ARM loans.[250] It is unclear what monetary settlement there was, other than a reference of $10 million to Massachusetts.[251]

Several U.S. cities have filed claims against a number of financial institutions alleging that the banks' predatory lending practices caused a dramatic spike in the number of foreclosures in neighbourhoods that were intentionally targeted.[252] This targeting, according to the cities, increased the number of abandoned and vacant homes in already vulnerable communities. The cities sued to hold banks accountable for money spent to maintain the properties, and for municipal expenses incurred because of the need to call police officers and firefighters to abandoned properties to address problems caused by squatters and criminal activity.

In 2017, the U.S. Supreme Court ruled that cities have standing to sue under the Fair Housing Act[253] and remanded the case to the United States District Court to clarify and define the Fair Housing Act's proximate causation requirement.[254] When the case returned to the District Court in May 2019, Miami argued that Bank of America targeted black and Latinx borrowers for predatory loans that "resulted in disproportionate foreclosures on homeowners of those races, diminished property values in predominantly minority neighbourhoods, substantially reduced tax revenue for the City, and increased expenditures by the City for municipal services."[255] The District Court found that the city adequately pled the proximate causation element, thus avoiding a motion to dismiss.[256] The case will proceed. This finding,

[250] *Re Fremont Investment & Loan et al*, No 7-035b, Order to Cease and Desist (FDIC filed 7 March 2007).

[251] Megan Woolhouse, "Lender Settles with State for $10m" *Boston Globe* (10 June 2009), http://archive.boston.com/business/articles/2009/06/10/subprime_lender_settles_suit_with_mass_for_10m/.

[252] See *Bank of America* v *City of Miami, Florida*, 137 S Ct 1296, 197 L Ed 2d 678 (2017) (hereafter *Bank of America* v *Miami*). See also Thom Weidlich, "Foreclosures Prompt Cities to Sue Banks Over Mowing, Repairs" *Bloomberg* (11 May 2011), http://.bloomberg.com/news/2011-05-12/foreclosures-prompt-four-u-s-cities-to-sue-banks-for-mowing-home-repairs.html (hereafter Weidlich, "Foreclosures").

[253] Weidlich, "Foreclosures," citing the Fair Housing Act, 42 USC § 3605 (1968) (as amended in 1988 by Pub L No 100-430, 102 Stat 1619); also known as Title VIII of the Civil Rights Act, prohibits discrimination on the basis of race when making or purchasing loans for purchasing, constructing, or improving a dwelling.

[254] See *Bank of America* v *Miami*.

[255] *Bank of America* v *Miami*, 3.

[256] *City of Miami* v *Bank of America, NA*, No 14-14543 (11th Cir 2019). Miami also sued Wells Fargo: see *City of Miami* v *Wells Fargo Bank et al*, No 14-14544 (11th Cir 2019).

however, applied only to the city's claim that the bank's conduct reduced the city's tax base. The Court rejected the city's argument that the bank's predatory lending caused municipal losses due to increased expenditures relating to vacant, abandoned homes that were lost in foreclosure.

The book goes to press before this case has been litigated or settled. The litigation's outcome, however, is not pertinent to understanding the disregard for the economic plight of African Americans. By finding a causal link between Bank of America's predatory lending and the reduction in the city's tax base, the District Court allows for potential redress that relates primarily to the city's economic harm. Because the District Court found no proximate causation between the bank's lending practices and the worsened circumstances of Miami's blighted black communities, the economic plight of these neighbourhoods will continue to remain unaddressed.

One of the complaints by the Civil Rights Division of the DOJ against Countrywide, a subsidiary of Bank of America, was that 200,000 African-American and Latinx borrowers were steered to higher-cost sub-prime mortgages while white borrowers with similar creditworthiness were given traditional lower cost prime interest rate loans.[257] The DOJ gathered data that showed that Countrywide's lending decisions were based on race, not assessment of creditworthiness.[258] It had "reason to believe that Countrywide Home Loans engaged in a pattern or practice of discrimination based on race and ethnicity in violation of Section 701(a) of the Equal Credit Opportunity Act and the Fair Housing Act."[259] Countrywide's own underwriting criteria revealed African-American borrowers were steered into sub-prime mortgage products even when they had good credit ratings. The evidence revealed that Countrywide decided to specifically target African-American and Latinx borrowers as part of its business plan to expand its volume and thus its share of the sub-prime market.

The civil rights lawsuit alleged that Countrywide engaged in a pattern or practice of discrimination because African-American and Hispanic borrowers were more than twice as likely to be placed in sub-prime loans than non-Hispanic white wholesale borrowers who had similar credit qualifications.[260] Countrywide's marketing plan included aggressively persuading African-American and Latinx borrowers to take equity out of their homes in cash-out refinancing, offering time-limited teaser rates, and promising appreciation of house values. The evidence was that

[257] *United States of America* v *Countrywide Financial Corporation et al*, No 11-10540 (PSG), Document 4 Consent Order (CD Cal filed 28 December 2011), Civil Rights Litigation Clearinghouse, www.clearinghouse.net/chDocs/public/FH-CA-0007-0003.pdf (hereafter *USA* v *Countrywide*).

[258] Dickerson, *Homeownership*, 168.

[259] *USA* v *Countrywide*, 2.

[260] *USA* v *Countrywide*, 3.

Countrywide's loan officers never mentioned that homes located in largely non-white neighbourhoods were likely to see little or no appreciation in value.[261] A $335 million settlement was reached on the civil rights lawsuit.[262] The settlement agreement expressly states, "There has been no factual finding or adjudication with respect to any matter alleged by the United States."[263]

Other banks have been sued by cities alleging losses caused by predatory lending. In a separate suit, the mayor and city council of Baltimore, Maryland sued Wells Fargo, and as discussed in Chapter 3, Wells Fargo settled the suit. The cities of Philadelphia and Chicago also filed claims against Wells Fargo alleging discriminatory lending practices that targeted African-American and Latinx borrowers. In December 2018, a U.S. District Court Judge stayed Philadelphia's lawsuit so that the parties could seek resolution in mediation before a retired magistrate.[264] Chicago's potential recovery from Wells Fargo was limited "to the increase in costs of administering and processing foreclosures that allegedly multiplied due to Wells Fargo's 'equity stripping' practices."[265] A U.S. District Judge dismissed Chicago's claims that the bank's practices resulted in lost property taxes and expenditures to alleviate crime and deterioration in certain neighbourhoods, concluding that no plausible causal connection could be shown.[266] Los Angeles brought a claim against Deutsch Bank. Cleveland filed actions against JP Morgan Chase and Ameriquest. Birmingham, Alabama and Buffalo, New York filed and lost suits against Citigroup and ABN AMRO Mortgage, respectively.[267]

XVII SETTLEMENT MEANS NO ADMISSION OR FINDING OF LIABILITY

There is always a tension between notions of accountability and justice by court decisions finding liability and settlement of lawsuits without a judgment on the merits, the latter of which saves resources of the state and the parties and hopefully directs those resources towards relief. In the settlements described in this chapter, there are no admissions of illegal conduct and no findings of misconduct or fraudulent misrepresentations to mortgage borrowers. In the Bank of America

[261] Dickerson, *Homeownership*, 169.

[262] *USA* v *Countrywide*, 5.

[263] *USA* v *Countrywide*, 3.

[264] Max Mitchell, "Phila's Discriminatory Lending Suit against Wells Fargo Heads to Mediation" *The Legal Intelligencer* (13 December 2018), www.law.com/thelegalintelligencer/2018/12/13/phila-s-discriminatory-lending-suit-against-wells-fargo-heads-to-mediation/.

[265] Francis Monfort, "Judge Limits Chicago's Claims in Predatory Lending Suit against Wells Fargo" *Mortgage Professional America Magazine* (2 April 2018), www.mpamag.com/news/judge-limits-chicagos-claims-in-predatory-lending-suit-against-wells-fargo-96415.aspx (hereafter Monfort, "Judge Limits Chicago's Claims").

[266] Monfort, "Judge Limits Chicago's Claims."

[267] Weidlich, "Foreclosures."

settlement, the States prosecuting the files alleged that Citigroup Inc, Citibank NA, and CitiMortgage, Inc violated, among other laws, the Unfair and Deceptive Acts and Practices laws of the plaintiff States, the False Claims Act, the FIRREA, the Servicemembers Civil Relief Act, the Bankruptcy Code, and the Federal Rules of Bankruptcy Procedure.[268] The parties agreed to resolve their claims without litigation and the consent judgment specifically notes that the defendant, by entering into the judgment, did not admit the allegations.[269]

The settlement of the litigation brought by the city of Baltimore against Wells Fargo[270] that we describe earlier in this chapter and in Chapter 3 provides another example of a lender's failure to admit wrongdoing. The bank settled the Baltimore suit in the face of egregious misconduct. One former Wells Fargo loan officer provided an affidavit stating that "some [loan] officers told the underwriting department that their clients, even those with good credit scores, had not wanted to provide income documentation. 'By doing this, the loan flipped from prime to sub-prime'"[271] She also provided testimony claiming that Wells Fargo "loan officers cut and pasted credit reports from one applicant onto the application of another customer."[272] Yet on settling litigation filed by the city of Baltimore, Wells Fargo denied wrongdoing.

> Wells Fargo is settling this matter solely for the purpose of avoiding contested litigation with the DOJ, and to instead devote its resources to continuing to provide fair credit services and choices to eligible consumers, and important and meaningful assistance to borrowers in distressed U.S. real estate markets.[273]

Two years before Wells Fargo reached its settlement with the city of Baltimore, the bank settled a suit brought by the National Association for the Advancement of Colored People (NAACP) alleging violations of the Equal Credit Opportunity Act and Fair Housing Act.[274] The NAACP, seeking no monetary recovery, brought

[268] *United States of America, et al* v *Bank of America Corp, et al*, No 12-0361 (RMC), Document 12 Consent Judgment (DDC filed 4 April 2012), National Mortgage Settlements Digital Archive, https://scholarship.law.unc.edu/cgi/viewcontent.cgi?article=1002&context=mortgage-settlements (hereafter Citigroup NMS Consent Judgment).

[269] Citigroup NMS Consent Judgment.

[270] *City of Baltimore* v *Wells Fargo Bank*, No 8-062 (JFM), Document 222 Settlement Order (D Md filed 7 August 2012), Civil Rights Litigation Clearinghouse, www.clearinghouse.net/chDocs/public/FH-MD-0001-0013.pdf (hereafter *Baltimore* v *Wells Fargo* Settlement Order).

[271] Michael Powell, "Suit accuses Wells Fargo of steering blacks to subprime mortgages in Baltimore" *The New York Times* (7 June 2009), A16, www.nytimes.com/2009/06/07/us/07baltimore.html (hereafter Powell, "Suit Accuses").

[272] Powell, "Suit Accuses."

[273] Gary Haber, "Wells Fargo to Pay Baltimore $7.5 M in Discrimination Deal" *Baltimore Business Journal* (12 July 2012) (hereafter Haber, "Wells Fargo to Pay $7.5 M").

[274] Martha Neil, "Wells Fargo Settles With NAACP, But 2 Cities File New Fair Lending Suits" *ABA Journal* (8 April 2010), www.abajournal.com/news/article/wells_fargo_settles_with_naacp_but_2_cities_file_new_lender_discrimination_/ (hereafter Neil, "Wells Fargo Settles with NAACP");

the suit to "change patterns of unfair lending and discrimination in the mortgage industry."[275] The bank promised to work with the organization towards improving access to fair mortgage loans for people of colour by helping borrowers who faced foreclosure and educating consumers in financial matters.[276] In a statement from Wells Fargo announcing the settlement with the NAACP, the bank claimed to have "worked for generations to lend responsibly to minority communities and regarded the agreement with the [NAACP] as the 'next constructive step' toward that goal."[277]

Wells Fargo issued more denials of misconduct when it settled litigation brought by Memphis, claiming that the bank was committed to "fair and responsible lending practices." A Wells Fargo regional president said that, in settling the suit, both parties "agreed that it was in the best interests of everyone involved to work together rather than to continue to be involved in a protracted legal fight."[278]

Wells Fargo's denials are replete with doublespeak. William Lutz wrote a book about this type of discourse entitled, *Doublespeak: How Government, Business, Advertisers, and Others Use Language to Deceive You*.[279] Lutz defined 'doublespeak' as intentionally obfuscating and misleading language that makes negative conduct or events appear positive or tolerable in a way that allows the speaker to escape responsibility or accountability. When businesses engage in doublespeak, the content of what their spokespersons say does not match reality.[280]

In Wells Fargo's denials, we see how doublespeak sanitizes the conversation about racism and obscures the continuing problem of discrimination. Consider the bank's claims to have "worked for generations to lend responsibly to minority communities"[281] and to "devote its resources to continuing to provide fair credit services and choices to eligible consumers, and important and meaningful assistance to borrowers in distressed U.S. real estate markets"[282] in light of the testimony of former

Dan Fitzpatrick, "NAACP to Drop Suit against Wells Fargo" *Wall Street Journal* (8 April 2010), www.wsj.com/articles/SB10001424052702303591204575170332695249248. See also E. Scott Reckard, "Wells Fargo Agrees to Work with NAACP, Settling Accusation of Lending Bias" *LA Times* (8 April 2010), https://latimesblogs.latimes.com/money_co/2010/04/wells-fargo-agrees-to-work-with-naacp-settling-accusation-of-lending-bias.html.

[275] Neil, "Wells Fargo Settles with NAACP."

[276] Neil, "Wells Fargo Settles with NAACP."

[277] Neil, "Wells Fargo Settles with NAACP." The NAACP filed similar suits against JP Morgan Chase, Citigroup, HSBC, and GMAC.

[278] James O'Toole, "Wells Fargo Pledges $432.5M in Lending Payments to Settle Lawsuit" *CNN Money* (31 May 2012), https://money.cnn.com/2012/05/30/news/companies/wells-fargo-memphis/index.htm.

[279] William Lutz, *Doublespeak: How Government, Business, Advertisers, and Others Use Language to Deceive You* (New York: HarperCollins, 1989) (hereafter Lutz, *Doublespeak*).

[280] Lutz, *Doublespeak*, 1–2.

[281] See Haber, "Wells Fargo to Pay $7.5 M."

[282] Haber, "Wells Fargo to Pay $7.5 M." The NAACP filed similar suits against JP Morgan Chase, Citigroup, HSBC, and GMAC.

Wells Fargo loan officers. There is a significant gap between what the bank said about its relationship with minority borrowers and what really occurred. In general, doublespeak allows companies to avoid responsibility for enduring discrimination within their firms to save their firms' reputations. Because they did not move beyond superficial and mindless rhetoric, Wells Fargo and similarly situated lenders remain unable to address the problem of twenty-first century discrimination because they fail to acknowledge it.

The durability of corporate doublespeak even after a firm settles litigation may be attributable to the fact that the doublespeak begins before a suit is filed and increases when the firm is sued. The doublespeak is hard to reverse just because the case is settled. Consider several examples of Wells Fargo's pre-settlement doublespeak. In the months after Baltimore filed its claim against Wells Fargo, a spokesperson said that the bank "worked extremely hard to make homeownership possible for African-American borrowers. We absolutely do not tolerate team members treating our customers or others disrespectfully or unfairly, or who violate our ethics and lending practices."[283] In an email to media, another Wells Fargo spokesperson commented on the city of Chicago's suit against the bank. "We are prepared to defend our record as a fair and responsible lender."[284]

Wells Fargo's decree that it would defend its record as "a fair and responsible lender" was hollow rhetoric that may have prolonged the predation against consumers of colour while doing very little to prevent reputational harm to the firm. It seemed that its declaration to defend its record was made without seriously inquiring into allegations of predatory lending. A serious inquiry may have uncovered the pervasiveness of the predatory practices about which its former loan officers testified in subsequent litigation.

Only meaningful inquiry and monitoring of compliance with law can transform a predatory culture such as the one alleged to exist at Wells Fargo. Monitoring and inquiry processes should be rational. Consider an economist's definition of rational decision-making that is "based on deliberation, *i.e.*, on the collection and processing of information, and on the drawing of proper conclusions from it."[285] This definition of rational decision-making embodies the idea that directorial fiduciary duty imposes on boards an obligation to monitor compliance, which requires boards and managers to collect information.[286] Collecting the information, however, is only the first step. Once information is collected, boards and executives must analyze and draw conclusions from the information they have gathered. When serious or

283 Haber, "Wells Fargo to Pay $7.5 M."

284 Monfort, "Judge Limits Chicago's Claims."

285 Amitai Etzioni, *The Moral Dimension Toward a New Economics* (New York: The Free Press, 1988), 144.

286 See *Stone* v *Ritter*, 911 A2d 362 (2006).

pervasive noncompliance is uncovered, boards and executives should acknowledge the wrongdoing. Acknowledging corporate misconduct that is serious and pervasive is a prerequisite to correcting it. Unlawfulness that is not acknowledged will persist and may worsen. Corrective action is impossible without acknowledging the need for such action.

Firms should consider the strategy of acknowledging noncompliance when it is discovered. Acknowledgement, accompanied by an apology for harmed caused, may go a long way in helping to restore a company's reputation and minimize the likelihood that noncompliance will continue or recur. This strategy is one that many companies avoid in an attempt to protect themselves from liability. They fear that acknowledgement and apology will result in liability or higher settlement costs. These companies, however, fail to understand the value of compliance obligations to prevent litigation in the first place, or as part of a strategy to settle allegations quickly after taking corrective action, thereby avoiding more litigation and continuing harm to consumers.

Decades ago, this strategy worked well for Johnson & Johnson, "a corporation that used apology successfully and became a role model for handling a crisis during the Tylenol tampering case that killed seven people in 1982."[287] Johnson & Johnson made critically important organizational changes following its apology and re-established itself as a company deserving public and consumer trust.[288] The company did not avoid liability for the injuries that resulted from the tampering, but its apology, accompanied by corrective action, may have prevented additional litigation and negative publicity.[289]

> Over time, the public was willing to forgive Johnson & Johnson, and while no one will ever really forget the Tylenol scare, the corporation's credibility and reputation was restored by its ability to understand the consequences of its actions, take measures to fix the problem, and install measures to prevent similar incidents from occurring.[290]

It is also possible that an appropriate apology may help a company avoid litigation for its misconduct altogether.[291]

[287] Taryn Fuchs-Burnett, "Mass Public Corporate Apology" (May–July 2002) 57 *Disp Resol J*, 26–32 (hereafter Fuchs-Burnett, "Corporate Apology").

[288] See Fuchs-Burnett, "Corporate Apology."

[289] See Fuchs-Burnett, "Corporate Apology."

[290] Fuchs-Burnett, "Corporate Apology," 82–3.

[291] DOJ, "Bank of America to Pay $16.65 Billion." An African-American teenager sued an Eddie Bauer retail clothing store after having been falsely accused of stealing. The store's security guard made the accusation in public and in a degrading way, but the company offered no apology for the guard's conduct or the boy's embarrassment. The boy's father explained that "if they had apologized from the start or given some response, the lawsuit wouldn't happen. It feels like they don't care." DOJ, "Bank of America to Pay $16.65 Billion," 28.

Even though the financial institutions we discuss in this chapter settled various types of litigation without admitting any wrongdoing towards consumer borrowers, the harm to various constituencies impacted by the institutions' conduct is clear. Global economies were harmed. Investors, not just borrowers, were duped by institutions that securitized toxic mortgages and sold them without disclosing risks, or without performing due diligence. Our focus in this book, however, is on the harm to the mortgagors whose loans were packaged and sold to investors. Consumer borrowers had far more at stake than did investors. Investors suffered significant losses, but, in part because their investments were diversified, the losses were mitigated. The harm to mortgagors was far more devastating. Because of originators' predation, undertaken to provide mortgages that would be pooled to fulfil investors' and securitizing firm's desires for profit, many mortgagors lost everything. Moreover, investors in securitized sub-prime mortgages recovered much of their losses when the banks settled. Mortgagors did not.

The fact that disproportionately high numbers of the mortgagors are African Americans, and the fact that investors who recovered losses are predominantly white, is not irrelevant. This story is part of the larger historical narrative of the economic exploitation of African Americans for the profit of white Americans – mortgage originators, securitizing firms, and investors. Securitizing firms victimized investors, but these investors recovered losses while the mostly black mortgagors still suffer as a result of the victimization. This largely untold story is imperative to acknowledge if one is to understand the real reasons for the widening racial wealth gap between black and white Americans.

9

A Sub-prime Loan by Any Other Name Is Just as Predatory

There are now new iterations of predatory lending. Deeply disturbing is the re-emergence in 2018 and 2019 of sub-prime loans that are now called "non-prime."[1] These loans are widely offered in the mortgage market and the market has extended to non-prime auto loans and non-prime credit cards.[2] While the market boasts in its disclosures that the "illegal activities" on zero-deposit mortgages are no longer prevalent, much of the conduct found during the sub-prime debacle appears to be continuing today. The other recent development concerns mortgage modifications. This chapter connects this new burgeoning non-prime market with some of the structural features of financial markets and the treatment of African Americans, portending the risk of another significant financial crisis for African Americans and other borrowers.

I NON-PRIME MORTGAGES – THE NEW SUB-PRIME

Non-prime mortgages, just as with their predecessor sub-prime mortgages, are mortgages available to individuals with lower credit ratings and less disposable cash. Touted as making home ownership affordable for a larger group of people, the practice of securitizing the mortgages and selling them on to investors means that the same lack of oversight that occurred during the global financial crisis is occurring today.

[1] Mortgage Bankers' Association, "'One Mod:' Principles for Post-HAMP Loan Modifications" (September 2016), www.mba.org/Documents/Policy/16670_MBA_Public_Policy_One_Mod_Paper.pdf (hereafter Mortgage Bankers' Association).

[2] See Dustin McKissen, "The Subprime Mortgage is Back on the Market, and Has a Brand New Name" *Inc* (13 April 2018), www.inc.com/dustin-mckissen/subprime-mortgages-are-back-will-that-mean-another-recession.html (hereafter McKissen, "Subprime Mortgage is Back"). In this regard, it is important to remember that even African Americans who qualified for prime loans were targeted for and placed in predatory sub-prime loans. The lending predation that occurred in the years leading up to the 2008 recession negatively impacted credit scores, which means the individuals targeted before the recession are likely to be victimized again because of lowered credit scores and as new schemes emerge.

Reforms under the Dodd-Frank Act[3] now require securitization originators to retain not less than 5 per cent of the credit risk for an asset that is not a "qualified residential mortgage" (read sub-prime) when they securitize loans.[4] The Office of the Comptroller of the Currency, the Board of Governors of the Federal Reserve System, the Federal Deposit Insurance Corporation (FDIC), the U.S. Securities and Exchange Commission (SEC), the Federal Housing Finance Agency (FHFA), and the Department of Housing and Urban Development (HUD) in 2015 issued a final rule to implement the credit risk retention requirements of section 15G of the Securities Exchange Act of 1934,[5] as added by section 941 of the Dodd-Frank Act.[6] The final rule requires sponsors of asset-backed securities to retain at least 5 per cent of the credit risk of the assets underlying the securities and does not permit sponsors to transfer or hedge that credit risk during a specified period.[7]

The 5 per cent retention is aimed at the notion that if the originator has "skin in the game" (i.e. some of its own capital at risk in the transaction), it will be more responsible in its lending practices. However, retaining a 5 per cent interest when there are millions of dollars to be made in profit, is really the price of doing business in the mortgage-backed securities market and is far too small to actually change behaviour.[8]

As one media commentator observed: "The subprime mortgage industry vanished after the Great Recession but is now being reinvented as the nonprime market," offering mortgages to borrowers with less-than-perfect credit.[9] California-based Carrington Mortgage Services, a mid-sized lender, in 2018 announced an expansion into the non-prime market. It is originating and servicing the loans, but is securitizing them for sale to investors.[10] Borrowers can take out loans of up to

3 Dodd-Frank Act 2010. On 14 March 2018, the U.S. Senate passed a reform bill rolling back a number of requirements, easing financial regulations, and reducing oversight for banks with assets below $250 billion; the law passed the House of Representatives on 22 May 2018 and the legislation was then signed into law by President Donald Trump on 24 May 2018: the Dodd-Frank Act 2018.

4 Dodd-Frank Act. See also Mitchel Kider, Michael Kieval and Leslie Sowers, *Consumer Protection and Mortgage Regulation Under Dodd-Frank* (Eagan, MN: West, 2011), 540.

5 Securities Exchange Act of 1934, 15 USC § 78o-11 (hereafter Securities Exchange Act of 1934).

6 Office of the Comptroller of the Currency, "OCC Bulletin 2015–8 re: Credit Risk Retention – Final Rule" (29 January 2015), www.occ.treas.gov/news-issuances/bulletins/2015/bulletin-2015-8.html (hereafter OCC Bulletin 2015-8).

7 OCC Bulletin 2015-8. The rule applies to asset-backed securities issued on or after 24 December 2015, if the securities are backed by residential mortgages and to all other classes of asset-backed securities issued on or after 24 December 2016.

8 For a discussion generally of skin in the game, which pre-dates the financial crisis, see Janis Sarra, "Rose-Coloured Glasses, Opaque Financial Reporting and Investor Blues; Enron as Con and the Vulnerability of Canadian Corporate Law" (2002) 76:4 St Johns Law Rev, 715.

9 Diana Olick, "Subprime Mortgages Make a Comeback – With a New Name and Soaring Demand" *CNBC News* (12 April 2018), www.cnbc.com/2018/04/12/sub-prime-mortgages-morph-into-non-prime-loans-and-demand-soars.html (hereafter Olick, "Subprime Mortgages Make a Comeback").

10 Olick, "Subprime Mortgages Make a Comeback."

$1.5 million on single-family homes and condominiums and also can do cash-out refinances (home equity loans), where borrowers tap into equity in their homes, up to $500,000.[11]

Angel Oak also commenced offering and securitizing non-prime mortgages. Two securitizations were $329 million, comprised of 905 mortgages, with more than 80 per cent of the loans being non-prime,[12] and then in 2018, a $402 million securitization, almost entirely comprised of non-prime mortgages sourced through affiliated mortgage lenders, Angel Oak Mortgage Solutions LLC, Angel Oak Home Loans LLC, and Angel Oak Prime Bridge, LLC.[13] From 2015 to 2018, Angel Oak Capital Advisors completed seven non-qualifying (non-prime) mortgage securitizations, accounting for approximately $1.6 billion in total securitized residential loans, largely backed by mortgages originated through its affiliated mortgage lenders.[14] One media commentator observed: "Investors in Angel Oak's non-prime securitizations are, 'a who's who of Wall Street', according to company representatives," citing hedge funds and insurance companies.[15] Blackstone, a massive private equity fund, has a cluster of non-prime investments, including a stake in Bayview Asset Management mortgage service.[16]

Deephaven Mortgage, a Charlotte, North Carolina-based firm, was set up in 2013 by the person who ran Goldman Sach's residential mortgage business for a decade.[17] It has bought $1 billion of non-prime loans from a network of approximately 100 brokers and has resold about half of that into the mortgage-backed securities market.[18] In one $250 million mortgage-backed securities deal in June 2017, "more than 40 per cent of borrowers who got mortgages bought by Deephaven had had a prior 'credit event' such as a bankruptcy, foreclosure or short sale, according to Kroll, a credit rating agency"; yet the deal was roughly six times oversubscribed in the market.[19]

The former head of Fremont, the mortgage firm sanctioned by federal regulators for unsafe practices in March 2007, now runs a non-prime firm, HomeXpress, in Newport Beach, California, and a former Goldman Sachs trader mentioned more

[11] Olick, "Subprime Mortgages Make a Comeback."

[12] Olick, "Subprime Mortgages Make a Comeback."

[13] Businesswire, "Record Growth at Angel Oak Companies Leads to Numerous Milestones in Q2" (23 July 2018), www.businesswire.com/news/home/20180723005346/en/Angel-Oak-Companies-Continues-Set-Standard-Non-QM (hereafter Businesswire, "Angel Oak Growth").

[14] Businesswire, "Angel Oak Growth."

[15] Olick, "Subprime Mortgages Make a Comeback."

[16] Ben McLannahan, "'Nonprime Has a Nice Ring to It': The Return of the High-Risk Mortgage" *Financial Times* (30 August 2017), www.ft.com/content/3c245dee-8d0f-11e7-a352-e46f43c5825d (hereafter McLannahan, "Nonprime Has a Nice Ring to it"), reporting that Bayview Asset Management buys mortgages from Coral Gables, Florida.

[17] McLannahan, "Nonprime Has a Nice Ring to it."

[18] McLannahan, "Nonprime Has a Nice Ring to it."

[19] McLannahan, "Nonprime Has a Nice Ring to it."

than 500 times in a Senate report on the mortgage meltdown, is now buying non-prime loans from a hedge fund in Stamford, Connecticut.[20]

Why are investors flocking to these products again, notwithstanding what should have been the lessons learned from the financial crisis? Angel Oak says it is continuing to hold 5 to 10 per cent of its various mortgaged-backed securities deals to build trust with investors.[21] A few industry pundits have said that the banks "cannot afford not to get involved, given the profits being made by the securitizations," and even where they are not directly involved, banks such as Credit Suisse and Nomura are supplying lines of credit to originators and underwriting securitizations of non-prime mortgages.[22]

Moreover, credit rating agencies such as Fitch, DBRS, and Kroll have given their stamps of approval to a number of those securitization deals.[23] Fitch expected $3 billion of issuance of non-prime mortgage-backed securities in 2017 and 2018.[24] Even Standard & Poor, which paid $1.4 billion in 2015 to the U.S. Department of Justice (DOJ) to resolve a probe into ratings inflation, rated five non-prime mortgage deals in 2017.[25]

Richard Bowen, former Business Chief Underwriter for Citigroup, previously objected to the way the company certified poor mortgages as quality mortgages and sold them to Fannie Mae, Freddie Mac and other investors.[26] He testified before the SEC and gave the SEC 1,000 pages of evidence of fraudulent activities; and was also a key witness before the Financial Crisis Inquiry Commission.[27] Concerning the new market for non-prime, he observes that it is "happening without a proper reckoning from the last time around."[28] He contrasts the current situation with the savings and loan crisis in the United States in the 1980s, after which about 800 senior bankers went to jail; observing that the crisis since 2007 was many, many times worse, but no one has been held accountable, notwithstanding all the evidence.[29]

Dustin McKissen posits that non-prime mortgages, if properly regulated, can help borrowers who are saddled with low credit scores due to overwhelming medical expenses; however, if not properly regulated, lenders will drain even more wealth from the most economically vulnerable individuals.[30] He suggests that research has consistently shown that people of colour are disproportionately targeted for predatory loans and other risky financial products that make bad credit nearly inevitable,

20 McLannahan, "Nonprime Has a Nice Ring to it."
21 McLannahan, "Nonprime Has a Nice Ring to it."
22 Businesswire, "Angel Oak Growth."
23 McLannahan, "Nonprime Has a Nice Ring to it."
24 McLannahan, "Nonprime Has a Nice Ring to it."
25 McLannahan, "Nonprime Has a Nice Ring to it."
26 Richard Bowen, "About" (2019), www.richardmbowen.com/about/ (hereafter Bowen, "About").
27 Bowen, "About."
28 McLannahan, "Nonprime Has a Nice Ring to it."
29 McLannahan, "Nonprime Has a Nice Ring to it."
30 McKissen, "Subprime Mortgage is Back."

and more than 20 per cent of African-American borrowers have credit scores of less than 620. He suggests that a non-prime mortgage is just a tool, and like any tool, it can be used for good or bad. Thus, he argues that the problem is not the mere existence of sub-prime mortgages, it is "our tendency to let greed turn a good idea into a really bad one."[31] He argues that the key to allowing non-prime mortgages as part of the housing market is to regulate them tightly as tools aimed at giving otherwise reliable borrowers with low credit scores a second, or in some instances, a first chance; "and not a way for Wall Street to engage (again) in a temporary and ultimately destructive cash grab."[32]

Several of the most egregious features of sub-prime mortgages appear to be gone, specifically, zero deposits and failure of the lender to make any assessment of ability to repay. However, the terms continue to be onerous, thus setting borrowers up for failure.

II "ONE MOD" – THE LATEST ITERATION OF PRIVATE SECTOR "LOSS DISTRIBUTION STRATEGY"

The Home Affordable Modification Program (HAMP) ended in December 2016.[33] Essentially, the U.S. government determined that the private sector would step up to be more active in modification programs, and while it issued a statement that accessibility and transparency were important features, it did not set standards of protection for consumer borrowers or concerning the conduct of mortgage service providers.

The Mortgage Bankers' Association's Future of Loss Mitigation Taskforce, anticipating the end of HAMP in 2016, came up with the "One Mod" (one modification) program, aimed at creating a unified framework regarding loss mitigation.[34] One Mod is aimed at mitigating losses to investors through modification programs geared to investors not borrowers.[35] The taskforce involved 30 companies, "convened to draw upon the experiences of the financial crisis and HAMP to formulate universal principles that should be applied to a future loss mitigation program."[36] The language of the program is somewhat "valentine" in that it seeks to eliminate gaps that consumers fall through, suggesting that loss mitigation should focus on identifying and assessing consumer hardship and offering quick relief using reasonable, limited documentation.[37] The One Mod approach incorporates loan-to-value (LTV) ratios

[31] McKissen, "Subprime Mortgage is Back."
[32] McKissen, "Subprime Mortgage is Back."
[33] Making Home Affordable Program, "Need Mortgage Help?" (2019), United States Government, www.makinghomeaffordable.gov/need-help/Pages/default.aspx.
[34] Mortgage Bankers' Association.
[35] Mortgage Bankers' Association, 1.
[36] Mortgage Bankers' Association.
[37] Mortgage Bankers' Association, 7.

in the modification decision, which the taskforce states would provide more relief where a customer may have fewer options (negative/no equity) and where the local or regional housing market is distressed.[38]

It appears evident that some of the provisions may assist some borrowers, such as noting that "neither consumers nor servicers are well-served by requiring documentation that is not directly relevant to the final modification offering" and that mortgage servicers should only require the consumer to submit documentation that is directly related to their eligibility for the modification.[39] However, most of the One Mod provisions are aimed at protecting investors, not consumer mortgage borrowers.

The taskforce report observes: "Seeking a positive loss mitigation outcome for the investor is crucial to the success of a loan modification regime. It helps ensure continued availability of credit through a liquid mortgage market."[40] The taskforce developed a "One Mod waterfall proposal,"[41] which extended mortgages to 40 years as the primary strategy for modification. A 40-year mortgage means that most borrowers will not be able to pay off their mortgage during their entire working life.

The first step under One Mod is to "capitalize arrearages," which is adding the money that was past due on the mortgage, along with any interest and penalties the borrower has acquired, and tacking it on to the mortgage balance that the borrower owes. This step results in the mortgage being much larger, often larger than it was at the outset. Step 2 is to reduce the interest rate to the lower of market rate or current rate. Thus, while it is a reduction, it is an interest amount on a much larger new principal amount. Step 3 is then to extend the mortgage to 40 years. Such an extended period really resembles "rent by another name." The next step suggests that the mortgage servicer could provide principal forbearance; in other words, allowing the borrower to pay interest only and never beginning to pay off the mortgage. While there is brief mention of principal forgiveness, it is almost an afterthought and certainly not a recommended requirement. The taskforce notes that it is not suggesting using principal forgiveness in instances where a guarantor will not provide reimbursement.[42] The waterfall approach suggests options can be applied in succession to reach a desired outcome, or all at once to determine the resulting payment. Consumer Financial Protection Bureau regulations require that a servicer evaluate a consumer for all available loss mitigation options that they are eligible for once the servicer has received a complete loss mitigation request for assistance.[43]

38 Mortgage Bankers' Association, 9.
39 Mortgage Bankers' Association, 7.
40 Mortgage Bankers' Association, 7.
41 Mortgage Bankers' Association. The waterfall is split between pre-90 days delinquent and post-90 days delinquent.
42 Mortgage Bankers' Association, 10.
43 Consumer Financial Protection Bureau, "CFPB Finalizes Modifications to Mortgage Rules" (13 September 2013), www.consumerfinance.gov/about-us/newsroom/cfpb-finalizes-modifications-to-mortgage-rules/.

The One Mod waterfall program is thus a construct of the mortgage industry to continue to attract investors on the promise of profits that are made essentially on the backs of economically vulnerable borrowers. Each step in the waterfall process is aimed at mitigating losses to investors, not to borrowers. Not a single step requires the mortgage broker or servicer to consider forgiveness of a portion of the principal. One can juxtapose this outcome with debt forgiveness programs for businesses, where lenders acknowledge the value of a going-forward business and thus actually forgive parts of loans. Such a mindset is nowhere to be found in One Mod (i.e. a recognition that forgiveness of part of the loan might help preserve individuals' economic security and thus participation in the economy).

The U.S. Department of the Treasury, HUD, and FHFA released a white paper in July 2016 aimed at serving as a guide for future loss mitigation programs that said it drew on the lessons learned from the government's crisis-era housing recovery programs.[44] It reported that the foreclosure prevention programs established by Treasury, HUD, and FHFA "transformed the way in which the mortgage servicing industry has interacted with and assisted struggling homeowners."[45] These programs did lead to some relief for foreclosure, but it was far too little and far too late. In total, through government programs and private sector efforts, HUD reported that 10.5 million modification and mortgage assistance arrangements were completed between April 2009 and the end of May 2016,[46] although, as illustrated below, these global numbers reported by the government are deceiving.[47] Yet, 17 million people lost their homes, as discussed in Chapter 1, which indicates, at best, that these modifications were temporary and set borrowers up for future failure. The white paper by the U.S. Treasury, HUD, and FHFA states that the Making Home Affordable (MHA) program and other crisis-era homeowner assistance programs resulted in improved homeowner engagement in the loss mitigation process, new guidelines for the types of loss mitigation options offered to homeowners and standardized procedures for how such products are provided and support recovery of the housing market.[48] The following excerpt illustrates that its intentions were well meaning:

> Foreclosures can have severe consequences for families and communities. In addition to damaging a homeowner's access to credit, foreclosures can hinder children's educational success, increase crime in communities, and drain resources from local governments. Studies have shown that when families with children enter foreclosure, children are more likely to suffer in school and develop behavioral and health

44 Emergency Economic Stabilization Act of 2008, Pub L No 110–343, 110th Congress; Department of Treasury, "Treasury, HUD and FHFA White Paper on the Future of Foreclosure Prevention" (25 July 2016), U.S. Treasury, www.treasury.gov/press-center/press-releases/Pages/jl0527.aspx (hereafter Treasury, "White Paper").

45 Treasury, "White Paper."

46 Treasury, "White Paper," 3.

47 Treasury, "White Paper."

48 Treasury, "White Paper."

> issues. Widespread foreclosures not only depress housing prices in a community, but can create a contagion effect that can ripple through the local economy. Neighbourhoods may experience more crime when properties become vacant and local governments reduce police forces due to declining tax revenues.The personal and societal impacts of mass foreclosures highlight the importance of government-sponsored foreclosure prevention programs to help struggling homeowners.
>
> ...
>
> When the MHA programs terminate on December 31, 2016, there will no longer be a standard loss mitigation option that cuts across servicer and investor types. Other pieces of the infrastructure supported by MHA and HAMP, such as requirements to offer post-modification counseling, third party escalation centers, and public reporting of modification and servicer performance will also be phased out, or provided on a limited basis depending on investor or servicer. It is in this context that the Agencies look to continue their collaborative efforts and encourage stakeholders to design a framework for the future of loss mitigation.[49]

The white paper also sets out five guiding principles that should be a foundation for future loss mitigation programs: accessibility, affordability, sustainability, transparency, and accountability.

> Through their common experiences with loss mitigation programs over the past seven years, the agencies (U.S. Treasury, HUD, and FHFA) have identified five principles that should guide future loss mitigation programs. The guiding principles are:
>
> Accessibility: Ensuring that there is a simple process in place for homeowners to seek mortgage assistance and that as many homeowners as possible are able to easily obtain the needed and appropriate level of assistance.
>
> Affordability: Providing homeowners with meaningful payment relief that addresses the needs of the homeowner, the servicer and the investor, to support long-term performance.
>
> Sustainability: Offering solutions designed to resolve the delinquency and be effective long-term for the homeowner, the servicer, and the investor.
>
> Transparency: Ensuring that the process to obtain assistance, and the terms of that assistance, are as clear and understandable as possible to homeowners, and that information about options and their utilization is available to the appropriate parties.
>
> Accountability: Ensuring that there is an appropriate level of oversight of the process to obtain mortgage assistance for the protection of all parties.[50]

These excerpts make evident that U.S. government agencies understand the devastating effects of foreclosure and the report suggests principles for modification programs going forward. The agencies recognized that the MHA programs, as well as

[49] Treasury, "White Paper," 4, 5.

[50] Treasury, "White Paper," 9.

other types of infrastructure supported by MHA and HAMP, such as requirements to offer post-modification counselling, third-party escalation centers, and public reporting of modification and servicer performance, were to be phased out in 2016.[51] They acknowledged that the private sector would now "shoulder more responsibility for assisting struggling homeowners" through proprietary modifications and other loss mitigation programs,[52] and stated that there is need for an effective private sector framework that adopts best practices. However, it then proceeds to adopt the Mortgage Bankers' Association's Future of Loss Mitigation Taskforce recommendations, essentially in their entirety.

Thus, while the agencies' white paper principles look remarkably similar to the principles we articulated in Chapter 2 as fundamental to embedding fairness in financial markets, the endorsement of the Mortgage Bankers' Association recommendations essentially ignores the principles. It is the worst form of white washing – rhetoric about principles without any meaningful change. As this book has illustrated, modification and foreclosure practices since 2016 do not meet any of the fundamental substantive and procedural elements of fairness for African-American borrowers.

III MORTGAGE MODIFICATION STILL A SCAM

On the ground experience suggests that lack of proper regulatory oversight of the mortgage market continues. One lawyer sent us a denial letter from a mortgage servicer dated 19 October 2018.[53] The letter commences with: "You previously provided a complete Assistance Review Application and we are providing our response to that complete application," notwithstanding that the lawyer had yet to send in the information to complete the application on behalf of the Brooklyn, New York borrower and his family contributors. The signature is the mortgage servicer firm's name only, with no name on the signature, and no person to contact directly. The letter goes on to advise that "after careful review of your account, we find that there are no home retention loss mitigation options for which you are approved."[54]

Under "regulatory notice of non-approval," the letter gives reasons for ineligibility, which it says is based on "investor rules and based on your individual circumstances." Investor rules are, of course, what the company has decided that investors want as return on their investment – title to the property. The letter then lists the ineligibility as follows:

[51] Treasury, "White Paper," 6. HAMP was no longer an option for homeowners after 31 December 2016, except to those struggling homeowners with loans insured or guaranteed by the Federal Housing Administration (FHA), the U.S. Department of Agriculture's Rural Housing Service, and the U.S. Department of Veterans Affairs.

[52] Treasury, "White Paper," 18.

[53] Lawyer Alice Nicholson, letter on file with authors.

[54] Lawyer Alice Nicholson, letter on file with authors.

HAMP Tier 1 Trial Modification: Program expired; you are ineligible for this program as it has expired.
HAMP Tier 2 Trial Modification: Program expired; you are ineligible for this program as it has expired.
Proprietary Trial Modification, Insufficient Payment Reduction: We are unable to offer you this program because in performing our underwriting of a potential modification we could not reduce your principal and interest payment.
Home Affordable Unemployment Program (HAUP) – Program expired; you are ineligible for this program as it has expired.
SPS Unemployment Program, Not Currently Employed: Our records indicate that you are not currently receiving unemployment income. Therefore you are not eligible to be reviewed for this unemployment program.
Repayment Plan, Active Bankruptcy: We are unable to offer you this program at this time because there is an active bankruptcy filing referencing this account or property.

The mortgage servicer's letter goes on to state that the borrower, "H," is eligible for short sale and deed in lieu of foreclosure, both options leaving H homeless.

H, who received this denial letter, is receiving Social Security retirement income, but his daughter and son-in-law earn more than enough to get a restructured mortgage. H's lawyer observes that in this case, as in so many others, the borrower's family members are able to afford the payment and would like to stay in their home. "Mortgage servicers are sending these denial letters without seeing a scrap of paper from the borrower." H's lawyer observes that the denial prior to even getting the full application illustrates that the financial industry intends to auction most of the millions of homes that went into foreclosure due to predatory lending, another way of depriving people of intergenerational wealth. She notes that industry has come up with new names for the modification program – standard, one mod, proprietary – that continue to be aimed at default, foreclosure, and realization of the property on the default of the loan.

The lawyer also advises that in January 2019, mortgage servicers continue to add any delinquent interest and fees to the principal at the time of default, applying today's rising interest rate, and amortizing the new numbers over a 40-year period. The resulting payment almost always will be higher than the amount the borrower was paying on the date of default, in some instances eight, nine, or more times larger. The modification is then denied because, as evidenced in the servicer's letter: "in performing our underwriting," a service that generally does not exist at the mortgage servicer, "of a potential modification we could not reduce your principal and interest payment."[55]

55 Lawyer Alice Nicholson, letter on file with authors.

IV OTHER PREDATORY LENDING

Predatory lending is profitable and thus it is rapidly expanding to other consumer financing markets in the United States, with devastating consequences.

1 *Non-prime Home Equity Loans*

In the period leading up to the global financial crisis, many sub-prime mortgages were a form of refinancing where African-American homeowners had built up equity or paid off their mortgages. Here again, aggressive marketing made owners believe they could enjoy the benefits of having built up equity with some cash in hand. That practice continues today.

In principle, the idea of home equity loans or home equity lines of credit (HELOC) is not a bad one, in the sense that it can provide temporary bridge financing for a medical emergency, short-term loss of employment, unexpected home repairs, or supplement limited retirement income. However, there is a growing literature that home equity loans can deceptively impoverish older homeowners, thus leaving growing numbers without a sustainable means of living and even forcing them into bankruptcy.

In 2010, 41 per cent of borrowers over age 65 in the United States had mortgage debt and 24 per cent of homeowners over age 75 had mortgage debt.[56] These numbers stand in stark contrast to the 1950s through 1970s when homes tended to be fully paid for prior to retirement age. The difficulty with sub-prime home equity loans is exactly the same as the issues with sub-prime mortgages. If there are no payments, the interest is added on to the principal and re-amortized, quickly eating into the homeowner's equity, often their only life savings. Many older Americans who were persuaded to take out sub-prime home equity loans no longer had income or equity to pay property taxes, insurance, and for upkeep, and many lost their homes to foreclosure. By 2011, 1.5 million older Americans had lost their homes.[57] The increase in HELOC today places African Americans and other elderly Americans at serious risk of loss of their home as a financial safety net.

Mechele Dickerson writes at length about what she refers to as the "happy homeownership narrative." She describes how homeowners report being happier and more secure than renters, and that their children thrive better than children of renters.[58] However, she questions whether it is actual ownership that creates that happiness or just the better demographics for people that own homes.[59]

56 Mechele Dickerson, *Homeownership and America's Financial Underclass: Flawed Premises, Broken Promises, New Prescriptions* (Cambridge: Cambridge University Press, 2014), 89 (hereafter Dickerson, *Homeownership*).

57 Dickerson, *Homeownership*, 90.

58 Dickerson, *Homeownership*.

59 Dickerson, *Homeownership*, 31.

Dickerson argues that U.S. politicians have completely avoided answering the crucial question of whether it is sound public policy to make home ownership the centerpiece of U.S. housing policies given the economic realities of most Americans.[60] Dickerson wants governments to recognize and create a new housing narrative that says owning a home is risky and high cost for African Americans.[61] While we agree that co-housing, co-operative housing, and other forms of collective housing should be part of a range of effective housing options for all Americans, we do not endorse any strategy that dismantles the home ownership narrative solely for black Americans. We appreciate that is not what Dickerson is advocating, but absent careful and comprehensive policy change, there is risk that it could be a result. While Dickerson questions whether the American dream of homeownership is appropriate for some Americans, in this book, we explore and critique the impediments to wealth accumulation generally, and homeownership specifically, for African Americans.

2 *Contracts for Deed*

Schemes that erode the economic well being of African Americans continue in other contexts such as discretionary pricing in auto lending and rent-to-own transactions. In the mid-twentieth century, because discriminatory redlining precluded African Americans from access to traditional mortgages, many entered into arrangements known as contracts for deed or rent-to-own programs.[62] Twentieth-century statutes outlawed the discrimination that denied African Americans access to traditional mortgages, but, as we discuss in this book, many lost their homes as a result of reverse redlining of which predatory lending schemes were an integral part. Contract-for-deed programs have resurfaced in the twenty-first century to target homebuyers who cannot get traditional mortgages because they defaulted on predatory loans and their credit scores plummeted.[63] The twenty-first century contracts, however, are even more predatory than their predecessors. Not only do high interest rates make the contracts difficult, if not impossible, to pay, the homes are in a state of disrepair that is far worse than the conditions of most of the homes that would-be owners attempted to purchase in the 1950s and 1960s.[64]

60 Dickerson, *Homeownership*, 16.

61 Dickerson, *Homeownership*, 253–4.

62 See Ta-Nehisi Coates, "The Case for Reparations" *The Atlantic Magazine* (June 2014), www.theatlantic.com/magazine/archive/2014/06/the-case-for-reparations/361631/.

63 See Alexandra Stevenson and Matthew Goldstein, "Wall Street Veterans Bet on Low-Income Home Buyers" *New York Times* (17 April 2016), www.nytimes.com/2016/04/18/business/dealbook/wall-street-veterans-bet-on-low-income-homebuyers.html (hereafter Stevenson and Goldstein, "Wall Street Veterans Bet").

64 Alana Semuels, "A House You Can Buy, But Never Own" *The Atlantic Magazine* (10 April 2018), www.theatlantic.com/business/archive/2018/04/rent-to-own-redlining/557588/ (hereafter Semuels, "Buy, But Never Own").

A consumer who enters into a contract for deed "purchases an agreement for the deed rather than buying the deed itself."[65] Typically, the agreements require consumers to make timely payments for decades, pay taxes and insurance, make repairs to the home, and maintain the home. If consumers fail to fulfil the conditions enumerated in the agreement, they will not obtain the deed. Consumers who miss just one payment violate the agreement and can be evicted, thereby losing all of their capital investment in the home.[66]

Contracts for deed do not require consumers to have the home inspected. The individual signing the contract often does not know the extent of the home's disrepair until after he or she has signed. Then, in the process of purchasing the home insurance required under the contract, the insurance company may discover the need for extremely costly repairs.[67] The laws that protect homeowners who default on mortgages from eviction do not apply in this context.[68] If the individual is not evicted on default, the lender may convert the contract to a month-to-month tenancy.[69]

After sub-prime predatory mortgage lending drained wealth from African-American communities and destroyed the credit scores of millions of African Americans and others, private equity firms have started to target the same residents because they cannot get financing for a home purchase from traditional lenders.[70] These firms typically buy dilapidated homes that have stood vacant for several years and need a great deal of work. Because the properties are in disrepair, aspiring homebuyers find it extremely difficult to fulfil the conditions imposed under the contracts to make timely payments and pay for costly maintenance and repairs. Because of the extremely poor conditions of the homes, contract-for-deed arrangements in the twenty-first century are predatory in a way that the contracts for deed prevalent in the 1950s were not.[71]

In her article in *The Atlantic Magazine*, Alana Semuels describes the ordeal endured by Zachary Anderson, a consumer who entered into a contract for deed with a large private investment company, Harbour Portfolio Advisors (Harbour), which has made thousands of contract-for-deed deals with consumers across the country.[72] Semeul includes a map in her article that was used in litigation against Harbour, showing the racial makeup of the communities in which the private equity firm has purchased property. Harbour owns no properties in all or predominantly white areas. Almost all of its properties subject to contracts for deed are located in communities

65 Semuels, "Buy, But Never Own." Alana Semuels describes a victim who "spent tens of thousands of dollars repairing a hole in the roof, replacing a cracked sidewalk, fixing ceilings."

66 Semuels, "Buy, But Never Own."

67 Semuels, "Buy, But Never Own."

68 See Stevenson and Goldstein "Wall Street Veterans Bet."

69 Stevenson and Goldstein "Wall Street Veterans Bet."

70 Semuels, "Buy, But Never Own."

71 Semuels, "Buy, But Never Own."

72 Semuels, "Buy, But Never Own."

that are 80 to 100 per cent African-American, and a few are in neighbourhoods that are 60–79.9 per cent African-American.[73] Anderson, the consumer that Semuels describes in her article, learned about Harbour and its contract-for-deed arrangements when he saw signs posted in the predominantly African-American Atlanta suburb where he worked. The signs "listed the amounts buyers would have to put down—often as low as $700—and the amount they'd have to pay per month—often as low as $375. …"[74] The signs revealed nothing about Harbour's interest rates, which were more than twice the rates charged for traditional home loans.[75] Nor did Anderson know that Harbour "sells the homes for four to five times what it paid for them … even though the company does not invest money into fixing up the homes. The contracts are designed to fail … because they require tenants to do so many repairs so rapidly."[76]

The contract required Anderson to make the home habitable within four months after signing and he spent approximately $35,000 to do so.[77] Most of his payments went to interest and, approximately seven years after he signed the contract, he found that he owed Harbour only $100 less in principal.[78] After he was injured at work, Anderson had to retire early. While in the hospital, he missed a payment and Harbour threatened to evict him. He was able to pay what he owed Harbour under the contract and, as of the time Semuel's article was published, he was current on his payments, but his disability disbursements barely cover his Harbour payments and utility bills. He is now on food stamps and borrows money from family.[79]

In 2018, Anderson joined with others to file a suit alleging that Harbour violated state and federal law when it marketed its predatory contracts for deed to African Americans.[80] The African-American plaintiffs survived Harbour's motion to dismiss by establishing a *prima facie* case that included evidence that Harbour violated the FHA by intentionally targeting them on the basis of race. The plaintiffs did so by showing that "defendants solicited brokers who operated mainly in the black community, distributed flyers and advertisements in black communities and put their offices in black communities."[81] Harbour's marketing was unlikely to reach white

73 Semuels, "Buy, But Never Own."
74 Semuels, "Buy, But Never Own."
75 Semuels, "Buy, But Never Own."
76 Semuels, "Buy, But Never Own."
77 Semuels, "Buy, But Never Own." In addition to roof repairs and cutting tree limbs that were too close to the house, he repaired the sidewalk, purchased a hot-water tank, a stove, and refrigerator, lowered the ceilings to reduce his electricity bills, which were initially about $500 a month. He also painted, screened in his porch, installed a fireplace to lower heating bills, and added solar panels.
78 Semuels, "Buy, But Never Own."
79 Semuels, "Buy, But Never Own."
80 *Horne* v *Harbour Portfolio VI*, LP, 304 F Supp 3d 1332 (ND Ga 2018) (hereafter *Horne* v *Harbor*) Plaintiffs claimed that Harbor violated the Fair Housing Act, the Equal Credit Opportunity Act, the Georgia Fair Housing Act, the Truth in Lending Act, the Georgia Fair Business Practices Act, the Unfair and Deceptive Practices Towards the Elderly Act, and the Georgia Residential Mortgage Act. *Horne* v *Harbor*, *1337–8.
81 *Horne* v *Harbor*, *1341–2.

would-be homebuyers because the firm did not advertise its contracts for deeds on television or radio or in the media,[82] nor were they likely to have placed signs in white communities. To support its motion to dismiss, Harbour claimed that the decision to refrain from advertising in the media was evidence that it had "no marketing plan at all."[83] The case is pending as this book goes to press.

3 *Predatory Auto Loans*

Other twenty-first century discriminatory practices threaten wealth in communities of colour. In the aftermath of predatory mortgage lending that targeted African-American and Latinx communities, and even after the passage of the Dodd-Frank Act, enacted, in part, to address this misconduct, predatory auto lenders target African-American consumers.[84] Auto dealers often connect auto buyers to lenders. Both dealers and lenders profit by making "auto loans that contain hidden figure charges and other essentially useless add-ons like credit insurance."[85]

Finance companies provide "objective, credit-based interest rates" that auto dealers are free to ignore. Dealers can increase the interest rate of a borrower's loan by several percentage points. This markup is entirely within the dealers' discretion. Not surprisingly, this discretionary markup is applied in a way that unfairly disadvantages people of colour. Many people of colour pay more for their car loans even though they are as creditworthy as their white counterparts. There is "solid evidence that black, Latino, and Asian-American car buyers are charged higher interest rates than white Americans with similar credit histories."[86]

As was true in the mortgage context, these predatory loans are assigned to other institutions. Ally Bank, Honda Finance, and Fifth Third Bank settled with the Consumer Financial Protection Bureau (CFPB) and the DOJ concerning some predatory auto loans and paid back victimized consumers.[87] As part of the settlement, Fifth Third Bank agreed to limit, but not eliminate, the dealer markup.[88]

82 Semuels, "Buy, But Never Own."
83 Semuels, "Buy, But Never Own."
84 See the Editorial Board, "Putting an End to Abusive Car Loans" *New York Times* (13 June 2015), www.nytimes.com/2015/06/14/opinion/sunday/putting-an-end-to-abusive-car-loans.html?_r=0 (hereafter New York Times, "Abusive Car Loans") (beginning the article by declaring auto loans to be a "bastion of predatory lending and racial discrimination").
85 New York Times, "Abusive Car Loans."
86 Van Jones, "Congress Says 'OK' to Racist Auto Lenders" *CNN* (16 December 2015), www.cnncom/2015/12/16/opinions/jones-discrimination-auto-lenders/ (hereafter Jones, "Racist Auto Lenders").
87 When it was created, the CFPB covered auto lenders, but only if they do not assign the loan, thus leaving unprotected consumers whose auto loans were assigned.
88 Jones, "Racist Auto Lenders."

Toyota agreed to pay $21.9 million in restitution to thousands of consumers of colour after charging them interest rates that were higher than those charged to white borrowers with similar credit histories.[89]

4 *Continuing Discriminatory Practices*

Predatory servicing is another type of discriminatory practice that victimizes borrowers of colour. Predatory servicing exists "when collection procedures on 'prime' accounts differ from collection procedures employed on 'non-prime' or 'sub-prime' accounts."[90] Predatory servicing impacts borrowers after a loan has been originated. It affects communities of colour in ways that it does not impact white borrowers because a disproportionately higher number of non-prime or sub-prime loans are held by people of colour, who may hold these types of loans because of predatory lending practices. These borrowers face aggressive discriminatory collection procedures at disproportionately higher rates than white borrowers because their original loans were sub-prime and predatory and less likely to be repaid. Borrowers were far more likely to default on the predatory mortgages, and therefore these consumers were more likely to be further victimized by predatory collection processes. Since people of colour were targeted by lenders who originated predatory loans, they are more likely to face discriminatory servicing and collection processes when they default on loans that seemed to have been designed for failure. The failure to which we refer here is a loan designed in a way that will make repayment extremely difficult, if not impossible. The loan is designed to fail from the borrower's perspective, but from the lender's perspective, the loan is designed for success in the form of higher fees and interest rates that inure only to the benefit of originators and servicers.

Plaintiffs who have brought predatory servicing claims argue that disparate servicing or collection processes violate the Equal Credit Opportunity Act.[91] In 2017, the CFPB filed a claim against Ocwen Financial Corporation and affiliated firms in the Southern District of Florida.[92] The CFPB alleged that Ocwen violated federal consumer financial laws in servicing the loans of defaulting borrowers.[93] The CFPB claimed that Ocwen "improperly calculated loan balances, misapplied borrower

89 See Lisa Lambert, "Toyota Motor Credit Settles with US over Racial Bias in Auto Loans" *Reuters* (2 February 2016), www.reuters.com/article/us-consumers-autofinance-toyota-idUSKCN0VB2EO.

90 Scott J. Hyman and Erin S. Kubota, "Predatory Servicing" (2018) 72 *Conf Cons Fin L Q* 43 (hereafter Hyman and Kubota, "Predatory Servicing").

91 Hyman and Kubota, "Predatory Servicing."

92 See *Consumer Financial Protection Bureau* v *Ocwen Financial Corporation et al*, No 17-80495, Document 1 Complaint (SD Fla, W Palm Beach Div filed 20 April 2017), https://files.consumerfinance.gov/f/documents/20170420_cfpb_Ocwen-Complaint.pdf (hereafter *CFPB* v *Ocwen* Complaint).

93 *CFPB* v *Ocwen* Complaint, 1.

payments, failed to correctly process escrow and insurance payments, and failed to properly investigate and make corrections in response to consumer complaints."[94] In addition to these claims, the CFPB alleged that Ocwen had "illegally foreclose[ed] upon borrowers' loans and [sold] loan servicing rights to servicers without fully disclosing or correcting errors in borrowers' loan files."[95] More than twenty state regulators filed similar claims against Ocwen claiming that the firm's mortgage servicing violated consumer protection laws.[96] Ocwen quickly negotiated settlements and consent agreements with state regulators so that it would not be precluded from new business that included originating new loans and additional mortgage servicing rights.[97] The CFPB suit against Ocwen continues amidst motions to dismiss the CFPB's case along with arguments that the case should be dismissed because the CFPB's very existence is unconstitutional.[98]

Along with new iterations of exploitation, redlining, a twentieth-century practice, has re-emerged in the twenty-first century. As discussed in Chapter 3, in the 1950s and 1960s, redlining was a system employed by real estate agents to exclude black and Latinx families from white neighbourhoods and used by banks to exclude borrowers of colour from access to home loans. Banks refused to provide home mortgages to African-American and Latinx borrowers for reasons unrelated to creditworthiness.[99] Twentieth-century federal and state legislation outlawed redlining, but the practice persists in 2019.

For example, Hudson City Savings Bank settled a case with the DOJ for almost $33 million "after an investigation found that it was avoiding doing mortgage business with African Americans and Latinos between 2009 and 2013."[100] In 2014, Hudson "approved 1,886 mortgages in the market that includes New Jersey and sections of New York and Connecticut.... Only 25 of those loans went to black borrowers."[101] Even though it settled the suit, Hudson denied all wrongdoing.[102]

94 *CFPB* v *Ocwen* Complaint.

95 *CFPB* v *Ocwen* Complaint.

96 See Ben Lane, "Ocwen Begins Settling with States to Remove Mortgage Servicing Restrictions" *Housing Wire* (28 September 2017), www.housingwire.com/articles/41433-ocwen-begins-settling-with-states-to-remove-mortgage-servicing-restrictions (hereafter Lane, "Ocwen Begins Settling").

97 Lane, "Ocwen Begins Settling."

98 See Nexsen Pruet, "The CFPB's Enforcement Case against Ocwen Financial Corporation – 18-month Checkup" (4 October 2018), www.nexsenpruet.com/uploads/1593/doc/Bossong_Ocwen___CFPB0.pdf.

99 Real estate agents refused to show homes in white neighborhoods to black and Latinx would-be homebuyers.

100 Brentin Mock, "Redlining is Alive and Well – and Evolving" *City Lab* (28 September 2015), www.citylab.com/equity/2015/09/redlining-is-alive-and-welland-evolving/407497/. According to the DOJ, this was the "largest residential mortgage redlining settlement in its history."

101 Rachel L. Swarns, "Biased Lending Evolves, and Blacks Face Trouble Getting Mortgages" *The New York Times* (30 October 2015), www.nytimes.com/2015/10/31/nyregion/hudson-city-bank-settlement.html (hereafter Swarns, "Biases Lending Evolves").

102 Swarns, "Biases Lending Evolves."

The banks' narrative focuses only on borrowers. "Fallout from the excesses of the sub-prime era in mortgage lending has, in some ways, set the stage for the discriminatory practices of today. As banks have tightened their credit lending standards to avoid risky loans, the percentage of blacks and Hispanics getting approved for mortgages has plunged."[103] Borrowers of colour fail to qualify for mortgages because of past foreclosures, job losses, and credit scores that plummeted because of these circumstances.

Evans Bank also settled a case with then New York Attorney General Eric Schneiderman after "discovering that the bank erased black neighbourhoods from maps used for determining mortgage lending. ... of the over 1,100 mortgage applications the bank received between 2009 and 2012, only four were from African Americans."[104] Associated Bank settled for $200 million with HUD for denying mortgage loans to black and Latinx applicants in Chicago and Milwaukee between 2008 and 2010.[105] Both Hudson City Savings Bank and Associated Bank are supposed to open branches in predominantly black and Latinx communities under the settlement terms.[106]

A *New York Times* editorial discussed a federal housing discrimination complaint filed in early September 2015 describing the practices of real estate agents who discriminated against African Americans by failing to show them properties in neighbourhoods that were predominantly or all white.[107] The African Americans who endured this discrimination had higher incomes, superior credit scores, and more money available for down payments than white potential homebuyers.[108] White and African-American testers uncovered these discriminatory practices when they pretended to shop for homes. The white testers also discovered that real estate agents steered them into predominantly white neighbourhoods even when the testers expressed interest in homes in predominantly black areas. The organization that conducted these tests uncovered housing discrimination in Atlanta, Austin, Birmingham, Chicago, Dayton, Detroit, New York, Philadelphia, San Antonio, the District of Columbia, and Jackson, Mississippi.[109]

Agents also showed African-American testers fewer homes than were shown to their white counterparts. Pertinent information that would make home buying easier was not given to the African-American testers. The black testers were asked to provide documents such as loan pre-approval letters even though similarly situated or less qualified whites were not. As we explored in Chapter 3, redlining causes

[103] Swarns, "Biases Lending Evolves."
[104] Swarns, "Biases Lending Evolves."
[105] Swarns, "Biases Lending Evolves."
[106] Swarns, "Biases Lending Evolves."
[107] New York Times, "Abusive Car Loans."
[108] New York Times, "Abusive Car Loans."
[109] New York Times, "Abusive Car Loans."

residential segregation that results in the undervaluation of homes in predominantly black and Latinx communities. That this type of discrimination endures decades after the passage of an extensive array of civil rights and fair housing and lending laws is remarkable. Also pertinent is the fact that middle- and upper-middle-class African Americans suffer this type of discrimination.

There is, unfortunately, another type of opportunistic predation that falls into a gray area of conduct that may not be illegal. Professor Ann Goldweber, Director of Clinical Legal Education at St John's School of Law and Director of the Consumer Justice for the Elderly Litigation Clinic,[110] shared with us copies of several letters and flyers that were distributed in African-American neighbourhoods in New York City in the years right before and immediately after the 2008 financial crisis.[111] The flyers purported to offer help for homeowners having trouble paying mortgages. One of the letters, addressed "Dear Homeowner" and signed by a Moses Crawford, III, informed recipients that they had "been selected to take advantage of a limited opportunity to reinstate [homeowner's] mortgage and discontinue you (sic) foreclosure action." The letter described what was referred to as "a special Test Pilot Program designed to help homeowners who have fallen behind on their monthly payments and cannot catch up." The flyer promised that, "program participants" would "be able to remain in their homes and will be provided an affordable financing package." Also promised was that participation in the program would require no cash payments from homeowners, that the participant's credit rating would not be used in determining eligibility, and the flyer suggested that participants may be able to "preserve ... credit rating[s] by avoiding a foreclosure sale." Recipients of this flyer were urged to call right away because the program was limited to 40 pre-selected families. In May 2019, we called the phone number on the flyer but the number was no longer working.

Another flyer was sent by fax encouraging individuals to refinance mortgages to get cash for home improvements, debt consolidation, or "for any reason" at all. The notice promised, "rates as low as 1.25%," that income would not be verified, and that individuals who were self-employed or had declared bankruptcy were welcome to apply. On another flyer, a similar refinancing offer was extended to homeowners with a promise to give the borrower two free airline tickets for any U.S. destination (with the airline to be chosen by lender). This flyer was also faxed, described special services that included "unlimited cash out" and "100% financing" and declared that bankruptcy and bad credit were no impediments to refinancing. Neither of these two flyers had letterhead or the name of a business or individual.

Another fax, sent in 2007, offered refinancing opportunities to homeowners under terms that were similar to the two described in the preceding paragraph – unlimited

[110] Ann Goldweber, Professor of Clinical Education and the Director of the Consumer Justice for the Elderly: Litigation Clinic and Gina Calabrese, Professor of Clinical Education, "Interview" *John's University School of Law, New York City*, 25 March 2019, quoted with permission.

[111] Letters and flyers on file with the authors.

cash out, no income verification, 100 per cent financing – and made clear that foreclosure and bankruptcy were not impediments to participation. This fax also encouraged recipients to ask about "credit restoration mortgage loans" and offered to remove recipients from "our database" upon request. No names, of either an individual or a company, were provided, just a phone number. This phone number was working in May 2019, but, when we called, an answering service connected us to a car dealership.

Ann Goldweber also provided us with a flyer that had a Manhattan address announcing in all caps, "GOOD NEWS ... YOUR INVITATION IS ENCLOSED." Recipients were told that they qualified for a "quick refinance lending program to avoid foreclosure." This notice encouraged homeowners to act quickly to "help maintain ... good credit and thus get a lower rate on any financing." Also included were the following statements: "Call now to reinstate your mortgage and stop foreclosure"; and "Get a fresh start and get time to get back on track"; along with promises to make new loans "even if you have filed Bankruptcy, even if you have numerous Judgments and other debts" and "without charging ANY up-front fees, nor any cash outlay" to get the new loan. This flyer also stated, "we will ... make you a loan in a matter of days not weeks or months so that you can avoid the Auction or Bankruptcy."

This flyer, unlike the others, listed no business name, but did provide the first name of an individual to call and a working cell phone number. Co-author Wade called, and after leaving a message asking for help concerning a delinquent mortgage, the person listed on the flyer called back immediately on 21 May 2019. In the next few paragraphs, co-author Wade recounts the conversation during which she pretended to be a homeowner in distress:

> Just a minute or two into the conversation, the person listed on the flyer asked me to give her the address of the property about which I was calling so that she could check on the location and the details of my situation. I told her that I did not want to give my address. I was simply calling to inquire about the 'Express Service Program' for which, according to the flyer, I qualified. The woman with whom I was speaking then asked for the name of my mortgage lender and whether I had requested a modification. Trying to sound like a distressed mortgagor rather than a law professor, I asked her to tell me what a modification is and then told her that I wasn't sure whether I had made that request. She advised me to call the bank myself to ask for a modification package and that the bank would be required to send it, but not required to do the modification. When I expressed hesitation about making the call, she told me that she has an excellent team with experience negotiating with banks on behalf of borrowers.
>
> When the woman with whom I was speaking asked whether a judgment had been entered regarding my property, I asked her to explain, and after she did, I told her that I wasn't sure whether a judgment had been entered. She then revealed that the next best step for me, once she confirmed my situation, would be a short sale of my home. Of course, I asked what this meant, and she told me that my home would be sold for less than what I owe, and she clearly stated that I would lose the house.

> When I reminded her that I had called about the loan that was advertised on the flyer, she asked me about my income and pointed out that if my income were not sufficient, a loan would not work for me. At that point she explained that she was a consultant and that she attempts to get the best situation for each individual. She disclosed that her company does short sales and that it would cost me nothing. The bank would pay commissions, she said, and attorneys' fees. "It's a legal way to get out of a situation." The 'consultant' said that if I authorized her and her attorneys to deal with the bank, she would do so, get a buyer, check the buyers' finances and submit everything to the bank. "All of this takes time, anywhere from six months to a year", she said. She promised that she would stay in 'direct contact' with me while dealing with the bank and that I would be able to stay in my house during that time period without paying a mortgage. I could save my money, she said, so that I can rent something suitable once the short sale is completed.
>
> The 'consultant' advised me that a short sale would avoid harm to my credit history, and that typically, two months after a short sale, a borrower's credit score is quickly restored. But, she warned, "Time is not on your side. If you wait too long, the bank may secure a judgment of foreclosure. Once a judgment is entered, you will not be able to force the bank to do a short sale."
>
> As our conversation came to an end, the 'consultant' asked, "how did you hear about us? We send out a lot of information." I told her that a friend had given me the flyer. In response to my questions about her, the 'consultant' revealed her last name and the name of her company. She then explained that her firm is very honest and warned me to be careful because there are lots of scams out there.

We found the consultant's bio online. She is described as a Limited Liability Company Broker who is licensed and who works "with conventional sales with a specialty in short sale foreclosures."[112] The webpage also says that she holds a Master's degree in counselling and a Doctorate in education, and that she counsels homeowners facing foreclosure through her not-for-profit company, but includes no name or information regarding the not-for-profit firm. By clicking on several links, we came to a page listing thousands of homes in Queens, New York.[113] Of the 59 new listings, 41 were in predominantly black neighbourhoods. The consultant/broker's profile on the National Ethics Association website has expired and is inactive.[114]

We make no claim about the appropriateness or legality of the consultant's conversation with Wade other than to note that she admitted to "sending out information" about her services. Because she represents many black homeowners in Queens, New York, Ann Goldweber was able to confirm that the flyers we describe,

112 New York State MLS, "Profiles" (2019), nystatemls.com.

113 Homes.com, "Simply Smarter Home Search" (2019), homes.com.

114 The National Ethics Association assists business professionals by providing information that helps to promote ethical practices and is "also devoted to aiding consumers with the increasingly complex task of conducting due diligence on business professionals." National Ethics Association, "FAQ" (2019), www.ethics.net/faq.

including the consultant with whom Wade spoke, were distributed in predominantly or all-black communities. Notably, while the consultant's flyer describes the possibility of refinancing, reinstating one's mortgage, and stopping the foreclosure process, her discussion with Wade as the tester posing as a distressed homeowner was all about the short-sale option that would require the homeowner to leave her home and lose any equity she had in the home. During the conversation, the consultant mentioned that the lender would pay commissions. When asked to provide detail about the commissions, the consultant readily revealed that she would receive the commission.

The exchange with the consultant/broker uncovers the vast breadth of opportunities for certain actors to make money by exploiting African-American homeowners.

5 *"Smart" Loans*

Rapid changes in technology have radically changed the process of applying for and obtaining mortgages. Borrowers can apply for a mortgage online and be approved within minutes after the borrower clicks submit.[115] Credit is increasingly automatically scored, and while designed for credit cards, it is being used extensively in mortgage approval decisions. Lenders then charge much higher interest rates, given their inability to verify income, thus continuing to exacerbate issues of high interest, high risk mortgages.[116]

While the use of technology, from "robo-lender" to "robo-advisors" is beyond the scope of this book, it is important to note two ways in which these developments could disproportionately and negatively affect African Americans. First, the online application processes gather a lot of information from applicants, including employment, income, address (read postal code of predominantly black neighbourhoods), and banking information – information that could be used in the same racist way to deny mortgages and other loans. The higher interest rates that are already being charged could be even higher for African Americans, and it would be difficult to establish a case of discrimination because the criteria for setting the interest rate could be embedded in complex algorithms. Some firms report that they are using thousands of data points on lending decisions now.

The second major issue has to do with lack of transparency and accountability of the lender as counterparty to the online mortgage. The applicant borrower, in giving information on bank accounts and other liquid assets, can expose himself or herself to online fraud. There is no requirement for the smart mortgage lender to disclose where it is located, including whether or not in the United States, or where any concerns by the borrower may be directed. Where a question or dispute arises in respect of the mortgage, the applicant cannot find someone to complain to or seek

[115] Dickerson, *Homeownership*, 74.
[116] Dickerson, *Homeownership*.

advice from, similar to issues discussed earlier concerning securitized mortgages. The borrower already has given a right to access his or her bank account and the lender can go in and take funds without permission, even if there is an outstanding dispute regarding the amount owed. Such new barriers to enforcing rights may be insurmountable. Even if the mortgage borrower could figure out who the actual lender is, the lender may be located anywhere in the world, taking the mortgage contract out of the purview of U.S. domestic law.

The issue of online standard form contracts was debated contentiously at the 2019 annual meeting of The American Law Institute (ALI). Established in 1923, the ALI's mission is "to promote the clarification and simplification of the law and its better adaptation to social needs, to secure the better administration of justice, and to encourage and carry on scholarly and scientific legal work."[117] In its annual report, the ALI notes that "courts have come to trust and rely on ALI's work due to its careful drafting process, [and] its independence and integrity.… Federal and state courts routinely look to ALI's work for guidance in resolving questions of law." Courts rely on the ALI's Restatements of the Law as unambiguous expressions of common and statutory law.

At the 2019 ALI meeting, a drafting committee submitted a tentative draft of The Restatement of the Law of Consumer Contracts to ALI members. In anticipation of the discussion, State Attorneys General of 22 states[118] and the District of Columbia submitted to ALI members a memorandum stating their concerns regarding the tentative draft.[119] The State Attorneys General acknowledged the goal of the drafters to efficiently streamline the online contracting process while balancing the interests of consumers in being protected from patently unfair terms in online contracts. The Attorneys General concluded, however, that the drafters failed to achieve this balance because of inaccurate interpretations of the common law that abandoned important principles intended to protect consumers.[120] The Attorneys General noted "the reality of consumer contracts in the digital age, including consumers' complete lack of bargaining power over contractual terms, consumers' relative lack of business sophistication, and the nearly insurmountable barriers most consumers face to seeking redress through litigation."[121] After amendments were made, only parts of

[117] American Law Institute, "2017–2018 Annual Report" (28 November 2018), 3, www.ali.org/news/articles/2017-2018-annual-report/.

[118] See State of New York Office of the Attorney General, letter to the members of the American Law Institute re Restatement of the Law of Consumer Contracts, 14 May 2019, https://ag.ny.gov/sites/default/files/letter_to_ali_members.pdf (hereafter (NY Attorneys General Letter). Attorneys General who signed onto the memorandum were from the following states: New York; California, Delaware, Hawaii, Idaho, Illinois, Iowa, Kentucky, Maine, Maryland, Massachusetts, Michigan, Minnesota, Mississippi, Nevada, New Jersey, New Mexico, Oregon, Pennsylvania, Rhode Island Vermont, and Virginia.

[119] NY Attorneys General Letter.

[120] NY Attorneys General Letter.

[121] NY Attorneys General Letter.

the tentative draft were approved. We may not know the final result of this attempt to restate the law on consumer contracts until the next ALI annual meeting, but we offer this brief description of the process to note that some influential jurists would take the law in a direction that moves dangerously away from longstanding consumer protections. They propose to do so to make the online contracting process more efficient and easier for businesses.

The impact of interpretations of the law that chip away at important consumer protections such as the doctrines of mutual assent[122] and unconscionability would be devastating for African-American mortgagors. Analysis under the mutual assent doctrine to determine the contractual terms to which a consumer actually assented is fact sensitive because of the need to determine whether a consumer had notice of the term. The ALI draft would abandon this fact-sensitive inquiry because, in the drafters estimation, "the costs of the doctrine outweigh the benefits because consumers do not read standard form contracts and, even if they did, could not make informed decisions about the terms given that most form contracts are drafted in unintelligible legalese."[123] The ALI drafters asserted that the doctrine of unconscionability offers sufficient protection for consumers. Among other things in this regard, the State Attorneys General objected to the idea that the doctrine provides enough protection for consumers because the "burden of demonstrating unconscionability is generally high, and courts rarely find consumer contracts to be unconscionable."[124]

6 *Public Sector Predation*

In this book, we describe and analyze predatory and discriminatory practices in the context of home mortgages and ownership. While our focus is on private sector firms, it is imperative that we briefly mention the alarming possibility of twenty-first century predation on the part of municipalities. For example, the community activist we interviewed in Detroit described situations where African Americans lost homes in tax foreclosures. In 2018, the city of Detroit, Michigan settled a lawsuit

122 The mutual assent doctrine provides that a party to a contract is "bound to only those contractual terms to which she assented." NY Attorneys General Letter, 2. The attorneys general wrote, "our States have brought numerous enforcement action, under our respective consumer protection statutes and laws, where material terms of a consumer contract are buried in the fine print under circumstances where consumers would never have assented to them. These actions have included … predatory mortgage loans with teaser rates that are unaffordable in the long-term. … Any presumption that consumers have assented to these material terms is a fiction." NY Attorneys General Letter, 4–5.

123 NY Attorneys General Letter, 2.

124 NY Attorneys General Letter, 6. The foundational case on unconscionability, decided in 1965, involves a contract between a retail furniture store and Ora Lee Williams, an African-American woman with limited income. See Amy H. Kastely, "Out of the Whiteness: On Raced Codes and White Race Consciousness in Some Tort, Criminal, and Contract Law" (1994) 63 *U Cin L Rev* 269 at 305–10.

brought by the American Civil Liberties Union. One commentator described how difficult it was for Detroit property owners to take advantage of property tax exemptions for impoverished homeowners because the city impeded homeowners' ability to discover and qualify for the exemptions. When thousands of Detroit homeowners paid property taxes they did not owe, the city did not inform them about the exemptions for which they qualified. Other homeowners who qualified for the exemptions, but were unable to pay the taxes, lost their homes at tax foreclosure auctions.[125]

In New York City, the Third Party Transfer Program (TPT) threatens black homeownership for families and individuals on all socio-economic levels.[126] The TPT program was created decades ago to address a rise in vacant and abandoned homes in certain neighbourhoods.[127] The program allows the city to transfer ownership of homes from homeowners to selected for-profit and not-for-profit developers when homeowners become delinquent on water bills or property taxes.[128] The developers do not have to pay the delinquent bills and are given extremely low interest rates on financing for redevelopment.[129] Once the property is redeveloped, it is rented out at affordable rates.[130] The program, ostensibly created to provide affordable housing and reduce the urban blight that is exacerbated when homes are abandoned and left vacant, has primarily impacted black homeowners who lose all equity in their homes. At a packed three-hour legislative hearing in Brooklyn, New York in March 2019 that we describe further in Chapter 10, many former homeowners, all of whom were African American, described homes lost to or threatened by the TPT program.[131]

New York City's predation in this regard impacted a solidly middle-class black homeowner who was not delinquent in paying property taxes or utility bills and whose home was maintained in pristine condition. Marlene Saunders, a 74-year-old retired nurse who is African American, almost lost her house under the TPT program. Ms. Saunders and her family had owned the home for more than thirty years and it was "free from loans, [a] mortgage and had no … Department of Building violations."[132] The city used its in-rem process to transfer Ms. Saunder's home because

[125] Tracy Samilton, "Detroit settles ACLU tax foreclosure lawsuit to keep impoverished residents in their homes" *Michigan Radio* (4 July 2018), www.michiganradio.org/post/detroit-settles-aclu-tax-foreclosure-lawsuit-keep-impoverished-residents-their-homes.

[126] NYC, Department of Housing Preservation and Development, "Multifamily Disposition and Finance Programs Term Sheet" (29 March 2019), www.nyc.gov/assets/hpd/downloads/pdf/developers/term-sheets/multifamily-disposition-and-finance-term-sheet.pdf.

[127] See Stephen Witt and Kelly Mena, "TPT Horror Stories Aired at Packed Borough Hall" *King's County Politics* (18 March 2019), www.kingscountypolitics.com/tpt-horror-stories-aired-at-packed-borough-hall/ (hereafter Witt and Mena, "TPT Horror Stories").

[128] Witt and Mena, "TPT Horror Stories."

[129] Witt and Mena, "TPT Horror Stories."

[130] Witt and Mena, "TPT Horror Stories."

[131] Witt and Mena, "TPT Horror Stories."

[132] Stephen Witt, "City Caught Trying to Grab Senior Citizen's Brownstone" *King's County Politics* (17 September 2018), www.kingscountypolitics.com/1217-dean-street/ (hereafter Witt, "City Caught").

of an almost $4,000 water bill.[133] Ms. Saunders' family was not aware that owing this amount would risk foreclosure.[134] They immediately paid the water bill but were told that the home was already in the process of being transferred to a non-profit third party called Neighborhood Restore.[135] The process had been initiated through a court proceeding about which Ms. Saunders was given no notice.[136] With the help of local activists and a city council member, the city attributed the transfer to the owner's "mistake in applying the necessary payment to the wrong property" and reversed the transfer.[137] The council member who assisted the Saunders' family adamantly disputed the city's claim that Ms. Saunders, the homeowner, committed the error and attributes the mistake to the city.[138]

Consider the name of the third party to whom Marlene Saunders' property was transferred – Neighborhood Restore.[139] The name suggests that the third party will pursue the laudable goal of restoring a blighted neighbourhood, but Ms. Saunders' home was in excellent condition. In reality, Neighborhood Restore will restore ownership of homes in what has become a black community after white flight that occurred decades ago, with a newly coveted location because of its proximity to commercial centres like downtown and midtown Manhattan, to white developers and homebuyers. A thriving, desirable black community is "restored" by gentrification and the transfer of ownership from blacks to whites. The name, Neighborhood Restore, is intentionally obfuscating.

According to the council member who assisted Ms. Saunders, there is "at least one other property in Brooklyn … where there is a similar situation, and perhaps more across the city."[140] In March 2019, a Brooklyn Supreme Court Judge found that New York City's seizure of six properties from black and Latinx homeowners under the TPT program was unconstitutional and reversed the transfers.[141] Almost all of the properties were paid for and were not subject to mortgages.[142] The judge found that the homeowners were not properly notified about the transfers.[143] He also concluded that the homes were not distressed as is required under the TPT

133 Witt, "City Caught."
134 Witt, "City Caught."
135 Witt, "City Caught."
136 Witt, "City Caught."
137 Witt, "City Caught."
138 Witt, "City Caught."
139 Housing Development Fund Corporation, "Neighbourhood Restore" (2019), neighborhoodrestore.org. Under this program private homes were and continue to be designated to Neighborhood Restore Housing Development Fund Corporation, which was formed in 1999.
140 Witt, "City Caught."
141 See Stephen Witt and Kelly Mena, "Court Rules against City, Millions of Dollars of Wealth Restored" *King's County Politics* (29 March 2019), www.kingscountypolitics.com/courts-rules-against-city-millions-of-dollars-of-wealth-restored/ (hereafter Witt and Mena, "Court Rules against City").
142 Witt and Mena, "Court Rules against City."
143 Witt and Mena, "Court Rules against City."

program for homes to be transferred.[144] The judge observed that, "[t]he City has particularly targeted properties that are owned by minorities."[145] Additionally, 66 homeowners sought class certification in New York Federal District Court to pursue a claim that New York City improperly seized their property under the TPT program. According to the filing, New York City violated the equal protection clause of the U.S. Constitution when it:

> Improperly engaged in acts and transactions that intended to, or that resulted in, a redistribution of property ownership and wealth away from individuals that are of African-American and/or Hispanic American descent, or buildings that are owned predominantly by individuals of African-American or Hispanic American descent, to private companies and partners of the ... defendants.[146]

In New York City's TPT program, we see a dangerous partnership between a municipality and private sector firms that redevelop buildings in communities of colour that are in the process of being gentrified. Journalists Stephen Witt and Kelly Mena described this partnership in an investigative series of articles to which we cite in the preceding paragraphs. Witt warns that the public sector must be carefully monitored and rejects "the idea that predatory lending is only a private sector enterprise."[147] Mena concludes that black homeowners were intentionally targeted under the TPT program as part of gentrification efforts focused on previously all-black neighbourhoods.[148] She believes that the targeting of black homeowners is grounded in racism and is aimed at assisting white developers to take properties without compensating the homeowners, renovate them, and profit from sales to more affluent homebuyers, almost all of whom are white.[149] In her investigation, Mena found that 90–95 per cent of the homeowners targeted under the TPT program are black, some were Latinx homeowners, but "none were white."[150] Mena explained that the lack of attention to, and reporting on, the impact of New York's TPT program on black homeowners derives from racist assumptions that black homeowners cannot afford the homes they purchase.[151]

This chapter reveals that predatory lending continues in different forms and African Americans continue to be specifically targeted. In addition, mortgage borrowers are being exposed to new forms of fraudulent conduct. For example, the Federal Bureau of Investigation (FBI) has reported that sophisticated phishing

[144] Witt and Mena, "Court Rules against City."
[145] Witt and Mena, "Court Rules against City."
[146] Stephen Witt and Kelly Mena, "City Faces $66M Class Action Lawsuit on Taking of Private Property," *King's County Politics* (13 March 2019), www.kingscountypolitics.com/city-faces-66m-class-action-lawsuit-on-taking-of-private-property/.
[147] Stephen Witt, telephone interview, 5 July 2019, quoted with permission.
[148] Kelly Mena, telephone interview, 3 July 2019, quoted with permission.
[149] Witt and Mena, "Court Rules against City."
[150] Witt and Mena, "Court Rules against City."
[151] Witt and Mena, "Court Rules against City."

scams are increasingly taking advantage of homebuyers during the closing process, in which they attempt to divert the consumer's down payment and closing costs into a fraudulent account by confirming or suggesting last-minute changes to wiring instructions.[152] Reports of these scams have risen 1,100 per cent between 2015 and 2017, and in 2017 alone, there was an estimated loss of nearly $1 billion in real estate transaction costs.[153]

To date, regulatory reform has not been effective in curbing racially discriminatory predatory practices. African Americans in Queens, a borough of New York City, were especially hard hit during the foreclosure crisis that was precipitated by predatory lending and examination of some of the details relating to the June 2019 Democratic Primary for Queens District Attorney provides one example that helps to explain why the targeting of black homeowners persists. The successful candidate, Melinda Katz, issued a position paper on predatory lending that came alarmingly close to the type of victim-blaming discourse that we describe in Chapter 4. The candidate acknowledged that communities of colour were targeted for predatory loans and that rates of foreclosure in the all-black neighbourhood of Southeast Queens continued to go up in 2018.[154] Most of her discussion in the position paper, however, on this issue was devoted to the availability of financial literacy programs for consumers and the fact that many homebuyers signed mortgage loans without taking advantage of financial literacy programs.[155] Katz claimed that homebuyers often failed to understand the risks of mortgage loans and promised that if successful, her office would provide resources to help to educate consumers and make it easier for them to report predatory and fraudulent lending practices by way of a consumer hotline that would allow them to record their stories if a lender is prosecuted.[156]

It is unfortunate that Katz's position statement fails to address the fact that the predatory lenders also targeted homeowners in refinancing schemes. Most troubling, however, is the fact that the candidate focuses primarily on the need for consumers to change by promising to provide workshops aimed at informing consumers about how to protect themselves from predatory practices. She focuses on what victims should do – educate themselves – and not sufficiently on the notion of holding predatory lenders accountable. In her position paper, she acknowledges that predators frequently go to the homes of potential victims and that some of the homeowners who are targeted escape the predation because they "know enough" to refuse the lender's offer. This statement suggests that homebuyers and homeowners who are

152 Melissa Yu, "Mortgage Closing Scams: How to Protect Yourself and Your Closing Funds" (3 June 2019), Consumer Finance Protection Bureau, www.consumerfinance.gov/about-us/blog/mortgage-closing-scams-how-protect-yourself-and-your-closing-funds/ (hereafter Yu, "Mortgage Closing Scams").

153 Yu, "Mortgage Closing Scams."

154 Melinda Katz, "Position Paper 2: Housing Fraud, Predatory Small Business Lending and Landlord Abuse" (27 March 2019), katz4da.com (hereafter Katz, "Position Paper 2")

155 Katz, "Position Paper 2."

156 Katz, "Position Paper 2."

victimized do not "know enough" to avoid traps, and it fails to focus sufficiently on the predatory behaviour. No amount of financial literacy training would assist consumers confronted by sophisticated and experienced lenders intent on scamming them. The focus must be on the predatory practices and not primarily on educating consumers and providing avenues for them to report predation.

Katz's position paper briefly mentions prosecuting predators, but observes that it is difficult to provide evidence that can be used in a criminal case.[157] If successful, Katz promised to create a Bureau of Housing and Loan Fraud to gather information to provide a record of predators who target multiple victims in the same community. Evidence of a track record of deceptive practices and lies on the part of one predator in a single community would, according to Katz, more likely result in litigation outcomes that provide justice for victims.[158] Based on the tone of Katz' position paper, it seems unlikely that she would aggressively prosecute predatory lenders.

Katz was backed by the Queens Democratic Party establishment, and she won her bid for the party's nomination. One of her rivals, Tiffany Caban, in an interview with *The Nation*, promised to prioritize the prosecution of predatory lenders.[159] This focus on deceptive lenders rather than requiring victims to educate themselves is sensible and dramatically contrasts with Katz' focus on victims' behaviour. Katz won the 2019 election for Queens district attorney. Unfortunately, her focus on borrowers' deficiencies, rather than on lenders' predatory conduct, demonstrates why reform efforts have failed to mitigate the impact of predatory lending practices on the consumers who were targeted.

[157] Katz, "Position Paper 2."
[158] Katz, "Position Paper 2."
[159] Isabel Cristo, "Tiffany Caban Wants to Transform What It Means to Be a DA" *The Nation* (13 June 2019), www.thenation.com/article/tiffany-caban-queens-da-interview/.

10

"Forgiveness" rather than Forbearance or Foreclosure

In this concluding chapter, we turn to a normative discussion of how we should approach default for home borrowers. It considers the dissonance between the oft-stated public policy goals of U.S. governmental agencies regarding home ownership and the policies and practices they have sanctioned on the ground. The chapter explores whether there is space for a paradigm shift, a complete reconceptualization of mortgage lending, conditions, response on default, and prevention of foreclosures. It examines whether the law can be responsive to contemporary developments in mortgage lending, and whether it can be designed to recognize the legacy of racism in its application.

There have been many important policy recommendations aimed at protecting consumers.[1] It makes sense to strengthen state consumer protection laws considerably and to place resources behind their enforcement. Consumer protection laws have been effective in shifting at least some conduct of non-bank lenders.[2]

Kathleen Engel and Patricia McCoy argue for federal support for savings towards home ownership:

> the key to helping cash-constrained people buy homes is savings programs where they can accumulate money for down payments, FHA insurance premiums, and unexpected expenses like home repairs. The government should finance a matched

[1] See, for example, American Civil Liberties Union, "Justice Foreclosed: How Wall Street's Appetite for Subprime Mortgages Ended Up Hurting Black and Latino Communities" (October 2012), www.aclu.org/sites/default/files/field_document/justiceforclosed-singlepage-rel4.pdf (hereafter American Civil Liberties Union, "Justice Foreclosed").

[2] See the discussion in Manisha Padi, "Consumer Protection Laws and the Mortgage Market: Evidence from Ohio" (2018) (Working Paper), 3, Manisha Padi, https://manishapadi.com/working-papers/, referencing the National Low Income Housing Coalition, "Findings from the HB 4050 Predatory Lending Database Pilot Program" (1 April 2007), https://nlihc.org/resource/findings-hb-4050-predatory-lending-database-pilot-program (hereafter Padi, "Consumer Protection Ohio").

savings program for lower-income households. In addition, the government should give tax credits to people in lower tax brackets who salt away money in special home ownership funds.[3]

Meshra Baradaran has a bolder proposal, arguing for reparation of the harms caused financially. She suggests that one needs only to follow the 'red lines' to focus on home-ownership reform, as these neighbourhoods have long been denied credit and remain impoverished;[4] and we would add, have been the most directly targeted for predatory lending. Baradaran observes that reparation could take the form of direct cash payments, subsidized college tuition, housing vouchers, subsidized mortgage credit, or other "creative proposals that garner full and meaningful financial inclusion that reverse the effects of historic exclusions from wealth creation."[5] She suggests a reparation program that focuses on geography and home ownership, involving reparations to people living in historically redlined areas, which has the potential to lead to longer term benefits as intergenerational wealth is passed through home and land ownership.[6]

Much less discussed are changes to financial market regulation to prevent predatory lending. The Center for Responsible Lending recommends policy changes that would curtail steering African Americans into predatory loans by requiring objective pricing standards, holding lenders and brokers responsible for providing loans that are suitable for their customers, ensuring that adequate resources are dedicated to fully enforcing fair lending laws, and creating incentives and supporting a policy framework that lead the market to better serve African-American and Latinx communities.[7] Mandatory disclosures have the potential to reduce misconduct in mortgage contract formation; however, transparency of terms and conditions is meaningless if consumers do not have the skills to understand the financial impact of the terms on their capacity to repay the mortgage. All are important suggestions for reform. We add our recommendations to this list.

I EFFECTIVE STRUCTURAL REFORM IS ONLY POSSIBLE IF THERE IS WIDESPREAD RECOGNITION OF THE PERMANENCE OF RACISM

It is important to note that proposed policy reforms focus, appropriately, on all consumer borrowers and not just African-American consumer borrowers. Of course, policies designed to help consumers in general will help African-American consumers.

3 Kathleen Engel and Patricia McCoy, *The Subprime Virus: Reckless Credit, Regulatory Failure, and Next Steps* (New York: Oxford University Press, 2011), 232 (hereafter Engel and McCoy, *The Subprime Virus*).

4 Meshra Baradaran, *The Color of Money: Black Banks and the Racial Wealth Gap* (Cambridge: Belknap Press, 2017), 282 (hereafter Baradaran "Color of Money"). Redlining was discussed in Chapter 3.

5 Baradaran "Color of Money."

6 Baradaran "Color of Money," 283.

7 D. Gruenstein Bocian, K. S. Ernst and W. Li, "Unfair Lending, the Effect of Race and Ethnicity on the Price of Subprime Mortgages," 4 (2006) Center for Responsible Lending, www.responsiblelending.org/research-publication/unfair-lending-effect-race-and-ethnicity-price-subprime-mortgages (hereafter Bocian et al, "Unfair Lending").

But it is imperative that proponents for reform acknowledge the unique historical and social position of African Americans and the economic exploitation they faced in the past, and continue to face in the twenty-first century. The work of Derrick Bell, one of critical race theory's originators, is invaluable in this respect. In his book, *Faces at the Bottom of the Well*, Bell writes that, "racism is an integral, permanent, and indestructible component" of U.S. society.[8] According to Bell, African Americans "are doomed to fail as long as the majority of whites do not see their own well-being threatened by the *status quo*."[9] In other words, African Americans' success – financial, social, and existential – depends upon the willingness of white Americans to relinquish privileges their whiteness provides.[10]

Why would white Americans give up systemic privilege, most of which is invisible to them? Bell's answer to this question is that white Americans will relinquish privilege and dismantle systems that oppress black Americans when the interests of blacks and whites converge.[11] Mary Dudziak invokes Bell's interest convergence theory by suggesting that desegregation was driven in large measure by America's Cold War policy around 1947, rather than a commitment to human rights and racial equality.[12] The Court's decision in *Brown* v *Board of Education*[13] was influential in the U.S. government's efforts to combat communism.[14] She reports that during the Cold War years, international perceptions of American democracy were thought to affect the United States' ability to maintain its international leadership role.[15] There were huge contradictions between racism and the ideology of democracy and the essential dignity of human beings.[16] Dudziak argues that civil rights reform was, in part, a product of the Cold War because continuing racial discrimination in the United States received high profile and considerably negative attention internationally.[17] Lynching and racial segregation led to international outrage, and by 1949, race in America was a Soviet propaganda theme, the Soviets arguing that America's professing of liberty and equality under democracy was a sham.[18] Dudziak examines *amicus curiae* briefs in civil rights cases, where the Truman administration stressed to the U.S. Supreme

[8] Derrick Bell, *Faces at the Bottom of the Well: The Permanence of Racism* (New York: Basic Books, 1992) (hereafter Bell, *Faces at the Bottom of the Well*).

[9] Bell, *Faces at the Bottom of the* Well.

[10] See, for example, Peggy McIntosh, "White Privilege: Unpacking the Invisible Knapsack" (1989) *Peace and Freedom Magazine* 10, The National SEED Project, https://nationalseedproject.org/images/documents/Knapsack_plus_Notes-Peggy_McIntosh.pdf, describing the daily and systemic privileges that white Americans enjoy.

[11] See Derrick A. Bell, Jr, "*Brown v Board of Education* and the Interest Convergence Dilemma" (1980) 93 *Harvard L Rev* 518 (hereafter Bell, "*Brown v Board of Education*").

[12] Mary Dudziak, *Cold War Civil Rights: Race and the Image of American Democracy* (Princeton, NJ: *Princeton University Press*, 2000) (hereafter Dudziak, *Cold War*).

[13] *Brown* v *The Board of Education*, 347 US 483 (1954) (hereafter *Brown* v *Board of Education*).

[14] Dudziak, *Cold War*, xvii.

[15] Dudziak, *Cold War*, 6.

[16] Dudziak, *Cold War*, 9.

[17] Dudziak, *Cold War*, 11.

[18] Dudziak, *Cold War*, 15, 37.

Court the international implications of race discrimination and the negative impacts on U.S. foreign relations that a pro-segregation decision might have.[19]

The violent events in Little Rock, defying court orders to desegregate, are testimony to the courage of the student protesters, but also the endemic racism of the United States.[20] The equal protection clause and the constitutional ideal of equal justice under the law were severely challenged.[21] The Supreme Court unanimously reaffirmed its holding in *Brown* that segregated schools violated the 14th amendment. Dudziak suggests that the story of civil rights and the Cold War is part of the story of a struggle over the narrative of race and democracy.[22] As the civil rights movement gained strength, it faced the brutality of massive resistance.[23]

The 17 of May 2019 marked the 65th anniversary of the U.S. Supreme Court's decision in *Brown* v *Board of Education*, and while it is considered a foundational constitutional decision in respect of U.S. democracy and desegregation, segregation continues. A recent report found that over the past three decades, black students attend intensely segregated schools, defined as being 90 to 100 per cent non-white.[24] By 2016, 40 per cent of all black students were in schools with 90 per cent or more students of colour.[25] New York, California, Illinois and Maryland are the four states in which a majority of black students attend extremely segregated schools. 90 to 100 per cent of the students who attend predominantly black schools are from low-income households.[26]

Sherrilyn Ifill, president and director-counsel of the National Association for the Advancement of Colored People ('NAACP') Legal Defense and Educational Fund recently observed that for 65 years, the legal consensus around *Brown* v *Board of Education* was unequivocal, noting that even the most conservative judges affirmed its centrality to the nation's democratic character.[27] Then in April 2018, Trump

19 Dudziak, *Cold War*, 90.

20 Dudziak, *Cold War*, 45–7.

21 Dudziak, *Cold War*, 147.

22 Dudziak, *Cold War*, 250.

23 Dudziak, *Cold War*.

24 Erica Frankenberg et al, "Harming our Common Future: America's Segregated Schools 65 Years after Brown" (10 May 2019), University of California, Los Angeles, www.civilrightsproject.ucla.edu/research/k-12-education/integration-and-diversity/harming-our-common-future-americas-segregated-schools-65-years-after-brown/Brown-65-050919v4-final.pdf (hereafter Frankenberg et al, "Common Future"). The Report was issued by the Civil Rights Project at UCLA and the Center for Education and Civil Rights at Pennsylvania State University with input from researchers at Loyola Marymount University and North Carolina State University.

25 Frankenberg et al, "Common Future," 25.

26 Frankenberg et al, "Common Future," 23. See also Valerie Strauss, "The Promise of Historic Brown v Board School Desegregation Ruling Is 'At Grave Risk,' Report Says" *Washington Post* (10 May 2019), www.washingtonpost.com/education/2019/05/10/promise-historic-brown-v-board-school-desegregation-ruling-is-at-grave-risk-report-says/.

27 Sherrilyn Ifill, "If Judicial Nominees Don't Support 'Brown v Board,' They Don't Support the Rule of Law" *Washington Post* (12 May 2019), www.washingtonpost.com/opinions/if-judicial-nominees-dont-support-brown-v-board-they-dont-support-the-rule-of-law/2019/05/12/d12c542a-734d-11e9-8be0-ca575670e91c_story.html (hereafter Ifill, "Judicial Nominees").

judicial nominee Wendy Vitter bucked more than a half-century of unanimity by failing to offer support for the *Brown* decision, and since then, more than two dozen executive and judicial nominees have declined to endorse the U.S. Supreme Court's unanimous decision in *Brown* v *Board of Education*.[28] She writes:

> The ugly truth is that declining to offer approval of *Brown* signals a willingness to question the project of democracy that *Brown* created — one in which African Americans and other marginalized groups compelled the federal courts to honor the spirit of equal justice embodied in the words of the 14th Amendment. And this isn't just deeply troubling; it's also downright dangerous.[29]

Unfortunately, the type of interest convergence that occurred in the mid-twentieth century that led to the *Brown* decision will not happen in the predatory lending context. Too many white Americans profit from the economic exploitation of African Americans, even in the twenty-first century. It is true, however, that interests converged, at least momentarily. This convergence occurred briefly when African Americans defaulted on mortgages and faced foreclosure, investors in the securitized mortgages lost money and global economic systems were at risk. However, the convergence was short-lived as remedies were skewed racially. African Americans lost homes, or some held onto homes by adhering to the onerous terms of modification agreements. Investors and financial institutions were bailed out, but foreclosed-upon homeowners were not. Investors and lenders, most of whom are white, largely recovered their investments and their interests no longer converged with the interests of individuals victimized by predatory lending who recovered little to none of their losses.

At first glance, Bell's permanence of racism thesis seems hopeless. It is not. Bell's position focuses reform efforts in a practical and realistic direction. Effective policy reform is only possible with the acknowledgement of the history and persistence of the economic exploitation of African Americans. The insight that Bell offers is that proposals for reform will never work for African Americans without acknowledging the anti-black bias of centuries past and its endurance in the twenty-first century. If historical context and twenty-first century racial reality are ignored, reformists will labour in futility. Meaningful change can occur only if lenders, jurists, legislators, regulators, and policymakers acknowledge that proposed reforms must be able to operate in the context of what Bell describes as "integral, permanent, and indestructible" racism in the United States. Without this acknowledgement, reform will be useless.

An effective foundation for reform depends also on Cheryl Harris' work.

> Whiteness and property share a common premise—a conceptual nucleus—of a right to exclude. This conceptual nucleus has proven to be a powerful center around which whiteness as property has taken shape. Following the period of slavery and conquest, white identity became the basis of racialized privilege that was

[28] Ifill, "Judicial Nominees."
[29] Ifill, "Judicial Nominees."

> ratified and legitimated in law as a type of status property. After legalized segregation was overturned, whiteness as property evolved into a more modern form through the law's ratification of the settled expectations of relative white privilege as a legitimate and natural baseline.[30]

Harris describes the continuing reality of whiteness as property even in the last decade of the twentieth century:

> Whiteness as property has taken on more subtle forms, but retains its core characteristic—the legal legitimation of expectations of power and control that enshrine the *status quo* as a neutral baseline, while masking the maintenance of white privilege and domination.[31]

The seeming intractability of economic oppression may have led historian Manning Marable to conclude that it was not possible for African Americans to be free from exploitation in a capitalist society.[32] He suggests a radical shift towards socialist policy. On the other hand, even though both Bell and Harris write about the interest of white Americans in maintaining a system that privileges them, they indicate that they seek reform within the system already in place. Bell concludes that the entrenchment of white Americans in upholding the *status quo* should not preclude attempts to dismantle white privilege. He saw value in the activism itself. Harris concentrated on ways to reinterpret law in order to "de-legitimate" the implicitly held belief of many white Americans that they are entitled to "the unfettered right to exclude as a legitimate aspect of identity and property."[33]

We align with Bell and Harris in this book. We believe that effective reform is possible even while we accept Bell's thesis about the permanence of racism. Reform will not eradicate racism, but it can mitigate its impact on vulnerable individuals and communities. Reform will work only if the historical context of the economic exploitation of African Americans is acknowledged and understood. Effective reform has been elusive, in large part, because, as we discuss in Chapter 8, lenders have settled litigation that provided convincing evidence of their predation without acknowledging their wrongdoing. Settlements expedite resolution of lawsuits, but without judgments on the merits, there are no established "facts" and the perpetrators of abusive or fraudulent conduct are not held accountable.

Reformists labour in a twenty-first century context distorted by erroneous post-racial ideology. The radical social and economic progress of African Americans in

[30] Cheryl I. Harris, "Whiteness as Property" (1993) 106 Harvard L Rev, 1709–14 (hereafter Harris, "Whiteness as Property").

[31] Harris, "Whiteness as Property," 1715.

[32] Manning Marable, *How Capitalism Underdeveloped Black America* (Boston, MA: South End Press, 1983), 228 (hereafter Marable, *Capitalism Underdeveloped Black America*).

[33] Marable, *Capitalism Underdeveloped Black America.*

the nineteenth and twentieth centuries was unburdened by claims of post-racialism. The advances were possible because it was largely impossible for rational Americans to ignore the racism of that era.

We agree with Marable's insightful observation about the relevance of race to the human activities of accumulation and dispossession.[34] We see this connection in the predatory lending context where lenders and investors in securitized mortgages accumulate wealth by dispossessing African Americans. Marable observed that the economic exploitation of the labour and expertise of African Americans by enslaving, segregating, and otherwise discriminating against them is inextricably linked to the foundation of U.S. capitalism.[35] He vividly described the indispensability of the exploitation of African Americans to one of the most remarkably rapid accumulations of wealth (for white Americans only) in the history of humanity.[36]

More than thirty years later, Marable's book describing the connection between wealth accumulation and the exploitation of African Americans was republished with a new foreword written by Leith Mullings. Mullings illustrated Marable's prescience by noting the ways that racism continues to profit white Americans and contributes to the widening income and wealth gaps through the twenty-first century practices of gentrification and land dispossession.[37] Mullings connected Marable's three-decades old commentary about the indispensability of African-American exploitation to advance wealth accumulation for white Americans to the predatory lending context and noted the pecuniary benefits that fraudulent real-estate practices yielded for financial institutions. She described the fact that foreclosure rates in African-American and Latinx communities, where financial firms steered borrowers of colour into sub-prime mortgages, are three times higher than those in white neighbourhoods where the extension of sub-prime loans was disproportionately lower.[38]

Professor Steven A. Ramirez calls for the rule of law to constrain the economic and political power wielded by elite Americans at the expense of economically vulnerable individuals.[39] Unlike Marable, however, Ramirez' work cogently calls for a reconstruction of capitalism rather than a shift towards socialism. Professors Todd Clark and andré douglas pond cummings also look to reform of the system in place and persuasively insist that all constituents involved in corporate activity pursue profits without harming or depleting human potential.[40]

34 Marable, *Capitalism Underdeveloped Black America*, xiii.
35 Marable, *Capitalism Underdeveloped Black America*, xi.
36 Marable, *Capitalism Underdeveloped Black America*, 1–2.
37 Marable, *Capitalism Underdeveloped Black America*, x.
38 Marable, *Capitalism Underdeveloped Black America*, xiii.
39 See, generally, Steven A. Ramirez, *Lawless Capitalism: The Subprime Crisis and the Case for an Economic Rule of Law* (New York: New York University Press, 2012).
40 Todd J. Clark and andré douglas pond cummings, *Corporate Justice* (Durham, NC: Carolina Academic Press, 2016).

II IMPOSE RIGOROUS LIMITS ON THE TYPE AND NATURE OF PRODUCTS AND SERVICES

While post-2009 policy reform has imposed new measures on banks in terms of capital adequacy and liquidity, as well as creating a few new restrictions on consumer mortgage lending, the discussion in Chapter 9 on new forms of predatory lending reveals that little substantive reform has occurred concerning mortgage products and practices. The requirement for financial firms to retain 5 per cent of securitized mortgages is fairly meaningless, because the originator can hold the safest part of the pooled mortgages, which means no potential loss at all. Much more powerful measures could be enacted that would require proactive change by mortgage lenders and their agents. We suggest several types of reform that could be effective.

Recommendation 1: Eliminate or Restrict Residential Mortgage-backed Securities

One effective strategy would be to ban securitization of residential mortgages completely, as securitizations fuel investor pressure for short-term returns, which in turn creates incentives for predatory and non-prime lending to expand product sales as rapidly as possible. Such a prohibition would create a decline in the market for mortgages and mortgage-backed securities, particularly the new burgeoning market for "non-prime" residential mortgage-backed securities. However, the lost profits would accrue to financial firms and their investors, and it would prevent the devastating losses that continue to occur to consumer borrowers. Securitization does little to create meaningful access to credit for African-American mortgage borrowers, given all the issues discussed in this book. Such a ban would force lenders back to relational lending, because they could not immediately shed their risk of mortgage loans in the market. They would have to engage in careful assessment of mortgage applications and their servicing agents would have to monitor compliance on an ongoing basis. Since they could not shed the risk, they are more likely to develop ongoing relationships with the borrowers.

Notwithstanding the large amounts paid out in settlements, the amounts did little to deter these financial firms. All of the penalties and settlement amounts "paid" by Bank of America, for example, totalled less than one year's profit, and while the settlements were a short-term hit to investors (paid in the form of diminished dividends), the bank continues to have record profits.[41] The 5 per cent "skin in the game" is currently just the price of doing business.

If not a ban, then the U.S. Government could require mortgage originators to hold 25 per cent of the mortgage for the life of the loan, being allowed to securitize

[41] Fred Imbert, "Bank of America Shares Jump 7% after Record Earnings Report" *CNBC News* (16 January 2019).

75 per cent at most. While it would not stop the incentives for selling predatory mortgages, it would slow the market. Importantly, the law should then require that any losses be borne proportionally across all investors holding these mortgage-backed assets. In other words, the 25 per cent retained could not be the most secure part of the pooled mortgages; the financial firm would be proportionally at risk if there is default and foreclosure. Such a requirement would benefit investors as well as requiring an adequate level of capitalization of originators.

Recommendation 2: Impose a Positive Duty of Care on Mortgage Originators and Servicers

Even if one accepts that there is a place for non-prime mortgage lending in the commercial market, another reform would be to impose an express duty of care on mortgage lenders not to sell *predatory* sub-prime or non-prime mortgages to consumer borrowers. A positive duty should include making both directors and officers personally liable for breaches of the duty, as well as making the company liable for the actions of its employees that breach the duty. That duty of care should be owed to both investors and consumer borrowers.

An important reform to accompany such a duty would be to allocate resources to consumer organizations or legal clinics to pursue remedies for breach of the duty of care. While no duties are owed to these organizations or clinics, they can advise persons to whom duties are owed – the consumers and investors. These resources could be raised by levies on the industry as a whole. Just as the banks contribute annual amounts to the Federal Deposit Insurance Corporation to provide funds to protect depositors, there could be annual required contributions by financial firms to organizations entrusted with responsibility to monitor compliance with the duty of care and hold firms accountable for any breaches.

In addition, imposing a duty of loyalty would provide a related mechanism to discourage lenders from selling predatory loans, which would also be accompanied by reform that would provide resources to enforce such a duty. Under U.S. common law, directors are obliged under the duty of loyalty to monitor compliance with law. This duty is breached when boards act in bad faith by consciously disregarding compliance obligations or engaging in intentional derelictions of monitoring requirements.[42] The duty of loyalty in this context would impose liability on firms, boards and executives who look the other way when mid-level loan officers make predatory loans or when managers engage in racist predatory lending practices. Consideration should be given also to imposing a duty of loyalty on firms that purchase securitized mortgages without performing the type of due diligence that would reveal the predatory nature of the pooled mortgages.

[42] See *Stone* v *Ritter*, 911 A2d 362 (Del 2006).

Recommendation 3: Require Affirmative Action on Mortgage Accessibility
Another strategy that could be an effective start to redressing the harms of the sub-prime mortgage debacle would be to require the financial firms in the mortgage market to proactively market and grant low-interest traditional prime mortgages to African-American borrowers and to report annually on their efforts. Since little of the penalties and relief went to families that were foreclosed on, such an affirmative strategy could be aimed at these former mortgagors and their now adult children. Here again, one would have to ensure that there are remedies and sanctions for failure to shift mortgage lending practices. In other words, this recommendation would acknowledge the structural racism across the market and require an affirmative action strategy that offers traditional mortgages to African Americans.

Recommendation 4: Enhance Transparency during the Lending Process
Mortgage lenders should be required to have a uniform set of clear and accessible disclosures regarding all mortgage loans, including the real impact of interest rates and other terms. While some disclosures have improved in the decade after the financial crisis with guidance from the Consumer Financial Protection Bureau (CFPB), disclosures are not uniformly accurate or comprehensible, as evidenced throughout this book. As discussed in Chapter 7, recent amendments to the Home Mortgage Disclosure Act have exempted smaller mortgage lenders from reporting requirements, arguably making them less accountable for disclosures to consumer borrowers due to the diminished regulatory oversight.

Lessons can be taken from the warnings required by the tobacco industry. Mortgage documents could warn up front that the mortgage could be hazardous to the consumer's financial viability and specify the reasons why. It could require, as has been done in some places concerning credit card interest rates, the lender to disclose the entire cost of the mortgage over the amortized period, as well as clear disclosure in respect of fees and other charges, including what agents are receiving in fees at each stage of the loan process, how much principal is paid, and whether any prepayment penalties are imposed.

Another recommendation is to require all mortgage originators and brokers to always offer consumer borrowers a fixed-rate mortgage with no prepayment penalties or hidden fees. The consumer could then undertake a comparison of fully transparent mortgage product options.

Recommendation 5: Impose an Outright Ban on Contracts for Deeds
Chapter 9 revealed how misleading contracts for deeds are and illustrated the financial hardship that is created when consumer borrowers spend thousands of dollars to repair their homes, only to discover later that they are not the owners and do not have title. Just as securities law prohibits publicly traded corporations

and investment firms from selling retail investors specified types of products, an important reform would be to prohibit contracts for deeds, as well as mortgage and other property-related structured financial products from being sold to consumer borrowers.

Recommendation 6: Bankruptcy Reform

Bankruptcy as a debt relief tool needs a comprehensive reassessment, beyond the scope of this book. But one important immediate recommendation is to amend the United States Bankruptcy Code to allow for forgiveness of part of mortgage principal as part of consumer "fresh start," authorizing the bankruptcy court during a consumer bankruptcy proceeding to impose mortgage principal forgiveness where the lender has not made a fair and reasonable offer of principal forgiveness. There would have to be guidance in the statute or regulations as to what constituted fairness and reasonableness, but such an assessment could take account of the consumer debtor's income, budget, medical expenses, and family needs, and allow the court to weigh the equities in the circumstances. Currently the bankruptcy court has no ability to order principal forgiveness, so the authority to order forgiveness using these criteria would be a huge step forward.

Such an amendment would bring mortgage lenders to the negotiation table for consumer plans under Chapter 13, because it would be in their interests to try to find a fair and reasonable amount of principal forgiveness rather than have the court impose it. The backstop authority of the bankruptcy court would be a driver for lenders to reach reasonable settlements with consumer borrowers, something that has not occurred with mortgage modification programs.

Another tool would be to impose tax consequences on mortgage originators and servicers where they fail to negotiate the terms of these workouts in good faith or in requisite numbers. Arguably, this recommendation should apply both in and outside of bankruptcy to mortgage forgiveness. There would have to be work done to unpack the principles that should inform the imposition of tax consequences, their scope, and the mechanisms that would initiate and apply these tax consequences, but the aim would be to reform the tax structure away from current incentives that drive foreclosures.

Recommendation 7: Overhaul Modification Programs and Place Oversight Back with Government

Mortgage modification programs should require mortgage lenders and servicers to forgive a percentage of principal owing on mortgages in default, prior to allowing negotiations of other forms of modification or prior to allowing them to move for foreclosure. The evidence in this book is that the vast majority of consumer borrowers act in good faith in their efforts to have their mortgage terms modified to accommodate job loss, losses to property from extreme weather events, and financial losses due to large medical bills. Assuming good faith, some portion of principal and interest forgiveness would be the best way to allow mortgagors to stay in their home during financial setbacks. Remedies could be crafted to deal with the outlier 'bad actors'.

Oversight of mortgage modification programs and policies should be handed back to a government agency, reversing the privatization of this oversight that occurred in 2016. The current "waterfall modification" approach needs to be reconceptualized to protect consumers rather than primarily investors.

Recommendation 8: Create More Effective Oversight and Relief for Mortgage Fraud and Abusive Conduct

For any future settlement of any mortgage fraud or abusive conduct cases, mortgage lenders and servicers should no longer be permitted to implement the agreed remedy themselves. The very individuals and firms engaging in the misconduct should not control the decisions on relief. Such a prohibition is the only way there can be meaningful relief to consumer borrowers. Consumer organizations or agencies of the government should be used to directly administer the funds to consumer borrowers. All future resolution of abusive conduct cases should require a substantial proportion of the relief to be outright principal forgiveness. Rather than "credit" incentives for timeliness, which reduced actual relief paid by up to 30 per cent in the case of some settlements, personal liability should be imposed on financial firm directors and officers for failure to comply in a timely manner.

On the investor protection side, another recommendation is to allow credit in settlements by modifying investor loans only when it is determined to be in the investors' best economic interests.[43] The Urban Institute suggests that future settlements need to be explicit about the terms under which investor loans can be used to meet the financial firm's settlement obligations and there should be considerable transparency on the models used for modification decisions.[44]

Recommendation 9: Consider More Innovative Interventions for Financial-firm-owned Empty Homes

Two of the most serious outcomes of the foreclosure tragedy discussed in this book are that many people lost both their homes and life savings and that good accommodation at a reasonable price continues to be scarce. Instead of contracts for deeds, whereby the firm reaps all the benefits, as discussed in Chapter 9, there could be more creative measures that make housing available.

[43] Laurie Goodman and Maia Woluchem, "National Mortgage Settlement: Lessons Learned," 8, (15 April 2014) Urban Institute, www.urban.org/research/publication/national-mortgage-settlement-lessons-learned (hereafter Goodman and Woluchem, "National Mortgage Settlement").

[44] Goodman and Woluchem, "National Mortgage Settlement."

Ideas can be drawn from international developments. For example, the Mayor of Barcelona, Spain used a law passed by the Catalan parliament in 2016 under which local authorities can claim homes owned by companies that have many properties in their portfolios, if they are left vacant for two years or more, and where there is strong demand for housing.[45] The municipal council must first ask the owner to allow the property to be used as social housing, but then can proceed to an expropriation in the case of a refusal or no reply. Homes then become part of the municipality's housing stock for up to ten years.[46]

In the United States, rather than the New York Third Party Transfer Program that takes homes away from individuals, discussed in Chapter 9, why not have a program in which homes and apartments that have been vacant for two years can be used for up to ten years as part of municipal social housing stock? It would open up accommodations, and might create an additional incentive for lenders not to foreclose, as the rents under such a program would accrue to the municipality not the lenders.

An even bolder option would be to require mortgage lenders to return foreclosed homes to the former mortgagor on a mortgage-free basis when they have been vacant for two years. While the consumer would have to spend resources to repair the home, given the serious damage that occurs when the homes are left unattended, at least they would have full title to the home and could work to restore the condition of the home. Some of the moneys given for community restoration in the settlements discussed in Chapter 8 could then be directed to restoring these homes, but with the consumers (or their children) who suffered the loss of the home deriving the benefit. It would be better to use the community restoration funds in this way rather than using these funds to restore homes and then giving them to consumer borrowers who did not go through the devastating foreclosures and thus have resources still to make down payments. This approach would be fairer and more equitable.

These measures are just a few ideas for how there could be meaningful structural reform of mortgage markets to end the predatory lending that continues today. These recommendations would directly benefit consumer borrowers, but they would require active monitoring and enforcement to ensure that they are meaningful. While they would not address the myriad of other challenges such as barriers to employment, education, and in-community banking, they could accompany reforms in these areas as the first steps towards addressing the embedded racism discussed earlier in this chapter.

45 James Badcock, "Barcelona Orders First Expropriation of 'Empty' Flat Owned by a Bank" *The Telegraph* (24 June 2019) (hereafter Badcock, "Barcelona Orders Expropriation"), www.telegraph.co.uk/news/2019/06/24/barcelona-orders-first-expropriation-empty-flat-owned-bank/?fbclid=IwAR2rtodG2boswelPQXn-PAYu8_LvWYgNTze6kST79oJ12czQ14Si9J5Y3yA.

46 Badcock, "Barcelona Orders Expropriation." The law survived a constitutional challenge in 2018.

III EFFECTIVE CORPORATE GOVERNANCE AND OVERSIGHT IS NEEDED AS WELL

In addition to recommendations that look to policies, regulation, and legislation that are exogenous to lending firms, we suggest an approach that focuses on internal corporate governance matters[47] as a way to protect African-American consumer borrowers. There are numerous federal and state statutes aimed at protecting consumers of colour from housing and lending discrimination. Predatory lenders are subject to mandates to comply with those laws. It is hard to imagine why lending institutions had not installed compliance programs to encourage and measure compliance with antidiscrimination law in the years leading up to the foreclosure crisis. If lenders had such programs, why did the programs fail to uncover the lending practices that intentionally targeted African-American consumers? Or, if predatory practices were uncovered, why did lenders ignore them?

Lenders can mitigate harm to consumers of colour by installing robust compliance programs that take seriously the substance of legal strictures that prohibit housing and lending discrimination.[48] The installation of such programs is only the first step. Lenders must demonstrate a commitment to take compliance obligations seriously in a way that makes them part of the fabric of their firm's culture. Compliance can be achieved by addressing problems that are uncovered in a timely manner, working hard to prevent recurring misconduct, measuring the effectiveness of compliance measures on a regular basis, and encouraging employees to report wrongdoing and protecting them when they do so.[49]

In his 2016 speech to the Consumer Bankers Association, Richard Cordray, former Director of the CFPB, appointed by then President Obama, described the CFPB's focus on banking firms' compliance with federal consumer financial laws and regulations.[50] Cordray recommended that compliance officers pay close attention to the CFPB's guidance with respect to adhering to consumer finance law and warned that executives who fail to work to understand the CFPB's guidance

[47] Lynne Dallas provides an excellent discussion of some of the corporate governance failures that contributed to the financial crises by describing corporate managers' and investors' obsessive focus on short-term results. Lynne Dallas, "Short-Termism, the Financial Crisis and Corporate Governance" (2012) 37 *J Corp L*, 265.

[48] Compliance involves "the processes by which an organization seeks to ensure that employees and other constituents conform to applicable norms—which can include either the requirements of laws or regulations or the internal rules of the organization." Geoffrey P. Miller, *The Law of Governance, Risk Management and Compliance* (Alphen aan den Rijn, the Netherlands: Wolters Kluwer Law & Business, 2014), 3.

[49] See Cheryl L. Wade, "Effective Compliance with Antidiscrimination Law: Corporate Personhood, Purpose and Social Responsibility" (2017) 74 *Wash & Lee L Rev*, 1187, 1197–9.

[50] See CFPB Director Richard Cordray, "Prepared Remarks" (speech delivered at the Consumer Bankers Association, Phoenix, Arizona, 9 March 2016), Consumer Finance Protection Bureau, (hereafter Cordray, Consumer Bankers Association Speech), www.consumerfinance.gov/about-us/newsroom/prepared-remarks-of-cfpb-director-richard-cordray-at-the-consumer-bankers-association/.

would be committing "compliance malpractice."[51] In his speech, Cordray eventually focused specifically on the U.S. mortgage market and the "highly irregular and irresponsible practices in this market that blew up the U.S. economy and brought on the financial crisis."[52] Cordray acknowledged the occurrence of predatory mortgage lending in the speech, but he never mentioned the targeting of consumers of colour.

Cordray claimed that the CFPB's work with banking leaders inspired companies "to realize that if they are going to make sure they are treating their customers fairly, it is not enough to rely solely on their own subjective impressions. Instead, they have to listen closely to what consumers are telling them, think carefully about what they are hearing, and act accordingly."[53] Unfortunately, Cordray did not discuss the bankers' "subjective impressions" about African Americans and the evidence that disproportionately high numbers of them were targeted for predatory loans. It would have been helpful for Cordray to mention consumers of colour who complained about predatory lending when he encouraged the group of banking leaders to "listen closely to what consumers are telling them." Interestingly, just four months after his speech to the Consumer Bankers Association, Cordray delivered a speech at the National Association of Colored People (NAACP) annual convention where he stated that the "discrimination, fuelled by conscious or unconscious prejudice, has hindered millions of African-American consumers from getting ahead, or even keeping up."[54] He discussed redlining and reverse redlining when he appeared before the NAACP audience.[55]

When he spoke to the Consumer Bankers Association, Cordray missed an invaluable opportunity to spur effective compliance with the laws that prohibit discrimination in housing and lending markets. His silence regarding consumers of colour aligned with lenders' denials of discrimination and wrongdoing even when lenders settled litigation. This denial rendered invisible the African Americans who were targeted for predatory loans. When a firm's executives refuse or fail to acknowledge misconduct, its compliance program will be merely cosmetic. Protecting African Americans from predatory lending practices requires acknowledgment that race discrimination is a twenty-first century problem.

1 *Worker-sponsored Capital Could Press for Enhanced Corporate Governance and Protection of African-American and Other Consumer Borrowers*

Another avenue by which to enhance corporate governance and oversight of the mortgage market is to try to tap into the growing activism of large institutional

[51] Cordray, Consumer Bankers Association Speech.

[52] Cordray, Consumer Bankers Association Speech.

[53] Cordray, Consumer Bankers Association Speech.

[54] CFPB Director Richard Cordray, "Prepared Remarks" (speech delivered at the NAACP Annual Convention, Cincinnati, Ohio, 19 July 2016), Consumer Finance Protection Bureau (hereafter Cordray, NAACP Speech. www.consumerfinance.gov/about-us/newsroom/prepared-remarks-cfpb-director-richard-cordray-naacp-annual-convention/.

[55] See Cordray, NAACP Speech.

investors that own and/or manage billions in employees' pension savings. Pension fund asset ownership in the United States amounts to more than $5.6 trillion, most in defined-benefit pension plans.[56] The power of this capital could ensure meaningful governance change at the financial services companies in which they are invested.

The investors that incurred huge losses in Citigroup residential mortgage-backed securities included federally insured financial institutions, as well as a host of states, cities, public pension funds, union pension and benefit funds, universities, religious charities, and hospitals, among others.[57] As noted in Chapter 8, JP Morgan Chase admitted to giving California's pension funds incomplete information about mortgage investments, and it agreed to return to California's pension funds the money that it wrongfully took from them.[58] Thus, worker-sponsored capital and other not-for-profit institutional investors have aligned interest in preventing predatory lending.

Arguably, a compelling case can be made for pension funds to press the companies they invest in to stop racist and abusive mortgage lending practices. New alliances could be formed between pension funds and consumer protection organizations. Consider the prudential obligation of pension trustees, which is to discharge their duties with respect to a pension plan solely in the interest of the participants and beneficiaries for the exclusive purpose of providing benefits to participants and their beneficiaries, acting with care, skill, prudence, and diligence under the circumstances and diversifying the investments of the plan so as to minimize the risk of large losses. The case would have to be made that capital invested in a fairer and more equitable mortgage market meets this prudential standard. Capital that is invested in the non-prime mortgage market is arguably not in the best interests of pension members and beneficiaries, many of whom were victimized by the subprime mortgage debacle. Predatory lending and abusive conduct directly threatens the long-term investment strategies that pension fiduciaries engage in because massive financial settlements from misconduct by mortgage originators and servicers detract from returns on investment, and market meltdowns create risks for the

[56] David Webber, *The Rise of the Working-Class Shareholder* (Cambridge, MA: Harvard University Press, 2018), xii (hereafter Webber, *Rise of Working-Class Shareholder*). In the 1960s, one-third of the American workforce was unionized; it is now less than 10 per cent, primarily in the public sector; Webber, *Rise of Working-Class Shareholder*, 9, citing Board of Governors of the Federal Reserve System Financial Accounts of the United States, 2016.

[57] Citigroup DOJ Settlement, paras. 1–2. Department of Justice, "Justice Department, Federal and State Partners Secure Record $7 Billion Global Settlement with Citigroup for Misleading Investors about Securities Containing Toxic Mortgages" (14 July 2014), www.justice.gov/opa/pr/justice-department-federal-and-state-partners-secure-record-7-billion-global-settlement (hereafter DOJ, "Record $7 Billion Global Settlement with Citigroup").

[58] Department of Justice, "Justice Department, Federal and State Partners Secure Record $13 Billion Global Settlement with JPMorgan for Misleading Investors about Securities Containing Toxic Mortgages" (19 November 2013), www.justice.gov/opa/pr/justice-department-federal-and-state-partners-secure-record-13-billion-global-settlement (hereafter DOJ, "Record Settlement with JP Morgan").

pension fund mandate of protecting intergenerational wealth. In our view, that case could be made effectively.

David Webber has analysed how the power of pension funds can be used to thwart self-serving managers and directors, as well as be used to benefit workers directly, fend off attacks on pension plans, and create jobs, thus advancing workers' interests as workers saving for retirement and as long-term shareholders.[59] He posits what he calls a worker-centric legal and policy vision that considers the full range of workers' real interests when determining how their powerful pension funds make investment decisions.[60] He gives a number of examples where pension funds, as large institutional investors, have cooperated to push back on poor management and self-dealing transactions,[61] and how interests can align. Webber argues that shareholder power is a vehicle for reintroducing the voices of middle and working-class people to produce two basic changes: many more people could retain more of the economic surpluses that they themselves have created, thus restoring wealth to the parties that generated it; and markets, which are structured to respond to investors, will respond to middle- and working-class shareholders in ways that, by extension, will make them more responsive to middle- and working-class people more generally.[62] This reasoning applies to pension funds concerned about protection of mortgage consumer borrowers in that these consumers are many of their current and future pensioners, and because there is a convergence of interest in not having the kind of financial meltdown experienced during the global financial crisis.

Civil rights organizations such as the NAACP also can join in the type of firm-based activism we describe here. These organizations can invest minimal amounts to purchase the stock of mortgage firms and engage in shareholder activism. As shareholders, the organizations would, under certain circumstances, be entitled to shareholder inspection rights that would provide them with the information they would need to structure and target their activism.[63] As shareholder activists, these civil rights organizations can draft demand letters to the boards of mortgage firms that describe the type of corrective action that would prevent predatory practices.[64]

59 Webber, *Rise of Working-Class Shareholder*, 21.

60 Webber, *Rise of Working-Class Shareholder*, xiii.

61 Webber, *Rise of Working-Class Shareholder*.

62 Webber, *Rise of Working-Class Shareholder*, 17–18. See also Lisa Fairfax, *Shareholder Democracy: A Primer on Shareholder Activism and Participation* (Durham, NC: Carolina Academic Press, 2011) and Dalia Tsuk Mitchell, "Shareholders as Proxies: The Contours of Shareholder Democracy" (2006) 63:4 *Wash & Lee L Rev*, 1503.

63 See Del Code title 8 § 220 Corporations – Inspection of books and records.

64 These letters are required in the derivative litigation context where shareholders must demand that boards file litigation to redress harm to the corporation. Demand is required when boards are able to exercise independent business judgment and can be expected to make a decision about whether a suit should be filed that will be in the corporation's best interest. Shareholders, in these cases, cannot file the suits themselves because they lack standing because the harm that is alleged impacts the corporation and not the shareholders directly.

Many times boards respond to these demand letters by taking the action that shareholders suggest. Shareholder activists may also submit shareholder proposals under federal rules.[65] Again, there is no requirement that corporate boards do what shareholders propose, but they often acquiesce to prevent protracted discussion of issues or social media visibility that would harm the firm's reputation.

2 *Tax Incentives Could Also Assist*

Dickerson helpfully recommends amending federal tax law to not allow homeowners to deduct interest on sub-prime and exotic mortgages such as negatively amortizing, interest-only, and no down payment mortgages.[66] She also recommends policies that provide additional financial assistance to homeowners who live in neighbourhoods disproportionately harmed by the foreclosure crisis in the form of direct relief or substantial tax relief.[67] Equally, Dickerson suggests that homeowners should not be able to receive a tax benefit of deducting interest for high-cost and high-risk mortgages that triggered the financial crisis.[68] She argues that since second mortgages and home equity loans do not increase home ownership rates, the original public policy goals of such tax breaks do not apply, and U.S. tax policies should not subsidize or in any way encourage these financial products.[69] Rather than across-the-board mortgage tax benefits, which disproportionately benefit higher-income taxpayers with large mortgages, Dickerson argues that the U.S. government could provide ways to subsidize the interest rates or give the greatest tax benefits to low and middle income earners, including possibly lump sum payments annually for 3–5 years where the borrower is financially responsible and has been making mortgage payments for a specified period of time.[70] She also suggests that tax policy should encourage cooperative housing and communal or joint ownership of homes.[71]

In addition to direct tax relief to consumer borrowers, the law could shift the tax benefits given to mortgage lenders and servicers. The law could prohibit lenders from having any tax write-offs for mortgages foreclosed on, and instead could only allow for a deduction actual for amounts of principal forgiven on a mortgage. These two measures would immediately create incentives to consider principal forgiveness rather than foreclosure.

65 Securities Exchange Act of 1934, Rule 14a-8(i).

66 Mechele Dickerson, *Homeownership and America's Financial Underclass: Flawed Premises, Broken Promises, New Prescriptions* (Cambridge: *Cambridge University Press*, 2014), 262 (hereafter Dickerson, *Homeownership*).

67 Dickerson, *Homeownership*. She advocates that government insurance or purchase of mortgages should be limited to mortgage products that are long-term and self-amortizing, not to sub-prime mortgages.

68 Dickerson, *Homeownership*, 265.

69 Dickerson, *Homeownership*.

70 Dickerson, *Homeownership*, 266–7.

71 Dickerson, *Homeownership*, 267.

3 *Finding Innovative Ways of Delivering Mortgage and Banking Services*

Another, more structural reform, would be to address head-on the racial discrimination in mortgage and other banking services by considering new ways to ensure African Americans and other individuals of colour have access to those services in their communities.

For example, Baradaran proposes using the existing U.S. Postal Service (USPS) post office framework to develop a new form of banking and small loan financing, drawing on experiences globally and from a White Paper report from the USPS in 2014.[72] She envisions that the USPS post offices could house a public bank offering a wide range of services, including deposit taking and lending. She observes that USPS post offices already have a prolific number of locations, and the infrastructure, and economics of scale to effectively service unbanked and underbanked communities. Baradaran suggests that the loans would be available without life-crushing fees and interest, in turn helping advance democracy.[73] She notes that the unbanked currently spend $89 billion each year on financial fees and services, all going to payday lenders, check-cashers, and similar predatory lenders.[74] Why not allow those fees to accrue directly to a public bank that gives effective service to all communities?

IV HOMES AND HEARTS

In this book, we are privileged to share the narratives of people targeted by predatory lending practices – people who typically have no voice and no platform. After we interviewed them, we worked with composer Alex Silverman, who created the song entitled *Homes and Hearts*, encapsulating the stories of the individuals we interviewed in their own words. Here are the lyrics:

Home is where the heart is
So the saying goes
You chase your dreams in poetry
and pay for them in prose
Then comes the dreadful day you find
that you've been sold a lie:
It was just a little loan
Now they've taken everything you own,

72 Baradaran "Color of Money," 211, citing USPS, Office of the Inspector General, "Providing Non-bank Financial Services for the Underserved" (27 January 2014) White Paper Report No RARC-WP-14-007, www.uspsoig.gov/sites/default/files/document-library-files/2015/rarc-wp-14-007_0.pdf.

73 Baradaran "Color of Money," 211–12.

74 Baradaran "Color of Money," 212.

and you're standing on your own wondering 'why?'
What did I do wrong?
What happened to our family?
When the pressure knocked me to the floor
How can there be more?
More than ten million people like me?

***

I followed my dreams here
To the rainbow's end
To get a place I shared a loan
With my daughter and a friend
Time came for them to move on,
To set up on their own,
I signed the papers at the library,
Oh ... the things I wish I'd known.
The effects of the recession
They get every where:
When everyone is struggling
No one wants to do their hair
The more I fell behind,
The more the bank put up their fees,
They sold my mortgage on and then,
put up the price and sold it on again,
and after nine long years they went
and took away the keys.

***

At first we were suspicious
Said we wouldn't sign,
They made another offer
and we figured it was fine
We lost our jobs,
Asked for help,
The bank agreed to meet
With a plan to drain our savings
and leave us on the street.
We sought an explanation
Knew the end was coming soon
When we drove to their head office
They gave us T-shirts and a balloon.
We've got no money,
No relationship,
But every single day
We will carry on the fight

Cos we know this can't be right
We no longer sleep at night,
But lie awake and pray.

***

They saw me as black
They saw me as a woman
They saw me as a nobody making a fuss
They saw me as poor
They saw me as easy
They said no need to hide that they just didn't care about us.

***

Struck by a passing car
Crossing the street
The least of my problems was being knocked off my feet.
Six months out of work
is a long time without pay
Then the bank says
"We got it wrong, we need five thousand dollars, right away"
that's when the charges
start getting out of hand
I can't keep up,
and in eighteen months
I owe them eighty grand
They pressure me to sell,
I resist, the market's low,
So they force me to accept
Another massive loan, the biggest yet,
A quarter of a million in debt
On a property I was months away
From calling my own!

We put together an *ad hoc* choir to sing and record *Homes and Hearts* at Bethany Baptist Church in Jamaica, Queens, a neighbourhood that is one of the epicenters of the predatory home mortgage debacle.[75] Surrounded by the church where we recorded were hundreds of homes in various stages of foreclosure.

Only one member of the choir, co-author Janis Sarra, is white. Everyone else who recorded the song is African American. We were a racially homogenous group, but in terms of socio-economic background, we were diverse. Two lawyers, a retired judge, a school administrator, a retired English teacher, a retired librarian, and other hardworking individuals recorded *Homes and Hearts*. Also in the choir was one participant who

75 To access the recording, see Live Canon, http://www.livecanon.co.uk/foreclosurefollies.

revealed that she was homeless at the time we rehearsed and recorded. Another choir member had a close family member who had lost her home to foreclosure, and yet another shared that because of medical costs, one of her loved ones was without a home.

In this book, we tell an integral part of an American story about African-American wealth accumulation and its subsequent destruction. U.S. history is replete with infrequently told narratives of wealth destruction in African-American communities and families. The Greenwood District of Tulsa, Oklahoma, where African Americans owned homes and businesses, became known as "The Black Wall Street of America." In 1921, white rioters burned this flourishing community to the ground.[76] Two years later, white rioters burned and destroyed another all-black town, Rosewood, Florida, where African Americans owned homes and businesses.[77] Moreover, few people know of Seneca Village, an almost entirely black community in the middle of what is now Central Park in New York City, where middle-class African Americans owned their own businesses and homes.[78] The city took the land on which Seneca Village existed through eminent domain.[79] Private land owned by white New Yorkers in other parts of the city was also taken for public use.[80] Seneca Village is unique, however, because very little is known about this once thriving community and its inhabitants.[81]

Tomashi Jackson is a visual artist who, in a 2019 exhibition of her work entitled Time Out of Mind, tells the story of Seneca Village along with present day narratives of lost and threatened homeownership in black communities under New York City's Third Party Transfer program that we described in Chapter 9. By helping to create and perform the *Homes and Hearts* song about predatory lending, like Jackson, we used the arts to share a complex story about the destruction of black wealth with as many people as possible. Like Jackson, we did so to avoid the erasure of these harrowing African-American narratives. We continue this effort in this book and we also acknowledge similarly overlooked stories about other people of colour such as Thomas Joo's poignant account and analysis of the demolition of Sacramento, California's Japantown in the late 1950s.[82]

[76] See Hannibal Johnson, *Black Wall Street: From Riot to Renaissance in Tulsa's Historic Greenwood District* (Fort Worth, TX: Eakin Press, 2007).

[77] Edward González-Tennant, *The Rosewood Massacre: An Archaeology and History of Intersectional Violence* (Gainesville, FL: University Press of Florida, 2018).

[78] See Marie Warsh, "Uncovering the Stories of Seneca Village" (7 February 2019), Central Park NYC, (hereafter Warsh, "Uncovering Stories"), www.centralparknyc.org/about/blog/uncovering-seneca-village.html.

[79] Warsh, "Uncovering Stories."

[80] Warsh, "Uncovering Stories."

[81] Warsh, "Uncovering Stories."

[82] See Thomas W. Joo, "Urban Renewal and Sacramento's Lost Japantown" (2018) 92 *Chi-Kent L Rev*, 1005 (hereafter Joo, "Lost Japantown"). In the pursuit of urban renewal, Sacramento used eminent domain to transfer private property in inner cities to private developers. Joo does not focus on whether the demolition of Japantown was motivated by unconscious racism. Instead, he focuses on the dignitary harm the taking inflicted upon Japanese and Japanese Americans and the manifestation of "official disregard for [their] human worth." Joo, "Lost Japantown," 1006.

Several months after we recorded *Homes and Hearts*, on 15 March 2019, a joint legislative hearing to examine NYC's homeownership housing crisis was held at the Brooklyn Borough Hall in New York. Brooklyn's borough president, state assembly members, and state senators invited New Yorkers to attend the open hearing. In the circular announcing the meeting, the legislators announced that, "many homeowners have lost their property and equity and have been left without support. This hearing will focus on the practices that have put homeowners and families in jeopardy." The notice described the topics that would be addressed as including: "predatory foreclosure practices; deed theft, redlining; equity theft; impact of municipal liens and properties lost due to sewer and water charges; and the Third Party Transfer program," discussed in Chapter 9.

About 500 people were huddled in a large room at Brooklyn Borough Hall where the hearing was held.[83] Almost all were African American. Many of the community activists and organization leaders who spoke to the audience about their work to protect consumers from predatory practices were white – including Sarah Ludwig, the founder and co-director of The New Economy Project. We interviewed Sarah more than two months after the hearing.

Sarah founded the New Economy Project (Project) to pursue economic justice for New Yorkers and in the 1990s attempted to sound the alarm regarding predatory practices that targeted communities of colour.[84] The work of the Project included meeting with the Federal Reserve, the State Banking Department, bond-rating agencies, regulators at the DOJ, and several banks, but concerns were dismissed as merely anecdotal. In our interview, Sarah stated that she had a clear understanding of the role that race played during decades of predatory lending that targeted predominantly black neighbourhoods in southeast Queens, central Brooklyn, and parts of the Bronx. An integral part of the Project's work included forming relationships with legal services, advocating for individuals victimized by predatory lending, and creating maps that showed that, starting in the 1990s, incredibly high numbers of predatory home loans were made in mostly black communities. In our interview, Sarah described many of the specifics about the targeting of African Americans. "People knocked on doors to offer home repairs and sat at kitchen tables where individuals signed documents to refinance mortgages that were almost paid off."

At the hearing, Sarah Ludwig was eloquent and passionate as she described the Project's work. Other speakers offered suggestions, including: a study of the disparate racial impact of the Third Party Transfer program under which occupied

83 Another hearing on the Third Party Transfer program was convened in Manhattan by The Council of the City of New York. The announcement for the hearing contained a statement explaining that the Third Party Transfer program "is under fire for wrongfully seizing properties from black and brown homeowners." The announcement also quoted Council Member Robert Cornegy explaining that mistakes under the program "can lead to the loss of a generation of wealth for a family." City Council to Hold Joint Oversight Hearing on HPD's Third Party Transfer Program, 3 July 2019.

84 Sarah Ludwig, telephone interview, 24 May 2019, quoted with permission.

single-family homes had been taken away from homeowners because they looked abandoned after falling into a state of disrepair; and forming a civilian review board. But one African American who spoke at the hearing said, "We want to tell our own stories. Many who speak on these issues have white privilege." Several attendees had in fact been invited to tell their personal horror stories about predatory practices that left them homeless or penniless or both, and some struggled to articulate their narratives in the three minutes they were given. One of the men we interviewed for this book haltingly shared the ordeal he had already told us when we interviewed him. Some speakers wept as they described their stories, and others in the audience shouted in support and agreement with those at the podium. The pain, frustration, and desperation were palpable.

We understand that Americans typically prefer stories with happy endings. But, after describing narratives of continuing predation and proposing recommendations for reform, we struggle to find a happy ending. Perhaps there is hope in Sarah Ludwig's comment that in her years of work through the New Economy Project, she never referred to the people for whom she advocated as victims. When she said this, we were reminded of the men and women we interviewed for this book. They expressed disappointment in themselves and in a system that victimized them, but not one referred to himself or herself as a victim. Nor did they behave and speak like victims. We end here, however, with a description of a legislative hearing replete with profound human suffering.

Even in mid-2019, as we drove through black communities in Southeast Queens where we recorded *Homes and Hearts*, we saw signs, posters, and billboards that placed struggling African-American homeowners in the crosshairs of predators. One sign asked, "Are you 3 months behind in your mortgage payments?" Prominently printed on the sign were the words "foreclosure specialists" and "short sale specialists" promising to "buy your house—all cash" and that the sale would "close in 5 days." There is no happy ending. There is no end in sight.

Appendix[1]

TABLE A.1 *Ally Financial, ResCap, and GMAC settlements*

MONETARY PENALTIES – Actual Payments by Bank	
U.S. Department of Justice (DOJ) and Independent Settlements	
U.S. Treasury General Fund, pursuant to the Financial Institutions Reform, Recovery and Enforcement Act of 1989 (FIRREA) (DOJ)[2]	$52,000,000
National Credit Union Administration (NCUA)[3]	$9,102,637
Federal Housing Finance Agency (FHFA)[4]	$574,500,000
Subtotal – Settlement Monetary Penalties	$635,602,637
National Mortgage Settlement (NMS)	
Subtotal – NMS Monetary Penalties[5]	$109,628,425
TOTAL MONETARY PENALTIES – ACTUALS	$745,231,062

(continued)

1 This appendix was compiled by MaryGrace Johnstone, JD, Peter A. Allard School of Law, University of British Columbia, after analyzing thousands of pages of settlement agreements, monitors' reports, and financial firm disclosures, and contacting monitors for clarification of the numbers. The authors are deeply appreciative of the extensive amount of time it took MaryGrace to verify the figures.

2 Ally Settlement Agreement (21 November 2016), United States Department of Justice, para 1, www.justice.gov/usao-cdca/case-document/file/912531/download (hereafter Ally DOJ Settlement).

3 National Credit Union Administration, "AME Allocations for Legal Recoveries, Fees and Expenses" (11 August 2017), www.ncua.gov/Legal/Documents/legal-recoveries-allocations.pdf (hereafter NCUA Settlements).

4 Federal Housing Finance Agency, "Fact Sheet: FHFA Final Update on Private Label Securities Actions" (17 September 2018), FHFA, www.fhfa.gov/Media/PublicAffairs/Pages/FHFA-Final-Update-on-Private-Label-Securities-Actions-9172018.aspx (hereafter FHFA Private Label Securities Actions).

5 *United States of America, et al* v *Bank of America Corp, et al*, No 12-0361 (RMC), Document 13 Consent Judgment (DDC filed 4 April 2012), para. 3, National Mortgage Settlements, https://scholarship.law.unc.edu/cgi/viewcontent.cgi?article=1003&context=mortgage-settlements (hereafter Ally NMS Consent Judgment).

TABLE A.1 *(continued)*

NMS CONSUMER RELIEF OBLIGATIONS – Credit Adjusted Per Settlement Terms	
TOTAL CONSUMER RELIEF CREDIT EARNED	$257,411,785
TOTAL SETTLEMENT (Monetary Penalties + Consumer Relief Credit)	$1,002,642,847

The National Mortgage Settlement (NMS) was a cumulative settlement between the 5 largest mortgage servicers: Ally, ResCap and GMAC ('Ally'); Bank of America; Citigroup; JP Morgan Chase; and Wells Fargo.[6] For the monetary penalties, each bank paid an amount into escrow; Ally contributed $109,628,425, and the total $5,031,507,456[7] was divided among the recipients as follows:

- Federal Payment Settlement Amounts
  - $684,090,417 distributed to the Federal Housing Administration Capital Reserve, Veterans Housing Benefit Program Fund, or otherwise as directed by the U.S. Department of Justice (DOJ).[8]
  - $227,687,500 to resolve five civil settlements.[9]
- State Payment Settlement Amounts: $2,539,915,614 distributed among fifty states party to the settlement.[10]
- Other Payments
  - $1,489,813,925 (including cost of distribution) distributed as remedial payment to borrowers whose homes were finally sold/foreclosed between 1 January 2008 and 31 December 2011 (inclusive);[11] borrowers eligible to submit claims for harm allegedly arising under Covered Conduct;[12] and borrowers who otherwise met certain criteria set forth by the State members of the Monitoring Committee.[13]
  - $15 million provided to the Financial Services and Consumer Protection Enforcement, Education, and Training Fund to be administered by the National Association of Attorneys General.[14]

6 Joseph A. Smith, Monitor, "Initial Report" (29 August 2012), 3, National Mortgage Settlements, https://scholarship.law.unc.edu/cgi/viewcontent.cgi?article=1034&context=mortgage-settlements (hereafter NMS Initial Report).

7 Ally NMS Consent Judgment, para. 3. Exhibits B, D and D1 of the Consent Judgments are identical.

8 Ally NMS Consent Judgment, Exhibit B, para. 1(a)(i).

9 Ally NMS Consent Judgment, Exhibit B, para. 1(a)(ii).

10 Ally NMS Consent Judgment, Exhibit B, para. 1(b). Complete breakdown of state payments listed at Exhibit B-1 and described at Exhibit B-2.

11 Ally NMS Consent Judgment, para. 4, Exhibit B, para. 2(a), and Exhibit C.

12 Ally NMS Consent Judgment, para. 4 and Exhibit G(I).

13 Ally NMS Consent Judgment, para. 4.

14 Ally NMS Consent Judgment, Exhibit B, para. 2(b).

- $10 million provided to the Ameriquest Financial Services Fund for reimbursement of costs and fees during the investigation of this case.[15]
- $65 million provided to the Conference of State Bank Supervisors: $15 million to establish the State Financial Regulation Fund, and $1 million to each state financial regulator of the States party to this agreement.[16]

- Interest earned on funds while they were held by the escrow agent were to be used for administrative costs and expenses, or for any other housing related purpose, at the discretion of the State members of the Monitoring Committee.[17]

TABLE A.2 *Ally Financial, ResCap, and GMAC National Mortgage settlement – consumer relief*[18]

Type of Relief	Credit Earned	Actual Relief
First-Lien Mortgage Modifications	$130,324,492	$108,686,970
Second-Lien Portfolio Modifications	$22,589,924	$86,452,677
Subtotal – Modifications/Forgiveness	$152,914,416	$195,139,647
Subtotal – Refinancing Program	$48,349,699	$38,055,289
Short Sales/Deeds in Lieu	$39,425,927	$168,074,388
Deficiency Waivers	$15,121,743	$151,217,425
Contribution to Borrower HOPE Loan Portal	$1,600,000	$1,600,000
Subtotal – Other Creditable Items	$56,147,670	$320,891,813
Total Consumer Relief	$257,411,785	$554,086,749

Under the National Mortgage Settlement, Ally was required to earn a minimum of $185 million in consumer relief credit, as well as $15 million in refinancing relief credit.[19] The credited amount was derived from the actual relief the bank provided to borrowers; the monitor took each dollar of actual relief and made various upward and downward adjustments to determine how much of each dollar would be counted toward the total consumer relief credit, according to the terms of the settlement in the following outline.

15 Ally NMS Consent Judgment, Exhibit B, para. 2(c).
16 Ally NMS Consent Judgment, Exhibit B, para. 2(d).
17 Ally NMS Consent Judgment, Exhibit B, para. 3.
18 NMS Digital Archive, "Final Crediting Report" (18 March 2014), NMS, 17, https://scholarship.law.unc.edu/mortgage-settlements/servicing/publications/30/ (hereafter NMS Final Report).
19 Ally NMS Consent Judgment, para. 5.

MINIMUMS AND MAXIMUMS

The terms placed maximum and minimum obligations for earning credit in certain categories of relief[20]:

- Minimum 60 per cent in first- and second-lien modifications, with a minimum 30 per cent in first-lien modifications,
- Maximum 12.5 per cent in forgiveness of forbearance amounts on existing modifications,
- Maximum 5 per cent in enhanced borrower transitional funds,
- Maximum 10 per cent in deficiency waivers, and
- Maximum 12 per cent in anti-blight provisions.

TERMS OVERALL

- Additional 25 per cent incentive credit for any first- or second-lien principal reduction and amounts credited pursuant to the refinancing program within 12 months of the start date.[21]

TERMS BY CATEGORY

First-Lien Mortgage Modifications: $108,686,970 actual relief provided to consumers in first-lien mortgage modifications, earning $130,324,492 credit for[22]:

- First-lien principal forgiveness modification, earned subject to certain eligibility requirements to ensure the necessity and sufficiency of relief, at a rate of:

  a. $1 write-down = $1 credit on loans with loan to value (LTV) at or below 175 per cent, or
  b. $1 write-down = $0.50 credit for the portion of principal forgiven over LTV 175 per cent.

- Forgiveness of forbearance amounts on existing modifications at a rate of $1 write-down = $0.40 credit.
- Earned forgiveness over a period of no greater than 3 years, provided it was consistent with principal reduction alternative ('PRA') modification, at a rate of:

  a. $1 write-down = $0.85 credit on loans with LTV at or below 175 per cent, or
  b. $1 write-down = $0.45 credit for the portion of principal forgiven over LTV 175 per cent.

20 Ally NMS Consent Judgment, Exhibit D1.
21 Ally NMS Consent Judgment, Exhibit D-11, para. 10(b).
22 Ally NMS Consent Judgment, Exhibit D1, 1–2.

- First-lien principal forgiveness modification on investor loans (forgiveness by an investor, not the bank), at a rate of $1 write-down = $0.45 credit.
- Earned forgiveness over a period of no greater than three years on investor loans, provided it was consistent with PRA, at a rate of:

  a. $1 write-down = $0.40 credit on loans with LTV at or below 175 per cent, or
  b. $1 write-down = $0.20 credit for the portion of principal forgiven over LTV 175 per cent.

Second-Lien Portfolio Modifications: $86,452,677 actual relief provided to consumers in second-lien portfolio modifications, earning $22,589,924 credit for[23]:

- Performing second liens (0–90 days delinquent), at a rate of $1 write-down = $0.90 credit.
- Seriously delinquent second liens (91–179 days delinquent), at a rate of $1 write-down = $0.50 credit.
- Non-performing second liens (180+ days delinquent), at a rate of $1 write-down = $0.10 credit.

Refinancing Program: $38,055,289 actual relief provided to eligible borrowers under the refinancing program, subject to certain conditions to ensure the necessity and sufficiency of relief, earning $48,349,699 credit calculated as the difference between the pre-existing interest rate and the offered interest rate times the unpaid principal balance times a multiplier based on the life of the loan.[24]

Short Sales/Deeds in Lieu: $168,074,388 actual relief provided to consumers in incentive payments for a dignified exit from a property via short sale or similar program, subject to certain conditions to ensure the necessity and sufficiency of relief,[25] earning $39,425,927 credit for[26]:

- Payments by the bank to unrelated second-lien holders for the release of the lien, at a rate of $1 payment = $1 credit.
- Forgiveness of deficiency and release on first-lien portfolio loans by the bank, at a rate of $1 write-down = $0.45 credit.
- Forgiveness of deficiency and release on first-lien investor loans by investors, at a rate of $1 write-down = $0.20 credit.
- Forgiveness of deficiency and release on performing second-lien portfolio loans by the bank, at a rate of $1 write-down = $0.90 credit.
- Forgiveness of deficiency and release on seriously delinquent second-lien portfolio loans by the bank, at a rate of $1 write-down = $0.50 credit.

[23] Ally NMS Consent Judgment, Exhibit D1, 2–3.
[24] Ally NMS Consent Judgment, Exhibit D, 9–11.
[25] Ally NMS Consent Judgment, Exhibit D, 6–7.
[26] Ally NMS Consent Judgment, Exhibit D1, 3–4.

- Forgiveness of deficiency and release on non-performing second-lien portfolio loans by the bank, at a rate of $1 write-down = $0.10 credit.

Deficiency Waivers: $151,217,425 actual relief provided to consumers in deficiency waived on first- and second-lien loans where the bank could have pursued the deficiency but did not after completion of the foreclosure sale,[27] earning $15,121,743 credit, at a rate of $1 write-down = $0.10 credit.[28]

Contribution to Borrower HOPE Loan Portal: $1.6 million actual relief provided and credit claimed in contributions to the HOPE Loan Portal servicing system to enhance communications with housing counselors, at a rate of $1 payment = $1 credit.[29]

TABLE A.3 *Bank of America settlements*

MONETARY PENALTIES – Actual Payments by Bank	
U.S. Department of Justice (DOJ) and Independent Settlements[30]	
U.S. Treasury General Fund, pursuant to the Financial Institutions Reform, Recovery and Enforcement Act of 1989 (FIRREA)	$5,000,000,000
National Credit Union Administration (NCUA)[31]	$165,000,000
Federal Deposit Insurance Corporation (FDIC)	$1,031,000,000
Federal Housing Finance Agency (FHFA)[32]	$5,828,883,292
Federal Housing Administration (FHA)	$2,050,000,000
Securities Exchange Commission (SEC)	$135,840,000
State of New York	$300,000,000
State of California	$300,000,000
State of Illinois	$200,000,000
State of Delaware	$45,000,000
State of Maryland	$75,000,000
Commonwealth of Kentucky	$23,000,000
Tax Relief	$490,160,000
Subtotal – Settlement Monetary Penalties	$15,643,883,292

[27] Ally NMS Consent Judgment, Exhibit D-7.
[28] Ally NMS Consent Judgment, Exhibit D1-4.
[29] Ally NMS Consent Judgment, Exhibit A-25.
[30] Bank of America Settlement Agreement Recitals (21 August 2014), paras. 1–2, Department of Justice, www.justice.gov/iso/opa/resources/3392014829141150385241.pdf (hereafter Bank of America DOJ Settlement). A complete breakdown of monetary penalties paid to the listed litigants is provided at para. 3.
[31] NCUA Settlements.
[32] FHFA Private Label Securities Actions.

National Mortgage Settlement (NMS)[33]	
Subtotal – NMS Monetary Penalties	$2,382,415,075
TOTAL MONETARY PENALTIES – ACTUALS	$18,026,298,367
CONSUMER RELIEF OBLIGATIONS – Credit Adjusted Per Settlement Terms	
DOJ Credit Earned	$7,005,373,353
NMS Credit Earned	$9,610,418,492
TOTAL CONSUMER RELIEF CREDIT EARNED	$16,615,791,845
TOTAL SETTLEMENT (Monetary Penalties + Consumer Relief Credit)	$34,642,090,212

TABLE A.4 *Bank of America – U.S. Department of Justice settlement – consumer relief*

Type of Relief	Credit Earned	Actual Relief
First-Lien Principal Forgiveness	$3,031,552,456	$1,253,550,146
Principal Forgiveness of Forbearance	$565,181,334	$444,444,974
First-Lien Forbearance	$170,422,953	$675,515,566
Second-Lien Extinguishment	$76,521,480	$67,274,425
Junior Liens – Unsecured Principal Forgiveness Extinguishment	$1,534,521,483	$3,402,660,476
Subtotal – Modifications/Forgiveness	$5,378,199,706	$5,843,445,587
Subtotal – Low- to Moderate-Income Lending and Other Lending	$416,999,000	$0[34]
Principal Extinguishment	$296,594,622	$258,040,915
Donations of Mortgages and Real-Estate Owned Properties	$68,703,427	$60,507,316

(continued)

33 *United States of America, et al* v *Bank of America Corp, et al,* No. 12-0361 (RMC), Document 11 Consent Judgment (DDC filed 4 April 2012), para. 3, National Mortgage Settlements, https://scholarship.law.unc.edu/cgi/viewcontent.cgi?article=1000&context=mortgage-settlements (hereafter Bank of America NMS Consent Judgment). The NMS was a cumulative settlement; a complete breakdown of monetary penalties and parties are described previously under the Ally DOJ Settlement, referencing the NMS Initial Report, 3, and the Ally NMS Consent Judgment, para. 3 and Exhibit B, which is identical to the Bank of America NMS Consent Judgment, Exhibit B.

34 The bank earned $417 billion credit at a rate of $10,000 credit, plus incentive credit, for each purchase money loan sold to credit worthy borrowers in hardest hit areas; who lost a primary residence to foreclosure or short sale; or who were first time LMI homebuyers with an income at or below the area median income. The value of the loans is not included as actual relief, because the borrowers were required to repay the loans with interest. See Bank of America Settlement Agreement Annex 2, Consumer Relief (21 August 2014), 6, Department of Justice, www.justice.gov/iso/opa/resources/8492014829141239967961.pdf (hereafter Bank of America DOJ Settlement, Annex 2).

TABLE A.4 *(continued)*

Donations for Rehabilitation/Maintenance of Donated Property	$14,094,058	$6,150,188
Donations to Community Development Funds and HUD-Approved Housing Counselling Agencies	$156,283,564	$70,000,000
Donations for Legal Assistance	$69,000,000	$30,000,000
Subtotal – Community Reinvestment and Neighbourhood Stabilization	$604,675,671	$424,698,419
Subtotal – Affordable Rental Housing	$441,865,938	$109,565,000
Subtotal – Additional Credit for Exceeding Minimum	$163,633,038	$0
Total Consumer Relief	$7,005,373,353	$6,377,709,006

Under the DOJ Settlement, Bank of America was required to earn a minimum of $7 billion in consumer relief "credit,"[35] derived from the actual relief by the same method as described previously in the Ally Settlement,[36] and according to the terms of the settlement in the following outline. The terms placed minimum and maximum relief obligations on certain categories of relief as discussed in detail in Chapter 8.

TABLE A.5 *Bank of America National Mortgage settlement – consumer relief*[37]

Type of Relief	Credit Earned	Actual Relief
First-Lien Mortgage Modifications	$3,365,196,272	$4,869,347,311
Second-Lien Portfolio Modifications	$2,210,934,257	$9,655,705,939
Subtotal – Modifications/Forgiveness	$5,576,130,529	$14,525,053,250
Subtotal – Refinancing Program	$1,013,769,682	$811,006,154
Enhanced Borrower Transitional Funds	$68,349,672	$162,354,522
Short Sales/Deeds in Lieu	$2,952,168,609	$11,846,419,147
Subtotal – Other Creditable Items	$3,020,518,281	$12,008,773,669
Total Consumer Relief	$9,610,418,492	$27,344,833,073

Credit was earned at the same rates described previously under the Ally Settlement,[38] and the terms for Bank of America were discussed at length in Chapter 8.

35 Bank of America DOJ Settlement, para. 2.
36 See Table A.2 description.
37 NMS Final Report, 11.
38 Referencing the Ally NMS Consent Judgment, Exhibits D and D1, which are identical to the Bank of America NMS Consent Judgment, Exhibits D and D1.

TABLE A.6 *Citigroup settlements*

MONETARY PENALTIES – Actual Payments by Bank	
U.S. Department of Justice (DOJ) and Independent Settlements[39]	
U.S. Treasury General Fund, pursuant to the Financial Institutions Reform, Recovery and Enforcement Act of 1989 (FIRREA)	$4,000,000,000
National Credit Union Administration (NCUA)	$20,500,000
Federal Deposit Insurance Corporation (FDIC)	$208,250,000
Federal Housing Finance Agency (FHFA)	$250,000,000
Federal Housing Administration (FHA)[40]	$158,300,000
Securities Exchange Commission (SEC)	$360,000,000
State of New York	$92,000,000
State of California	$102,700,000
State of Illinois	$44,000,000
Commonwealth of Massachusetts	$45,700,000
State of Delaware	$7,350,000
Subtotal – Settlement Monetary Penalties	$5,288,800,000
National Mortgage Settlement (NMS)[41]	
Subtotal – NMS Monetary Penalties	$413,041,577
TOTAL MONETARY PENALTIES – ACTUALS	$5,701,841,577
CONSUMER RELIEF OBLIGATIONS – Credit Adjusted Per Settlement Terms	
DOJ Credit Earned*	$1,891,254,913
NMS Credit Earned	$1,792,967,705
TOTAL CONSUMER RELIEF CREDIT EARNED	$3,684,222,618
TOTAL SETTLEMENT (Monetary Penalties + Consumer Relief Credit)	$9,358,533,016

* *Current through May 2019:* DOJ Settlement due for completion by 31 December 2018, finals not yet available. Note that actuals are not available under the Rate Reduction category.

39 Citigroup Settlement Agreement Recitals (14 July 2014), Department of Justice, www.justice.gov/iso/opa/resources/471201471413656848428.pdf (hereafter Citigroup DOJ Settlement). A complete breakdown of monetary penalties paid to the listed litigants is provided at para. 3.

40 Andrew Scoggin, "Citi Settles FHA Mortgage Suit for $158 Million" *Housing Wire* (15 February 2012), online: www.housingwire.com/articles/citi-settles-fha-mortgage-suit-158-million.

41 *United States of America, et al* v *Bank of America Corp, et al*, No 12-0361 (RMC), Document 12 Consent Judgment (DDC filed 4 April 2012), National Mortgage Settlements Digital Archive, https://scholarship.law.unc.edu/cgi/viewcontent.cgi?article=1002&context=mortgage-settlements (hereafter Citigroup NMS Consent Judgment). The NMS was a cumulative settlement; a complete breakdown of monetary penalties and parties are described previously under the Ally DOJ Settlement, referencing the NMS Initial Report, at 3 and the Ally NMS Consent Judgment, para. 3 and Exhibit B, which is identical to the Citigroup NMS Consent Judgment, Exhibit B.

TABLE A.7 *Citigroup – U.S. Department of Justice settlement – consumer relief*

Type of Relief	Credit Earned[42]	Actual Relief
First-Lien Principal Forgiveness	$27,531,179	$23,879,526
Assistance to Refinance Outside Citigroup	$31,172,235	$27,146,255
Junior Liens (Less Than Second Position)	$36,586,150	$79,786,217
Unsecured Mortgage Debt – Principal Forgiveness	$274,000,933	$598,655,080
Subtotal – Modifications/Forgiveness	$369,290,497	$729,467,078
Subtotal – Rate Reduction*	$371,304,201	*Not available*
Entire Principal Forgiveness without Foreclosure	$275,955,575	$241,795,343
Donations	$115,000,000	$50,000,000
Affordable Rental Housing	$759,704,640	$194,207,520
Subtotal – Community Investment and Neighbourhood Stabilization	$1,150,660,215	$486,002,863
Total Consumer Relief*	$1,891,254,913	$1,215,469,940

* *Excluding Rate Reduction Actuals; not included in monitor's reports. Data as of May 2019.*

Under the DOJ Settlement, Citigroup was required to earn a minimum of $2.5 billion in consumer relief credit,[43] derived from the actual relief by the same method as described previously in the Ally Settlement[44] and according to the terms of the settlement in the following outline.

MINIMUMS

The terms placed minimum relief obligations on certain categories of relief:

- Minimum $820 million credit earned in modifications and forgiveness of entire principal without foreclosure cumulatively, with a minimum 50 per cent of modifications earned in hardest hit areas, and a maximum of $553 million credit in forgiveness of entire principal without foreclosure.[45]
- Minimum $299 million credit earned in rate reduction, with principal or balance forgiveness beyond $74 million credit earned under Modifications.[46]

[42] Thomas J. Perrelli, Monitor, "Citi Monitorship: Tenth Report" (May 2019), 14, Citigroup Monitorship, 14, www.citigroupmonitorship.com/wp-content/uploads/2019/05/Citigroup Monitor_10thReport.pdf (hereafter Citigroup DOJ Tenth Report).

[43] Citigroup DOJ Settlement, para. 2.

[44] See Table A.2 description.

[45] Citigroup DOJ Settlement, Annex 2, 7, 11.

[46] Citigroup DOJ Settlement, Annex 2, 8.

- Minimum $25 million credit earned for donations to certain community development funds.[47]
- Minimum $15 million credit earned for donations towards legal assistance.[48]
- Minimum $10 million credit earned for donations to HUD-approved housing counselling agencies.[49]
- Minimum $180 million credit earned in the financing of affordable rental housing.[50]
- Minimum $90 million credit each earned in California and in New York.[51]
- Minimum $40 million credit earned in Illinois.[52]
- Minimum $10 million credit each earned in Massachusetts and in Delaware.[53]

TERMS OVERALL

- All bonus credit is cumulative.[54]
- 115 per cent credit for all consumer relief offered by 1 October 2015.[55]
- 115 per cent credit for credit amounts in excess of the Participating State Minimum Amounts for each Participating State (see Minimums, shown previously) in the categories described in the categories of Modifications, Rate Reduction/Refinancing, and entire principal forgiveness without foreclosure, below.[56]

TERMS BY CATEGORY

Modifications

- $23,879,526 actual relief[57] provided in first-lien principal forgiveness, tentatively earning $27,531,179 credit. Subject to certain eligibility requirements to ensure the necessity and sufficiency of relief, credit was earned as a rate of $1 financing = $1 credit.[58]
- $27,146,255 actual relief[59] provided to assist borrowers in refinancing outside Citigroup, tentatively earning $31,172,235 credit. Subject to certain eligibility

[47] Citigroup DOJ Settlement, Annex 2, 11.
[48] Citigroup DOJ Settlement, Annex 2, 12.
[49] Citigroup DOJ Settlement, Annex 2, 12.
[50] Citigroup DOJ Settlement, Annex 2, 13.
[51] Citigroup DOJ Settlement, Annex 2, 14.
[52] Citigroup DOJ Settlement, Annex 2, 14.
[53] Citigroup DOJ Settlement, Annex 2, 14.
[54] Citigroup DOJ Settlement, Annex 2, 2.
[55] Citigroup DOJ Settlement, Annex 2, 2.
[56] Citigroup DOJ Settlement, Annex 2, 14.
[57] Citigroup DOJ Tenth Report, 9.
[58] Citigroup DOJ Settlement, Annex 2, 2.
[59] Citigroup DOJ Tenth Report, 9. Thomas J. Perrelli, Monitor, "Citi Monitorship: Eighth Report" (April 2018), 11–12, Citigroup Monitorship, 11-12, www.citigroupmonitorship.com/wp-content/uploads/2018/04/CitigroupMonitor_8thReport_FINAL-3-red.pdf (hereafter Citigroup DOJ Eighth Report).

requirements to ensure the necessity and sufficiency of relief, credit was earned as a rate of $1 financing = $1 credit.[60]

- $79,786,217 actual relief[61] provided to consumers in modification of secured junior liens, tentatively earning $36,586,150 credit. Subject to certain eligibility requirements to ensure the necessity and sufficiency of relief, credit was earned at a rate of $1 forgiveness = $0.40 credit.[62]
- $598,655,080 actual relief[63] provided in principal forgiveness of unsecured mortgage debt, tentatively earning $274,000,933 credit. Subject to certain eligibility requirements to ensure the necessity and sufficiency of relief, credit was earned at a rate of $1 forgiveness = $0.40 credit.[64]

Rate Reduction: $371,304,201 credit was tentatively earned for rate reduction (actuals not available)[65] as follows:[66]

- For rate reductions between 200 and 400 basis points (bps) (exclusive), the difference between the pre-existing rate and the offered interest rate times the unpaid principal balance times an average life of 8 years, or
- For rate reductions between 200 and 400 bps (exclusive), the difference between the pre-existing rate and the offered interest rate times the unpaid principal balance times an average life of 8 years times 1.25, or
- To facilitate refinancing, $1 costs = $1 credit for costs paid to lienholders other than the bank; for closing costs paid to third party originators; and for principal or balance forgiveness; and
- 115 per cent credit for LTV reduction below 100 per cent.

Community Reinvestment and Neighbourhood Stabilization

- $241,795,343 actual relief provided to consumers in forgiveness of entire principal associated with a property where foreclosure was not pursued and the liens released, tentatively earning $275,955,575 credit at a rate of $1 forgiveness = $1 credit.[67]

[60] Citigroup DOJ Settlement, Annex 2, 2, 6–7.

[61] Thomas J. Perrelli, Monitor, "Citi Monitorship: Ninth Report" (November 2018), 25–6, Citigroup Monitorship, www.citigroupmonitorship.com/wp-content/uploads/2018/11/citigroupmonitor_ 9threport_final.pdf (hereafter Citigroup DOJ Ninth Report).

[62] Citigroup DOJ Settlement, Annex 2, 2, 7.

[63] Citigroup DOJ Ninth Report, 26–7.

[64] Citigroup DOJ Settlement, Annex 2, 2, 7.

[65] Thomas J. Perrelli, Monitor, "Citi Monitorship: Seventh Report" (June 2017), 4, Citigroup Monitorship, www.citigroupmonitorship.com/wp-content/uploads/2017/06/Citi_Monitorship_seventh_report_6-15-2017.pdf (hereafter Citigroup DOJ Seventh Report).

[66] Citigroup DOJ Settlement, Annex 2, 8.

[67] Citigroup DOJ Ninth Report, 21; Citigroup DOJ Settlement, Annex 2, 11.

- $25 million actual relief provided to consumers in donations to Community Development Financial Institutions, land banks subject to state or local regulation, or community development funds administered by non-profits or local governments; tentatively earning $57.5 million credit at a rate of $1 payment = $2 credit.[68]
- $10 million actual relief provided to consumers in donations to HUD-approved housing counselling agencies, tentatively earning $23 million credit at a rate of $1 payment = $2 credit.[69]
- $15 million actual relief provided to consumers in donations for legal assistance, tentatively earning $34.5 million credit at a rate of $1 payment = $2 credit.[70]
- $194,207,520 actual relief provided to consumers in affordable rental housing, tentatively earning $759,704,640 credit[71] according to the following terms[72]:
  - $1 loss = $3.25 credit, or
  - $1 loss = $3.75 credit for critical need family housing developments, subject to certain requirements to ensure that size and affordability meets a reasonable standard.

TABLE A.8 *Citigroup National Mortgage settlement – consumer relief*[73]

Type of Relief	Credit Earned	Actual Relief
First-Lien Mortgage Modifications	$524,062,757	$695,316,336
Second-Lien Portfolio Modifications	$348,564,573	$1,530,203,988
Subtotal – Modifications/Forgiveness	$872,627,330	$2,225,520,324
Subtotal – Refinancing Program	$519,098,690	$404,795,612
Enhanced Borrower Transitional Funds	$842,377	$1,253,377
Short Sales/Deeds in Lieu	$316,159,020	$569,472,785
Payment to an Unrelated Second-Lien Holder	$1,614,481	$1,853,943
Forgiveness in Lieu of Foreclosure	$82,625,807	$312,812,924
Subtotal – Other Creditable Items	$401,241,685	$885,393,029
Total Consumer Relief	$1,792,967,705	$3,515,708,965

68 Thomas J. Perrelli, Monitor, "Citi Monitorship: Fifth Report" (June 2016), 11, Citigroup Monitorship, www.citigroupmonitorship.com/wp-content/uploads/2016/06/Citi_Monitorship_fifth_report_6-27-2016.pdf (hereafter Citigroup DOJ Fifth Report). Citigroup DOJ Settlement, Annex 2, 11.

69 Citigroup DOJ Fifth Report, 11; Citigroup DOJ Settlement, Annex 2, 12.

70 Citigroup DOJ Fifth Report, 11; Citigroup DOJ Settlement, Annex 2, 12.

71 Citigroup DOJ Seventh Report, 9.

72 Citigroup DOJ Settlement, Annex 2, 13.

73 NMS Final Report, 15.

Under the National Mortgage Settlement, Citigroup was required to earn a minimum of $1.41 billion in consumer relief credit, as well as $378 million in refinancing relief credit.[74] The terms placed additional maximum and minimum relief obligations on certain categories of relief, and provided for an early incentive credit.[75]

TERMS BY CATEGORY

Credit was earned at the same rates described previously under the Ally and Bank of America Settlements[76] with the following additions:

> Short Sales/Deeds in Lieu (B): $569,472,785 actual relief provided to consumers in payments to unrelated second-lien holders to facilitate short sales or deeds in lieu of foreclosure and releases of liens, earning $316,159,020.[77] The rate at which credit was provided is not available.
>
> Anti-blight provision: $312,812,924 actual relief provided to consumers in forgiveness of principal associated with a property where the bank does not pursue foreclosure, earning $82,625,807 at a rate of $1 property value = $0.50 credit.[78]

TABLE A.9 *Credit Suisse settlements*

MONETARY PENALTIES – Actual Payments by Bank	
U.S. Treasury General Fund, pursuant to the Financial Institutions Reform, Recovery and Enforcement Act of 1989 (FIRREA) (DOJ)[79]	$2,480,000,000
National Credit Union Administration (NCUA)[80]	$460,062,048
Federal Deposit Insurance Corporation (FDIC)[81]	*Not available*
Federal Housing Finance Agency (FHFA)[82]	$885,000,000

74 Citigroup NMS Consent Judgment, para. 5.

75 Terms are described previously under the Ally DOJ Settlement, referencing the Ally NMS Consent Judgment, Exhibits D1-1 through D1-4, which is identical to the Citigroup NMS Consent Judgment, Exhibit D1.

76 Referencing the Ally NMS Consent Judgment, and Bank of America NMS Consent Judgment, Exhibits D and D1, which are identical to the Citigroup NMS Consent Judgment, Exhibits D and D1.

77 Citigroup NMS Consent Judgment, Exhibits D1-3 through D1-4.

78 Citigroup NMS Consent Judgment, Exhibit D1-4.

79 DOJ, "Credit Suisse Agrees to Pay $5.28 Billion." Credit Suisse Settlement Agreement Recitals (18 January 2017), para. 1–2, United States Department of Justice, para. 1, www.justice.gov/opa/press-release/file/928521/download (hereafter Credit Suisse DOJ Settlement).

80 NCUA Settlements.

81 Federal Deposit Insurance Corporation Settlement and Release Agreement (26 May 2016), para. 1, FDIC, www.fdic.gov/about/freedom/plsa/colonialbankreditsuissesecuritiesubssecurities.pdf (hereafter FDIC Settlement). The settlement required a cumulative $190 million to be paid by eight banks; the division is not available.

82 FHFA Private Label Securities Actions.

Securities Exchange Commission (SEC)[83]	$120,004,330
State of New York[84]	*Not available*
TOTAL MONETARY PENALTIES – ACTUALS*	$3,945,066,378
DOJ CONSUMER RELIEF OBLIGATIONS – Credit Adjusted Per Settlement Terms	
TOTAL CONSUMER RELIEF CREDIT EARNED**	$73,379,895
TOTAL SETTLEMENT (Monetary Penalties + Consumer Relief Credit)**	$4,018,446,273

* Excluding FDIC and New York State Settlements – not publicly released.

** Current through February 2019 – DOJ Settlement consumer relief must be completed by 31 December 2021.

Under the DOJ Settlement, Credit Suisse was required to earn a minimum of $2.8 billion in consumer relief credit,[85] derived from the actual relief by the same method as described previously in the Ally Settlement[86] and according to the terms of the settlement in the following outline.

TABLE A.10 *Credit Suisse – U.S. Department of Justice settlement – consumer relief*

Type of Relief – Modifications/Forgiveness	Credit Earned	Actual Relief
First-Lien Principal Forgiveness	$15,517,735	$10,546,157
First-Lien Forbearance – Payment Forgiveness	$57,862,160	$132,620,501
Total Consumer Relief *	$73,379,895	$143,166,658

* As of February 2019.

MINIMUMS

The terms placed maximum and minimum relief obligations on certain categories of relief[87]:

- Minimum $1.75 billion credit earned in modifications, with $980 million in first-lien principal forgiveness.

83 *In the Matter of Credit Suisse Securities et al*, No 3-15098, Order (SEC filed 16 November 2012), IV(c) and (d), SEC, www.sec.gov/litigation/admin/2012/33-9368.pdf (hereafter Credit Suisse SEC Settlement).

84 "Credit Suisse settles New York State RMBS lawsuit," *Reuters* (7 January 2019), online: Reuters, www.reuters.com/article/us-credit-suisse-gp-new-york/credit-suisse-settles-new-york-state-rmbs-lawsuit-idUSKCN1P1119.

85 Credit Suisse DOJ Settlement, para. 2.

86 See Table A.2 description.

87 Credit Suisse Settlement Agreement Annex 2 Consumer Relief (18 January 2017) at 2, 5, online (pdf): United States Department of Justice, www.justice.gov/opa/press-release/file/928486/download (hereafter Credit Suisse DOJ Settlement, Annex 2).

- Minimum $240 million credit earned in the financing of affordable rental housing, with at least 50 per cent in Critical Need Family Housing Developments.

TERMS OVERALL[88]

- All bonus credit is cumulative.
- 115 per cent credit for all consumer relief offered by 1 March 2018.

TERMS BY CATEGORY

Modifications

- $10,546,157 actual relief provided to consumers in first-lien principal forgiveness, tentatively earning $15,517,735 credit.[89] Subject to certain eligibility requirements to ensure the necessity and sufficiency of relief, credit was earned as follows[90]:
  - $1 forgiveness = $1 credit, and
  - 150 per cent credit for forgiveness completed by 1 November 2017, and
  - 115 per cent credit for incremental LTV reduction between 90 and 100 per cent, and
  - 120 per cent credit for incremental LTV reduction between 76 and 90 per cent, and
  - 125 per cent credit for entire amount of principal forgiven if post-modification LTV equal to or less than 75 per cent.
- $132,620,501 actual relief provided to consumers in first-lien forbearance payment forgiveness, tentatively earning $57,862,160 credit.[91] Subject to certain eligibility requirements to ensure the necessity and sufficiency of relief, credit calculated as the difference between the pre-existing rate and the offered interest rate times the unpaid principal balance times an average life of 8 years.[92]

88 Credit Suisse DOJ Settlement, Annex 2, 2.

89 Neil M. Barofsky, "Monitor for the Credit Suisse RMBS Settlement: Third Report" (31 August 2018) at 37, online (pdf): Credit Suisse RMBS Settlement Monitor, http://d3cvzjdoxgm4sc.cloudfront.net/uploads/report/pdf_upload/4c7cd9c9-dfb8-4cb4-8584-7b1bcb55dbc1/2dc39497-ddf1-493e-a910-6336a13d5ca4.pdf (hereafter Credit Suisse DOJ Third Report); Neil M. Barofsky, "Monitor for the Credit Suisse RMBS Settlement: Fourth Report" (28 February 2019) at 20, online (pdf): Credit Suisse RMBS Settlement Monitor, http://d3cvzjdoxgm4sc.cloudfront.net/uploads/report/pdf_upload/93720065-75f1-4d99-adaa-845dbeeab466/25ef7cc3-84ea-456b-bb1a-58e69013764b.pdf (hereafter Credit Suisse DOJ Fourth Report).

90 Credit Suisse DOJ Settlement, Annex 2, 2–3.

91 Credit Suisse DOJ Third Report, 52; Credit Suisse DOJ Fourth Report, 33.

92 Credit Suisse DOJ Settlement, Annex 2, 2–3.

Affordable Housing: $51,879,335 actual relief[93] provided to consumers in affordable rental housing, pending approval by the monitor. If approved, credit will be calculated according to the following terms[94]:

- $1 loss = $3.25 credit, or
- $1 loss = $3.75 credit for critical need family housing developments, subject to certain requirements to ensure that size and affordability meets a reasonable standard.

TABLE A.11 *Deutsche Bank settlements*

MONETARY PENALTIES – Actual Payments by Bank	
U.S. Treasury General Fund, pursuant to the Financial Institutions Reform, Recovery and Enforcement Act of 1989 (FIRREA) (DOJ)[95]	$3,100,000,000
National Credit Union Administration (NCUA)[96]	$145,000,000
Federal Deposit Insurance Corporation (FDIC)*[97]	*Not available*
Federal Housing Finance Agency (FHFA)[98]	$1,925,000,000
Securities Exchange Commission (SEC)[99]	$3,729,743
Multi-State[100]	$220,000,000
TOTAL MONETARY PENALTIES – ACTUALS*	$5,393,729,743
DOJ CONSUMER RELIEF OBLIGATIONS – Credit Adjusted Per Settlement Terms	
TOTAL CONSUMER RELIEF CREDIT EARNED**	$2,207,476,000
TOTAL SETTLEMENT (Monetary Penalties + Consumer Relief Credit)**	$7,601,205,743

* Excluding FDIC Settlement; not publicly released.
** Current through May 2019; DOJ Settlement consumer relief must be completed by 31 March 2022.

93 Credit Suisse DOJ Fourth Report, 59.

94 Credit Suisse DOJ Settlement, Annex 2, 5–6.

95 Deutsche Bank Settlement Agreement Recitals (17 January 2017), paras. 1–2, United States Department of Justice, para. 1, www.justice.gov/opa/press-release/file/928096/download (hereafter Deutsche Bank DOJ Settlement).

96 NCUA Settlements.

97 FDIC Settlement. The settlement required a cumulative $190 million to be paid by eight banks; the division is not available.

98 Deutsche Bank FHFA Settlement Agreement (19 December 2013), 2, FHFA, www.fhfa.gov/Media/PublicAffairs/Documents/FHFADeutscheBankSettlementAgreement122013.pdf (hereafter Deutsche Bank FHFA Settlement).

99 *In the Matter of Deutsche Bank Securities Inc and Benjamin Solomon*, No. 3-18367, Order (SEC filed 12 February 2018), para. 22, SEC, www.sec.gov/litigation/admin/2018/34-82686.pdf (hereafter Deutsche Bank SEC Settlement).

100 Deutsche Bank Multi-State Settlement Agreement (25 October 2017), para. 71, NY Government, https://ag.ny.gov/sites/default/files/db_settlement_agreement_signed.pdf (hereafter Deutsche Bank State Settlement).

Under the DOJ Settlement, Deutsche Bank was required to earn a minimum of $4.1 billion in consumer relief credit.[101]

Deutsche Bank has elected to fulfil its entire relief obligation by facilitating the origination of new residential mortgages to first-time low-to-moderate income homebuyers and borrowers in hardest hit areas.[102] The bank earns $10,000 credit for each purchase money loan, plus an additional 115 per cent credit for all consumer relief offered by 1 September 2018.[103] The total actual relief received by borrowers will be $0, as they will repay the loans with interest.

To date, Deutsche Bank has earned $2,207,476,000 credit, representing $42 billion in principal loaned.[104]

TABLE A.12 *Goldman Sachs settlements*

MONETARY PENALTIES – Actual Payments by Bank	
U.S. Treasury General Fund, pursuant to the Financial Institutions Reform, Recovery and Enforcement Act of 1989 (FIRREA) (DOJ)[105]	$2,385,000,000
National Credit Union Administration (NCUA)[106]	$575,000,000
Federal Deposit Insurance Corporation (FDIC)*[107]	*Not available*
Federal Housing Finance Agency (FHFA)[108]	$1,200,000,000
Securities Exchange Commission (SEC)[109]	$550,000,000
State of New York[110]	$190,000,000
State of California[111]	$10,000,000

[101] Deutsche Bank DOJ Settlement, para. 2.

[102] Michael J. Bresnick, "Monitor of the 2017 Deutsche Bank Mortgage Settlement: Sixth Report" (May 2019) at 1, online (pdf): Deutsche Bank Mortgage Monitor, https://deutschebankmortgagemonitor.com/wp-content/uploads/2019/05/46560300-v1-Deutsche-Bank-Monitor-Sixth-Report-May-2019.pdf (hereafter Deutsche Bank DOJ Sixth Report).

[103] Deutsche Bank Settlement Agreement, Annex 2 Consumer Relief (17 January 2017) at paras. 3, 6, online (pdf): United States Department of Justice, www.justice.gov/opa/press-release/file/927281/download.

[104] Deutsche Bank DOJ Sixth Report, 1.

[105] Goldman Sachs Settlement Agreement Recitals (11 April 2016), para. 1(a)(i), Department of Justice, www.justice.gov/opa/file/839891/download (hereafter Goldman Sachs DOJ Settlement).

[106] NCUA Settlements.

[107] FDIC Settlement, para. 1. The settlement required a cumulative $190 million to be paid by eight banks; the division is not available.

[108] FHFA Private Label Securities Actions.

[109] *Securities and Exchange Commission* v *Goldman, Sachs & Co and Fabrice Tourre*, No 10-3229 Consent Judgment (SDNY filed 15 July 2010), para. 2, SEC, www.sec.gov/litigation/litreleases/2010/consent-pr2010-123.pdf (hereafter Goldman Sachs SEC Consent Judgment). See also U.S. Securities and Exchange Commission, "Financial Crisis Enforcement Actions: SEC Monetary Recoveries" (19 October 2011), SEC, www.sec.gov/news/press/2011/2011-214-chart-recoveries.pdf (hereafter SEC Monetary Recoveries).

[110] Goldman Sachs DOJ Settlement, para. 1(d).

[111] Goldman Sachs DOJ Settlement, para. 1(b).

State of Illinois[112]	$25,000,000
Federal Home Loan Bank of Chicago[113]	$75,000,000
TOTAL MONETARY PENALTIES – ACTUALS*	$5,010,000,000
DOJ CONSUMER RELIEF OBLIGATIONS – Credit Adjusted Per Settlement Terms	
TOTAL CONSUMER RELIEF CREDIT EARNED **	$1,378,599,289
TOTAL SETTLEMENT (Monetary Penalties + Consumer Relief Credit)**	$6,388,599,289

* Excluding FDIC Settlement; not publicly released.
** Current through May 2019; DOJ Settlement consumer relief must be completed by 31 January 2021.

TABLE A.13 *Goldman Sachs – U.S. Department of Justice settlement – consumer relief*

Type of Relief	Credit Earned	Actual Relief
First-Lien Principal Forgiveness	$697,573,606	$604,542,708
Principal Forgiveness of Forbearance	$10,386,397	$9,370,714
First-Lien Forbearance (Payment Forgiveness)	$2,162,457	$0
Second-Lien Extinguishment	$28,344,186	$62,766,502
Junior Lien Unsecured Principal Forgiveness/ Extinguishment	$120,132,387	$267,428,015
Subtotal – Modifications/Forgiveness	$858,599,033	$944,107,939
Subtotal – Affordable and For-Sale Housing	$240,000,256	$60,518,900
Grants – Certified Land Banks/Trusts	$30,000,000	$13,043,479
Grants – Housing Quality Improvement/ Enforcement	$30,000,000	$13,043,479
Debt Restructuring – Homeowners with Foreclosure Risk	$220,000,000	$95,652,174
Subtotal – State of New York Settlement	$280,000,000	$121,739,132
Total Consumer Relief *	$1,378,599,289	$1,126,365,971

* As of May 2019.

Under the DOJ Settlement, Goldman Sachs was required to earn a minimum of $1.8 billion in consumer relief credit,[114] derived from the actual relief by the same method as described previously in the Ally Settlement[115] and according to the terms of the settlement in the following outline.

[112] Goldman Sachs DOJ Settlement, para. 1(c).
[113] Goldman Sachs DOJ Settlement, 1(d) and (f).
[114] Goldman Sachs DOJ Settlement, para. 2.
[115] See Table A.2 description.

MINIMUMS AND MAXIMUMS

The terms placed minimum and maximum relief obligations on certain categories of relief:

- Minimum $1.52 billion credit earned in modifications and affordable and for-sale housing, with a minimum of $1.28 billion credit earned in modifications.[116]
- Minimum $240 million credit earned in affordable and for-sale housing, with at least 50 per cent in Critical Need Family Housing developments.[117]
- Minimum $200 million credit earned in New York, in addition to $280 million earned under the New York Settlement, Appendix A category.[118]
- Minimum $30 million credit earned in California.[119]
- Minimum $16 million credit earned in Illinois.[120]
- Maximum $630 million credit earned cumulatively in second-lien extinguishments and junior liens.[121]

TERMS OVERALL

- All bonus credit is cumulative.[122]
- 115 per cent credit for all consumer relief offered by 30 June 2017.[123]
- 115 per cent credit for credit amounts in excess of the Participating State Minimum Amounts for each Participating State (see Minimums, shown previously) in modifications and affordable and for-sale housing.[124]

TERMS BY CATEGORY

Modifications

- $604,542,708 actual relief provided to consumers in first-lien principal forgiveness, tentatively earning $697,573,606 credit.[125] Subject to certain eligibility

[116] Goldman Sachs Settlement Agreement Annex 2 Consumer Relief (11 April 2016), 2, 6, Department of Justice, www.justice.gov/opa/file/839906/download (hereafter Goldman Sachs DOJ Settlement, Annex 2).
[117] Goldman Sachs DOJ Settlement, Annex 2, 5.
[118] Goldman Sachs DOJ Settlement, Annex 2, 7; Goldman Sachs DOJ Settlement, para. 2; see also Goldman Sachs Settlement Agreement, Appendix A New York Settlement (11 April 2016) at 1, online (pdf): New York Attorney General, https://ag.ny.gov/pdfs/GS-NYAG-Settlement.pdf (hereafter Goldman Sachs New York Settlement).
[119] Goldman Sachs DOJ Settlement, Annex 2, 7.
[120] Goldman Sachs DOJ Settlement, Annex 2, 7.
[121] Goldman Sachs DOJ Settlement, Annex 2, 4.
[122] Goldman Sachs DOJ Settlement, Annex 2, 3.
[123] Goldman Sachs DOJ Settlement, Annex 2, 2.
[124] Goldman Sachs DOJ Settlement, Annex 2, 7.
[125] Eric D. Green, "Monitor of the 2016 Goldman Sachs Settlement Agreement: Eleventh Report" (1 May 2019) at 33, online (pdf): Goldman Sachs Mortgage Settlement Monitor, https://goldmansachs.mortgagesettlementmonitor.com/Reports/May-01-2019-Report-2016-Goldman-Sachs-Mortgage-Settlement.pdf (hereafter Goldman Sachs DOJ Eleventh Report). In the Monitor Reports, "forgiveness"

requirements to ensure the necessity and sufficiency of relief, credit was earned as follows[126]:

- $1 forgiveness = $1 credit, and
- 150 per cent credit for forgiveness completed by 30 November 2016, and
- 115 per cent credit for incremental LTV reduction below 100 per cent.

- $9,370,714 actual relief provided to consumers in first-lien principal forgiveness of forbearance, tentatively earning $10,386,397 credit.[127] Subject to certain eligibility requirements to ensure the necessity and sufficiency of relief, credit was earned as follows[128]:
  - $1 forgiveness = $1 credit, and
  - 115 per cent credit for incremental LTV reduction below 100 per cent.
- $2,162,457 credit was tentatively earned in first-lien forbearance payment forgiveness.[129] Subject to certain eligibility requirements to ensure the necessity and sufficiency of relief, credit was calculated as the difference between the pre-existing rate and the offered interest rate times the unpaid principal balance times an average life of 10 years.[130]
- $62,766,502 actual relief provided to consumers in second-lien extinguishment, tentatively earning $28,344,186 credit.[131] Subject to certain eligibility requirements to ensure the necessity and sufficiency of relief, credit was earned as follows[132]:
  - For performing loans (maximum 90 days past due), $1 forgiveness = $1 credit, or
  - For seriously delinquent and non-performing loans (more than 90 days past due), $1 forgiveness = $0.40 credit.
- $267,428,015 actual relief provided to consumers in outstanding unsecured mortgage debt principal forgiveness and extinguishment of junior liens, tentatively earning $120,132,387 credit.[133] Subject to certain eligibility requirements to ensure the necessity and sufficiency of relief, credit was earned at a rate of $1 forgiveness = $0.40 credit.[134]

is the equivalent of actual relief: "Forgiveness is the amount prior to any adjustments required to determine credit," according to Thomas Cooper of BDO USA LLP, email message to MaryGrace Johnstone, 16 May 2019.

126 Goldman Sachs DOJ Settlement, Annex 2, 2–3.
127 Goldman Sachs DOJ Eleventh Report, 34.
128 Goldman Sachs DOJ Settlement, Annex 2, 2–3.
129 Goldman Sachs DOJ Eleventh Report, 35.
130 Goldman Sachs DOJ Settlement, Annex 2, 2–3.
131 Goldman Sachs DOJ Eleventh Report, 36.
132 Goldman Sachs DOJ Settlement, Annex 2, 2, 4.
133 Goldman Sachs DOJ Eleventh Report, 39.
134 Goldman Sachs DOJ Settlement, Annex 2, 2, 4.

Affordable Housing: $60,518,900 actual relief provided to consumers in affordable rental housing, tentatively earning $240,000,256 credit,[135] as follows[136]:

- $1 loss = $3.25 credit, or
- $1 loss = $3.75 credit for critical need family housing developments, subject to certain requirements to ensure that size and affordability meets a reasonable standard.

NEW YORK SETTLEMENT

In addition to relief provided to New York borrowers under the other categories of the DOJ Settlement consumer relief component, Goldman Sachs came to a separate agreement with the New York Attorney General, the total of which is included in the DOJ Settlement. At a rate of $1 grant/restructuring = $2 credit,[137] the bank earned $280 million credit as follows:

- $13,043,479 actual relief provided to consumers in grants for certified land banks or trusts, tentatively earning $30 million credit.[138]
- $13,043,479 actual relief provided to consumers in grants to municipalities or their housing or finance agencies to support housing quality improvement and enforcement programs, tentatively earning $30 million credit.[139]
- $95,652,174 actual relief provided in debt restructuring for homeowners at risk of foreclosure, tentatively earning $220 million credit.[140]

TABLE A.14 *HSBC settlements*

MONETARY PENALTIES – Actual Payments by Bank	
U.S. Treasury General Fund, pursuant to the Financial Institutions Reform, Recovery and Enforcement Act of 1989 (FIRREA) (DOJ)[141]	$765,000,000
National Credit Union Administration (NCUA)[142]	$5,250,000
Federal Housing Finance Agency (FHFA)[143]	$550,000,000

135 Goldman Sachs DOJ Eleventh Report, 40.
136 Goldman Sachs DOJ Settlement, Annex 2, 5.
137 Goldman Sachs New York Settlement, 1.
138 Eric D. Green, "Monitor of the 2016 Goldman Sachs Settlement Agreement: Third Report" (1 May 2017) at 16, online (pdf): Goldman Sachs Mortgage Settlement Monitor https://goldmansachs.mortgagesettlementmonitor.com/Reports/May-01-2017-Report-2016-Goldman-Sachs-Mortgage-Settlement.pdf (hereafter Goldman Sachs Settlement Agreement Third Report).
139 Goldman Sachs Settlement Agreement Third Report, 17.
140 Goldman Sachs Settlement Agreement Third Report, 18.
141 Department of Justice, "HSBC Agrees to Pay $765 Million in Connection with Its Sale of Residential Mortgage-Backed Securities" (9 October 2018), online: www.justice.gov/usao-co/pr/hsbc-agrees-pay-765-million-connection-its-sale-residential-mortgage-backed-securities.
142 NCUA Settlements.
143 FHFA Private Label Securities Actions.

Federal (U.S.)[144]	$40,500,000
Multi-State (U.S.)[145]	$59,500,000
TOTAL MONETARY PENALTIES – ACTUALS	$1,420,250,000
U.S. CONSUMER RELIEF OBLIGATIONS – Credit Adjusted Per Settlement Terms	
TOTAL CONSUMER RELIEF CREDIT EARNED	$371,075,290
TOTAL SETTLEMENT (Monetary Penalties + Consumer Relief Credit)	$1,791,325,290

TABLE A.15 *HSBC U.S. settlement – consumer relief*

Type of Relief	Credit Earned
First-Lien Principal Forgiveness	$214,614,828
Forgiveness of Forbearance	$7,986,483
Subtotal – Modifications/Forgiveness[146]	$222,601,311
Short Sales	$101,443,516
Deeds in Lieu	$47,030,463
Subtotal – Other Creditable Items[147]	$148,473,979
Total Consumer Relief	$371,075,290

Under the U.S. Settlement, HSBC was required to earn a minimum of $370 million in consumer relief credit,[148] derived from the actual relief by the same method as described previously in the Ally Settlement.[149] Actuals are not available for this settlement.[150]

[144] *United States of America, et al* v *HSBC North America Holdings, et al*, No 16-00199 (RJL), Document 8 Consent Judgment (DDC filed 14 March 2016), para. 3, National Mortgage Settlements, https://scholarship.law.unc.edu/cgi/viewcontent.cgi?article=1116&context=mortgage-settlements (hereafter HSBC Consent Judgment). HSBC paid the amount into escrow, to be distributed according to undisclosed instructions from the DOJ.

[145] HSBC Consent Judgment, para. 3. HSBC paid the amount into escrow; $59,300,000 was to be distributed according to the same terms as the NMS Borrower Payments described in Table A.1. The remaining $200,000 was to be paid into the Ameriquest Financial Services Fund for reimbursement of costs and fees during the investigation of the case as set out in Exhibit B, para. 2 and as seen in the NMS described in Table A.1. HSBC Consent Judgment, para. 4.

[146] *United States of America, et al* v *HSBC North America Holdings, et al*, No 16-0199 (RJL), Document 26 Final Consumer Relief Report (DDC filed 14 March 2017) at 8, s II(d) Consumer Relief Requirements: Monitor's Obligations, online (pdf): National Mortgage Settlements, https://scholarship.law.unc.edu/cgi/viewcontent.cgi?article=1181&context=mortgage-settlements (hereafter HSBC Final Report).

[147] HSBC Final Report, 11, III(c) Review: Servicer's Assertions.

[148] HSBC Consent Judgment, para. 5.

[149] See Table A.2 description.

[150] HSBC Final Report, II(D) Consumer Relief and V Total Consumer Relief, referring to actual relief data in Schedule. Schedule Y is not in the public record.

MINIMUMS

The terms placed maximum and minimum relief obligations on certain categories of relief as described previously under the Ally Settlement.[151] The terms also required that a minimum of $88 million credit be earned through first-lien principal forgiveness, and an additional minimum of $104 million credit be earned through first-lien principal forgiveness and forgiveness of forbearance cumulatively (among other categories not used by HSBC).[152]

TERMS BY CATEGORY

Credit was earned at the same rates described previously under the Ally Settlement, including the early incentive credit.[153]

TABLE A.16 *JP Morgan & Chase Co. settlements*

MONETARY PENALTIES – Actual Payments by Bank	
U.S. Department of Justice (DOJ) and Independent Settlements[154]	
U.S. Treasury General Fund, pursuant to the *Financial Institutions Reform, Recovery and Enforcement Act of 1989 (FIRREA)* (DOJ)	$2,000,000,000
National Credit Union Administration (NCUA)	$1,417,525,773
Federal Deposit Insurance Corporation (FDIC)	$515,463,917
Federal Housing Finance Agency (FHFA)	$4,000,000,000
Securities Exchange Commission (SEC)	$210,361,214
State of New York	$613,000,235
State of California	$298,973,006
State of Illinois	$100,911,813
Commonwealth of Massachusetts	$34,400,000
State of Delaware	$19,725,255

151 Referencing the Ally NMS Consent Judgment, Exhibit D1, which is identical to the HSBC Final Report, Exhibit D1.

152 HSBC Final Report, s II(c) Consumer Relief Requirements: Servicer's Obligations.

153 Referencing the Ally NMS Consent Judgment, Exhibit D1, which is identical to the HSBC Final Report, Exhibit D1.

154 JP Morgan Chase Bank et al, Settlement Agreement Recitals (19 November 2013), paras. 1–2, United States Department of Justice, www.justice.gov/iso/opa/resources/69520131119191246941958.pdf (hereafter JP Morgan Chase DOJ Settlement). A complete breakdown of monetary penalties paid to the listed litigants is provided at para. 1. Additionally, JP Morgan Chase came to an independent settlement with the SEC: U.S. Securities and Exchange Commission, "JP Morgan to Pay $153.6 Million to Settle SEC Charges of Misleading Investors in CDO Tied to US Housing Market" (21 June 2011), online: SEC, www.sec.gov/news/press/2011/2011-131.htm; and SEC Monetary Recoveries.

Subtotal – DOJ Settlement Monetary Penalties	$9,210,361,214
National Mortgage Settlement (NMS)[155]	
Subtotal – NMS Monetary Penalties	$1,121,188,661
TOTAL MONETARY PENALTIES – ACTUALS	$10,331,549,875
CONSUMER RELIEF OBLIGATIONS – Credit Adjusted Per Settlement Terms	
DOJ Credit Earned	$4,063,880,724
NMS Credit Earned	$4,463,524,210
TOTAL CONSUMER RELIEF CREDIT EARNED	$8,527,404,934
TOTAL SETTLEMENT (Monetary Penalties + Consumer Relief Credit)	$18,858,954,809

TABLE A.17 *JP Morgan & Chase Co. – U.S. Department of Justice settlement – consumer relief*[156]

Type of Relief	Credit Earned	Actual Relief
First-Lien Principal Forgiveness	$1,057,668,869	$1,278,869,890
Principal Forgiveness of Forbearance	$300,000,000	$231,487,510
First-Lien Forbearance	$300,000,000	$1,080,338,478
Second-Lien Principal Forgiveness and Extinguishments	$360,785,046	$737,147,863
Subtotal – Modifications/Forgiveness	$2,018,453,915	$3,327,843,741
Subtotal – Rate Reduction	$874,470,934	$1,115,656,744
Subtotal – Low- to Moderate-Income Disaster Area Lending	$1,170,955,875	$0[157]
Total Consumer Relief	$4,063,880,724	$4,443,500,485

155 *United States of America, et al* v *Bank of America Corp, et al*, No 12-0361 (RMC), Consent Judgment (DDC filed 4 April 2012), para. 3, National Mortgage Settlements, https://scholarship.law.unc.edu/cgi/viewcontent.cgi?article=1001&context=mortgage-settlements (hereafter JP Morgan Chase NMS Consent Judgment). The NMS was a cumulative settlement; a complete breakdown of monetary penalties and parties are described previously under the Ally DOJ Settlement, referencing the NMS Initial Report, 3 and the Ally NMS Consent Judgment, para. 3 and Exhibit B, which is identical to the JP Morgan Chase NMS Consent Judgment at Exhibit B.

156 Joseph A. Smith Jr., Monitor, “Chase RMBS Settlement: Consumer Relief through March 31, 2016” (2016), 3, 8, National Mortgage Settlements, https://scholarship.law.unc.edu/cgi/viewcontent.cgi?article=1178&context=mortgage-settlements (hereafter JP Morgan Chase DOJ Final Report).

157 The purchase money loans sold to credit-worthy borrowers were valued at a total of $15.77 billion. However, this was not actual relief as the borrowers were required to repay the loans with interest. See explanation at *supra* note 29 referencing the Bank of America DOJ Settlement, Annex 2, 6, which corresponds to the JP Morgan Chase DOJ Settlement, Annex 2, 4.

Under the Department of Justice Settlement, JP Morgan Chase was required to earn a minimum of $4 billion in consumer relief credit,[158] derived from the actual relief by the same method as described previously in the Ally Settlement[159] and according to the terms of the settlement as follows.

MINIMUMS AND MAXIMUMS

The terms placed minimum and maximum relief obligations on certain categories of relief[160]:

- Minimum $2 billion credit earned in modifications, including $1.2 billion in first-lien principal forgiveness and principal forgiveness of forbearance cumulatively, and with a maximum of $300 million in principal forgiveness of forbearance.
- Maximum $300 million in first-lien forbearance (payment forgiveness).
- Maximum $165 million in lending to borrowers in areas declared as major disasters by the Federal Emergency Management Agency (FEMA).

TERMS OVERALL[161]

- All bonus credit is cumulative.
- 115 per cent credit for all consumer relief offered by 1 October 2014.
- 125 per cent credit for relief in hardest hit areas.
- 50 per cent credit reduction for first-lien principal forgiveness and forbearance of loans serviced for others.

TERMS BY CATEGORY

Modifications

- $1,278,869,890 actual relief provided to consumers in first-lien principal forgiveness, earning $1,057,668,869 credit.[162] Subject to certain eligibility requirements to ensure the necessity and sufficiency of relief, credit was earned at a rate of $1 write-down = $1 credit.[163]

158 JP Morgan Chase DOJ Settlement, para. 2.

159 See Table A.2 description.

160 JP Morgan Chase DOJ Final Report, 3, 8; see also JP Morgan Chase Bank et al, Settlement Agreement Annex 2, Consumer Relief (19 November 2013), 2–4, Department of Justice, www.justice.gov/iso/opa/resources/6442013111916475916 3425.pdf (hereafter JP Morgan Chase DOJ Settlement, Annex 2).

161 JP Morgan Chase DOJ Settlement, Annex 2, 2–4.

162 JP Morgan Chase DOJ Final Report, 3, 8.

163 JP Morgan Chase DOJ Settlement, Annex 2, 2.

- $231,487,510 actual relief provided to consumers in principal forgiveness of forbearance, earning $300 million credit.[164] Subject to certain eligibility requirements to ensure the necessity and sufficiency of relief, credit was earned at a rate of $1 write-down = $1 credit.[165]
- $1,080,338,478 actual relief provided to consumers in forgiveness of first-lien forbearance, earning $300 million credit,[166] calculated as a product of the loan's pre-modification rate, forborne unpaid principal balance, and an average life of eight years.[167]
- $737,147,863 actual relief provided to consumers in second-lien principal forgiveness, including extinguishments,[168] earning $360,785,046 credit as follows:[169]
  - $1 forgiveness = $1 credit for performing loans (90 days or less past due), and
  - 40 per cent credit (60 per cent reduction) for seriously delinquent and nonperforming loans (more than 90 days past due).

RATE REDUCTION/REFINANCING

- $1,115,656,744 actual relief provided to eligible borrowers for rate reduction or for refinancing under the Home Affordability Refinance Program (HARP), earning $874,470,934 credit, calculated as follows[170]:
  - For rate reduction, the difference between the pre-existing rate and the offered interest rate times the unpaid principal balance times a multiplier based on the life of the loan (five or eight years), or
  - For HARP, the difference between the pre-existing rate and the offered interest rate times the unpaid principal balance times an average life of five years.

LENDING

- The bank earned $1,170,955,875 credit for selling loans worth a total of $15,771,381,912 to eligible borrowers,[171] according to the same terms as the Bank of America consumer relief lending category.[172]

164 JP Morgan Chase DOJ Final Report, 3, 8.
165 JP Morgan Chase DOJ Settlement, Annex 2, 2.
166 JP Morgan Chase DOJ Final Report, 3, 8.
167 JP Morgan Chase DOJ Settlement, Annex 2, 2.
168 JP Morgan Chase DOJ Final Report, 3, 8.
169 JP Morgan Chase DOJ Settlement, Annex 2, 3.
170 JP Morgan Chase DOJ Settlement, Annex 2, 3; JP Morgan Chase DOJ Final Report, 3, 8.
171 JP Morgan Chase DOJ Final Report, 3, 8.
172 Referencing the Bank of America DOJ Settlement, Annex 2, 6, which corresponds to the JP Morgan Chase DOJ Settlement, Annex 2, 4.

TABLE A.18 *JP Morgan & Chase Co. National Mortgage settlement – consumer relief*[173]

Type of Relief	Credit Earned	Actual Relief
First-Lien Mortgage Modifications	$1,851,496,721	$2,914,871,594
Second-Lien Portfolio Modifications	$308,672,792	$2,234,144,451
Subtotal – Modifications/Forgiveness	$2,160,169,513	$5,149,016,045
Subtotal – Refinancing Program	$623,424,705	$492,247,276
Enhanced Borrower Transitional Funds	$136,957,159	$170,177,249
Short Sales/Deeds in Lieu	$1,495,692,789	$5,259,532,309
Payment to an Unrelated Second-Lien Holder	$9,780,918	$15,962,950
REO Properties Donated	$37,499,126	$37,499,126
Subtotal – Other Creditable Items	$1,679,929,992	$5,483,171,634
Total Consumer Relief	$4,463,524,210	$11,124,434,955

Under the National Mortgage Settlement, JP Morgan Chase was required to earn a minimum of $3,675,400,000 in consumer relief credit, as well as $537 million in refinancing relief.[174] The terms placed additional maximum and minimum relief obligations on certain categories of relief, and provided for an early incentive credit.[175]

TERMS BY CATEGORY

Credit was earned at the same rates described previously under the Ally, Bank of America, and Citigroup Settlements[176] with the following addition:

> Anti-Blight Provision: $37,499,126 actual relief provided to consumers and credit earned in REO properties donated, at a rate of $1 payment = $1 credit.[177]

[173] NMS Final Report, 13.

[174] JP Morgan Chase NMS Consent Judgment, para. 5.

[175] Terms are described previously under the Ally DOJ Settlement, referencing the Ally NMS Consent Judgment, Exhibits D and D1, which are identical to the JP Morgan Chase NMS Consent Judgment, Exhibits D and D1.

[176] Referencing the Ally NMS Consent Judgment, Bank of America NMS Consent Judgment, and Citigroup NMS Consent Judgment, Exhibits D and D1, which are identical to the JP Morgan Chase NMS Consent Judgment, Exhibits D and D1.

[177] NMS Final Report, Exhibits D1-4, D1-5.

TABLE A.19 *Morgan Stanley settlements*

MONETARY PENALTIES – Actual Payments by Bank	
U.S. Treasury General Fund, pursuant to the Financial Institutions Reform, Recovery and Enforcement Act of 1989 (FIRREA) (DOJ)[178]	$2,600,000,000
National Credit Union Administration (NCUA)[179]	$225,000,000
Federal Deposit Insurance Corporation (FDIC)[180]	$86,950,000
Federal Housing Finance Agency (FHFA)[181]	$1,250,000,000
Securities Exchange Commission (SEC)[182]	$275,000,000
State of New York[183]	$150,000,000
State of Illinois[184]	$22,500,000
TOTAL MONETARY PENALTIES – ACTUALS	$4,609,450,000
NEW YORK CONSUMER RELIEF OBLIGATIONS – Credit Adjusted Per Settlement Terms	
TOTAL CONSUMER RELIEF CREDIT EARNED	$401,690,163
TOTAL SETTLEMENT (Monetary Penalties + Consumer Relief Credit)	$5,011,140,163

178 Morgan Stanley Settlement Agreement and Statement of Facts (11 February 2016), para. 1, United States Department of Justice, www.justice.gov/opa/file/823671/download (hereafter Morgan Stanley DOJ Settlement).

179 NCUA Settlements.

180 Federal Deposit Insurance Corporation, "FDIC Announces $62.95 Million Settlement with Morgan Stanley Related to RMBS Claims" (2 February 2016), online: FDIC, www.fdic.gov/news/news/press/2016/pr16007.html.

181 FHFA Private Label Securities Actions.

182 *In the Matter of Morgan Stanley and Co LLC et al*, No 3-15982, Order Instituting Cease-and-Desist Proceedings (SEC filed 24 July 2014) at para. 40(b), online (pdf): SEC, www.sec.gov/litigation/admin/2014/33-9617.pdf.

183 Morgan Stanley Settlement Agreement (11 February 2016), paras. 1–2, New York Attorney General, https://ag.ny.gov/pdfs/Final_NYAG_Settlement_Agreement.pdf (hereafter Morgan Stanley New York Settlement).

184 Illinois Attorney General Pressroom, "Madigan Announces $22.5 Million Morgan Stanley Settlement" (11 February 2016), online: Illinois Attorney General, www.illinoisattorneygeneral.gov/pressroom/2016_02/20160211.html.

TABLE A.20 *Morgan Stanley New York settlement – consumer relief*

Type of Relief	Credit Earned
First-Lien Balance Forgiveness	$12,418,114
Second-Lien Balance Forgiveness Including Extinguishments	$57,587,469
Subtotal – Modifications/Forgiveness	$70,005,583
Subtotal – Financing for Acquisition and Remediation of Non-performing Loans	$66,412,500
Grants for Certified Land Banks	$30,202,136
Grants for Housing Quality Improvement and Enforcement Programs	$30,057,865
Subtotal – Community Reinvestment and Neighbourhood Stabilization	$60,260,001
Subtotal – Affordable Rental Housing	$205,012,079
Total Consumer Relief	$401,690,163

Under the New York Settlement, Morgan Stanley was required to earn a minimum of $400 million in consumer relief credit,[185] derived from the actual relief by the same method as described previously in the Ally Settlement[186] and according to the terms of the settlement as follows.

MINIMUMS

The terms placed minimum relief obligations on certain categories of relief[187]:

- Minimum $70 million credit earned in modifications.
- Minimum $30 million credit earned in each of grants for certified land banks and grants housing quality improvement and enforcement programs.
- Minimum $125 million credit earned cumulatively in financing for acquisition and remediation of non-performing loans and community reinvestment and neighbourhood stabilization.
- Minimum $150 million credit earned in financing for affordable rental housing.

[185] Morgan Stanley New York Settlement, para. 2.

[186] See Table A.2 description.

[187] Eric D. Green, "Monitor of the 2016 Morgan Stanley Mortgage Settlement – Final Report" (20 December 2017) at 13 [on file with author] (hereafter Morgan Stanley New York Final Report). Actual relief given to individual borrowers is not available for this settlement, according to James Patton of Young Conaway Stargatt & Taylor LLP, email message to MaryGrace Johnstone, 20 May 2019.

TERMS OVERALL[188]

- All bonus credits are cumulative.
- 115 per cent credit for all consumer relief offered by 30 January 2016.

TERMS BY CATEGORY

Modifications

- Morgan Stanley earned $12,418,114 credit in first-lien balance forgiveness,[189] subject to certain conditions to ensure the necessity and sufficiency of relief, as follows[190]:
  - $1 forgiveness = $1 credit, or
  - $1 forgiveness = $0.50 credit on loans serviced by the bank but owned by other investors, or
  - $1 Housing Affordability Modification Program (HAMP) incentive payments for principal reduction of first liens = $1 credit, and
  - 115 per cent credit for reduction of LTV below 100 per cent.
- Morgan Stanley earned $57,587,469 credit in second-lien balance forgiveness,[191] subject to certain conditions to ensure the necessity and sufficiency of relief, as follows[192]:
  - $1 forgiveness = $1 credit, or
  - $1 forgiveness = $0.50 credit on loans serviced by the bank but owned by other investors, or
  - $1 HAMP incentive payments for principal reduction of first liens = $1 credit.

Morgan Stanley earned $66,412,500 credit in financing for the acquisition and remediation of non-performing loans,[193] subject to certain conditions to ensure the necessity and sufficiency of relief, at a rate of[194]:

- $1 financing = $2 credit, or
- $1 grant = $2.50 credit.

Community Reinvestment and Neighbourhood Stabilization

[188] Morgan Stanley Settlement Agreement Appendix B (11 February 2016) at 2, online (pdf): New York Attorney General, https://ag.ny.gov/pdfs/Final_Consumer_Relief_AppendixB.pdf (hereafter Morgan Stanley New York Settlement, Appendix B).

[189] Morgan Stanley New York Final Report, 7.

[190] Morgan Stanley New York Settlement, Appendix B, 2–4.

[191] Morgan Stanley New York Final Report, at 7.

[192] Morgan Stanley New York Settlement, Appendix B, 2–4.

[193] Morgan Stanley New York Final Report, 7.

[194] Morgan Stanley New York Settlement, Appendix B, 2, 4–5.

- Morgan Stanley earned $30,202,136 credit in grants for certified land banks, at a rate of:[195]
  - $1 grant = $2 credit, and
  - 115 per cent early incentive credit for grants provided by 10 February 2017 to the Local Initiatives Support Corporation.
- Morgan Stanley earned $30,057,865 credit in grants housing quality improvement and enforcement programs, at a rate of $1 grant = $2 credit.[196]

Morgan Stanley earned $205,012,079 credit in financing and/or grants to municipalities or counties to fund Critical Need Housing Developments and/or support services or programs for such developments, at a rate of[197]:

- $1 loss = $3.75 credit up to $100,000 per grant, and
- 115 per cent credit for projects where the bank has not funded a Critical Need Housing Development in the past four years.

TABLE A.21 *Ocwen U.S. settlement*[198]

Monetary Penalties – Actual Payments by Bank	$127,300,000
Consumer Relief Obligations – Credit Earned, Adjusted Per Settlement Terms	$2,127,661,400
TOTAL SETTLEMENT	$2,254,961,400

According to the consumer relief component of the U.S. multi-state settlement, Ocwen was required to earn a minimum of $2 billion in consumer relief credit,[199] derived from the actual relief by the same method as described previously in the Ally Settlement.[200] Actuals are not available for this settlement.[201]

195 Morgan Stanley New York Final Report, 7, 10; Morgan Stanley New York Settlement, Appendix B, 7.
196 Morgan Stanley New York Final Report, 7; Morgan Stanley New York Settlement, Appendix B, 7.
197 Morgan Stanley New York Final Report, 7, 12; Morgan Stanley New York Settlement, Appendix B, 8.
198 *Consumer Financial Protection Bureau et al* v *Ocwen Financial Corporation and Ocwen Loan Servicing, LLC*, No. 13-02025 (RMC), Document 12 Consent Judgment (DDC filed 26 February 2014), paras. 4–5, Department of Justice, Ocwen Consent Judgment (26 February 2014), paras. 4–5, National Ocwen Settlement, www.nationalocwensettlement.com/Portals/0/Documents/Consent Judgement.pdf (hereafter Ocwen Consent Judgment). Ocwen paid the amount into escrow, to be distributed according to the same terms as the NMS Borrower Payments, described in Table A.5.
199 Ocwen Consent Judgment, para. 5.
200 See Table A.2 description.
201 *Consumer Financial Protection Bureau, et al* v *Ocwen Financial Corporation and Ocwen Loan Servicing, LLC*, No 13-02025 (RMC), Document 38 Final Consumer Relief Report (DDC filed 28 April 2016), Schedule Y, National Mortgage Settlements, II(D) Consumer Relief and V Total Consumer Relief, https://scholarship.law.unc.edu/cgi/viewcontent.cgi?article=1118&context=mortgage-settlements (hereafter Ocwen Final Report). Referring to actual relief data in Schedule Y. Schedule Y is not in the public record.

Ocwen earned $2,127,661,400 credit,[202] the entirety of which was required to be earned through principal reduction loan modifications on first-lien residential mortgage loans, subject to certain eligibility requirements to ensure the necessity and sufficiency of relief, at a rate of[203]:

- $1 write-down = $1 credit, or
- $1 earned forgiveness over three years (minimum 1/3 forgiveness annually) = $1 credit.

TABLE A.22 *Royal Bank of Scotland settlements*

MONETARY PENALTIES – Actual Payments by Bank	
U.S. Treasury General Fund, pursuant to the Financial Institutions Reform, Recovery and Enforcement Act of 1989 (FIRREA) (DOJ)[204]	$4,944,000,000
National Credit Union Administration (NCUA)[205]	$1,239,100,000
Federal Deposit Insurance Corporation (FDIC)*[206]	*Not available*
Federal Housing Finance Agency (FHFA)[207]	$5,500,000,000
Securities Exchange Commission (SEC)[208]	$153,700,000
State of New York[209]	$100,000,000
State of California[210]	$125,000,000
State of Connecticut[211]	$120,000,000

(continued)

202 Ocwen Final Report, 16.

203 Ocwen Final Report, Exhibit C-1.

204 RBS Settlement Agreement Recitals (14 August 2018), para. 1, Department of Justice, www.justice.gov/opa/press-release/file/1087146/download (hereafter RBS DOJ Settlement); Jonathan Stempel, "RBS to Pay $44 Million to Settle US Charges It Defrauded Customers," *Reuters* (26 October 2017), www.reuters.com/article/us-rbs-settlement/rbs-to-pay-44-million-to-settle-u-s-charges-it-defrauded-customers-idUSKBN1CV2QD (hereafter Stempel, "RBS to Pay $44 Million").

205 NCUA Settlements.

206 FDIC Settlement, para. 1. The settlement required a cumulative $190 million to be paid by eight banks; the division is not available.

207 FHFA Private Label Securities Actions.

208 U.S. Securities and Exchange Commission, "SEC Charges Royal Bank of Scotland Subsidiary with Misleading Investors in Subprime RMBS Offering" (7 November 2013), www.sec.gov/news/press-release/2013-239 (hereafter RBS SEC Settlement).

209 RBS Financial Products Settlement Agreement (6 March 2018), para. 2, RBS Monitor, https://rbs.mortgagesettlementmonitor.com/Settlement-Agreement-Documents/RBS-Settlement-Agreement-3-6-18.pdf (hereafter RBS New York Settlement).

210 California Attorney General Pressroom, "Attorney General Xavier Becerra Announces $125 Million Settlement against Royal Bank of Scotland for Misleading California's Pension Funds" (22 December 2017), California Attorney General, https://oag.ca.gov/news/press-releases/attorney-general-xavier-becerra-announces-125-million-settlement-against-royal (hereafter RBS California Settlement).

211 Nate Raymond, "RBS to Pay $120 Million to Resolve Connecticut Mortgage Bond Probe", *Reuters* (3 October 2016), www.reuters.com/article/us-royal-bank-scot-settlement/rbs-to-pay-120-million-to-resolve-connecticut-mortgage-bond-probe-idUSKCN1231PQ (hereafter RBS Connecticut Settlement).

TABLE A.22 *(continued)*

TOTAL MONETARY PENALTIES – ACTUALS*	$12,181,800,000
NEW YORK CONSUMER RELIEF OBLIGATIONS – Credit Adjusted Per Settlement Terms	
TOTAL CONSUMER RELIEF CREDIT EARNED	$400,005,578
TOTAL SETTLEMENT (Monetary Penalties + Consumer Relief Credit)	$12,581,805,578

* *Excluding FDIC Settlement; not publicly released.*

TABLE A.23 *Royal Bank of Scotland New York settlement – consumer relief*[212]

Type of Relief	Credit Earned	Actual Relief
Subtotal – Financing for Acquisition and Remediation of Non-performing Loans	$65,000,012	$22,608,700
Grants for Certified Land Banks or Land Trusts	$60,000,100	$26,087,000
Grants for Housing Quality Improvement and Enforcement Programs	$110,002,100	$47,827,000
Subtotal – Community Reinvestment and Neighbourhood Stabilization	$170,002,200	$73,914,000
Subtotal – Affordable Rental Housing	$165,003,366	$33,271,000
Total Consumer Relief	$400,005,578	$129,793,700

Under the New York Settlement, the Royal Bank of Scotland was required to earn a minimum of $400 million in consumer relief credit,[213] derived from the actual relief by the same method as described previously in the Ally Settlement[214] and according to the terms of the settlement as outlined below.

[212] Eric D. Green, "Monitor of the 2018 RBS Financial Products Mortgage Settlement – Final Report" (31 August 2018) at 19, online (pdf): RBS Mortgage Settlement Monitor, https://rbs.mortgagesettlementmonitor.com/Reports/Aug-31-2018-Report-2018-RBS-Financial-Products-Settlement.pdf (hereafter RBS New York Final Report). The total amount of grants made was $129,793,700, corresponding to just over $400 million credit; RBS New York Final Report, 19, Table 4. The bank earned 115 per cent early incentive credit for the entire amount, and in each category: Menu Item 1 Community Restoration and Loan Remediation, $2.50 credit per $1 grant made to agencies for the acquisition and remediation of non-performing loan; Menu Item 2 Community Reinvestment and Neighbourhood Stabilization, $2 credit per $1 grant made to capitalize or support eligible land banks/trusts and agencies to support housing quality improvement and enforcement programs; Menu Item 3 Affordable Rental Housing, $3.75 credit per $1 grant, plus a 115 per cent cumulative bonus location-related credit, for funding Critical Need Housing Developments: descriptions pursuant to the RBS New York Settlement, Appendix B.

[213] RBS New York Settlement, para. 3.

[214] See Table A.2 description.

MINIMUMS

The terms placed minimum relief obligations on certain categories of relief:[215]

- Minimum $65 million credit earned in community restoration and loan remediation.
- Minimum $60 million credit earned in grants for certified land banks or land trusts.
- Minimum $110 million credit earned in grants to municipalities or their housing or finance agencies to support housing quality improvement and enforcement programs.
- Minimum $165 million credit earned in financing and/or grants for affordable rental housing.

TERMS OVERALL[216]

- All bonus credits are cumulative.
- 115 per cent credit for all consumer relief offered by 30 September 2018.

TERMS BY CATEGORY

Credit was earned at the same rates described previously under the Morgan Stanley New York Settlement.[217]

TABLE A.24 *SunTrust U.S. settlement*[218]

Monetary Penalties – Actual Payments by Bank	$468,271,986
Consumer Relief Obligations – Credit Earned, Adjusted Per Settlement Terms	$502,756,425
TOTAL SETTLEMENT	$971,028,411

215 RBS New York Settlement, Appendix B, 1–2.

216 RBS New York Settlement, 1.

217 Referencing the Morgan Stanley New York Settlement, Appendix B, which is identical to the RBS New York Settlement, Appendix B.

218 *United States of America, et al* v *SunTrust Mortgage, Inc*, No. 14-01028 (RMC), Document 65 Consent Judgment (DDC filed 30 September 2014), paras. 3–5, Department of Justice, www.justice.gov/opa/file/831121/download (hereafter SunTrust Consent Judgment). $418 million plus $280 thousand interest was to be distributed according to undisclosed instructions from the Department of Justice. SunTrust additionally paid $50 million into escrow, $40 million of which was to be distributed according to the same terms as the NMS Borrower Payments described in Table A.1; SunTrust Consent Judgment, para. 4.

TABLE A.25 *SunTrust U.S. settlement – consumer relief*[219]

Type of Relief	Credit Earned
First-Lien Principal Forgiveness	$38,101,662
First-Lien Streamline Modifications	$67,223,257
Second-Lien Portfolio Modifications	$5,939,817
Second-Lien Portfolio Modifications – Extinguishments	$149,678,698
Subtotal – Modifications/Forgiveness	$260,943,434
First-Lien Refinance	$37,778,138
Second-Lien Loan Rate Reduction	$8,707,728
Subtotal – Refinancing Program	$46,485,866
Enhanced Borrower Transitional Funds	$282,757
Short Sales/Deeds in Lieu	$91,280,325
Payment to an Unrelated Second-Lien Holder	$2,100,043
REO Properties Donated	$1,664,000
Subtotal – Other Creditable Items	$95,327,125
First Time Homebuyer	$52,931,250
Hardest Hit Areas Homebuyer	$47,056,250
Previously Liquidated Homebuyer	$12,500
Subtotal – Low- to Moderate-Income and Hardest Hit Area Lending Program	$100,000,000
Total Consumer Relief	$502,756,425

According to the consumer relief component of the settlement, SunTrust was required to earn a minimum of $500 million in consumer relief credit,[220] derived from the actual relief by the same method as described previously in the Ally Settlement.[221] Actuals are not available for this settlement.[222]

[219] *United States of America, et al* v *SunTrust Mortgage, Inc*, No 14-01028 (RMC), Document 74 Final Consumer Relief Report (DDC filed 10 August 2017), 28, Exhibits D and D1, National Mortgage Settlements, https://scholarship.law.unc.edu/cgi/viewcontent.cgi?article=1182&context=mortgage-settlements (hereafter SunTrust Final Report). s V(a) Validated Consumer Relief Credit. The same kinds of minimum and maximum relief obligations as discussed for Bank of America are set out in the Appendix. As with the other settlements, it is difficult to determine what actual relief went to consumer borrowers.

[220] SunTrust Consent Judgment, para. 5.

[221] See Table A.2 description.

[222] SunTrust Final Report, II(D) Consumer Relief and V Total Consumer Relief, referring to actual relief data in Schedule Y. Schedule Y is not in the public record.

MINIMUMS AND MAXIMUMS

The terms placed minimum and maximum relief obligations on certain categories of relief as described previously under the Ally Settlement[223] in addition to the following requirements[224]:

- Minimum $187.5 million credit earned through first-lien principal forgiveness and second-lien portfolio modifications, including a minimum $93.75 million credit through first-lien principal forgiveness.
- Minimum $25 million credit earned through the refinancing program, including a maximum $5 million through second-lien refinancing.
- Minimum $25 million and maximum $100 million credit earned through the new lending program.

TERMS BY CATEGORY

Credit was earned at the same rates described previously under the Ally, Bank of America, Citigroup, and JP Morgan Chase Settlements, including the early incentive credit,[225] with the following addition:

New Lending Program: The bank earned $100 million credit[226] for selling loans to eligible borrowers who intend to occupy the home, and who are first time homebuyers, are buying a home in a hardest hit area, or who lost a home foreclosure or short sale, calculated as follows[227]:

- $10,000 credit for each purchase money loan, and
- 125 per cent credit for homes in hardest hit areas, and
- 125 per cent credit for loans made between 1 January 2014 and 1 January 2015.

[223] Referencing the Ally NMS Consent Judgment, Exhibit D1, which is identical to the SunTrust Final Report, Exhibit D1.

[224] SunTrust Final Report, 9–10, s II(b) Consumer Relief Requirements: Eligibility Criteria and Earned Credits.

[225] Referencing the Ally NMS Consent Judgment, Bank of America NMS Consent Judgment, Citigroup NMS Consent Judgment, and JP Morgan Chase NMS Consent Judgment, Exhibits D and D1, which are identical to the SunTrust Final Report, D and D1.

[226] SunTrust Final Report, 28, s V(a) Validated Consumer Relief Credit.

[227] SunTrust Final Report, Exhibit I-3, I-4.

TABLE A.26 *UBS settlements*

MONETARY PENALTIES – Actual Payments by Bank[228]	
National Credit Union Administration (NCUA)[229]	$524,321,500
Federal Housing Finance Agency (FHFA)[230]	$885,000,000
Federal Deposit Insurance Corporation (FDIC)[231]	*Not available*
State of New York[232]	$41,000,000
TOTAL MONETARY PENALTIES – ACTUALS	$1,450,321,500
NEW YORK CONSUMER RELIEF OBLIGATIONS – Credit Adjusted Per Settlement Terms	
TOTAL CONSUMER RELIEF CREDIT EARNED*	$0
TOTAL SETTLEMENT (Monetary Penalties + Consumer Relief Credit)	$1,450,321,500

* *Current through August 2019; consumer relief must be completed by 31 December 2019.*

Under the New York Settlement, UBS is required to earn a minimum of $189 million in consumer relief credit,[233] derived from the actual relief by the same method as described previously in the Ally Settlement[234] and according to the terms of the settlement as follows.

MINIMUMS

The terms place minimum relief obligations on certain categories of relief:[235]

- Minimum $35 million credit earned in grants for certified land banks or land trusts.
- Minimum $59.5 million credit earned in grants to housing quality improvement and enforcement programs.
- Minimum $94.5 million credit earned in financing and/or grants for affordable rental housing.

[228] The Department of Justice is pursuing a settlement, which has not yet been resolved; *United States* v *UBS Securities LLC*, No 18-06369 (MKB), Document 1 Complaint (EDNY filed 8 November 2018), Court Listener, www.courtlistener.com/docket/8161829/united-states-v-ubs -securities-llc/ (hereafter UBS DOJ Settlement).

[229] NCUA Settlements.

[230] FHFA Private Label Securities Actions.

[231] Federal Deposit Insurance Corporation Settlement and Release Agreement (26 May 2016), para. 1, FDIC, www.fdic.gov/about/freedom/plsa/colonialbankreditsuissesecuritiesubssecurities.pdf (hereafter FDIC Settlement). The settlement required a cumulative $190 million to be paid by eight banks; the division is not available.

[232] New York Attorney General UBS Settlement Agreement (20 March 2018), New York Attorney General, https://ag.ny.gov/sites/default/files/ubs_settlement.pdf (hereafter UBS New York Settlement).

[233] UBS New York Settlement, para. 3.

[234] See Table A.2 description.

[235] UBS New York Settlement, Appendix B-2.

TERMS OVERALL[236]

- All bonus credits are cumulative.
- 115 per cent credit for all consumer relief offered by 30 September 2018.
- 106 per cent early resolution credit for all consumer relief.

TERMS BY CATEGORY

Credit will be earned at the same rates described previously under the Morgan Stanley New York Settlement.[237]

TABLE A.27 *Wells Fargo settlements*

MONETARY PENALTIES – ACTUALS	
U.S. Department of Justice (DOJ) and Independent Settlements	
U.S. Treasury General Fund, Pursuant to the Financial Institutions Reform, Recovery and Enforcement Act of 1989 (FIRREA) (DOJ)[238]	$2,090,000,000
National Credit Union Administration (NCUA)[239]	$53,000,000
Federal Housing Finance Agency (FHFA)[240]	$335,230,000
Federal Housing Administration (FHA)[241]	$1,200,000,000
Securities Exchange Commission (SEC)[242]	$6,606,572

(continued)

236 UBS New York Settlement, 2.

237 Referencing the Morgan Stanley New York Settlement, Appendix B, which is identical to the UBS New York Settlement, Appendix B.

238 *United States of America et al* v *Bank of America Corp et al*, No 12-0361 (RMC), Document 14 Consent Judgment (DDC filed 4 April 2012), para. 1, Exhibits D-7, D1-4, D1-5, National Mortgage Settlement Digital Archive, www.nationalmortgagesettlement.com/files/Consent_Judgment_WellsFargo-4-11-12.pdf (hereafter Wells Fargo NMS Consent Judgment). A complete breakdown of monetary penalties paid to the listed litigants is provided at para. 3.

239 NCUA Settlements. Wells Fargo was responsible for the Wachovia settlement.

240 FHFA Private Label Securities Actions.

241 *United States of America* v *Wells Fargo Bank, NA and Kurt Lofrano*, No 12-07527 (JMF), Document 320 Stipulation and Order of Settlement and Dismissal with Prejudice (SDNY filed 8 April 2016) at Attachment B, online: DOJ, www.justice.gov/opa/pr/wells-fargo-bank-agrees-pay-12-billion-improper-mortgage-lending-practices.

242 *In the Matter of Wells Fargo Brokerage Services, LLC n/k/a Wells Fargo Securities, LLC and Shawn Patrick McMurtry*, No 3-14982, Order (SEC filed 14 August 2012) at IV(c) and (g), online (pdf): SEC, www.sec.gov/litigation/admin/2012/33-9349.pdf.

TABLE A.27 *(continued)*

Subtotal – Settlement Monetary Penalties	$3,684,836,572
National Mortgage Settlement (NMS)[243]	
Subtotal – NMS Monetary Penalties	$1,005,233,716
TOTAL MONETARY PENALTIES – ACTUALS	$4,690,070,288
NMS CONSUMER RELIEF OBLIGATIONS – Credit Adjusted Per Settlement Terms	
TOTAL CONSUMER RELIEF CREDIT EARNED	$4,568,334,894
TOTAL SETTLEMENT (Monetary Penalties + Consumer Relief Credit)	$9,258,405,182

TABLE A.28 *Wells Fargo National Mortgage settlement – consumer relief*[244]

Type of Relief	Credit Earned	Actual Relief
First-Lien Mortgage Modifications	$1,718,197,498	$1,762,406,092
Second-Lien Portfolio Modifications	$214,390,813	$1,616,236,125
Subtotal – Modifications/Forgiveness	$1,932,588,311	$3,378,642,217
Subtotal – Refinancing Program	$1,383,030,038	$1,107,251,002
Enhanced Borrower Transitional Funds	$12,675,400	$12,675,400
Short Sales/Deeds in Lieu	$1,186,566,813	$3,017,246,010
Payments to Unrelated Second-Lien Holders	$9,133,711	$9,133,711
Deficiency Waivers	$39,397,160	$393,971,597
Payments of Cash for Demolition of Property	$82,463	$82,463
REO Properties Donated	$4,860,998	$4,860,998
Subtotal – Other Creditable Items	$1,252,716,545	$3,437,970,179
Total Consumer Relief	$4,568,334,894	$7,923,863,398

243 *United States of America et al* v *Bank of America Corp et al*, No 12-0361 (RMC), Document 14 Consent Judgment (DDC filed 4 April 2012), para. 3, Exhibits D-7, D1-4, D1-5, National Mortgage Settlement Digital Archive, www.nationalmortgagesettlement.com/files/Consent_Judgment_WellsFargo-4-11-12.pdf (hereafter Wells Fargo NMS Consent Judgment). The NMS was a cumulative settlement; a complete breakdown of monetary penalties and parties are described previously under the Ally DOJ Settlement, referencing the NMS Initial Report, 3 and the Ally NMS Consent Judgment, para. 3 and Exhibit B, which is identical to the Wells Fargo NMS Consent Judgment, Exhibit B.

244 NMS Final Report, 19.

Under the National Mortgage Settlement, Wells Fargo was required to earn a minimum of $3.434 billion in consumer relief credit, as well as $903 million in refinancing relief credit,[245] derived from the actual relief by the same method as described previously in the Ally Settlement.[246] The terms placed additional maximum and minimum relief obligations on certain categories of relief, and provided for an early incentive credit.[247]

TERMS BY CATEGORY

Credit was earned at the same rates described previously under the Ally, Bank of America, Citigroup, and JP Morgan Chase Settlements, including the early incentive credit.[248]*continued*

[245] Wells Fargo NMS Consent Judgment, para. 5.

[246] See Table A.2 description.

[247] Terms are described previously under the Ally DOJ Settlement, referencing the Ally NMS Consent Judgment, Exhibits D1-1 through D1-4, which is identical to the Wells Fargo NMS Consent Judgment, Exhibit D1.

[248] Referencing the Ally NMS Consent Judgment, Bank of America NMS Consent Judgment, Citigroup NMS Consent Judgment, and JP Morgan Chase NMS Consent Judgment, Exhibits D and D1, which are identical to the Wells Fargo NMS Consent Judgment, Exhibits D and D1.

Index

Note: Page numbers in italic and bold refer to figures and tables, respectively.

For EU product safety concerns, contact us at Calle de José Abascal, 56–1°, 28003 Madrid, Spain or eugpsr@cambridge.org.

www.ingramcontent.com/pod-product-compliance
Ingram Content Group UK Ltd.
Pitfield, Milton Keynes, MK11 3LW, UK
UKHW022152080726
473066UK00010B/900

* 9 7 8 1 1 0 8 8 1 1 5 8 3 *